DREW S   H'S

FOOD
watch

The Essential Consumer Guide to What We Eat

HarperCollins*Publishers*

For Sue, Grace and Oliver

Nearly all the foods tested for this book were bought independently from supermarkets and delicatessens between May 1993 and April 1994. A small number were tasted at exhibitions or tastings organized by third parties.

The prices quoted are those charged or displayed to us as consumers in that period. The tasting notes are my own, from batched comparison tastings usually in conjunction with one or two colleagues with specialist knowledge.

First published in 1994
by HarperCollins*Publishers*, London

A catalogue record for this book is available from the British Library.

ISBN 0 00 412710 2

Typeset in Helvetica
Printed and bound in Great Britain by
Butler & Tanner Ltd, Frome and London

Editor: Lewis Esson
Designer: Siân Keogh
Editorial Director: Polly Powell
Project Editor: Barbara Dixon

Acknowledgements
A great many people have helped in the putting together of this book: answering questions, checking facts or just allowing me to put ideas and thoughts to them. There are special thank-yous due to Juliet Harbutt, Patrick Rance and Randolph Hodgson for the dairy sections; Paul Fry for the fruit and vegetables; Simon Watson, Lawrence Alderson and Alastair Cuthbertson for the meat; Dr Eric Edwards for shellfish; Alan Davidson, Ninnette Lyon and Rick Stein for their excellent writing on fish; Helen Conn, Charles Carey and Judy Ridgeway for the larder section; John Lister for bread. There are smaller, but no less grateful, thanks to George Benyon, Colin Boswell, Tim Clarke, Sue Cloke, Colin Creese, John Dewesbury, Wilson Dyer, Mike Ford, David Frost, Peter Hadaad, John Hassal, Dorothy Hollingsworth, Peter Hudson, Martin Keeble, Monica Lavery, Trevor Paveley, Nick Reed, Ron Smith, William Tullberg and Adam Wells. Also thanks to a number of specialist shops that unwittingly have been supplying much of the better produce: Camisa, Carluccio's, I Camisa, Fromagerie, Harvey Nichols, Harrods, Jeroboams, Langman's, Lena's, Loon Fung, Mortimer & Bennett, Neal's Yard, Tom's, William's Kitchen, Wing Yip, Wild Oats, and to everyone at Billingsgate, Nine Elms and Smithfield Markets.

On a personal level my thanks go to Emma Bland and to Sam Dobson, who did some heroic shopping trips; Lewis Esson for his noble efforts in organizing and editing the text, and Polly Powell and Robin Wood for having the vision to commission it in the first place.

CONTENTS

THE QUALITY OF CHOICE

I wrote this book because I wanted to read it, to be able to use it and to refer back to it. I wanted a portrait of what we were doing to this planet and to ourselves in the name of food. The modern supermarket sells anything up to 15,000 foods, and is introducing, at a conservative estimate, around 1,500 new lines a year. The food market has become dynamic in a way that impinges on our lives in a way that has never been seen before. While it may seem, superficially, that we are a nation of conservative eaters who rarely change our foods, the statistics argue differently. Our diet has gone – and is going – through unparalleled change.

Twenty years ago this book might have been impossible to compile. There were so many different foods produced in so many different areas in so many different ways that it would have stretched into volume upon volume, if anyone could have lived long enough to chronicle all its vagaries. However, the world trade routes have become discernible highways, the move to mass standardization of products to serve huge urban populations has brought a sense of rationality, and the rise of the modern supermarket has made it possible to focus on all the effort and ingenuity that contributes to the food chain. We have leapt from local parochial food chains into the stratosphere of a global food machine that sucks foods from one corner of the earth and delivers them the next day to the other.

This country is perhaps uniquely placed to witness these massive changes. If the UK is not quite a junction box on the world food superhighway – because we put very little back – it is certainly a major terminus. There are historic reasons for this: a tradition of global trading; the long-standing partnerships with the former colonial world being exchanged for new links with Europe; a relatively affluent urban population that has shown itself to be receptive to new foods; and trade agreements that have been as much about bananas and cocoa as they are about the more publicized tanks and nuclear waste. We have had a grandstand seat on the greatest market the world has ever seen – delivered right to a supermarket near you every day.

The scale of change has been awesome. It is easy to point to foods like pasta, courgettes, basil, chilli peppers, olive oil, wine vinegar, avo-cados etc – central, almost everyday, foods which even in the '60s were unknown to most people. Nor at that time were artificial colours, nature-identical flavourings or emulsifiers in common use. The change is, in fact, deeper and more fundamental. Basic foods are not the same anymore. The major varieties of potato all changed in the '80s... so did the breeds of cattle... indigenous breeds of pig are now rare breeds, because a docile foreigner was more adaptable to intensive farming... the list goes on.

Popular issues such as the (waning) support for organic foods, con-cern over pesticides, the emergence of food-related diseases like sal-monella and listeria, the latent and ongoing threat from BSE, the reac-tion to food itself as in anorexia and bulimia, might all be said to be symptoms of a much larger, more important upheaval. The Global Food Machine demands a response.

THE QUALITY OF SECRECY

It is too simplistic to question simply whether all this change has been for the good. It is hard to deny we have now one of the most entertain-ing, nutritious and versatile diets ever available to us. Food has become an international language, and a peaceful one. The ability to buy fresh food is ultimately an act of emancipation, arguably democ-racy's greatest achievement.

However, the language of food is also the language of the propa-gandist. For this book, huge tracts of industry refused to talk or to con-firm facts, or asked for payments to answer simple questions. Two organizations even asked to be paid to use their libraries. Others were not available, or too fearful of what their paymasters might say. The culture of confidentiality and secrecy is ingrained.

Whatever smiling face the GFM (Global Food Machine) adopts in public, in private it is inclined to furtiveness and paranoia and does not take kindly to having the stone under which it is hiding removed – even though it expects the rest of us to buy and eat its products. The analogy with the infamous Derby cheese-makers who were so secre-tive they never divulged the recipe to anyone, until they all died and the cheese became extinct, is not far from the point.

The quality of information is an important issue. How is any government supposed to formulate policy without having access to market information? And surely consumers are entitled to know what it is they are eating? If the labels on packets do not exactly lie, they certainly, as we all know, enjoy avoiding the truth. We have all become accustomed to half truths.

The law has been subverted. To take a few isolated examples from the entries that follow: Why is it that a packet of butter actually seems to suggest that the recommended daily intake for an adult is 100 g, when 100 g on a daily basis might lead to dietary disability? Or that the nutritional advice on a carton of cream is in grams, when the carton is labelled in pints? Or that supermarkets can sell the same foods labelled either in grams or in lbs to make easy price comparison as difficult as possible? These are all indications that genuine choice is being undermined.

THE QUALITY OF SUPERMARKETS

When I began writing this book, like many people I felt indebted to supermarkets for introducing me to the whole range of foods they now sell. And I still do, except in one regard.

It is hard to respect supermarkets as honest brokers when without exception they play a variation on roulette with their pricing. It is not surely right to sell the same thing in the same shop at different prices, just by packing one up in grams and the other in lbs. In one **Tesco**, Parmesan was sold in three different places at three different prices. Some goods, especially brands, are calculated in such minute fractions of grams that price comparisons between two items are almost impossible without a PhD in mathematics, or at least a decent calculator. Take these prices from the otherwise commendable **Marks & Spencer**: smoked salmon in six different guises, 454 g, 113 g, 85 g, 5 oz, 100 g and 6 oz… with these kind of fractions, who can compare?

Nor are these price differentials small. Often they can be double. It is hard to escape the conclusion that the main reason to do this is to deceive the customer. It is hardly a fair trade. The EC will ban such practice next year, but even though supermarkets have known this ban was coming they have persisted up to the last minute.

The customer only really has a choice in the market where there is genuine variety. Many of these price differentials are being applied to products where the main difference is the packaging not the product. Cheddar is a good example where the process is so internationally standardized that there can be no real justification for selling one factory produced Cheddar for twice the price of another. In some supermarkets you can find upwards of 15 different factory Cheddars masquerading in different weights and packages at nearly £2 difference in price. Of course, they are different – or marginally so – but they are not £2 different. Bacon is another example where there seems no rhyme or reason behind the pricing other than profiteering. These are artificial pricing scales that have been introduced to suggest that there is a difference in the product when in reality there is hardly any. The consumers' choice is a fiction.

The least anyone of us has to expect is that prices conform to a single scale and that if there are differences between products that they should be demonstrable.

The old corner shop argument that they just happened to buy something cheap or they wanted to loss-leader an item as a special event hardly holds water in these days when the packaging design alone might cost £30,000 and where supermarkets are so fundamentally involved in the industry itself – in many cases having been instrumental in creating the companies that supply them.

WHAT IS CHOICE?

Faced with a global market, the central issue is the quality of choice. Variety ceases to be an indolent expression of affluence, rather it creates an organic and necessary positive influence. It obstructs the imperialistic tendencies of governments and large corporations. It provides some insurance against the implicit dangers of mass-production and it gives consumers a genuine voice in the market place.

The recognition of a healthy market place is that a pear is not just a pear... it is a *Comice*, an *Anjou*, a *Conference*, a *Packham's Triumph* etc, and that each one has some economic and social meaning to a region and the people who work there.

The most convincing example of this is French wine. The imposition of *appellation contrôlée*, whereby the names and regions are strictly controlled in line with the historical performance of those vineyards, has seen French wines dominate the world market. There is an important declaration in this principle. You buy a bottle of wine secure in the knowledge that someone in France is having his livelihood endorsed by that purchase. Compare that to buying a ready-prepared chicken, for about the same price, and knowing that you are endorsing a low-paid factory line cruelty in the name of nobody in particular.

Of course, it is fashionable to argue now that New World wines from Australia, New Zealand or Chile are better value than French, but that is a point about price. If the French had not laid down the principles of quality in *appellation contrôlée* and opened up the world market, then the New World could not have followed. One has only to look at another European country, say Portugal, where wine is no less important but its reputation has not been protected by a scheme like *appellation contrôlée* and the trade is minimal.

IS FOOD TOO EXPENSIVE?

Alastair Grant, head of **Safeway**, famously remarked, 'pricing is like the missionary position, there are more interesting positions, but you are expected to be able to do it'.

Price is also about philosophy and expectation. Some of us may well pay more for free-range eggs than battery as a point of principle. **Sainsbury** undercuts most wholefood shops by about three times on brown egg price, but on Greek virgin olive oil it may charge three times more than a Greek delicatessen. Beyond the range of basic goods, where **Sainsbury** and **Tesco** in particular have made a point of reducing prices to a level where it is hard to see anyone undercutting them, prices seem more opportunistic. The mark-ups on designer salads are breathtakingly audacious. Even more depressing is **Gateway** selling breast of chicken for more than **Waitrose** as if trying to underline a class distinction. **Waitrose**, for its part, would be very hard pushed to justify its parent company **John Lewis's** boast that it is 'never knowingly undersold'.

The cost of buying branded foods against own-labels is punitive enough to beg some serious questions as to what is going to happen to independent food manufacturers in the next decade.

Archie Norman, head of **Asda**, let the cat out of the bag when he announced in March that his price cutting would long-term be funded by netting down, 'promotional bonuses and fees'. What used to be called euphemistically 'hello money', or listings allowance or more commonly now just the retail support budget must account for significant revenues to the larger retailers and is almost certainly responsible for the enormous range of choice in some sectors.

The normal shopping basket surveys don't really take account of this very real difference. In any case, many price surveys are undertaken by firms that owe a lot of their business to supermarkets, and may well often have even been commissioned by the supermarket. Invariably they will only assess the cheapest items in each range. That may be one reason why the £30 shopping basket, beloved of statisticians' weekly shop, often turns out to be £60 when the rest of us go.

Cheapness does not equate to value. The 'big five' – **Sainsbury**, **Waitrose**, **Asda**, **Tesco** and **Safeway** – do not really bear comparison with the cut-price warehouses like **Costco** and **Cargo**, where the overlap is essentially in toiletries and tins. The supermarkets have pioneered the introduction of fresh fruit and fresh vegetables and other staples that go to make a balanced diet. They have done it by protecting quality. Most of what they sell is class 1. Class 2 tends to end up in Nine Elms or in street markets. In that sense standardization has culled much poor practice.

Producers argue that supermarkets are too powerful. They are. But they are also, in this country, the only credible influence on what we eat and will go on being so until there is a sea change in political thinking on food. They have seized the means of production, and importantly understood the idea that a fresh food economy is intrinsically about transport and getting fresh foods still in their prime to the market as swiftly as possible.

THE QUALITY OF DIET

The scale of the global food industry is such that in many areas customers cannot really be said to have a true choice. When all the milk is controlled by a monopoly, when 80% of the flour for our bread is milled by three firms, when whole nations plant a single variety of potato, when governments both here and abroad invest huge sums of public money to establish monolithic monocultures, in all honesty who really is going to care what the customer thinks? That freedom of choice has been passed, by proxy, to the large supermarkets who wield it with some discernment but also often with some financial inducement.

We will also be told, politely, that our preferences as customers are subjective. This is a pernicious argument. It suggests that there are no defined criteria for quality – or none that the consumer is grown-up enough to appreciate.

We know what good food is. There is a certain reassurance in the results of the 30 year study of 80,000 American nurses which showed that the trans-fatty acids created by hydrogenation for margarines is linked to increased levels of heart disease. The dietary evidence is plain enough in its broad consensus and has been known for the best part of 50 years, only the weight of documentation gets larger and the goal posts move bit by bit as our diet is forced through these massive changes. Producers are fully aware usually of the quality thresholds of their own products.

This book is really about the junction where good food meets healthy food, or at least foods that are known to be good for us. Textbooks up to the '50s spoke freely of how different foods were stomachic, carminative or otherwise therapeutic. Many foods listed here survive only because they were historically seen as medicines. This is no longer allowed in law and such foods would have to be classed as drugs and sold for twice or three times as much. The result is that any old rubbish can declare that it is loaded up with vitamins and iron whereas a food known for centuries to be positive, like say porridge, cannot declare its medical record. It is folly in the extreme to suggest that what we put in our bodies does not have some effect on how they perform.

There is another issue which has become almost a subtext in writing the individual stories of these foods and it is a political one. Was it right to abandon our fishing fleets, to pollute our inland rivers and estuaries, to grub up our apple orchards, to abandon cherries and nuts as industries, to give the world the machinery for Cheddar cheese, to allow bread to have additives put back into it rather than encouraging bakers to stay with a loaf that has all its wholesomeness left in? We might ask if it might not have been more intelligent to sustain our own trades so that we do not spend huge sums importing other foods? And might it not have been more constructive to hang on to these crafts and skilled roles rather than having people on the dole or on check-out tills?

The perceived economic imperative was always to feed the nation. This seems to have been allowed to take over other considerations, but it is also out of date. Already most of our food is bought on the world market. What we have forgotten politically is where food fits in our society and how it might be used to create the kind of world we want. That is the next great intellectual leap. The customers' opinions seem to have been taken for granted. Manufacturers have been – no, are – intent on using the cheapest possible ingredients, cutting as many corners as possible, often with total disregard for quality or tradition. They hide behind a veneer of sophistication provided by advertising executives and PR firms. The peddling of rubbish has become an institution.

I wanted this book at least to provide the facts by which foods can be judged. If it makes manufacturers think harder about what they are selling; or inspires supermarket buyers to demand better standards; or empowers consumers to articulate their case better; or helps legislators to see the historical impact of what they are doing – or not doing – then it will have achieved something. This book will be revised next year to take on board any comments. The debate continues...

FOODS OF THE YEAR

A personal note:
For the most part in this book I have tried to be as objective as was possible, checking texts, talking to experts, triple-checking value judgements. In the course of that work I have probably had to judge more than 10,000 different food products in the last eighteen months. There are two foods that stay in my mind and have been benchmarks against which all other foods have really stood or fallen, whatever the category. These are the most subjective of all awards but, at the same time, if I had to hang my hat on just two foods that have represented for me what this book is about they would be these. One is a variety to which doubtless a great many people have contributed. The other is down to the vision of one man.

CHARLOTTE POTATOES

HUGH LILLINGSTONE'S BOSWORTH GOATS' CHEESE

SUPERMARKETS OF THE YEAR

BEST CHEESES	Sainsbury (French)
	Tesco (display)
BEST EFFORTS TO ENCOURAGE FRUIT AND VEGETABLE VARIETIES	Safeway
BEST FISH	Waitrose
BEST FRUIT	Marks & Spencer
	Waitrose
BEST LARDER	Waitrose
BEST MEAT	Tesco
BEST NEWCOMER	Somerfield
BEST OWN-LABEL	Sainsbury
BEST READY-MEALS	Marks & Spencer
BEST VEGETABLES	Waitrose

FOOD WATCH CHECKLISTS

1 FOODS OF THE YEAR

Foods marked with ** in the text are defining examples of the best of their kind.

BREAD — Innes
Manoucher
Sally Clarke

BRISLING (TINS) — King Oscar

BUTTER — Echiré
Isigny

CAPERS — Tornatore

CAVIAR — Caviar House

CHEESES

British

Caerphilly
Duckett's
Cheddar
Green's
Keen's
Montgomery's
Quicke's
Cheshire
Appleby
Double Gloucester
Appleby
Quicke's
Smart's
Lancashire
Kirkham
New
Beenleigh Blue
Bosworth (goats')
Little Rydings (sheep's)
Tymsboro' (goats')
Waterloo (wash-rind)
Stilton
Colston Bassett

French

Brie de Meaux
Brie de Melun
Coulommiers
Fleur de Maquise
Livarot
Roquefort
Selles-sur-Cher

Irish

Cashel Blue
Gubbeen
Milleens

Spanish

Montenebro
Rey Cabra

CHOCOLATE — Bonnat
Ménier
Valronna
(supermarket) Marks & Spencer

CREME FRAICHE — Isigny
Neal's Yard

FROMAGE FRAIS — Neal's Yard
Onken

HAM (air-dried) — Jamon de Jabugo
Parma
San Danielle

ICE-CREAM — Bowman's
Godiva
Häagen-Dazs

MUSTARD — Beaufor
Colman's dry mustard powder

Maille	SALAMI — Negroni (blue label)
Poupon	SALT — Maldon
Wiltshire Tracklements	Salines de Guerande
OLIVE OILS	SARDINES — Connetable
Spanish	SAUSAGES — Bill O'Hagan
Lerida	SESAME OIL — Koon Yick Wah Kee
Nunez de Prado	SOY SAUCE — Kikkoman
Tuscan	TOMATO KETCHUP — Heinz
Avignonese	TUNA (tinned) — Busto
Carluccio	Zarotti
Colonna	VINEGAR
Dell 'Ugo	*Balsamic*
Monte Vertine	Carluccio
Ornellia	Fortnum & Mason
Podere Cogno	*Cider*
Other Italian	Côteaux Nantais
Bottarelli	*Wine*
Carluccio (Apulia)	Edmond Fallot
Montiferru	Doktorenhof
Ravida	Martin Pouret
PULSES	WORCESTERSHIRE SAUCE — Lea & Perrins
Tormesina, Sierra de Gredos	YOGHURT ICE-CREAM — Häagen-Dazs

2 THE BARGAIN HUNTER'S LIST

Foods marked with an * in the text offer particularly good value or interest in their sector.

ANCHOVY (fillets in tins)
Rizzoli Emanuelli

BUTTER Channel Islands
President
Rachel's Dairy
Surgères

CAVIAR Chinese malossol

CHEESE
British
Martell's Single Gloucester
J.M. Nuttal's Lancashire
French (supermarket)
L'Edel de Cleron
Pavé d'affinois
Italian
Crottin, Piedmont

CHESTNUTS (tinned) Bridge House

CREME FRAICHE Waitrose

GRAPESEED OIL Dufrais

HAZELNUT OIL Asda

ICE-CREAM Hingston's

LUMPFISH CAVIAR Macrae's

MILK
UHT Milk can

OLIVE OILS
Greek
Illiada
Mani (organic)
Sainsbury
Solon
Spanish
L'Estornell

ROLLMOP HERRINGS Laurel farm
Konserver
Varefakta gaffelbidder

SAUSAGES Safeway Traditional
Tesco Traditional
Waitrose Traditional

SMOKED MUSSELS John West

SOY SAUCE Fo Shan
Pearl River

VINEGAR
Balsamic
Luigi Ugolotti & Figli
Mazzarretti
Rice
Chinkiang

YEAST Allinson's yeast pellets

3 BEST OF BREEDS/VARIETIES

** denotes best of category, * denotes of special interest or value

DAIRY

MILK		Jersey***

FRUIT

APPLE	(import)	Braeburn*
	(native)	Cox**
		Kid's Orange**
		Worcester Pearmain**
CITRUS		Clementine**
		Ortanique*
DATE		Medjoul**
GOOSEBERRY		Leveller**
GRAPE		Dan Ben Hannah**
		Muscat**
GRAPEFRUIT		Sweetie**
MANGO		Bombay**
		Ruby (Gambia)*
MELON		Charentais**
NECTARINE		Honegold (France)*
		Silvery (Spain)*
ORANGE		Navel**
PEACH	French branch-picked (Tesco)	
PEAR	(import)	Abate Fetel**
		Comice**
		Red Williams**
PLUM	(import)	Ruby Nell*
		Santa Rosa**
	(native)	Marjorie Seedling*
		Victoria**
UGLI		Uniq**

VEGETABLES

ASPARAGUS	Evesham**
	Extra Fine (Thailand)*
AVOCADO	Hass*

BEANS	Cannellini
	Flageolet
BROCCOLI	Purple sprouting*
GARLIC	Beaumont (white)**
	Lautrec (pink)**
	Venice (white)**
LENTILS	de Puy
MUSHROOMS	Cep
	Morel
POTATOES	Belle de Fontenay**
	Carlingford*
	Charlotte**
	Jersey Royal**
	La Ratte**
	Roseval**
SALAD LEAVES	Butterhead lettuce**
	Oak Leaf**
	Raddichio*
	Rocket**
TOMATO	Ailsa*
	Cherry*
	Melrow*
	Sicilian on the vine**

MEAT, POULTRY & GAME

BACON	Collar*
	Knuckle/hock*
BEEF	LMC (Leg of mutton cut)*
	Jacob's ladder*
	Fillet**
	Oxtail*
	Calves' liver**
	Calves' sweetbreads
CHICKEN	Bresse**
DUCK	Barbary**
	Mallard**

GAME			Grouse**
			Partridge**
			Rabbit*
			Squab**
LAMB			Leg**
			Liver*
			Loin**

FISH & SHELLFISH

FLAT FISH			Sole**
			Turbot**
KIPPERS			Craster*
			Manx*
LOBSTER	*(native)*		Scottish**

OILY FISH	*(import)*	Canadian*
		Herring*
		Mackerel*
		Tuna (fresh)**
OYSTERS	*(native)*	Helford
		West Mersea
	(pacific)	Ireland
SEA FISH		John Dory*
		Red mullet**
		Sea bass**
		Sea trout**
		Shark*
WHITE FISH		Cod**
		Smoked haddock**

SHOPPING CALENDAR

A selective month-by-month shopping guide to the main fresh produce as it arrives.

January is bolstered by the first flush of the citrus fruits, the traditional dried Levantine fruits from the autumn, the last of the game – often quite cheap – and the big white fish near their prime, if the boats can get out in the rough seas.

Almond	Nuts (Brazil)
Chestnut	Oranges (blood, Navelina, Seville)
Clementine	Pheasant
Cod	Pomegranate
Date	Rhubarb
Grapefruit (Sweeties)	Satsuma
Gurnard	Sprat
Haddock	Ugli (Uniq)
Herring	Walnut
Mackerel	Whiting

February is the hiatus in the year, which even Southern-Hemisphere imports struggle to conceal. There are one or two surprises: the citrus fruits are in their full glory, the trade originally encouraged to offset the risk of scurvy and other diseases caused by lack of greenery, and white fish are still good.

Cod	Oranges (blood, navel)
Ginger (Hawaiian)	Pears (Red Anjou, Ruby Nell)
Grapes (Dan ben Hannah)	Red mullet
Haddock	Salmon (wild – first catches from
Hake	Scottish rivers)
Herring	Sea trout (the first catches)
Lemon Sole	Sole
Mackerel	Squid
Mandarin	

March is often said to be the hardest month of all for the cook, waiting for the promise of spring which usually comes with the first stems of purple sprouting broccoli. A time to give more respect to foods overshadowed at other times of the year. The diet becomes strangely balanced between New World exotics and familiar stand-bys. Potatoes and apples have been in store for a long time, and the early new potatoes seem forced and lack character or flavour. Fish depends on the weather.

Aubergine (baby – from Uganda)
Broccoli (Purple sprouting)
Guinea fowl
Lemon sole
Mackerel
Mussel

Orange (blood)
Oyster
Pear (Asian)
Rhubarb (green)
Ugli
Salmon (wild)

April starts with a stutter not a shout, heralded by a few of the finest – and most expensive – foods of the year in their first flush. There are also the first signs of greenery, offset against the off-loading of the stored vegetables and fruits.

Cauliflower
Guinea fowl
Lamb (spring – expensive)
Lambs' liver
Lambs' kidneys
Mangosteen
Morel
Oysters (best of natives)
Pear (Asian)

Plum (Sonagold)
Potatoes (Jersey Royal – officially
    from April 26, but not usually
    found before)
Rabbit
Radish
Spring greens
Swiss chard
Turbot

May, and still summer waits before giving up her full bounty. Fish start to change, spring lamb is at its peak, so is asparagus. Other fresh foods are still not plentiful... a time for careful shopping, for checking that carrots are new-season and not stored.

Almond (green)
Asparagus (English)
Carrot (first of new season)
Chinese vegetables (the first imports
    from Spain)
Cockle
Garlic (first shoots for salad)
Herbs (rosemary, mint, thyme, chives
    – first of the outdoor crop)
Herring (first of the spring runs)
Lamb
Lambs' liver
Lambs' kidneys

Lambs' heart
Lobster (Scottish)
Mango (Bombay)
Morel
Potatoes (Jersey Royal)
Samphire
Sea bass
Sea trout
Sorrel
Spring cabbage
Tomato (first of UK under glass)
Watermelon

June and at last summer comes on line, with the first broad beans, strawberries and all the salad crops. A wealth of summer fish and imports of New World fruits. The first herbs push through outside rather than under glass.

Apples (Braeburn, Fuji)
Asparagus (English and French)
Bream
Brill
Broad bean
Carrot
Caviar (first of spring imports)
Currant
Elderflower
Flounder
Garlic (fresh)
Gooseberry
Grey mullet
Grilse

Hake
Kohlrabi
Lobster (Scottish)
Melons (Honeydew leads the crop)
Plums (Royston, Santa Rosa)
Pineapple
Potatoes (Jersey Royal, Charlotte)
Radishes
Shrimp
Sorrel
Turnip
Tomato (outdoor)
Whitebait
Watercress

July is rampant. Italy is sending fruit by the crate. The French are holding back the best orchards for harvesting later in the year. Suddenly tomatoes have flavour. The berry fruits are in full flight.

Artichoke
Aubergine
Bream
Broad bean
Beetroot
Cabbage (Hispi)
Fennel
Gooseberry (Levellers)
Pear
Radish

Squash
Lettuces
Mango (ruby)
Peach
Plum (Santa Rosa)
Raspberry
Strawberry
Tomatoes (plum from Italy and best
    natives)
Turnip

August swells up to one of the great months of the year, still replete with the summer harvests, but the first of the autumn foods coming on line with the opening of the game season and the promise of the first new-season apples.

Apple (Discovery)
Crab (hen)
Cucumber
Garlic (first of the French)
Melon (Galia)

Mushrooms (pied de mouton, hedgehog)
Pea
Plums (Santa Rosa, Victoria, greengage)
Sweetcorn
Tomato

September is the height of the fruit and vegetable year: the finest peaches, the first native blackberries, apples starting their prime. Shellfish is good too.

Cheese (Beenleigh Blue)
Garlic
Goose
Grey mullet
Grouse
Melon (Galia)
Mussel

Nuts (Kent cobs)
Onion
Oyster (native)
Peach (French on the tree)
Pears (Abate Fetel, France)
Plums (Victoria, Santa Rosa)
Sweetcorn

October is as abundant as March is scarce, as the full force of the harvest is unloaded on the market. There is good fish as the waters start to turn cool at the end of the month. Game is at its best, the first of the winter roots, lamb arguably better than in the spring.

Apple (Cox)
Celeriac
Hake
Jerusalem artichoke
Lamb
Partridge
Pheasant

Pomegranate
Pumpkin
Salsify
Snipe
Walnut
Woodcock

November, and the first imports from the Near East start to arrive for Christmas – bringing figs, nuts and dates. The winter vegetables are at their peak, the start of the citrus season, and the cold seas mean the return of the big white fish.

Apples (Cox)
Cabbages (January King, Savoy)
Chestnut
Fig (Bursa from Turkey)
Haddock
Orange (Navelina)

Pheasant
Swede
Truffle (white from Alba)
Walnut
Woodcock

December, by tradition or design, marks the resplendent climax of the year before the cold of winter sets in properly. Foods that have been unseen for most of the year suddenly manifest themselves, many at their very peak.

Apples (Cox, Egremont)
Caviar (autumn harvest from Iran)
Clementines
Cod
Cheese (Stilton)
Chestnut
Cranberry
Date (Medjoul)

Fig (Bursa from Turkey)
Geese
Grapefruit (Sweetie)
Lychee
Nuts (Brazil)
Salsify
Scallop
Turkey

All year: the best farmed or cultivated foods available most of the year.

Courgette	Mussel
Cucumber	Oyster
Herbs (in pots)	Salad leaves
Lobster (Canadian)	Salmon (farmed – best in summer)
Mushroom (button)	Trout

SUPERMARKET BY SUPERMARKET

ASDA is a bit like a pair of those '50s trousers they actually sell – practical but old-fashioned and dull. Its chief virtues tend to be that it is not over-expensive and that it often has a high percentage of good brands that don't penetrate the other big five.

Formed in 1965 out of a small supermarket chain and a dairy group, it grew swiftly into one of the most powerful chains by the late '70s. It was, however, badly hit by its move away from good value to value-added, a point even accepted in the company report. Now in a state of transition, it is still the biggest operator in Scotland. A quarter of the 30,000 lines are own-label. It has also publicly committed itself to a policy of improving the price and quality of its fresh foods – which would be welcome.

The **CO-OP** was started in 1844 by 28 disaffected workers fed up with adulterated food in the Rochdale area. The first shop is now a museum in Toad Lane. Not only was the food they sold then fresh, but profits were shared out among the members at the end of the year according to how much they had spent.

It still claims to be the largest retailer in the UK, with 8 million members, but each region now has separate policies. Beyond its 1,000-plus stores it also has the biggest milk round – delivering to one-third of homes – and is the biggest undertaker, doing a quarter of all funerals.

The big show-piece stores are a match for any supermarket, but the original pioneering zeal seems to have ebbed badly and there is little evidence of a policy either in favour of fresh foods or of unadulterated foods as the founders might have wished. Application forms for those who wish to join are available in the stores.

GATEWAY is going to change its stores into the style of its younger son, **SOMERFIELD**, which can only be good news. If ever there was evidence needed that a supermarket could not survive indefinitely selling cheap, second-rate brands – while rival stores developed own-label, ready meals and fresh foods – then Gateway was it.

Its solitary virtue was cheapness, but for what? **Somerfield** by contrast has invested heavily in its own-label lines, which by and large are innovative and forward-looking. Some of the meat buying, especially of ham and Welsh lamb in western stores, has been inspired. In other respects it has taken on some of the character of a miniature **Safeway**.

MARKS & SPENCER does not properly qualify to be listed alongside other supermarkets because its contribution is much smaller. The stores are places for one-stop shopping, not stock-up shopping – unless you are very extravagant and have a very large freezer. There is a minimum of larder products and the accent is firmly on convenience.

Its ready meals are still more enterprising and dynamic than rivals. The butchery section has been developing different gimmicky ways of selling meat to make it yet easier – ready-sliced roasts with the sauces in a packet, or whole roasts sold in a roasting tin. The fruit section is impeccable and the fruit, by and large, more likely to be ripe than **Sainsbury** – also varieties are invariably detailed. There is little arguing with the freshly shelled peas from Kenya in February.

It is expensive, but there is very little trickery with the pricing and the convenience and quality are genuine enough.

SAFEWAY is the corporate raider of the supermarkets, born out of the vicious price wars of the late '70s, and assembled by acquisition of small retail outlets and industrialized food businesses.

Like **Tesco**, it suffers from a mish-mash of old- and new-generation stores. It has backed some high-publicity varietal causes, notably apples, melons, strawberries, lemons and venison, but how deep the commitment goes is not clear. At heart, it seems committed to having a bit of everything without really leading in any field. The investment is currently behind the scenes in distribution and computerization, but a new management team may impose a stronger philosophy.

The original company was American, opening its first purpose-built supermarket in Bedford in June 1963. Its style was American – wide aisles, money-back guarantees, in-store bakeries, sell-by dates and chill displays. More than one-third of what was sold was own-label. By 1986 it was the sixth largest retailer, with strongholds in London, the South and Scotland.

A hostile take-over bid for the American parent led to the UK stores being put up for sale. Enter **Argyll** – representing all shades of the patchwork quilt of UK retailing in the period since the First World War, notably strong in the Midlands and North-west. Shrewdly put together, they had grown out of a loss-making grocery distribution company in Shrewsbury in 1978, with a few almost-bankrupt stores called **Supavalu**. By a deliberate and brilliant campaign of acquiring ailing businesses, Argyll grew to take over well-known shops like **Pricerite**, **Presto** and **Liptons**, plus a range of smaller freezer centres like **Snow King** and **Cordon Bleu**.

SAINSBURY remains the benchmark by which other supermarket chains are judged. It is the oldest, originating out of a North London dairy in the 1860s. It has consistently pursued a policy of own-labels since then and has remained a family-owned and -run business. Its heartland is Surrey, but it has started to expand in the North.

Some of the quality does not live up to the brilliance of its marketing, but for the most part it achieves its slogan of 'good food costs less'. It excels at French products, notably wine, dairy and even bread. Fruit and vegetables are extensive, if not always in as good nick as they might be. The limited fresh fish range is supported by a solid frozen section. Own-label lines, on which it depends, are for the most part carefully thought out. It does not overstock with different varieties, but tends to polarize between a good quality example and often a down-market brand name.

It tends to stick to its principles – for example, veal has been stocked throughout the past two decades of controversy, albeit neither Dutch nor crated. It is proud of its integrated crop management, for example introducing wasps (*Encarsia formosa*) to tomato greenhouses. The wasps lay their eggs in the eggs of the pest whitefly, where previously pesticides were used. These pesticides also killed bees and pollination had to be done artificially. With the introduction of the wasps, the bees happily pollinate again. It is also fond of its innovations, introducing crème fraîche and, more recently, a new less expensive dry cure for bacon.

TESCO tends to change in perception according to the size of the store. The big new-generation stores and the streamlined inner-city '**Tesco Metro**' – symbolically the first on the site of the Old Moss Bros in Covent Garden – are probably a match for anywhere.

The **Tesco** ethics tend to be sound and honest, with a genuine desire to develop new forms of variety and also to keep the costs in check. This is considerably more obvious where they have the space to show off. In those areas that they have worked on they might well consider themselves market-leaders – fruit and vegetables are wideranging but increasingly without the overly exotic, although there may well be a choice of, say, five kinds of oranges in February. Fish is smaller than **Waitrose** and less adventurous, but typically sensible and mainline. The new initiative last year on meat has improved quality considerably for pork, lamb and beef. Cheese and dairy are developing enterprisingly. Its commitment to healthy eating has to be read against the greater razzmatazz of 4% fat oven-ready chips and the Christmas Double Cream with Cointreau. It does, however, seem less cynical than some of its competitors, and more thorough in, say, its bread flours which have sufficient protein in them to bake a sound loaf.

Its major ethical stances on computers for schools and a positive approach to the environment are not without some commitment. Improvements are introduced across the board and not just lobbed in as extra-high premium earners. Amazingly, the Swindon branch has been selling Sevruga caviar at £11.99 an ounce.

There is a sense of honesty and straightforwardness in the flagship stores, though this might be seen as dullness in the older generation of shops, where lack of space cramps a not-inconsiderable vision or the attempt to offer a large range of choices. It is said to have been worse hit than rivals in the recession because larger stores are not necessarily attracting higher spends. The size of bigger stores means similar items are often placed on different aisles, which makes price comparisons difficult.

FISH
&
SHELLFISH

The recent history of fishing is a story of nationalistic greed, war, mindless pollution and decimation of the marine environment. On shore, whole communities have been wiped out by draconian edicts of bureaucrats and ministers; at sea, the Russians and the Americans have hoovered up all life forms and spewed them out as low-cost food or fertiliser.

All the while, the numbers of fish have declined. In 1948, Billingsgate fish market handled 3,800 tonnes of fish in a week, in 1960 this was halved to 1,700, in 1970 down to 1,100, in 1980 only 800 and in 1990 a mere 600 tons. The downward trend in white fish is worse: the 1980 and 1990 figures are buoyed up by imports of exotic fish. Just as our waters have been ravaged, so now are the tropical coral reefs.

The river authorities have accepted that UK rivers are too polluted with sewage to sustain breeding populations of healthy fish. The campaigning zeal that led to salmon being caught again in the Thames seems to have dissipated. On some salmon rivers, anglers have been buying net-men out in a desperate effort to protect the waters for themselves.

Some efforts at conservation have been made. The ban on herring fishing has seen this once staple food return safely to the market. Other species are threatened, however, and the litany of EC legislation for tying up boats in harbour, quota limits and pollution controls of sorts does not seem to convince

THE TRADE IN BRITAIN

The biggest port is Peterhead, north of Aberdeen. Hull tends to take the bigger ships from further afield. Billingsgate notionally takes most of the fish, but this has been a slow, sluggish artery where fish has tended to hang around before getting to the fishmonger. In itself, Billingsgate is an endangered species due to the new health regulations. It is, however, an excellent place to buy inexpensively in bulk for ordinary people with a rudimentary knowledge of good fish, prepared to get up in the morning and be there before eight. A number of smaller operations now run direct delivery from ports, dropping off fish to inland areas and many offer a higher quality of fish than otherwise washes through the conventional trade, if for no other reason than it is fresher.

For packing and presentation, the Dutch (who else) and the French at Rungis set a considerably higher standard than is commonly found here. Much of the fish trade seems stuck in the 19th century and has not assimilated ideas from other areas of the food industry – most obviously the value of fresh food, properly looked after. Fish, of all foods, needs to be fresh, carefully handled and kept well iced. These may be obvious points, but they are too rarely followed. A more innocent explanation of the decline in sales of fresh fish might simply be that really fresh fish has become harder and harder to find.

The traditional advice to those buying fresh fish is to check that the eyes are bright, the skin still slimy and the flesh is resilient and does not ply to the touch.

anyone. What is still outstanding is an international strategy, or at the very least a European one. This would certainly include far tougher pollution controls and a commitment to reviving rivers and inshore waters.

There should also be an acceptance of fishing as a smaller-scale cottage industry to ensure its long-term future and the survival of marine life. Coastline towns, many of which have lost their identity, might hope for some regeneration.

THE BIG WHITES

COD

Cod may vary from greenish-grey to khaki in colour, depending on where they come from: those brownish-green with brown or yellow spots tend to come from the North Sea; the darker from near the Faeroes, and the almost black from further north, although they all seem to share the look of earnest sadness and the courtier's smart little goatee fin under the mouth. Food writer Frances Bissell calls cod 'the patriarch of the (big white) family'.

Most are found on the Newfoundland Bank, a submarine plateau 800 km (500 miles) long and 500 km (200 miles) wide, but they will stray as far afield as Britain and Iceland. At their best in winter, they range from 35 to 100 cm (14 inches to 3 ft) in length, larger fish tasting discernibly different from the younger sweeter, more delicate smaller inshore fish, known as CODLING. They can grow as big as 45 kg (100 lb), but over-fishing has made these giants increasingly rare.

In 1948, 300,000 tonnes were landed. (This figure included the salt cod sold in barrels where the boats went north for much of the summer and preserved the fish on board.) By 1987, only 90,000 tonnes were landed and in 1992 that figure was halved. Massive fishing by Russian factory ships is one potent factor in this decline.

Scarcity has rehabilitated the culinary reputation of the cod and it has increasingly appeared on restaurant menus. Short and plump fish are the best. Steaks are more tender if taken from nearer the tail, but shoulder cuts have more flavour. Cheap cod is off-loaded on the English markets from the Atlantic and can be as much as four weeks

Cod
Coley
Haddock
Hake
Ling
Whiting

FOOD *watch*

Fish in Supermarkets

The best supermarket for fresh fish is **Waitrose. Asda** is probably the cheapest. **Sainsbury** is content to stock mostly frozen fish, but often at competitive prices compared to Billingsgate. **Tesco** and **Marks & Spencer** tend to be expensive. There is some truth in the claim that fish frozen at sea within hours of catching may be in better condition than much of what passes for 'fresh'. Frozen fish is best cooked straight from the freezer, without thawing as this allows nutrients and flavour to leak out.

old, so more than other fish it is worth checking for freshness. Cod deserves more attention than simply deep-frying in batter; grilled or poached, it lends itself to strong sauces, even curry. It is good cold with *aïoli* and is excellent in stews, like the classic French *bourride*

SALT COD

Today, this is principally prepared in Norway. The fish are gutted, soaked in brine and then kept in salt. They are then dried for export – mostly to southern Europe. In Portugal, salt cod is hung along the streets of fishing ports to dry. STOCKFISH is the dried variation and was a feature of the pre-war diet in this part of the world. It needs to be soaked for 48 hours to remove the bulk of the salt before cooking.

COD'S ROE

Available from November to March, these are usually already boiled by the fishmonger. Raw, they are sold in pairs. Handle carefully so as not to break the outer membrane, and poach for 10 minutes. Dry well, then shallow-fry or make into fish-cakes. They can be baked with strong sauces, like shrimp or anchovy, mixed with cream as a filling for omelettes, or rolled in bacon slices and grilled. For a salad, chop and mix with chopped with hard-boiled eggs, fresh herbs, spring onion, and diced ham.

COLEY

Sometimes called COALFISH, BLACKJACK or SAITHE and sold still as ROCK SALMON, these blackish or dark green paling to silver fish, 60-100 cm (2-3 ft) in length, are best in summer. They are clean creatures, preying on other fish, notably herring. Translucent pink-grey flesh turns a more attractive white on cooking, but tends to dryness and breaks up easily in cooking. Coley was always decried as rather a second-rate fish, but it does not really deserve this poor standing. A good everyday fish, it can be about £1 per lb cheaper than cod, possibly more. It is best baked or braised with strong flavourings, or used in pies and fish-cakes. It can be found dyed orange and smoked.

HADDOCK

One in five fish taken from the North Sea used to be haddock, but serious over-fishing has seen catches halved in the five years from 1987 to 1992. Part of the cod family, it is similar in shape to the cod but the markings tend to be dark grey-black, with a silver underside; the head is more worldly, wider-eyed and smaller-mouthed. Legend has it that the thumbprint-like indentation on the side of the head is St Peter's mark. Smaller than cod, between 40-75 cm (16-30 in), it is available all year round, but best from colder waters in the months November to February. Large fish are now rare.

Some say haddock is superior to cod, especially the smaller fish which tend to have softer flesh, but the flakes are well-sized. Its blandness encourages bright saucing, like brown butter, and stronger flavours like mustard and cheese and the more old-fashioned flour-based sauces. Northern fish and chip shops prefer haddock to cod.

SMOKED HADDOCK

Haddock does not salt as well as cod, so the fish were instead smoked for eight hours over peat and sawdust after being left in brine for three hours, hence FINNAN HADDIES from the peat smokeries at 'Finnan', or Findon, eight miles south of Aberdeen. GLASGOW PALES are smoked just enough to turn the

FOOD *watch*

Haddock Prices
Sainsbury's frozen haddock has matched the Billingsgate price of fresh at £2.10 per lb, a margin of about 40p. Fresh **Somerfield** fillets are £2.99 against **Marks & Spencer** at £3.98 per lb.

colour to that of hay. ARBROATH SMOKIES are hot-smoked in pairs, originally in barrels but now in large kilns. There is still an active industry in Arbroath, which filched the idea from the tiny hamlet of Auchmithie further north. Smokies will keep up to two weeks. At other ports, more primitively, haddock were just sun-dried on the beach. Cod treated this way was never deemed as good.

HADDOCK ROE
This appears from November to March and is usually sold raw.

HAKE
Preferring deeper waters, these fish have long tapering bodies about 30-100 cm (1-3 ft), pointed heads, black mouths and ferocious teeth. Voracious cannibals, they sleep on the ocean bed by day and swim upwards to feed at night. The mouths are hinged, like monk-fish, which gives them a smug glare. They snare unsuspecting passing prey, usually herring and pilchards. Dark grey with large loose scales, they are best in the second half of the year, from June to December.

The flesh is more fragile than cod: soft and creamy and less well-flavoured, so it tends to suit stronger flavourings. When absolutely fresh, some argue hake is the finest of all the cod family. It is also inclined to break up, however, especially as it ages.

LING
Longer than the cod, ling has a green-brown mottled back and a grey belly. From 75 cm (30 in) long, the fish often goes for *bacalão* in Spain. It has a good flavour but is inclined to wateriness and marries with strong flavours in pies or fish cakes. Although not always avail-

Ways with Hake

Hake is well suited to being wrapped *en papillote* or in leaves, cooked briefly and served with garlicky *salsas* or green vegetables or stuffings. Hake is good cold and in fish pies, with lots of garlic and parsley. It is much appreciated in Spain, Italy and Portugal. Smaller fish are deep-fried. Basque *kokotxes* are hake throats marinated in oil, garlic and parsley.

able, it is cheaper than better-known fish and makes a good midweek buy – but avoid the bony tail cuts.

WHITING

Most whiting come from the sub-Arctic, though the best are attributed to Cornwall. Slim, silver-grey with white bellies, 30-60 cm (1-2 ft) in length, they are best from cold waters in winter. The sweet flesh is versatile and used to be recommended for invalids, but is worth more than that although some cooks are disparaging. It can be dry, so it is best not to grill whiting. It is useful for soufflès and mousses and may be braised or poached in wine for 15 minutes. An old recipe book declares the flesh 'delicate in flavour and easily digested'.

THE FLAT FISH

BRILL

With their ovoid disc-like bodies, light brown freckled to grey black markings and small scales, brill are 30-50 cm (12-20 in) in length and without the bony bumps under the skin found on the turbot, which they closely resemble. Although at their best in early summer, they are available most of the year. Sinistral fish, they lie on the seabed with their left sides uppermost and are voracious feeders, eating fry and eels. Their underrated creamy moist flesh is well-flavoured and makes a good alternative to turbot – indeed it was known and derided, wrongly, as 'poor man's turbot'. The best, and most expensive, are the larger fish which can be filleted and sauced. Otherwise grill or bake them. They go well with vegetables.

DAB

With a coarse, sandy brown back, white underside and 15-25 cm (6-10 in) in length, this is the smallest but fastest of the flat fish, and so enjoys a wider choice of prey than others in the plaice family. It is at its best in autumn, when it is sweet, tender and fragile, but may be found all year. Grill or shallow-fry in breadcrumbs. Larger fish are now quite a find; they can be filleted and take sauces as strong as soy, mustard or horseradish.

FLOUNDER

Also known as FLUKE, this fish migrates into estuaries in summer, but is found all year. Dull brown in colour, sometimes with a blotchy orange skin, it is akin to plaice, but less good (though passed off as such) – plaice has nodules on its head, flounder is smooth. Flounder is rarely found inland, because it must be eaten very fresh or the flesh suffers. Some cooks are disparaging, dismissing it as a filler for terrines; others attempt to sauce it for added flavour.

HALIBUT

The most magnificent and largest of all flat fish, and now also one of the most expensive – even more so than turbot. Before the war, fishing boats kept the halibut alive in tanks beneath the boats for up to eight weeks before bringing them back to port. Halibut feed on the floor of the Atlantic near Greenland, favouring rocky ground in the Arctic and North Sea. There they were usually caught on a line with live herring for bait. The duels of small boats landing huge fish were the stuff of fishermen's tales. Records exist in Grimsby of a halibut landed in 1957 weighing 137 kg (304 lb) and possibly 60 years old. Some report fish even larger, at six feet long and 225 kg (500 lb), although such monsters are rare now. Smaller fish, under 2.3 kg (5 lb), are called CHICKEN HALIBUT.

Halibut are best in spring but available most of the year, though some may be frozen imports. For a fish of such size it has a tiny glum boxer's face, white belly and blotchy olive-green rough skin. Its reputation has waxed and waned; most agree that the flesh is dry, but some recommend 'as little preparation as possible'. The tail end has more bones and these will conduct the heat in cooking and make it dry. What the fish needs is careful moist cooking, preferably poaching or shallow-frying, accompanied (not swamped) by other flavours, as with meat. Like brill, halibut tends to combine well with vegetables. Halibut farming is currently being developed in Norway.

SMOKED HALIBUT

This is usually GREENLAND or MOCK HALIBUT, a smaller fish without the white belly, with flesh that is drier and coarser. Some is sold in **Sainsbury** and occasionally fresh in some branches of **Somerfield**, where it is cheaper than haddock.

MEGRIM

Also known as MEG, WHIFF, SCARBOROUGH WHIFF or SCARBOROUGH SOLE, it is sandy in colour with spots, ovoid and snoutish mouth, white belly and 25-40 cm (10-16 in) in length. These fish blanket the deep ocean floor. The flesh is inclined to wateriness and needs quite strong sauces. The fish is best suited to deep-frying or fish-cakes.

PLAICE

From the same family as lemon sole, witch and flounder, this is a dextral flat fish, ie it lies right side uppermost, head twisted. The mouth is jaggedly awry, the eyes of different sizes. The plaice hunts either under cover of camouflage on the sand of the seabed or moving horizontally through the water, devouring molluscs and small crustacea. They have brown backs to merge with the sands in which they lie, with orange spots (they used to be called DIAMOND SOLES), white bellies, and are 30-45 cm (12-18 in) in length. They are at their best from June to December.

They have an iodinic smell when very fresh. The spots disappear in older fish, which are best cooked on the bone. Look for large fish and take a middle cut, using the rest for soup. 'More watery than flounder', but fish restaura-

FOOD *watch*

Plaice Prices
Smaller plaice sell for about 50p per lb wholesale, larger fish for just over the £1 mark. **Asda** sell them at £2.09, but **Somerfield** at £2.59 or fillets at a steep £3.29.

teur Rick Stein says, 'a fresh delicacy, I grow ever more fond of plaice, but its delicacy is soon lost as it stales'. Traditionally plaice was regarded as invalid food, steamed between two plates over boiling water. It is, however, best grill or shallow-fried.

SOLE

True soles are called DOVER SOLES because most destined for the London market were landed there to meet the train to the capital. Most are caught in the North and Irish seas as well as the English Channel and around the Mediterranean. They propel themselves just above the seabed, tapping the ground with the blind side of their head in search of worms, molluscs and small crustacea. The nose is blunt, the colouring surly grey, depending on its habitat. They have coarse, tough skin, compact flat bodies, lightly blotched, white underbelly, and are 25-55 cm (10-22 in) in length. Smaller fish, 20-25 cm (8-10 in) long, are termed SLIP SOLES; smaller still – under 20 cm (8 in) – are called TONGUES. They are available all year, but are best out of mid-winter. Witch and megrim are sometimes passed off as sole.

The only fish perfectly suited for serving on the bone, it is best grilled or *à la meunière*. The classical kitchen offers more sauces for sole than for any other fish, but at today's price this now seems almost irresponsible. Some say soles are best left a day or two before use.

LEMON SOLE are plump oval fish, with sandy brown backs, indistinct mottled markings, small heads and white belly. About 25-40 cm (10-16 in) in length and not related to Dover sole, they have a very good flavour, especially when very fresh, and are at their best from March to December. Cook them

FOOD *watch*

Sole Prices

The price of Dover sole is now so exorbitant, they have become almost entirely the preserve of the restaurant. **Marks & Spencer** sell them, on the bone, at £10.99 per lb. Underrated and good value, lemon sole cost between £1-£3 at Billingsgate, against £4.50 per lb frozen at **Sainsbury**, and £6.49 at **Marks & Spencer**. They are best bought from fishmongers at half that price.

simply: flour and grill them with butter, pan-fry or bake. Two people will need about 675 g (1½ lb) of fish.

The SAND SOLE, an oblong fish with a freckled sandy back and white belly, is simllar to Dover sole, but mostly goes for export. The flesh is creamy, moist and very good. WITCH SOLE, oval fish with pale-brown mottled backs and white bellies, are 30-40 cm (12-16in) in length, have white flesh and are a good value alternative to Dover sole, especially in heavily sauced dishes.

TURBOT

This king of the flat fish, like brill and megrim, has eyes on the left side of the head. It was held to be the finest fish, but is now rare and expensive. Mostly from the North Sea, it has a sandy or dark-brown grey back, no scales and a white belly. It is 50-100 cm (20-40 in) long and is almost circular, with thick moist flesh and an excellent flavour. Classical kitchens used diamond-shaped *turbotières* to accommodate them. Up to one-third of the fish is bones and waste. Bones for stock should be cooked longer than is usual – up to three hours to extract their gelatinousness. 'Two points ahead of sole,' declares fish expert Alan Davidson. Small fish, up to 1.35 kg (3 lb), are termed CHICKEN TURBOT.

Unlike sole, the skin is eaten. Whole fish should be slit along the backbone and the bone broken to stop it curling. Cook simply: poach for 6 minutes per 450 g (1 lb). It can look quite pallid and needs colourful accompaniments. Serve cold with mayonnaise.

THE OILY FISH

ANCHOVY

One of the herring family, this silver-skinned fish about 10-20 cm (4-8 in) long is distinguished by a deeply cleft mouth and long snout. Some reach the South-west coast of England in summer, but the trade is now centred on Spain, Morocco and Italy, where nearly all the canning is done (including some imports from Peru). In early summer the fish are attracted to the boats by lights and caught in nets.

Italy packs them in bottles, Spain in tins. Unlike sardines, preserved anchovies do not improve with age so look for far-off sell-by dates. Anchovies are only semi-cured in salt and, strictly speaking, ought to be kept chilled, but rarely are. The best fish used to come from the island of Gorgona off Livorno, one of the pre-war centres of the olive oil trade. The price is governed by the filleting. Hand-filleted anchovies are stripped in cold water and will often still have the skin on. Machines use hot water, which takes off skin and bone neatly. The former has personality, the other uniformity. Some arrive from Holland unsalted, but preserved in diluted sunflower oil, and are sold in specialist delicatessens. The contrast in the colouring – the one a grey white, the other a meat red – is testimony to the power of salt.

The two types need different strategies in the kitchen. Unsalted are ready to eat and go well with potatoes. They will be as good as the oil and vinegar in which they are kept. Usually they will be better for being rinsed out and put back in fresh oil. Brine-packed fish should be rinsed in cold water to rid them of the salt, then soaked in warm (not hot) water

Anchovy
Brisling
Herring
Mackerel
Pilchard
Sardine
Sprat
Tuna
Whitebait

**WAYS WITH
ANCHOVIES:**

British: Anchovy
butter.
French: *Anchoïade*,
mashed with oil, lemon
and garlic, then spread
on toast and flashed
under a grill.
*Anchoïade de Austin
de Croze:* this recipe
incorporates all the
flavours of Provence.
Mince 1 part each
fresh herbs, onion,
garlic, fennel leaves, to
3 parts dried figs,
stalks removed. Pound
a small chilli with a
dozen ground skinned
almonds (or 6 walnuts),
add a dozen anchovies
in oil, and a dozen
anchovies in brine,
lemon juice and orange
flower water. Slice an
unsweetened brioche
in half, spread the
paste on one side, oil
on the other, close up
and bake in a hot oven
for 5 minutes. Garnish
with black olives.

for 15 minutes and drained. Fresh fish should be filleted, salted for two hours, cooked very briefly in hot oil, drained and then marinated in olive oil, garlic and lemon for 48 hours. Salted they are used as a seasoning, as they are high in the glutamates associated with the fifth taste *umami*. From the Middle Ages they have been used to season pies, pastes and meat and, in classical *pâtisserie* for *canapés*.

TINNED ANCHOVIES

Prices range from 75p for 133 g or 6p a fillet, to £1.76 for the Italian **Zarotti** at 30p a fillet. *****Rizzoli Emanuelle** from Parma are low in salt and have 10 fillets in extra-virgin olive oil: 'chewy, texturous, delicate, salt building at the end.' The big brands like **John West**, **Epicure** and **Waitrose** have tended to outperform the more romantic colourful labels of smaller producers. Moroccan examples have been very scraggy and bony. **Princes** has also been cheap and poor, even greying. **Sainsbury** buy neat, meaty fillets from Spain; **Tesco's** from Italy are paler grey, less promising to look at but a good flavour in good oil (with an extravagant sell-by date of 18 months – nine more than Sainsbury's). The most expensive **Zarotti** are even poorer value on opening, with only seven fillets compared to Tesco's 12; they are bony, but with good flavour.

BOTTLED ANCHOVIES

Traditionally the Italians preserved anchovies in bottles. The best examples are from **Iasa**, in good oil and salt, still with some skin and bones but plenty of flavour and character.

BRISLING

The French successfully contested Norway's right to sell into Britain what they were calling 'sardines' under the **Skipper** label in 1912.

The name was changed to brisling or SILD. The Norwegians had their revenge by inventing the seamless tin can, and by the early '20s were selling more than a million cases a year into the UK.

The brisling is unique to Norway, coming close into the fjords in summer to feed near the surface in such numbers that the waters can seem to boil. Much of the fishing is still done by fourth-generation farmers, who form the main co-operative. The boats use fine-mesh purse seine nets, echo scanners and lights to attract the shoals. Two-year-old fish are taken at full maturity, when the fat content will be at its peak. The catch is impounded in nets in the fjord for several days so that the fish clean themselves of impurities. They are washed and then hung on steel rods to smoke for an hour over oak chippings. The heads are then removed and the fish packed, still by hand. Although small, they represent high sources of omega-3 oils (see page 23), as well as vitamins A, B and D.

> Brisling are sold tinned under the ****King Oscar** label. Norwegian brisling have not been sold widely into EC countries, since tariffs make them prohibitively expensive. **John West** sell brisling under the original **Skipper** label, but sourced now from Scotland. They lack the infusion of smoke and oil and are inferior to the Norwegian. The brisling mature in the can and after two years are markedly improved.

HERRING

Once second only to cod as the most important fish in the Northern-European economy, vast shoals of herring came inshore. 'Once seen, never to be forgotten,' said *Law's Grocer's Manual* in 1950. 'The sea for miles around shines with a silvery lustre from their glittering scales, for the herring swims near the surface, with its nose out of the water, as though enjoying the fresh air, and the effect is very peculiar. The myriad of little fish rushing along seem to affect the very sea itself, making a loud soughing noise, like a heavy fall of rain, the result of the rippling caused on the surface of the water. These great herring armies are also accompanied by various larger fish, gannets, hawks, gulls and other

WAYS WITH HERRING

Scotland: shallow-fried in bacon fat with coarse-cut oatmeal.
France: grilled with mustard; marinated in white wine (a good pairing).
Scandinavia: soused, pickled or salted.

Tinned Herring
John West has been putting herrings into tins, the results obscured by gunky sauces. They have also smoked small herrings and canned them as kippers in oil. The two processes fight each other, you just taste a lightly smoked oil. Far more successful, but only available in delicatessens, are ****Liflig Gaffelbidder** from **Varefakta**; packed in Denmark and confusingly called sild, they are marinated in sherry and vinegar.

sea birds, all of which feed on the herrings. Considering these and the raids made everywhere by fishermen, it is not easy to imagine how the brave little survivors, weakened, worn, and harassed, ever reach their icy home again; but each year the herring shoals come afresh...' Such phenomena sustained the history of northern European fishing for centuries. The Atlantic herring stocks were halved in the decade of the '50s; whether this was from over-fishing or a cyclical catastrophe – or both – is unclear. As many other fish feed on herring, the impact was two-edged. Since the lifting of the ban on fishing in '84, the catches have picked up dramatically. They remain cheap, as little as 40p per lb wholesale.

The herring has a dark blue-green back, silver sides, and a reddish tint to the eyes as if it is hungover (which accentuates as it gets older in the fishmonger's). It is best avoided in spring and autumn, after it has spawned, when it starves itself – such fish are known in the trade as SPENTS or SHOTTEN. They are a high-quality food with the same protein as beef and good vitamin A, B and D content. Levels of polyunsaturates alter through the year and with different species; the smaller Baltic herring being less fatty than the Atlantic. The flesh is fragile and needs careful cooking. It was said it is cooked when it sees the fire or in the time it takes to recite *Ave Maria*.

HERRING ROE

Roes are mostly taken from herring that go for kippers or are imported frozen from Canada. They are very high in vitamin D and underrated, both in price and value. Flour them and shallow-fry or bake or grill with mustard.

BLOATER

Most famously from Great Yarmouth, these are lightly smoked and bloated herrings, which gives a silvery cast. The guts are left in, which gives a gamy flavour. The curing process is not long enough to preserve or cook them. They are best grilled.

BUCKLING

Hot-smoked herring, traditionally imported from Germany and eaten as they are or dressed in a sharp vinaigrette with dill. Their smell is that of a clean kipper, but they tend to look off-puttingly squishy and soft. The flesh turns a bready dry, but is quite creamy. The irritating little bones seem to get everywhere.

KIPPER

These were reputedly invented by John Woodger, a Northumberland fish-curer, around 1843, though the history of smoking and curing haddock further north in the Scottish ports suggests it must have been earlier. Arbroath Smokies can show their history back to the 12th century and if haddock were being smoked, then surely herring were too.

The herrings are split, washed, put in brine, hung to dry and then smoked for 4-6 hours (even quite recently 6-18 seemed to be more usual). MANX and CRASTER kippers have long histories of careful smoking. Some others are artificially dyed with the controversial browning agent FK. Those cooked on the bone will have more flavour, but ironically they are more expensive – usually by 10p or more per lb – than fillets, a general recognition that the processing is not constructive.

Most cookbooks suggest grilling, but kippers can smell for a long time in small kitchens. Other safe strategies are to steep them in boiling water for 10 minutes, or microwave them. Though the smell still tends to linger.

RED HERRING

Originally designed for long keeping, these are heavily salted and then smoked. (One explanation of the use of their name to denote a diversion derives from the practice of hiding contraband in the bottom of the smelly barrel.) Such fish had to be soaked overnight before use. Today the few curers still active use much gentler cures, so 5 minutes soaking is enough. Treat them like kippers.

MATJE HERRING

The process for curing these in a light brine is credited to the Dutchman Willem Beukelzoom in the 14th century and was protected for centuries. The fish are packed in distinctive small barrels and were considered at their best in May, when the herrings returned after wintering further north. Traditionally they are eaten with French beans and chopped onions.

BISMARCK HERRING

These are flat fillets, marinated in vinegar and white wine with onions and juniper. The French reputedly gave them the name after the Franco-Prussian War of 1870.

ROLLMOP HERRING

These fillets are rolled around onion or gherkin and marinated in vinegar. Some may be frozen before marinating, which destroys the texture. The commercial recipe soaks the herring fillets in a solution of vinegar, sugar, salt, onions and spices for up to three weeks in a fridge. They are then drained and packed in bottles with a new marinade and spices. Swedish brands like **Laurel Farm** and **Konserver** are notably good. They ignore southern tradition and pragmatically cut the herring into chunks.

MACKEREL

At one time this was the only fish allowed to be sold on a Sunday as it keeps poorly. The French term for a pimp, '*maquereau*' is thought to come from a 17th-century manual which described mackerels as leading young female shad, which were also known as *vierges* (virgins), to their males. Another explanation is that their glistening green-blue markings resemble the bright clothes of pimps in the Middle Ages. The fish prefer the warmer currents and swim inshore as the summer draws in, but not further than the Wash or the Isle of Man. In winter they are trawled from deep seas. These fish tend to be fatter and oilier and usually go for smoking, which is one reason smoked mackerel shows so well in the omega-3 oil statistics (see page 23). Even at three and four times the wholesale price in the supermarket, mackerel still represent good value.

HORSE MACKEREL, or SCAD, are similar in flavour but, in fact, from a different family; both are distant relations of the tuna. They have no black markings but share the distinctive dark waves, torpedo shape and white belly of the mackerel. Similarly, they will be 30-45 cm (12-18 in) in length.

Mackerel are best in the first half of the year. The rich oily meat deteriorates quickly because of the high and healthy oil content when not fresh, but is an excellent source of vitamins and minerals. The mark-up for smoked fish is steep, with **Tesco** selling smoked mackerel at £2.69 per lb against 40p for unsmoked wholesale.

PILCHARD

This, the adult sardine, has larger and fewer scales than the herring and its habits are also different: it goes out to sea in spring and its

Ways with Mackerel

Mackerel is best simply cooked – usually grilled – with tart, assertive accompaniments, such as lemon, rhubarb, sorrel, gooseberry or mustard. Very fresh, it can be eaten raw in Japanese *sashimi*, or follow ideas for tuna. Preserved, soused or pickled, it shows an affinity with white wine or cider.

TINNED MACKEREL

Mostly from Denmark, the images on the packaging suggest clean brilliant white large fillets: in most cases, however, the contents tend to be grey-beige broken flakes. Either the cheap off-cuts go to brine or the brine actually breaks up the flesh. **Princes** and **Gerber** are notably guilty. The fat levels rise from around 15% for fillets in brine to 25% in soya oil. Good examples are **Marina** and **Sainsbury** in soya oil, though **Sainsbury Scottish** mackerel in brine still has the skin on and is in horizontal chunks not fillets. John West do an interesting canned wood-smoked and peppered mackerel fillet in oil.

eggs survive on the surface, unlike those of herring which sink. Pilchards are caught off the south-west coast of England from July to September. It was, however, the vast shoals of Pacific pilchards massing around California at the turn of the century that were historically important. Being so rich in oil, the canners sold the fish cheap in order to be allowed to extract the oil from the rest of the catch and sell on the debris as fish meal. Demand for this oil came from the emergent margarine and fats industry, ironically taking the oil in one acceptable form and putting it into another.

The pilchard makes great claims for health-giving attributes: more calcium than milk, more protein than beef and high in omega-3 oils. Over-fishing, as is the story the length of the Pacific coast of the Americas, destroyed the Californian industry. In the '50s, the same machinery was shipped to Peru to process another surge of fish, which in turn was over-fished and vanished. Pilchards are now usually found in tins from **Glenryck**, labelled 'south Atlantic' and arriving via Namibia. The brine does the bland breadiness little favours. They are oversized sardines without the flavour.

SARDINE

In summer, large quantities of sardines are caught off Cornwall. About 10-15 cm (4-6 in) long, with a blue-green back and silver belly, they are best barbecued or marinated in oil.

TINNED SARDINES

The trade began in Nantes about 1834, although the name derives from Sardinia, off whose shores huge quantities were once caught. As the waters warmed, the fish headed north in ever-growing shoals, either towards Provence in May and June or up the Atlantic coast arriving at Brittany in July and not leaving until October. The French boats used cod's roe as bait to attract the shoals and caught them in nets fine enough just to let the head through, but not the gills or fins. The fish were gutted, salted, left to dry on wooden slats, then raised on wire nets into vats of boiling olive oil to cook for 5-6 minutes. Once drained they were then hand-packed into tins. Further south in Spain, Portugal and North Africa, because of the heat, the fish were steamed and laid in olive oil in the tin. French sardines were considered better because the fish came from colder waters and the oil they used to cook was better. Often the oil in the tin was flavoured with bay, cloves or peppercorns.

Good sardines are judged firstly by the quality of the oil. Signs of redness on the flesh indicate it was not freshly packed. The bones should almost have dissolved. Smaller fish have more flavour and sardines improve in the tin with age. All the supermarkets sell them too young, in the same year that they have been caught.

SPRAT

This is sometimes known as BRISLING or SILD when canned, and is similar in appearance to – and often confused with – young herring. It is, in fact, a different species found mostly off the Norwegian coasts, East Anglia and previously around the Thames estuary. Catches have dwindled alarmingly in the last 20 years. With a dark blue-green back, silver sides and belly, and 7-12 cm (2¾-4¾ in) in length, they are at their best from September to March. Test for freshness by squeezing one between the fingers – it should slip out. Although a bit bony, they have very good flavour and are cheap – possibly, food writer Colin Spencer argues, because they smell

Tinned Sardines
Sainsbury favours Portuguese, which are good by our standards, but not in the same league as a brand like ****Piteu** in Portugal itself where the skins gleam unbroken and the fish are as delicate as brisling.

Connetable à l'Ancienne from Brittany have been made in the same way since 1853, and are sold either as fillets, in red cans , or with lemon, in yellow cans. 'The lemon is very pronounced and by some ingenious trick the bones are removed leaving the whole fish intact, skin and all. Very much like a fresh product and very good..' **Waitrose go to Italy where they have been palmed off with broken skinned fragments. The big canners, **John West** and **Princes** – and **Somerfield** – go to Morocco, which does not as yet appear to have ring-pulls. They are big clean fish, and **John West** bought the best last year.

strongly in the cooking. Shallow-fry or treat as anchovies, using the fillets in a brine of 2 parts salt to 10 of water for 30 minutes, then dry and preserve in olive oil with herbs. Pragmatically (less odour), they are excellent when smoked.

TUNA

This may well prove to be the fashionable fish of the '90s. High in the omega-3 oils, with a beautiful individual flavour, it is well suited to the cross-fertilization of Asian and European cooking and seems overdue for recognition. The neck and stomach cuts generally command higher prices.

From 150 cm (5 ft) long, ALBACORE TUNA, found in warm waters only, is long-finned and smaller than Blue and Yellow Fin, with chocolate rather than deep red flesh, which becomes paler on cooking and is not as dense. It is said to be sweetest of all tunas. It is best grilled, baked or braised.

BONITO is usually called SKIPJACK for tins, has steel stripes on a blue-black back, and is 30-50 cm (12-20 in) in length. Imported fresh from the Mediterranean or frozen from elsewhere, it is the least expensive of the tunas. Dried with *konbu* seaweed, it makes the Japanese stock *dashi*. Grill or bake the dark red flesh.

BLUE FIN and YELLOW FIN TUNAS are the large streamlined fish beloved of angling photographs, from 100 cm (40 in) long, with pointed heads and deep middle body. Their rich deep red flesh has few bones and is best grilled or stir-fried – be careful not to overcook. Yellow fin is used for *sashimi*.

MOJOMOA, from south-west Spain, is salted like ham, then cleaned and hung to dry on the factory rooftops under great sails. It keeps for six months in vacuum or oil. Orange in hue,

OMEGA-3 OIL RATINGS

Current thinking is not just that all fish have a positive effect on our bodies, but that the oily fish containing the omega-3 oils (also found in the livers of white fish) are exceptionally valuable. These oils are believed to relax the arteries and improve the flow of blood. With most fish, moreover, little is lost in the cooking, although tuna is an exception. The average recommended weekly intake of these beneficial oils is 8 g for women and 10 g for men – or roughly three meals a week. Smoking the fish increases the percentage of the oils as the water content evaporates, and smokers also tend to buy oilier fish than is usually sold in the supermarkets.

	%
Mackerel, smoked	6.6
Kippers, grilled	3.2
Pilchards, tinned	2.9
Mackerel, grilled	2.8
Sardines, grilled	2.4
Sprats, raw	2.4
Rock salmon	2.3
Conger eel	2
Sardines, canned	2
Salmon, farmed	1.8
Tuna, fresh	1.5
Trout	1
Cod, cooked	0.5
Tuna, canned	0.1

Table reproduced courtesy of Miriam Polunin and Taste magazine.

ham-like in taste and with a soft grainy texture, it is a cousin to anchovy in saltiness, but rather a clumsy and somewhat unsophisticated product.

TINNED TUNA

In Spain and the rest of the Mediterranean, the sardine fleets also caught tuna. It was packed in large tins to be repacked after the sardine season was over in October. Today most of the tinned tuna comes from the southern hemisphere.

The canners prefer skipjack because the meat is compact and the flesh deemed too dark to fetch a good price fresh. Cooking the tuna and draining off its oils reduces the omega-3 oils drastically. **Waitrose** sensibly makes no distinction between chunks and steaks which are now in practice the same thing, varying only in price. They are all skipjack, but landed in different ports: Seychelles (**Glenryck** and **Tesco**), Thailand (**John West**), Ecuador (**Heinz**). So too are the steaks: from Fiji (**Sainsbury**), Philippines (**Waitrose**), St Helena (**Tesco de luxe**). The flesh is more benefited by canning in oil rather than brine (**John West** claim spring water), but that may be subjective. The best examples have tended to be **Waitrose** and **Sainsbury** by a short distance.

More specialized tins deal in the discernibly different Albacore or yellow fin. These are confusingly called 'paler', 'deluxe' or (in **John West's** case) 'Jonggol', which does not appear in any other textbooks. **Tesco** confuse the issue further by selling skipjack in 185 g tins and deluxe in 150 g. These varieties respond differently to the oil and exchange the familiar mealiness of skipjack for an intense meatiness with an edge of lemons. There are good examples from **Tesco deluxe**, **Asda deluxe**, **Connetable**, **John West**, and two Italian sources, **Medusa** and *****Carluccio's yellow fin** – albeit at £3.50 for 250 g, against skipjack at 40-55p for 183 g, but as good an example as may be found on the market.

Zarotti from Italy can tuna from the Azores: the square designer box contains meaty sections which are 'chunky in good olive oil'; the limited-production **oval tin has the fillets of paler flesh, 'milder and more delicate, beautiful for cooking, superb for *vitello tonnato*.'

DOLPHIN-FRIENDLY

There are so many instances of dolphins helping fishermen, they collect credence. Pliny records an incident in a lake near Nîmes, where shoals of grey mullet were lured into the lake and the dolphins summoned others to guard the entrance and prevent their escape while the men netted the mullet. Similar incidents involving mullet have been recorded in America, only this time the dolphins ate the mullet. Off Brittany, there was a famous fable of dolphins pulling a row-boat of ship-wrecked sailors to shore. Dolphins, it seems, enjoy pushing things. Yellow fin tuna tend to swim underneath dolphins and fishermen follow the dolphins to find the tuna. Mexican fleets using massive drift nets caught the dolphins alongside the tuna. Conservationists have demanded the end of the small-mesh nets which capture both fish at the same time. Very little tuna is sold here now that does not claim to be dolphin-friendly.

WHITEBAIT

This term is normally used for a mix of the fry of herring, pilchard and sprats not more than 7 cm (2¾ in) in length. Whitebait used to be caught in the Thames: the great Cockney dish of deep-fried whitebait with lemon, salt and cayenne was a notable open-air feast in Greenwich in the 19th century. They are best from February to July, though invariably now they are frozen. They are very delicate, do not wash, but flour and shallow- or deep-fry.

OTHER SEA FISH

BREAM

These red and black fish live in warmer tropical waters; some come into the west coasts of England in summer and will stray into the North Sea. Young bream are known as CHAD. The best, GILT-HEADED BREAM or DAURADE, are imported from the Mediterranean or the Indian Ocean. Bream have strong crushing teeth and feed on hard-shelled molluscs. They can prise a limpet from inshore rocks. These teeth were imbued with mythical qualities: it was said they would render invisible a man who happened to have one in his mouth. They were embossed on tasting chalices and said to change colour on contact with poison.

The BLACK, or OLD WIFE BREAM, is actually blue-grey with gold markings; the RED BREAM is brown to silver and coarse-scaled. The Gilt-head is grey-black, with sad yellow bands on its face, and can grow to 30-40 cm (12-16 in). It is much favoured in Italian restaurants; the flesh is coarse, the fins sharp and the bones large. Usually dry cooked – baked or grilled, especially the black which is often char-grilled, with strong herbs – rather than poached.

More tropical species are given imperial names to mark their often strikingly beautiful appearance. BOGUE is popular in Malta, where it is known as VORPA, and usually barbecued. BLACK-BANDED, found in the Indian Ocean, are 20-30 cm (8-12 in) in length, oval, silver in colour with vertical black bands and with a yellow tail and fins. They are good white fleshy fish. CAPITAINE BLANC BREAM, silver grey with an orange hue to the fins and 15-30 cm (6-12 in) in length, are from Seychelles, hence the French name. The smaller version is called 'Sweet Lips' due to a red mouth, but is rarely seen. These are good, full-flavoured and big-boned. The EMPEROR BREAM, also found in the Indian Ocean as well as the Arabian Gulf, is grey-green, 15-30 cm (6-12 in) in length, with red-edged gills and large eyes, and it too has a good flavour.

CATFISH

Also known as WOLF FISH or (in fish and chip shops) as ROCKFISH, ROCK EEL or ROCK SALMON, the catfish has an elongated shark-like body, from 50 cm (20 in) long, a blue-grey-green back with vertical bars and a white belly. The more aggressive names come from the teeth and because it is so ugly the fish is usually sold head-off, providing steaks of pinky dense boneless meat. The versatile firm flesh has a good flavour. Fry, bake or grill – it responds well to stronger flavours.

The AMERICAN CATFISH is another fish entirely, raised on farms through the Mississippi delta, growing to 1.35 kg (3 lb) in 18 months. It is popular throughout the southern states. **Tesco** has started to use it in ready-made dishes.

GREY MULLET

These appear in shoals along the south and west coasts at the end of summer when they are at their best, although they are available all year. They are thick-lipped fish, with no teeth, and feed by sucking in the sand and mud and taking tiny crustaceans off weed in harbours and estuaries. The Greeks romantically regarded them as fine fish for being vegetarian (not strictly true), and gentle for the gallantry of the males who will follow a female on sight (they were caught with lures as a result). The pollution of inland waters affected their standing, but fish caught at sea are a fine buy; not as distinguished as sea bass, but not far behind and similar in shape and size. The head is flat and pointed, the body heavily scaled (the fishmonger will usually have brushed these off with metal brush), grey-blue-back in colour, with a silver underside and faint hoops, they are 20-40 cm (8-16 in) in length and quite princely. If you have an estuary fish that may be muddy, rinse it in vinegar. Recipes for sea bass are largely interchangeable. Grill smaller fish, stuff the larger and bake them. They are also good char-grilled, in casseroles or raw in *ceviche*.

GREY MULLET ROE

Mixed with soaked crustless bread, oil and lemon juice this is the traditional basis for Greek *taramasalata* (now more usually made with cod's roe). More commonly it was called BOTARGO, the roe salted, pressed, preserved in barrels and sliced to serve as an appetiser around the Mediterranean. Popular here in the 17th and 18th century, it has been usurped by smoked cod's roe and other variations on *taramasalata*. Use it as a flavouring ingredient, or grate it over pasta.

GROUPER

Highly regarded in Hong Kong for the meatiness of the flesh, grouper is used in flamboyant centrepieces for banquets. The fish are attracted to the warm waters of the Caribbean, Mexico, South-east Asia and the Indian Ocean, but can stray into the Mediterranean. Groupers grow to enormous sizes, up to 23 kg (50 lb). There are many varieties, with evocative pretty names – CORAL TROUT, CRESCENT TAIL, LEOPARD CORAL TROUT, VIEILLE MACONDE or

HONEYCOMB, VIEILLE ROUGE or RED. All are distinguished by the generosity of the flesh. They change their colour according to their habitat, often spectacularly so. Most keep their splendid colouring after cooking. Usually they will be flown in from the Seychelles within 24 hours of being caught (they can be fresher than many fish caught nearer to home). The taste alters fundamentally depending on whether it is served hot or cold, and the latter is not to be overlooked. The meat is robust and adaptable, but distinctive enough to be plainly steamed and lightly seasoned.

GURNARD

Also known as GURNET, there are three varieties of this fish: the smallest – at around 40 cm (16 in) – and best is the RED; and there are also the GREY and YELLOW (with a blue flash on the fin). The large angular bony head inhibits its swimming. To compensate it has three rays to the front which it is uses like stilts to walk across the sea bed. Found all the year, it is at its best outside of summer. Underrated and still often used for bait for lobsters, it does have firm white flesh, though it can be inclined to dryness. It suits poaching, frying and baking with strong flavours, as in a cheese gratin or wrapped in bacon and grilled. The head makes good stock.

JOHN DORY

ST PETER'S FISH, like the haddock, has finger and thumb marks on either side of its back, reputedly from where St Peter threw it back into the sea after it groaned so loudly in his hand – or perhaps because it looked so ferocious. The body is compressed, grey and ugly; 20-50 cm (8-20 in) in length, it has large

Ways with John Dory
Venice: cold with mayonnaise.
Devon: poached in cider and served with cream.

grimacing lips, tough spines and fins which are swept back like an aquatic teddy boy. It is a greedy hunter, using its slimness as camouflage. It approaches its prey with a wavering motion or – lying on the ocean bed with its dorsal fin as a lure – it attracts smaller fish. It has been known to eat six times its own length in other fish at one time. It is highly regarded by the restaurant kitchen, which will make it more expensive still. The resemblance of the flesh to lobster is one attraction. Allow about 675 g (1½ lb) per person, or buy steaks. The percentage of flesh to bone is poor (about 1:3), but the bones and head make excellent stock and soup. The versatile flesh may be fried, poached or lightly grilled and suits sauce recipes for either turbot or sole.

MONKFISH

Like the sea bass, the monkfish has risen to pre-eminence on the enthusiasm of restaurants and has become loftily priced as a result. Twenty years ago it was regarded as nothing. The enormous horny head and huge mouth, through which its unsuspecting prey are lured by the barbel on its head, was deemed off-putting on the slab. Today, hardly a self-respecting fishmonger would be without it. Apart from the occasional cheek, only the short tapering tail is sold, with its dirty brown, dark grey or browny-green skin, it is about 30-75 cm (1-2½ ft) in length – though it can grow to 2 m (6 ft). Best in winter, though available most of the year, the wholesale price will be between £3 and £4 per lb. The solitary central bone makes it good for roasts. The robust flesh will take strong flavours and forceful cooking. For more delicate saucing, it must be quite fresh and cut thinly. It is nearly all meat (take off the tough outer membrane before cooking). Traditionally used as an alternative to lobster or scampi, the head makes good stock and soup. If you can buy the whole fish, the liver is rare and excellent.

A French company, **de Cadenet** in Brest, has developed a *foie gras* of monkfish liver. The livers are marinated, then warmed and vacuum-packed to be sold fresh (they will keep 21 days) or bottled (these will keep for up to a year). The delicate flesh is white flecked with brown, which shows well in pâté combinations with salmon.

RED MULLET

The Greeks said the red mullet was sacred, stained by the blood of the goddess Hecate. This handsome red-scaled fish, 15-30 cm (6-12 in) in length, is available fresh in summer. They migrate from the Mediterranean around June to September, one species going as far as Norway. Cornish fish are often said to be among the best, as are the GOLDEN (in fact, red with a hue). There are more than 50 species in all. They are small-boned, so the bigger fish are at a premium, about £3.50 per lb wholesale. The liver, a prime delicacy, should be left in, hence the fish's nickname of 'the woodcock of the sea'. Serve the livers separately, or use to sauce. Red mullet is well established in top-class French restaurants, which does not help the price. The fish is best cooked simply: grilled or marinated in olive oil, lemon and fresh herbs for an hour and then baked in foil parcels. It is also one of the few fish that responds well to red wine in the cooking.

SEA BASS

An aristocrat with the expression of a nun, a steel-grey chain-mail mesh of large scales (which need to be brushed off) and white

---

Ways with Sea Bass

Chinese: Steamed with ginger and spring onion.

French: (*bar* or *loup de mer*) baked with fennel and pastis; with *beurre blanc*; poached with a classical *Maltaise* or *mousseline* sauce.

Spanish: (*lubina*) baked in salt.

---

underside, bass are found around the globe, but are most common in southern and western waters. They are usually 40-80 cm (16-32 in) in length, but can grow to more than 100 cm (40 in) and weigh up to 9 kg (20 lb). They are at their best from May to June, but still good until October. In early summer they come in from the deeper waters and head up river. Before pollution spread, the river fish were prized over those of the sea. The Romans claimed to be able to tell from which river a fish was caught. Farming has begun in France, Egypt and Greece. Often wrongly compared to salmon, the quite delicate flesh is soft but holds up well in cooking. Best baked, grilled or steamed, it is usually served hot.

SHARK

The smaller shark family go by rough-and-tumble, unflattering names like DOGFISH (or its equivalent in many different languages), FLAKE, HUSS, RIGG, and TOPE. Usually this will be the SPUR DOG, a sandy brown spotted shark, 50-100 cm (20-40 in) in length. Found most of the year, the boneless, underrated, strong-flavoured flesh stands up well for kebabs, curries and in soups, making it a useful cheaper alternative to monkfish. PORBEAGLE, caught off Cornwall, come in from the Mediterranean and are classically shark-like with rough skin, deep blue backs and white bellies. They may be anything from 150 cm (5 ft) in length. Whereas the dogfish is trawled up with other fish, porbeagle is hunted for itself. Its dense meat goes a long way and marries well with stronger flavours like ginger, soy and chilli. It does tend to be dry when frozen, but the French term for it, *veau de mer*, points to its quality and cooking strategies – marinate and then casserole or grill (good on kebabs) and serve with lemon.

SKATE

The nose on a skate is pointed, on a ray it is blunted. They swim with graceful waving flexes of their wings, but are voracious cannibals; slow but cunning, often swimming over their prey and smothering it into their mouth on the underside. The mottled THORNBACK is usually held to be the best. They mainly have brown skin with variations according to species and have no bones, just a cartilaginous well-fleshed skeleton to the wings and none in the nobs (cheeks). They may be found all year, but are at their best from colder waters in winter. Freshly caught skate, unless very young, tend to be tough (they were once dragged along behind the boats to tenderize them before cooking). Once tender, after two or three days, however, they can give off a smell of ammonia which should wash off (or it is off). There are different views prevailing on this, what seems to happen is that the ammonia inherent in the fish's system wears off for the first 2-3 days out of the water, but then begins to redevelop as it decomposes. The preponderance of recipes for deep-frying or with black butter is due to efforts to counter that ammonia. Wipe a finger along a fresh skate and the slime will reappear swiftly. They are best poached or pan-fried and are excellent cold and in salads, responding well to olive oil and lemon.

SKATE LIVERS

These used to be held to be a great delicacy, but are rare now as they are discarded at sea. Poach them in fish stock, then slice and serve on toast with butter and lemon.

Ways with Skate
French: poached and finished with *beurre noisette* – blackened (ie burnt) butter – and capers; braised with cider and onions; in a warm salad with olive oil, tomato, shallot and onions or bacon and croutons.

STURGEON

One fanciful explanation of the Loch Ness monster is that the sightings are of one of many different species of sturgeon which have been found migrating in UK rivers, like salmon, from the Baltic. Any caught are offered to the Queen. The taste is akin to veal. The Caspian Sea remains the epicentre of the caviar (sturgeon roe) industry, but farming is being developed in China and America. The French government has invested in projects to revive the fish in the Gironde and the Garonne, which produced caviar-bearing sturgeon before 1940. The fish spawn in the rivers and are then transferred to farms. The fish themselves are mostly sold as meat or smoked, but development continues on the eggs.

CAVIAR

Iranian caviar is now the best. The mullahs have fostered their industry on cottage fishing lines, while the former Soviet side of the Caspian Sea has been ravaged by pollution and indolent management. The fish are caught in spring and autumn and the best caviar will not be older than six months. Caviar should be packed at source, after salting; though the practice of the trade – and also the black market – is to re-pack large tins into smaller at the point where they are to be sold. Some is pasteurized to extend its shelf-life. Good caviar will not have a film of oil across the top and should hold its shape firmly in the tin. Restaurants and shops which serve it straight out of the larger tin do it no favours as it quickly oxidizes. Keep it chilled on ice and in the dark.

The names of different types of caviar derive from the type of sturgeon. BELUGA is the longest, reaching 4 m (12 ft). One fish gives about 15 kg (33 lb) of caviar. The eggs are large, at 50 per gram. Here and in

America, Beluga is prized above the others, less so in other countries. Although 1% of fish caught is Beluga, a quarter of all caviar sold is claimed as such. Often it is actually OSCI-ETRE, about a quarter the price. Oscietre can reach 2 m (6 ft) in length, and there will be 85 eggs per gram. Usually black when young, lightening through to shades of brown to gold, the taste is often likened to that of hazelnuts. *SEVRUGA is the most common and smallest of the sturgeons, not growing to more than 1.5 m (5 ft) and only giving 1-3 kg (2¼-6½ lb) of caviar, 115 eggs per gram. Distinctly less pebbled, almost a mush, these are not just the cheapest form of caviar but arguably the most interesting.

Good names are **R. G. White** and **Caviar House**. **Sainsbury** do an own-label caviar at Christmas. All varieties are best served simply on toast with lemon juice.

American caviar from **Carolyn Collins** is an imitation using the roes from Bowfin, hackleback sturgeon and paddlefish taken from Lake Crystal in Illinois. It is seasoned with chilli and Peppa vodka and smoked over mesquite, 'all of which translates into a weird jelly-like heat that destroys the roes'.

CHINESE MALOSSOL is a mix of eggs from different fish. Through the '80s, the Chinese have been developing a caviar industry: the first results were wayward, but recent batches have been impressive, especially for use in cooking. Lacking the finesse of Iranian caviar, but nevertheless strong fishy and ocean fresh, it is considerably cheaper and a good alternative.

MUJJOL

This is not strictly caviar at all, but a mix of herring, salmon and grey mullet roes from Spain. Black, squidgy, gelatinous and slightly sweet, it is an acquired taste.

LUMPFISH 'CAVIAR'

A derided fish, named after the lumps on its thick body, the lumpfish is occasionally found off the north-west coast. The male turns red at spawning time. It is a poor cooking fish and is caught mainly for the roe. The blackness is manipulated by the addition of E110, E151, and in the case of **Marina** of Denmark, then pumped up with flavour enhancers and citric acid. Examples from **Limford** and **Glenryck,** also from Denmark, were stale, the eggs dried out and without any natural oil, although the latter had the longest sell-by date of anything on the market. ***Macrae's** of Aberdeen show both up as poor: sold in plastic tubs with a greenish hue to the eggs, it is still moist with a wide taste, actually very salty and inky. It is easily the best of the batch.

FRESHWATER FISH

It is one of the ironies of our food culture that whereas angling remains one of the most active past times, little or none of the fish caught in this way has found its way to the kitchen or the market. The pollution of inland rivers has destroyed the natural habitats of our greatest fish, the trout and the salmon, both of which survive either through farming or the increasingly diligent efforts of enthusiastic anglers. The native crayfish and the brown trout have both lost their position to imports of different American species which have proved more responsive to farming. Perch, carp, roach and other small fish have all found their way into the cooking of other nations, but they will go on being of only academic interest until a more enlightened philosophy replaces our antiquated sewers and slack pollution controls.

Salmon
Trout
Pike
Crayfish

SALMON

The king of fish was once, as the well-worn story goes, so plentiful that workers asked not to be served it every day. The salmon is a river fish that feeds at sea and returns to spawn in the river – often the one in which it was born. The determination to return to their native spawning grounds is absolute: they will leap dams and obstacles to get up river. In 1913, millions of Pacific salmon died after a landslide blocked the upper estuary of the Fraser River in Canada – then the most famous salmon river in the western hemisphere – and the whole sockeye population was decimated.

Once in the fresh water, the sexual organs swell and the digestive tract shrinks so it does not eat again. As a result, salmon do not

GRAVLAX

has come to be more about the sauce than the fish. Most commercial versions are, disappointingly, just salted salmon with a little dill laced round the edges. They bear little comparison to home-made: For 450 g (1 lb) of salmon, make a paste with 450 g (1 lb) sugar, 450 g (1 lb) sea salt, 150 ml (¼ pt) of brandy or aquavit and 3 bunches of dill. Season generously with mustard and black peppercorns. Spread over the fish and leave 48 hours. Slice thinly and serve with mustard and dill sauce.

Ways with Salmon

Salmon are best slow-cooked: either poached, allowing 8 minutes to the 500 g (1 lb), or wrapped and baked slowly in the bottom of the oven for 1-2 hours. The tail cooks more quickly than the fatter belly. Vinegar spoils the coloration. There is an affinity with the acid tartness of fruits like rhubarb and the classic egg-based sauces. The salmon with sorrel-flavoured *beurre blanc* recipe from French master chefs, the Troisgros Brothers, is the dish often credited with the launch of *nouvelle cuisine*. Equally Raymond Blanc's salmon tartare helped establish his reputation. Traditionally, hot salmon (more effective grilled than poached) is served with hollandaise, cold with mayonnaise or, of course, it may be included in kedgeree.

prey on each other in rivers. At sea they swim at great depths often 100 km (60 miles) or more in a day, migrating on a 4,000 km (2,500 mile) pattern which is still not well understood.

Scottish – and, to a lesser extent, Norwegian – salmon are the finest. They can grow to well over 1 m (3 ft) and weigh 30 kg (66 lb), but the smaller fish are better. GRILSE, making their first return to the river, will be under 3.2 kg (7 lb). A good fish has a small head and large shoulders, the sleek steel blue silvery body scattered with black markings.

The Spey, the Tay, the Tweed, The Don and the Dee – the famous salmon rivers – are increasingly being bought back by the rod-and-line fishermen, who are putting a stop to netting. Wild salmon will become increasingly rare, except where caught by boat. Even now, wild represents only a few hundred tonnes a year compared with 40,000 tonnes of farmed, of which nearly a third goes for smoking. At sea, stocks have fallen dramatically in the last five years and salmon conservation organizations have also bought out fishermen.

Wild salmon are at their best when they have just entered the river and have the sea-lice still on their backs. Farmed are said to be better in summer. The tails of the wild fish are sleeker and a more defined triangle. The main differentiation among the farmed is whether the fish are kept in sheltered waters or more turbulent sea currents. The term 'organic' is misused to describe those farmed in sea pens. The **Scottish Quality Salmon** logo indicates fish that meet trade specifications: they should not be kept at densities greater than 15 kg to the cubic metre. Pollution from the *Braer* oil-tanker break-up led to the withdrawal from the scheme of Shetland fish in the area. The trade price for farmed fish is £1.60 per lb; wild will be at least 25% more.

SMOKED SALMON

Smoking was originally used as a means of preserving salmon, but has now become an end in itself. Smoked farmed fish are obviously fattier, almost like butter. Wild is usually 25% more expensive, and the quality can be erratic. Much farmed is passed off as wild, or so the figures suggest. The flesh will be firmer, less oily and subtler. It will also be paler, because the fish have not been fed on pigment supplementations. A good smoker will first salt his salmon – perhaps by as much as a ratio of 2:3 salt to salmon – for up 24 hours, in which time it can lose as much as 40% of its weight. The smoke is properly from oak, not strictly a flavouring process. William Pinney of the **Butley Orford Oysterage** and smokery in Suffolk who, like many, began smoking in the '70s argues: 'The oak's volatile components are released by the smoke. Every one of the chemicals in the wood has a different boiling point. A slow heat will not be sufficient, for example, to boil the pitch latent in the concentrated sap of oak. (This pitch would impart a bitter flavour.) But it may boil the antiseptic substance that yields acetic acid, or the one for formaldehyde, both good preservatives.' The salmon is exposed to these compounds and flavoured according to the time and the heat.

Traditionally, the salting and the smoking was much slower, at around 65°C (150°F) for up to 12 hours. Commercial expediency has tended to raise temperatures and cut smoking times. Many of the old kilns have been replaced on health grounds, indeed pressure from environmental health officers nearly led to a complete ban on mail-order smoked salmon until the government relented at the last minute. While bacteria levels can be above average, these are not necessarily hazardous. There have been no recorded

SMOKED SALMON BY MAIL ORDER

The rise of farmed salmon has questioned the supremacy of London smokers. Smoking has become a sizeable business, but some of the cures are purely cosmetic. All the best smokeries do mail order and deliver within 24 hours. Forman's of east London was first set up in 1908 and used traditional smoke-holes until 1973, when they modernized. Given the mark-ups in supermarkets, mail order is often a good value option. **Forman's wild salmon reputedly comes from the Tay and the Tweed, frozen out of season, which effectively makes it saltier. Two grades of salt are used and the fish can be more than two days in preparation before resting. Their farmed product is from the Shetlands, and makes a more buttery, less distinct, product. Scottish Eagle takes fish from the heavily tidal Ardvaar Loch and smokes in a traditional kiln at low heat.

Other good independent smokers are Ghillie & Glen of Aberdeen, Allean & Dey of Aberdeen, Minola of Lechlade, Gloucestershire, Inverawe of Taynuilt, Argyll, Loch Fyne of Ardkinglas, Argyll, Robson & Sons of Craster, Northumberland, and Salmon & Seafood Ltd of Clifden, Galway.

The three main suppliers are Joseph Johnson of Montrose, Pinney's of Scotland, Annan, Dumfriesshire, and Strathaird, Inverness, who all have histories of good smoking.

cases of food poisoning directly associated with smoked salmon.

Some Alaskan salmon is smoked in Somerset, but it lacks the delicacy of the Scottish although it has a compensatory mealiness. There is little price concession.

Balik salmon, developed by Hans Gerd Kubel, is reputedly modelled on the produce of old Russian smokehouses used by the Tsars, reconstructed in the Toggenburg mountains between Zurich and St Gall. At an altitude of 800 m (250 ft), they use mountain water and three woods for the slow smoker to give a result that is tender, but hardly worth the premium.

Ways with Smoked Salmon

Cooking: Serve chilled, not cold; with lemon and black pepper; with scrambled eggs; as a salad with new potatoes. It has an affinity with dill, horseradish, fresh cheese and cucumber.

HOT-SMOKED SALMON

Some supermarkets have been experimenting with hot-smoked fish, but the prices are giddily matched to smoked salmon rather than fresh, which makes them expensive, short-keeping *divertissements* for salads.

TINNED SALMON

The canning industry on the west coast of America began on the Sacramento River in 1849 and has moved north as rivers have been over-fished. Canada and Alaska began canning in 1866 and salmon canning was the first work for many immigrant Chinese. The fish are Pacific salmon. The finest for canning is the SOCKEYE, sometimes called BLUEBACK in Canada and RED FISH in Alaska. It weighs up to 4.5 kg (10 lb) and the depth of its redness has overshadowed other fish. It exudes a rich red oil – the more so after it has been in the can for a year. They follow upstream the larger spotted CHINHOOK, sometimes called KING, which have been known to weigh 40 kg (90 lb). Chinhook's size has given it commercial weight, but it is not as well-coloured as sockeye and goes very soft in the tin after a few months. The smaller and more beautiful COHO, sometimes called SILVER SALMON, is more delicate but disadvantaged because the flesh tends to pinkness and the quality has varied from river to river. Also prized, especially in Asia, is the smallest of the species, the HUMPBACK. Like the coho, however, it tends to pinkness and the quality varies from different rivers. The cheapest and least valued is DOG or CHUM SALMON, which has little oil, loses its colour quickly on entering the river and does not have an appetising flavour. In autumn, the males' jaws become enlarged at mating time, hence the name.

Tinned Salmon

Before the rise of cheap farmed salmon, tinned was regarded as a luxury. Increasingly, however, it looks like a poor alternative. The brines tend to win out and create a wet salt taste that predominates. Nearly all examples include skin and bone, and are messy and lacking in oil. Pink is particularly flavourless. **Socra** from Russia has the deepest coloured oil. **Sainsbury** buy a skinned and boned version from Canada, which at least aspires to some form of status. At twice the price, say of tinned tuna, tinned salmon seems an irrelevant relic of a past era.

The season is fixed by the return of the sockeye salmon to the Copper River at the beginning of June. Mostly reds and kings go to Japan. The big catch for the UK is that of the BRISTOL BAY REDS, on the far west point of the Alaskan shoreline, protected by the Alaskan peninsula.

SALMON TROUT

A confusing term, usually wrongly applied to large pink-fleshed trout.

TROUT

Prophetically, the brown trout is reputed to have been the first fish to have been artificially inseminated – as early as the 15th century. Before their rivers became polluted, trout were regarded as the freshwater equivalent of red mullet. Now they are almost exclusively farmed. These are RAINBOW TROUT or STEELHEADS, imported from California and first bred on this side of the Atlantic in France at the turn of the century. The silver skin is imbued with shades of olive green, a bluish back, and flecks of the rainbow. They usually grow from 20-60 cm (8-24 in) long, and smaller fish are preferable. The flesh should be white, but will be pink when fed on shrimp-enriched diet or just a dyed diet.

The density at which the fish are held in the farms varies according to the oxygen in the water. As they tend to shoal, however, there is little percentage in offering them more space. In the wild they are voracious hunters, taking fly and smaller fish – a large trout might even go for a small bird. Domesticated, they are fussy eaters and in recent years the conversion ratios of feed to meat have dropped dramatically due to farmers going from white fish meal to herring meal, and feed with a higher oil content. Smokers also want fish with higher oil levels than the ordinary kitchen.

Interestingly, the oils seem to concentrate at the head rather than the tail.

The artificial colour is due to astaxanthine, a nature-identical pigment made by **Roche** in Switzerland. The UK industry switched from canthaxanthin after (unrelated) concerns about eye problems in people who had over-dosed on tanning pills containing canthaxan-thin in Germany. The egg industry still uses it in their feed as does the American trout industry. The often attributed criticism of fish being muddy is more likely to be a problem with wild fish in overstocked lakes. Most farmed fish will be a year old, though larger ones can be as much as 15 months. Supermarkets mark farmed trout up by 100% over the trade price of around 90p per lb.

Shallow-frying remains the most effective cooking, although larger fish can be poached like salmon. However, the recipe culture, especially for rainbow, is strangely underde-veloped. The provenance of the bizarre trout with almonds is not known. Many of the regional recipes were designed for brown trout, not rainbows. It is cooked when the eyes turn white.

WILD BROWN TROUT are only caught pri-vately, mainly in the Test and Ichin and their tributaries. The sale of such fish has been banned in France since 1961.

SEA TROUT are not a separate species, but merely the common trout which goes wander-ing. They are caught as they return each year to their river to spawn from February to August. They do not migrate as far as salmon, return each year to the river and may only spawn once. The fish arrive at different rivers at different times, starting with the Tay in January. Once in their river they will not feed until spawning in autumn. The best are newly back from the sea at the start of each river's season. Bring out their superb flavour

WAYS WITH PIKE

Pike has a strong affinity with the egg and butter sauces of French regional cooking. For example this recipe from *Les Trois Faisans* in Dijon from the '20s: Lard the fillets as if they were beef, marinate in Madeira, white wine, cognac, shallots and herbs. Turn several times over a day or two. Bake in the juices in a hot oven with mushrooms for 20 minutes. Finish the sauce with cream or butter. French master chef, Fernand Point wiped the filets in flour, shallow-fried them and deglazed the pan simply with vinegar and then cream. More enduringly classic has been *quenelles de brochet*, served with a Nantua (crayfish) sauce: add 1 litre (1¾ pt) of cream to 1 kg (2¼ lb) of minced flesh, season. Add 4 whole eggs and leave for 24 hours. Roll into shapes on a floured surface, then poach in boiling water and refresh.

by baking them slowly in foil (with a little added butter, or olive oil if serving cold) in a very low oven for 1-2 hours.

PIKE

These predators of fresh waters can grow from 50-120 cm (20-48 in) in length. With a grey green back and a yellow hue to the belly, their long, duckbill mouth has very sharp teeth. Farming in Holland makes the pike increasingly available. Caught wild, it should be bled from the tails and gills to whiten the flesh. It is at its best out of spring. 'The old and very great pikes have in them more of state than goodness', Izaak Walton wrote. 'The smaller of middle-sized pikes being by the most the choicest... their life is maintained by the death of so many other fish, even those of their own kind, which has made him by some writers to be called the tyrant of the river, or the fresh water wolf'. Walton recommended stuffing pike with thyme, marjoram, its liver, pickled oysters, and anchovies in a pound of butter and roasting it over an open fire (tied up so the juices do not get lost for the sauce).

CRAYFISH

The largest freshwater invertebrates, these were widely found living in the banks and holes of inland rivers before pollution decimated their numbers. As with the red squirrels, the indigenous population has been wiped out – barring two or three protected colonies in the west country – by an introduced variety. The SIGNAL, imported from America, is 6-8 cm (2½-3¼ in) long. Some crayfish farming is being established. They are at their best in summer and used mainly as a garnish.

SHELLFISH ETC

The shellfish trade remains old-fashioned and individualistic. Each area still has its own language. At Billingsgate, lobsters are sold by the pound, crabs by the stone, oysters by the 100, Dublin Bay prawns by the gallon, scallops by the dozen, winkles by the hundredweight, mussels by the 25 kg and prawns by the box. The seaside stalls selling shellfish asphyxiated in baths of malt vinegar are a hangover from the costermongering of the 19th century, which has never really been thrown off. Shellfish has struggled to find a natural outlet – though some restaurants, notably the **Conran** group and others who have seen the value of mussels, have begun to reverse the trend.

Compare for a moment what has happened here with the story in Brittany, which shares the same waters and fishing. The restaurants of the coastline there are famous for their platters of shellfish and attract millions of francs in tourism each summer. Until very recently much of what appeared on those cork platters was thrown back by English boats. The few sheds that survive at Leigh on Sea in Essex provide a stark illustration – a ramshackle café culture, offering tea and brown bread and rickety tables in the open air. The comparison with France is shameful.

Serious London restaurants still take their shellfish from France, where the quality standards are more rigorously applied, though often it may have been landed or caught in UK waters and sent to Paris's Rungis rather than Billingsgate.

Shellfish are fashionably low in fat – lobster 1.9%, crab 2.8%, shrimp 1.4%, scallop 1.4%, oysters 2.1%. They can, however, pick up and pass on toxins that survive in the sum-

Clam
Cockle
Crab
Crawfish
Cuttlefish
Dublin Bay Prawn
Lobster
Mussel
Octopus
Oyster
Prawn
Scallop
Shrimp
Squid
Whelk

mer in the dinoflagellate algae, so beds are monitored weekly. Paralytic shellfish poisoning is rare but potentially fatal. Less serious is diarrhetic shellfish poisoning.

CLAM

The south coast and Channel Island waters are home to some of Europe's finest clams, but only the cockle has established itself on the fishmonger's slab. Until the '60s, other kinds of clam were only sold in tins. Clam bakes are a popular American picnic, using larger clams cooked over hot stones and covered with seaweed. The English names for the six varieties found underlie a sense of suspicion and unease that reflects the difficulty they have had making the transfer from scientific identification to the kitchen; the French names, by contrast, are almost poetic. All clams will open and cook with steaming. Recipes tend to be interchangeable, although some varieties have associated themselves with at least one enduring dish. Mostly imported from France, the COMMON CLAM (in French *palourde*, in Italian *vongole*) has a concave shell 3-6 cm (1¼-2½ in) across, marked with circular lines, light brown with dark mottling. The proper clam for *spaghetti vongole* or the Portuguese *cataplana*, with pork.

The HARD-SHELL CLAM or QUAHOG is the clam for chowder; grey beige, again concave with circular growth lines, it is slightly larger at 5-10 cm (2-4 in) and is best in July and August. They are thought to have been accidentally introduced around 1960, possibly by a liner from America throwing a consignment overboard in the Solent or simply carrying them attached to its hull. Older – hence larger – clams tend to be chewy and need marinating if they are to be eaten raw.

RAZORSHELL CLAMS are predictably named after a cut-throat razor because of its distinctive appearance; the shell is blue-green or beige and 10-20 cm (4-8 in) long. Widely caught off the Scottish coast and Channel Islands, these mainly go for export. Sweet and tender, serve them raw with just a drop of lemon juice, or steam them briefly. Some are smoked.

VENUS CLAMS, sometimes called VERNI, have a reddish-brown concave shell, 5-8 cm (2-3¼ in) across and are mostly imported. The smaller ones are better.

WARTY VENUS, the French *praire*, have a beige to brown shell 3-6 cm (1¼-2½ in) across, and can still be found on southern beaches by collectors. They are highly prized in Europe.

COCKLE

The edible cockle, *Cerastoderma edule*, forms great carpets of colonies between the mid- and the low-tide points of sandy beaches, sometimes as dense as 1,000 to a square metre. The rings on the outside of the shell indicate the age, as much as 10 years. They are now harvested at three to four years, when they will be 3-4 cm (1¼-1½ in) across. They are prey for plaice, flounders, crab and starfish, as well as gulls and waders. The Thames boats suck up the sea floor with hydraulic dredges. Other commercial beds are in the Wash, Morecambe Bay and on Barra, although many are imported from Holland. The best come from the **Gower Peninsula, where the extravagant tides of the Severn estuary wash over the beds with a rich supply of fresh, clean sea water. They are still harvested there by hand with cart and horse and are mostly sold in Swansea market. The DOG COCKLE (in

Ways with Cockles

Welsh: fry with bacon and laver bread.
Cockney: boiled with malt vinegar and pepper.

French *amande*) is beige with a zig-zag marking; 3-5 cm (1¼-2 in), it is larger than a UK cockle. It is not fished here, but is usually imported under the French name.

<u>BOTTLED COCKLES</u>
Invariably, the cheap vinegar used destroys their sweetness and delicacy.

CRAB

The crab is more developed than the lobster, and has central nerve cords. The EDIBLE CRAB, *Cancer pagurus*, is typically dirty rust-brown with a cream belly. It is a voracious eater and has a keen sense of smell to guide it across the ocean floor on its six legs. The male is flatter and its tail underneath is narrower, whereas in the female it is a triangular 'apron' to hold the eggs. The male has larger claws and therefore usually costs more. They must be 11 cm (4½ in) across the back to be sold. The major fisheries are Northumberland and Yorkshire, Devon and Cornwall, and the small, but well-known, area of Norfolk around Sheringham and Cromer. A crab moults to grow, shedding the old carapace and swelling up with water. Each moult may add an extra 2.5 cm (1 in) across the diameter. They mate when the female's shell is soft. She will have eggs from August to October and will be called 'berried'. The female will then move north, perhaps as much as 30 km (20 miles). Her eggs drift back to where they were conceived. Crabs are at their best between March and September, and at their peak in June when the warmer waters draw them closer to shore. In winter they become lethargic and go deeper.

A good crab should be heavy. If it is light it may be full of water from a recent moult. They are best eaten straight after cleaning. Ready-dressed crabs dry out quickly. To clean a crab: break open the shell horizontally; take off the grey fibrous fingers around the white head (these are inedible); separate the white meat from the brown in the larger shell and from the centre of the head; cut the head in half and, using a thin knife, work from the out-side in. The white shards are very sharp. The shell and trimmings make excellent stock. Underrated compared to lobster, perhaps because it is so labour intensive.

The SPIDER or SPINY CRAB is aptly named as the spindly claws and legs are roughly equally long, tucked under a rough cloth-cap-shaped carapace. The main flesh is in the body and legs. Wastefully, it has been thrown back by fishermen here for decades. Mostly they go straight to France and Spain, where they are more appreciated. The flesh is sweeter and more fibrous, and they are easier to clean. However, the ratio of meat to shell is lower than on the ordinary crab.

SOFT-SHELL CRABS are BLUE CRABS, *Callinectes sapidus*, from the American east coast, chiefly the Chesapeake Bay. They are caught as they moult their shell – hence the soft skin – usually in summer. The males are 'jimmies', the females 'sooks'. Rarely more than 15 cm (6 in) across, they are caught in pots and kept until they moult. Most found here are frozen, and have gone out to the restaurant trade as a novelty, usually deep-fried. In Louisiana there has also been seri-ous investment in soft-shelled crawfish since 1987.

TINNED CRAB

The meat is blasted off the shell with water canons and the flesh is crushed and rolled out of the claws. Much tinned crab is from ALASKAN KING CRABS, which can grow to 10 kg (22 lb) and are found round the Arctic rim of Alaska, Siberia and Greenland.

Tinned Crab

Essentially, canning removes the crab's greatest assets, its sweetness and freshness. **John West's** dressed crab from Scotland is 93% crab meat, extended with oil and wheat-flour. A 43 g tin might just stretch to two sides of a cricket-match-tea sandwich. It is dry, with a wheaty, biscuity and grainy filler, but at least distinct. Their white crab meat in brine comes from Thailand and has been boosted up with E621 (monosodium glutamate), sugar and salts, and then wrapped in some white paper inside the tin. The result is dry and pappy, desperately in need of mayonnaise, or anything at all to help it. Worse is **Armour,** again from Thailand and again with added MSG, which is particularly unpleasant with an acid taste and still some shell in the little pink clumps of vapid flesh.

CRAWFISH

Also sometimes called SPINY or ROCK LOB-
STER, crawfish like the warm waters around
the Mediterranean or the Gulf Stream currents
off Scotland. It has no claws – just two long
antennae – and can reach lengths of 50 cm
(18 in) or more. The colour changes with different habitats but, like lobster, turns bright
red after cooking. Caribbean and Brazilian
crawfish can be blue and reach weights as
much as 14 kg (33 lb). These make a spectacular centrepiece. Crawfish are expensive,
but 50% of the weight is edible. The texture is
more delicate than lobster, but loses flavour
swiftly after cooking, especially in the fridge.

CUTTLEFISH

Not to be confused with the squid, the cuttlefish has zebra-patterned skin, six long and
two short tentacles, and with the flat bone
beloved of budgerigars and previously used to
make toothpaste. The shape lends them to
stuffing and they may be poached, fried, or
grilled. Smaller ones, around 5 cm (2 in), are
prized. The ink sac is larger than that of the
squid or octopus and contains more ink; it is
valuable for saucing and is occasionally sold
separately in sachets.

DUBLIN BAY PRAWN

Sometimes known as NORWAY LOBSTER or
SCAMPI, from the Italian, properly they are
Nephrops norvegicus and *langoustine* to the
French. They are found from Iceland to
Morocco, but most abundantly around
Norway. Shaped like a miniature lobster, with
an orange hue to the carapace and hard brit-
tle incisors, they are 7-15 cm (2¾-6 in) long.
In summer they moult, making them watery.
Before 1950 they were usually thrown back.

Indeed, the Dublin market refused to take them and the fishermen used to have to give them away to street vendors, hence the name. They are now highly prized in French restaurants. All they need is two minutes in boiling water and then a quick plunge into cold. They are usually served as a garnish or on a platter of mixed shellfish with mayonnaise.

LOBSTER

Lobster are found from the Arctic Circle to Morocco, the main concentrations are around the UK, notably the north-west coast of Scotland, Norway and mid-channel. The female has smaller claws and a wider tail. They can live to become giant size, up to 15 kg (33 lb) – now uncommon – and 1 metre (3 ft) long. Smaller lobsters are sweeter, more intensely flavoured and better value; bigger specimens have thicker shells. Allow 450 g (1 lb) for one person, 1 kg (2¼ lb) for two; hens are a better buy than males. They are at their best from May to October. Hens from Scotland will have eggs in June and July. Lobsters moult, growing a second shell beneath the first. The shell is slipped off in 5-20 minutes and the lobster absorbs sea water and swells to its new size within 4-5 hours. They grow 50% larger with each moult. As they age this happens less frequently, perhaps every two or three years. The shell becomes rigid in 3-4 days and completely hard after 3-4 weeks. They mate when the female has just moulted and the eggs will take six years to develop to creatures weighing about 450 g (1 lb).

Attempts to farm lobsters have failed because they are quarrelsome and combative. Lobsters share the same territory as crabs, although one species tends to domi-

FOOD *watch*

Lobster Prices

The wholesale price of
Canadian lobster is
£3.50 per lb, which has
brought the price below
fillet steak and makes it
one of the more
surprising bargains
widely available in
supermarkets. Live
Canadian lobsters are
speckled down the
side. They have softer
shells and less colour
than the Scottish. The
Scottish lobster is a
better quality, but the
trade is less consistent
and the price £2-3
more per lb.

nate. The Canadians have revolutionized the trade in the last decade. Their canned lobster industry was based around Nova Scotia because of the clean sandy or gravel beds. As demand for canned lobster disappeared, the Canadians have gone into fresh. Fishing is organized on a rota system from different bays through the year and the taking of female lobsters with eggs is banned. They are rested in pounds, before being flown round the globe – notably here, America and Japan. The shells of Scottish lobsters are harder and have more carotene, which makes them more adaptable for classical recipes like mousses where the colour infused into the stock is important.

Cooked, the tail should be flexible not floppy and spring back to its original position. The tradition of cooking lobsters live is based on the principle that the flesh turns mushy quickly after death and does not keep well. There are different theories on how to kill a lobster humanely: place it in a carrier bag in a freezer at -10°C (14°F); put in cold water and let the temperature rise slowly to boiling; or, as in Hong Kong, behead it with a cleaver. From a culinary point of view they should go into rapidly boiling water and stay there for 12 minutes to the 450 g (1 lb).

FLATHEAD LOBSTERS are also known by the French as *cigale de mer* (sea grasshopper), which comes from its audible whistling underwater. Less flatteringly, they are called the 'Moreton Bay Bug' or the more southerly variation, 'Balmain Bug', in Australia. The sandy carapace folds over and the tiny claws and legs are tucked neatly underneath. They can grow to 1.8 kg (4 lb). The meat is all in the body and the smaller Mediterranean specimens go for soups. In America they are largely ignored. Some come from the Arabian Gulf and these are highly regarded. They have a reputation in Australia, and a few have begun to appear here frozen. A small slug of ungiving lobster-like flesh, they are still too costly to consider seriously, but likely to get cheaper as they are more widely available.

MUSSEL

The BLUE MUSSEL, *Mytilis edulis*, is highly fertile and responds to clean water by growing rapidly to 5 cm (2 in) in three years, clustering in the brackish waters of estuaries and harbour mouths by linking their beards. The shells are deep blue and opaque, the flesh creamy-beige to orange. The larger Mediterranean species, *M. galloprovincialis*, is sometimes found in the south-west. Wild mussels have thicker shells and less meat, 15-30% against 25%-45%. Most UK mussels are now seed taken from the wild and re-laid on prepared beds, mostly in North Wales and the Wash. The French technique of growing them on poles or ropes, known as *bouchots* (allegedly practised since the 13th century), is not used in UK. The story is that, in 1235, an Irishman, Patrick Walton, was shipwrecked near La Rochelle. He set nets out in the bay to catch fish on wooden poles and realised that colonies of mussels attached themselves to the poles.

Sold live, mussels are at their best from September to April. In summer they spawn, the male sending out a continuous stream of sperm to meet the eggs. Because of different cycles through the year, they are now also generally available in summer. They feed on the plankton in the water (hence the ban on the sale of wild, unpurified mussels, with which the danger from colonies feeding on sewage is acute) and grow rapidly. They will keep in a fridge at 5-8°C (41-46°F) or covered with a damp cloth for 5-7 days. To clean mussels: scrub them under running water, pull away the wiry beards – if they have already been de-bearded (by machine) they will not keep as long. Throw away any broken shells or any which stay morosely open before cooking. Wholesale, mussels are very cheap – £15 for 25 kg. They are sometimes sold by the pint, which equals 450 g (1 lb). Mussels are saltwater creatures and will not survive in a sink of tap water overnight.

Larger, 9x5 cm (3½x2 in), GREEN-SHELLED MUSSELS have a beautiful, completely smooth, pale brown shell with a vivid green edge. Inside, the cream or orange-hued flesh completely fills the shell. They have been associated with one case of listeria in New Zealand, from where they are mostly imported, but this has been linked to bad hygiene. They are now usually sold ready-cooked at around 11p each. Meaty, not subtle but generous, these are possibly a better buy than other preserved mussels.

OCTOPUS

The cephalopods are more advanced than other molluscs, with large mouths and beaks, well developed 'savage-looking eyes' and their organs contained in the sac they use to propel themselves through the water by contraction. They are found around Britain, though mostly imported from the Mediterranean. The eight tentacles have small suckers, either in one or two rows. They feed on other shellfish and this gives them a white, mild sweet taste. Do not over-cook (or salt) or they become rubbery. Larger specimens may need beating to tenderize the flesh. Only the tentacles are usually eaten. Coenders in his *Chemistry of Cooking* says, 'small octopus can be cooked by putting a wine cork in its mouth. This makes the octopus float and ensures even cooking. Drop in a potato. When the potato is cooked so is the octopus.' Peel off the skin and suckers to serve. The flavour is 'musky' and is best developed by slow braising. Marinating adds flavour and helps tenderize the flesh.

OYSTER

Two types of oyster are reared in Europe: the NATIVE, *Ostrea edulis*, which is flat and usually round, and the elongated PACIFIC, *Crassostrea gigas*. English natives are supreme, at a price, notably WEST MERSEA and HELFORD. Pacifics raised in Irish and Scottish waters are good value. The Pacific was introduced from Japan in the '70s to replace the Portuguese oysters wiped out by the perennial diseases that afflict oyster beds. More robust and less susceptible to disease and pollution, they are unlikely to spawn in our cooler waters and are eaten all year. Oysters grow fatter in different waters from those in which they spawn. Hence their name derives from the Greek *ostrakon*, to ostracize. Similarly, a Pacific oyster will grow much larger and more swiftly in Irish or Scottish waters than they do in France.

Native oysters, badly affected in the '80s by the disease bonamia, are slower to grow to maturity, taking 3-4 years – nearly twice that for a Pacific. They can be eaten in the summer, but as they spawn they become milky (this is why they are not usually sold when there is no 'r' in the month). Both are cultivated on the low-water mark of a spring tide and then brought into parks or on to trestles closer to the beach for harvesting. This hardens them off and teaches them to close their mouths out of water. (They can live for a week on a single gulp of water.) An oyster's age is told by the ridges on the shell – it will grow two a year, one in spring and one in autumn. They are graded by size and weight of the shell, but the French grading system does not correspond to the English.

BRITISH OYSTERS

LOCH RYAN:
No 1, natives, 4-5 years old, 10 cm (4 in) across the neatly crenellated shell (shells on Pacifics from Loch Ryan grow razor-sharp). Meat is about 5x6 cm (2x2½ in) and fills its shell generously with a clean, smooth beige body. Their salty, acid sourness – long in tannin – is very blunt and helped by saucing.

WEST MERSEA:
Blackwater natives, 3 years old, the shell discernibly lemon and green in the greys, 8x7 cm (3x2¾ in), but a small body of only 5x3 cm (2x1¼ in). Not as neat as the Ryan, pale-beige with a gritty edge to the shell, the central bouncy pouch of meat is surrounded by a drape of frills. Aristocratic, they have more punch than the Ryan, with little salt and a delicate sweet nuttiness that comes through straight away.

*IRISH: Pacific, 18 months old, 12x6 cm (4¾ x2½ in) shell, 9x3 cm (3½x1¼ in) beige flesh with a small frill. Sweet, salty, fleshy and delicate, with an aftertaste of iodine and nuts, they are good value for Pacifics.

IRISH: Native No 2, 9x7 cm (3½ -2¾ in) shell, 5x4 cm (2x1¼ in) meat. Although Irish Pacifics have a burgeoning reputation, the natives do not really match up to other natives. Chewy, sweet with a slightly fizzy edge, they can be dry, musty and salty and are best cooked.

WAITROSE: Scottish, Pacific, 45p, 9x5 cm (3½ x2 in) shell, 3x5 cm (1½x2 in) flesh, very young, lime green-grey shell, possibly under a year, black edge to the frill, milky white, salty, too soft-textured, but a taste of nuts. Cheap.

**HELFORD: natives, reputedly among the finest, still fished by sail, slightly metallic bitterness leading to a fresh saltiness, distinctive and aristocratic. Pacifics tend to be sweeter.

A healthy oyster will look like a lingerie commercial, its frilly skirt edging a silken plump body. They should be chewed, not swallowed whole. Natives have the subtlety of texture and meatiness, whereas Pacifics are inclined to softness. The exception tends to be oysters from Ireland, where the Pacifics can be as good as anywhere, but the natives are weak.

Supermarkets have started selling very young Pacifics for around 45-50p each.

You should never be poisoned by an oyster if you open it yourself. The smell of an off one is unmistakable. To open an oyster: place it in a cloth in your hand, hinge towards you and curved shell downwards to retain juices. Insert the tip of the knife to the side between top and lower shell and twist the blade to cut through the muscle. Separate the shells and finally cut underneath the meat to separate it from shell. Natives usually seem easier than Pacifics, which often grow razor-sharp horns.

Oysters were a staple from pre-Roman times, mostly in stews and often with lamb. These would have been much larger and older than those we see now. Lemon brings out the nuttiness of the flesh and seems to concentrate the flavour. Brown bread and butter is the traditional accompaniment. Other accessories, like Tabasco, ketchup and horseradish have been added over the years. Black velvet – Guinness and champagne – is an uncanny match. Breton restaurants dribble cream on oysters and grill them. In Essex they were fried with butter and bacon, a less formal version of Angel's on horseback.

SMOKED OYSTERS

These barely justify the premium over smoked mussels at three-quarters the price. The smoke and oil render them equals.

PRAWN

The NORTHERN, DEEPWATER or GREENLAND PRAWN, 3-10 cm (1¼-4 in) long, is usually frozen at sea. They are encased in a water glaze that will vary from 6 to 40% of their weight, so buy the lowest glaze percentage or by prawn weight. Such Atlantic prawns are said to have more flavour

MAIL ORDER OYSTERS

You can buy oysters by mail order directly from the beds. More expensive than at a supermarket or fishmonger, it is nevertheless the only way of ensuring a good supply from a choice source. Natives will usually be £5.00 more per dozen than gigas:
Loch Fyne, Argyll;
Auan Sea Fisheries, County Down;
Butley Orford Oysterage, Woodbridge, Suffolk;
Seasalter, Whitstable, Kent;
Scottish Shellfish, Loch Neil, Lynn of Lorn;
Carew, Dyfed;
Abbotsbury, Weymouth;
Rossmore County Cork, with London delivery.

FOOD *watch*

Prawn Prices
Waitrose has the widest selection of prawns. Prices can vary alarmingly for no apparent reason. **Asda**, usually very cheap with fish, has sold tiger prawns for twice the price of **Sainsbury**, whereas **Sainsbury** on ordinary prawns can be as much as £2 more than **Asda**.

than the cheaper ones from South-east Asia.

Larger TIGER PRAWNS, 12-30 cm (4¾-12 in), come from the Indian Ocean, the Gulf and South-east Asia. The dark-green shell with rings turn rosy red on cooking and the flesh is pale pink. They are expensive, at around £6 per lb unpeeled but cooked, but are chunkier and meatier than ordinary prawns and better for cooking. Some have extraordinarily long sell-by dates and can be very pappy and bready. Allow 2-3 per person.

SCALLOP

The scallop's fan-ribbed shell, usually 15-17 cm (5-7 in) across, is the symbol of pilgrims to the tomb of St James at Santiago de Compostela in Galicia, who eat a single scallop on arrival and wear the shell to attest to their journey.

Here the trade (which still sometimes refers to them as clams) is relatively young, gaining ground in Scotland in the '30s and in the English Channel in the '70s. Their top shell is reddish and flatter, the underside is bowl-shaped where it nestles into the ocean floor. They can propel themselves across the sea bed by opening and closing the shell. The orange roes (scallops are hermaphrodites, they release the sperm first and then, a few hours later, the eggs which fertilize in the water or stimulate other scallops nearby to start spawning) are eaten here but not in America. Scallops are best from cold water in December to March, when they will be about 30p each wholesale, but they are available all year. Frozen in the shell, however, they are often pumped with water to increase weight.

QUEENIES are, in fact, a different genus: only 5-8 cm (2-3 in) across, both parts of the shell are bowled. Available all year, they are usually cheaper and prettier and are very useful in cooking.

Ways with Scallops

To open a scallop: place curved side down in a warm oven. The shell will open enough to slip a knife inside and sever the muscle. Under cold running water, separate the white muscle and orange coral from the browny – sometimes black-edged – frill and intestinal thread. Throw the latter away.

Scallops can be eaten raw, or baked or grilled. Roe is more delicate and should be cooked briefly separately. Highly versatile, the scallop is a chameleon which will take on other flavours and complement them: often rigorous ones like brandy, bacon, ginger. They are good with high-quality butter sauces or in Cantonese cuisine they are steamed with ginger and spring onion.

SHRIMP

Almost transparent in water, shrimp are still fished around Britain. The larger variety, *Pandalus montagui*, sometimes called the AESOP PRAWN, has a pointed snout and turns red on cooking; the more delicate, but smaller and more highly prized, *Crangon crangon* turns brown.

Found all over the world, there are many sub species and sizes of shrimp, confusingly often with conflicting names in different regions. In America, the term shrimp has also come to mean prawn. Shrimp are at their best in summer and those from Morecambe Bay enjoy a rather inflated reputation. They are still fished on horseback at the Belgian village of Oostduinkeerke. The Far-Eastern fish sauces, *blakan* and *pattis*, are fermented shrimp pastes.

SQUID

Found in UK waters, squid are the tenderest of all cephalopods and good value with a wholesale price around £1 per lb. Boneless (as opposed to cuttlefish) and sweeter-fleshed, they are at their best in winter. Serve stuffed and sautéed or stir-fried.

WHELK

These small marine snails are usually thrown back by the English boats or exported. Only a few rise to seaside prominence with vinegar – usually the old rubbery ones. In Normandy, however, the young whelk is served with mayonnaise as a starter. Old recipes in this country talk of frying the larger ones. At their best in summer, they are usually (over)cooked by the fishmonger and this practice may have been their undoing. Gentle poaching in some sea water with some herbs, helps.

MEAT, POULTRY & GAME

❧ ⚜ ❧

E ngland has always been known as a nation of meat eaters, even before the rise of the urban centres.

The move to less fatty cuts of meat has seen the introduction, on a large scale, of Continental animals. The rise of the supermarket has seen traditional breeds abandoned unilaterally in favour of new hybrids. The move into the EC has broken links – in most cases established by the Victorians – with countries which have strong meat-rearing histories, without replacing it to advantage. There has been change, change and change again.

British lamb remains among the best in the world. The quality of pork has improved in the last two or three years, with more animals moving outside. Once the best in the world, British beef is for the most part now possibly inferior to American.

Supermarkets, notably **Tesco**, have quietly re-evaluated their policies and have introduced stricter quality and ethical guidelines across the board. **Sainsbury** has similar standards on its 'More Mature' label, where a degree of hanging has been encouraged again. The quality in other chains, especially in beef and pork, has not really kept up. **Waitrose** has innovatively been selling whole sides and half carcasses. **Marks & Spencer** has stuck with tradition for Aberdeen Angus beef, but elsewhere has embarked on a mindless quest for butchery novelty and gimmickry. **Safeway** seems to have concentrated its efforts on the more headline-grabbing lines of game and venison, rather than the mainstream.

MEAT

Meat is one of the most difficult foods for the consumer to judge. Price is a poor guide. Conflicting advice, changing breeds and uni-lateral changes in farming policy leave most of us completely in the hands of the butcher or the grocer.

Beef
Veal
Lamb
Pork
Sausages
Bacon
Ham
Salami etc

BEEF

The oldest surviving breed of cattle is the White Park. James I knighted his host as 'Sir Loin' after a banquet around a roast of beef, and this was surely White Park. Its ancestry may go back 2,000 years – possibly more. It was found mainly on the tougher grasses of the northern parklands and moors, and was known for its flavour and its leanness. It fell out of favour in the 19th century because it was slow to mature, not reaching its prime until two years old. Its leanness was also not what the 18th-century stock-breeders wanted; they wanted big fat animals to feed the cities.

These were to be the great triumvirate of the Hereford, Shorthorn and Aberdeen Angus. They were the first cattle to be exported, and were to be the great-grand-fathers of the American and Australian herds.

The Hereford's supremacy has slowly eroded over a century. Originally it was kept both as a dairy cow and for its meat. It lost its position as a milker to the more generous lactations of the Friesian, introduced in 1922, and completely with the arrival of pasteurization, which destroyed any quality argument. The arrival in the '60s of the leaner, larger and faster-matur-ing breeds from Europe – the Charolais, Simmenthal, Limousin and Belgian Blue – fur-ther undermined its commercial stature.

Q–GUILD BUTCHERS
Set up under the chairmanship of David Lidgate of **Lidgate's** in London's Holland Park in 1986, this organization now has more than 150 butchers nation–wide subscribing to independent inspection. The aim is to provide 'something different and something better'. Many of the better butchers in the UK have enlisted.

FOOD *watch*

HORMONES

The EC stopped the import of American beef because of their use of hormones. A small amount of prime beef – usually reared under the Hylton programme (a US version of *Appellation Contrôlée*) – gets through, but is prohibitively expensive as it carries a 20% levy. The best American beef is corn–fed and usually hung for as long as 40 days. Prime USA beef is probably now superior to Scotch.

Butchers prefer the traditional UK breeds. The smaller carcasses – around 180 kg (400 lb) for a heifer that has not calved, or 270 kg (600 lb) for a steer (usually fattened on for another six months) – are as much as an independent shop can handle. The bigger chains, the processors and the supermarkets favour crosses with the larger Continental breeds, which can weigh 450 kg (1,000 lb) in a heifer and up to 630 kg (1,400 lb) in a steer. The trade judges on backsides (front carcasses are often exported) and Charolais and Belgian Blue have double muscling, a second layer of meat on the valuable rump. There has been concern, however, at the large-scale breeding of animals that have difficulty giving birth to calves with such big hips.

REARING: calves are either suckled, left with the mother for a year, turned out in summer, and brought in for fattening when the mother is brought back into confinement; or, in the dairy method (used for six out of 10 calves), they are taken from their mothers at 10 days and fed on a concentrated diet of milk powder, wheat, barley and protein. They will only go outside if they are old enough in spring. Calves that have been outside will have darker flesh.

HANGING: as well as storing, this process was used to tenderize meat from older animals. Even 25 years ago much of the beef sold was four and five years old when slaughtered. Supermarkets rejected this practice on the grounds of cost, but **Sainsbury** and **Tesco** have begun to mature meat again for 10-12 days. Some of the more extravagant claims may also include the shelf-life. Independent butchers can hang beef for as long as three weeks.

COOKING: at 60˚C (140˚F), the connective tissues in beef begin to compress and squeeze out the juices. By 75˚C (170˚F) a quarter of all the juices have leached. Scientifically, it follows that rare steak will be juicier and more tender. The move to leaner, unhung cuts of beef favours French-style recipes for braises and casseroles, often where the fat and other flavours are added separately; or the short sharp stir-fries and flash-grilling of Oriental cooking. The classic English roast needs a level of fat to lubricate it, and few butchers accept that the move to leanness has improved flavour.

BEEF CUTS

The front cuts are out of fashion and offer good value, especially for longer cooking and older recipes. Clockwise from the head:

OX CHEEK is a poor-quality cut, sometimes used in mince, or it goes for pies and pet food. It needs up to six hours cooking and is best in a salad.

NECK, sometimes called CLOD or STICK-ING, is good for mince, stews and curries and needs long slow cooking. It can be sold as stewing steak and is good value.

CHUCK STEAK, sometimes called BLADE BONE, is sold as cubes or slices. It is good for braising but, as the seams run through it, it is an untidy joint. Use it for *daube de boeuf,* goulash or *carbonnade*.

BLADE STEAK is sold as steaks, which should not be more than 7.5 cm (5 in) across. They are good for braising.

*LMC or LEG OF MUTTON CUT, or some-times POOR MAN'S RUMP, weighs 1.8-2.7 kg (4–6 lb) but can sometimes be larger in Continental breeds. A complete muscle, it is lean and thus excellent for good casseroles. It is also good enough as a cheap steak, if cut thinly. Price should be about £2.50 per lb. If a butcher does not have this cut, he may be marking it up as topside at £3 per lb, or even frying steak. Use it flattened and rolled round a stuffing for beef olives.

*JACOB'S LADDER is usually boned and sold as stewing steak or mince, but can be rolled and sold as boneless brisket. Very lean, it is priced at about £2 per lb and is good to pot- or slow-roast.

SHIN is good value and ideal for long slow stews, where the flavour has time to develop. It is sometimes used in mince.

BRISKET is the breast, sold on or off the bone. It needs slow careful roasting or pot-roasting. It is good value, though bone (and fat) can account for 35% of weight. It can go for mince, or is cured in brine and salt. It is traditionally used for boiled beef and carrots.

FLANK is fatty and poor; best used in mince.

FORE-RIB is the first four ribs (sometimes five) taking one off the blade and the chuck, and weighs 4.5-6.8 kg (10-15 lb). It is excellent roast on the bone, but is sometimes sold off the bone. It is too tough to treat as steak or to stir-fry.

The back cuts are prized and priced ahead of the forequarters:

SIRLOIN is the classic English roasting cut. The continuation of the rib, it is sometimes sold as steaks off the bone for £1 per 1 lb less. It is excellent roasted on the bone (especially from British breeds); or grilled or pan-fried off the bone. The best ribs (there are 25) are towards the back. In French this is the *entrecôte or contrefilet*. The *aloyau* is the sirloin and the fillet as one cut, and this is always roasted. In beef from Charolais cattle, the grain is discernibly coarser. In American butchery three steaks are taken out of the section between the loin and the fillet: PORTERHOUSE is mostly loin, CLUB has no fillet, and the T-BONE straddles both sides.

**FILLET lies inside the rib and weighs 1.35-2.7 kg (3-6 lb). It is always tender because the muscle is hardly ever used.

Classically it is grilled, roasted or pan-fried (to make use of the juices). If stuffing it, always add a little extra fat. In French butchery, the head of the fillet is *biftek*; the middle is *Châteaubriand* and *filet*; the third section is *tournedos* or *medallions*, and the final, thickest, piece is *filet mignon*.

RUMP was originally only an English cut. In other countries this part was cubed for braising or boiling. Weighing about 3.5-5.5 kg (8-12 lb), it is always sold as steaks. With more flavour than fillet and sirloin, and a coarser grain (especially in Limousin), it is best fried or grilled. Well trimmed, it is ideal for *stroganoff* and high-quality casseroles.

H-BONE is the hip bone, which used to be sold on the bone but is usually now boneless. Leaner than rib, it is equal to topside, silverside and top rump together.

TOPSIDE is the top inside of the back legs, sold off the bone. As it tends to be lean and inclined to dryness, cooking time is critical: 10 minutes per 450 g (1 lb) maximum for rare, 14 minutes for well done. Although it is sold as a roasting joint, it is better to pot-braise it. Continental breeds will be grainier and larger than 15 cm (6 in) across. Some butchers will pass off top rump or silverside as topside. Use for *carbonnade de boeuf* or *daube de boeuf*.

TOP RUMP is the outside of the back leg and smaller than topside at 1.8-2.7 kg (4-6 lb), with a smaller diameter at around 10-12 cm (4-5 in), tapering at both ends and usually paler. It needs good butchering as it has more seams and is fattier in the centre.

SILVERSIDE is the back of the leg, weighing 2.7-4 kg (6-9 lb). The best cut is the 'eye', a tubular single muscle 7-10 cm (2¾-4 in) across. If it falls apart, other cuts have been rolled together to imitate it. Use it for salt beef.

Bresaola is air-dried beef, cured much like Parma Ham, but with a drier, tougher texture. The practice originated in Lombardy. Bresaola is served thinly sliced, with olive oil, lemon juice and black pepper.

BSE

First identified in November 1986, a quarter of all farms in the UK (some 27,000) have been affected by the virus Bovine Spongiform Encephalopathy, but in nearly half the cases only one animal has been infected. Repeated predictions of a fall in numbers of reported cases have been premature. The disease is one which has jumped the species barrier due to cow's being fed meat from lambs carrying the infection scrapie and has a four-year incubation period, so the 1988 ban on feeding 'ruminant protein to ruminants' should mean the peak of the epidemic has been reached.

The current theory is that the disease began because of changes in the meat-rendering industry in the late '70s. Solvents stopped being used to extract fat when the market for tallow collapsed. Importantly, this meant a move away from high-temperature steaming to clean off the solvent. Inadvertently this had prevented a cross-over of 'scrapie-like' infection.

Research is concentrating on the possibility that BSE may be being passed from mother to calf, possibly by the calf eating placenta in the field. Sporadic stories suggesting direct links to cases of Alzheimer's Disease are vigorously denied.

RUMP SKIRT, or GOOSE SKIRT, is the inside of the rump steak or the inside of the flank, and is ideal for stews and casseroles. It is also traditional in pasties because the crumbly texture cuts easily with a fork.

BEEF OFFAL

OX TONGUE weighs 1.35-2.3 kg (3-5 lb) and is usually sold cooked – either simmered for 3 hours with herbs and onions then cooled and skinned, or roasted – from a piece that has been lightly brined (it would need soaking beforehand). The price has risen to £2.50 per lb since the ban on American imports.

BRAINS are no longer sold in this country due to BSE (see above). Ironically, old books recommend them (along with the spinal marrow, also banned because of BSE) as nutritious for children and old people.

*OXTAIL is sold whole or by the pound. The butcher should cut between the joints; a whole tail should feed a family of four. It produces excellent jelly and is traditional in soup and stews.

*HEART used to be known as POOR MAN'S GOOSE. Weighing 1.35-2.7 kg (3-6 lb), it is lean and can be used in mince. It is also excellent value as a roast, stuffed with bread, garlic and herbs. It should be £1 per lb.

KIDNEYS have a very rich deep flavour. They are best used with other meats and cooked slowly, but they can also be thinly sliced and sautéed. They are traditionally used in steak and kidney pie or pudding.

LIVER should be soaked in milk for 4-5 hours to soften the flavour. Weighing 3.5-7 kg (8-16 lb), it is very rich and pungent and is best used alongside other meats in long slow casseroles. It is widely used in commercial processing to make pâtés etc.

MARROW BONES are ideal for stocks, soups and sauces. Reserve the jelly for spreading on toast or on top of steaks. Roast or boil for 2 hours and spoon out.

TRIPE is the stomach lining. Initially brown, it is first boiled to blanch it. The thick part is the seam between the stomach linings; the honeycomb (from the second stomach) is usually held to be the best, as it is softer. Blanket tripe is from the first stomach. If you have uncooked tripe, then boil it in salted water for 5 hours. In France it is traditional in *tripes à la mode de Caen*, in which ox feet (not calves') and the tripe from all the successive stomachs are cooked in a baker's oven.

SLAB is the rather obscure term for testicles. Boil in salted water for 30 minutes, skin and fry.

COW HEEL needs to be boiled for a long time to take off the jelly: the main use is for this gelatine.

Ways with Oxtail

A traditional butchers' recipe: Trim a whole oxtail leaving some fat, and dust in seasoned flour. Sweat 2 chopped onions in a pan, add 450 g (1 lb) sliced carrots and 115 g (4 oz) chopped streaky bacon. Brown the oxtail in a little lard or butter, cover with beef stock, season with herbs, such as parsley or sage, and slow cook overnight. Check that the meat is falling off the bone. Allow to cool and skim off the fat. Thicken the liquid to taste with flour. Add 1 tablespoon of redcurrant jelly and warm through for 1½ hours. Serve with mashed potatoes and winter vegetables.

BIV

BOVINE IMMUNODEFICIENCY VIRUS or BIV is an Aids–style virus that affects cattle. In 1993 there was an outbreak at a farm in Cheshire. The herd was destroyed.

VEAL

The outcry against the cruelty of Dutch crate-raised veal has almost stifled the trade, a testimony to the power of public opinion. The animals never see daylight and hardly have room enough to move. The immobility and the exclusively milk diet preserve the whiteness of the flesh. The culture comes from southern and central Europe, often mountain areas where keeping young animals in small spaces in winter did not seem so out of place. **Sainsbury** has pursued a solitary, more humane, approach on UK farms for the last 20 years – 'large airy barns, plenty of room to move freely, natural light, fed on a diet of milk and straw'. The flesh is distinguishably paler pink, not white.

Veal has the lowest fat content of all red meats and is high in iron. The calves are killed at just 16-20 weeks, so the butchery vocabulary is borrowed from lamb not beef. Guernsey and Jersey bulls were the main British breeds; by-products of the milk trade.

Veal is tender because it is young; but because it is so young it lacks flavour and has come to be cooked mostly with sauces. The stronger-tasting calves' offal is correspondingly prized for its delicacy compared to that of beef.

VEAL CUTS

The front part of the animal, the NECK, the SHOULDER and the BELLY are usually boned, trimmed and cubed for light stewing. Some butchers will leave the bone in a shoulder and sell it for roasting. Classically used for making *blanquette de veau*.

SHIN is usually boned and cubed for *ossobuco*.

LOIN is sold as a joint (the fillet still attached because its flavour has had so little time to develop) or occasionally as cutlets.

RUMP is sliced thinly, flattened and sold for escalopes. The prime steaks will be from the back end. Usually used for *wiener schnitzel.*

TOPSIDE, TOP RUMP and SILVERSIDE are sold as joints or escalopes.

VEAL OFFAL

VEAL KIDNEYS, weighing 115-225 g (4-8 oz), are very pale and very expensive. Ideal for frying, they are also good devilled.

**CALVES' LIVER is sold sliced and it has a marvellous creamy aristocratic flavour. Fry or grill very briefly.

**VEAL SWEETBREADS are the neck and gut glands, weighing 115-170 g (4-6 oz). As this book goes to press these have just joined the banned list because of recent developments re BSE.

LAMB

Lamb is the last of the domesticated animals to have maintained its freedom, and with which the idea of seasonality retains some stock. Hill lamb will be tougher but more flavoursome; downland animals raised on the lush easy-going pastures of Southern England will be the more tender. Imported frozen or chilled lamb from New Zealand makes up the weight in winter.

Spring lamb is tender and notoriously expensive, but most butchers hold that the lambs need a chance to get out on the spring pastures and the flavour is better in September. By autumn, older animals start to come to market. The colour of the meat is darker – brown rather than red. It should have been hung for a week to tenderize it, and needs the longer cooking of winter braises and casseroles, not the short sharp

FOOD *watch*

THE TRANSPORT OF LAMBS

The closing of local abattoirs to meet EC standards may affect the quality of much lamb. Like most animals, sheep do not like to travel; with larger and more centralized abattoirs, however, they travel further. The RSPCA has spoken out emphatically on the trade in Welsh lamb to France on the grounds of cruelty.

roasting and grillings of summer. Mountain or hill lamb will have less fat because it has been running around. The back legs will be muscular and lean, but the bone-to-meat ratio is high. Downland lamb tends to be larger and is killed younger, before the fat develops – from 90–120 days.

Few butchers label their lamb, or even know the breeds they sell. A lot of Welsh lamb goes to France, where it is better appreciated. However, **Gateway** and **Somerfield** stores seem to acquire the little that escapes for the English market.

LAMB CUTS

MIDDLE NECK, or SCRAG END, is fatty and bony and sold as one piece or chopped. It will, however, make excellent casseroles if generously spiced and seasoned and cooked slowly, for a long time.

BEST END, meaning the BEST END OF NECK, consists of the small eye and a long rib. Sometimes called CUTLETS, the first five bones near the loin are the best. They are good grilled or casseroled. Classically, grilled cutlets are served cold in aspic with mint jelly or sauce.

RACK is the complete set of best end chops and is usually roasted.

**LOIN, or in French NOISETTES, is the best cut of all. Usually boned and rolled, it is best grilled or roasted. When prices are cheap, look for a double chop.

*CHUMP is the underrated lamb equivalent of rump steak. The CHUMP END is the small cut by the join with the loin; it is too small to make a steak and is usually sold as stewing lamb.

SADDLE is the complete top section, including the best end, loin, chump and sometimes even the tail. It is always roasted.

*LEG is also often known by French term GIGOT. The nearer the foot, the more sinewy

RARE BREEDS OF LAMB

Conservationists argue that because lamb is slaughtered so young the difference between the flavour of different breeds that was crucial with mutton has been lost with lamb. It was the great 18th-century breeders Robert Bakewell and John Ellman who wanted sheep that had good wool and large fatty carcasses to feed the growing urban populations looking for work in the factories of the industrial revolution. Before then each region had its own breed and type of sheep.

The oldest were probably the Leicester, the Lincoln and the Teeswater, and the mountain breeds like Welsh, Soay and Hebridean. The Leicester and the Lincoln had large carcasses, and were bred primarily for their wool, which was still an important industry. It was Ellman, however, who adapted the principle. His own downland sheep were more compact and easier to develop on the lusher pastures of the south. His Southdowns became the great stock-improvers world-wide. They sired the flocks of Australia, New Zealand and Argentina and only lost their pre-eminence in this century, with the advent of the supermarkets who ruled that the Southdown was too fatty and slow-growing. So it was crossed with the Norfolk Horn to produce the Suffolk, today's most prevalent breed.

As with cattle, the native animals have increasingly been supplanted by the leaner Continental breeds, like Texel from Holland or Charollais (two 'l's in sheep, one in cattle). For British agriculture, joining the EC has seemed to have been a one-way street of importing foreign breeds, few of which have demonstrated much advantage in culinary terms.

the meat. The knuckle end is therefore the poorer cut on a half leg; the fillet end is the better bet. Usually now roasted, traditionally it was often boiled, especially if older meat as with mutton.

BARON is the saddle and the two legs sold as one joint. It is always served roasted, usually at banquets.

BREAST is cheap, fatty and bony. Best roasted to a crisp, it is also used in dishes like *navarin*, Irish stew and *cassoulet*; or cut

Lamb Ham

Unlike pork, lamb was rarely preserved, but seems to have been a prime source of fresh meat: Harry Fellows at **Ashdown Smokers** has developed a ham from the Lakelands sheep, which he calls **Herdwick Macon**. The legs are matured for up to eight months which gives it a powerful flavour. As with Bayonne, however, the smoking serves to obscure the subtlety and is not a northern tradition anyway.

Spring lamb: at one time this would always have been a cross with a Dorset Horn. They lamb early, in October, and so the first animals can be at market by February. Now it is more likely to be a hill or mountain ewe, perhaps a Cheviot, Swaledale or Welsh mountain, put to a prolific sire like a Blue or Border Leicester or a British Milk Sheep. Their lamb would then be mated to a meat sire such as a Charollais, Texel or Suffolk.

off the bone, egg-and-breadcrumbed and fried as *épigrammes*.

*SHOULDER is the cheapest joint on the lamb. The top half, the blade bone end, is better than the knuckle end which will be fattier and more sinewy. There is as much meat on half a shoulder as on a complete rack or best end – usually more. It is also a good cut for use in a curry. Classically, it was always boned out by the butcher and stuffed, a good practice that has gone out of vogue.

SHOULDER CHOPS are cut across the bone and often found in supermarkets, although usually poor value at 80p more per lb than the whole joint.

FILLET would more properly be called neck and is usually sold as barbecue or grilling meat in summer and for casseroles in winter.

LAMB OFFAL

Lamb offal benefits from being young to a greater degree even than the meat, so it is worth buying offal from spring lamb, even at a few pennies more, though this is more likely to be found at independent butchers than at supermarkets.

KIDNEYS are likely to be fresh as small butchers get them as part of the carcass (he will price by the kidney). They should be cored and the pipes taken out to stop any lingering taint of urine (occasionally the taste persists, a sign of infection). Buy them in the fat for roasting or barbecuing. Processing factories sell by weight, so the temptation is to leave in the pipes. New Zealand exports kidneys frozen in bulk and these are usually found in supermarkets. Sautéing or grilling is the best means of cooking them. By and large, kidneys do not freeze well, going mushy and losing texture.

*LIVER from spring lamb is almost as tender as that from calves, for about one-fifth the price. The whole liver tails off into a thumb shape at one end, unlike pigs (which is sometimes passed off as lamb). Grill or sauté it. Frozen livers are imported from New Zealand and sold by the tray in supermarkets (check for the tell-tale pool of blood). They are usually browner or, worse, develop a green glaze. Freezing affects the texture, making it coarser, so they are only good for casseroles with other meats.

HEART is an overlooked cut, too often sold as pet food or secreted away in mince, sausages and haggis. A stuffed and roasted heart from a young lamb makes a good meal. If it is crumpled and misshapen, it will have been frozen and will be the poorer.

SWEETBREADS are two separate glands – the thymus from the neck and one from the pancreas (the latter are called 'gut sweetbreads'). Boil them in salted water for 15 minutes and then peel off the outer membrane. They are at their best from spring lamb, when all good butchers should have them – but they are popular and scarce as a result.

BRAINS from lambs, unlike those from calves, can still be found on request.

FRY, or testicles, are rarer because most animals are castrated; though in country cooking they were prized. Halal butchers often stock the few that get away.

TONGUES are rarely found but can be cooked in the same way as calves' tongues, braising first and then skinning.

TROTTERS used to be cooked but are very rare now. Singed and split open, they are then cooked in stock with vinegar, traditionally covered so they do not discolour, and then finished with a white sauce, stuffed or deep-fried.

PAUNCH is the stomach used as casing with the PLUCK (heart, liver and lungs) mixed with oatmeal for haggis.

FOOD *watch*

LAMB JARGON

Teg: one-year-old female.

Hog or **hogget**: uncastrated male.

Weeder or **wether**: castrated male, usually a year old.

Milk-fed: all lamb is milk-fed.

Free-range: lamb is the last remaining animal not to be housed and caged. The exception is spring lamb that has never been outside.

In France, '**House Lamb**' has been deliberately kept inside and is not weaned, to give flesh that is almost white. The best example is Pauillac lamb.

The British Milk Sheep: 30 years ago this was a mix of Blue-Faced Leicester, Dorset Horn, LLeyn and Dutch Milk Sheep.

Ways with Fry

Recipes are interchangeable between the fry of different animals: poach them in stock with vinegar; slice, marinate in oil, vinegar and fresh herbs for 20 minutes, then dip in batter and deep-fry at the last minute before serving.

PORK

The commercial vision is of a fast-growing, long-legged pig who has plenty of babies; but, most importantly, it should have a long lean back which gives the lucrative bacon cuts. Breeders make little or no distinction between bacon and pork.

Pork pigs will be younger – from 16 weeks, before the boars reach maturity (and the flavour becomes tainted). By 21 weeks they weigh 50-60 kg (110-130 lb) – while full-grown, older breeds only ever reached 35 kg (80 lb) or so – and go either for bacon or pork, depending on the cut. Older animals, up to 27 weeks, will be bred on for their weight, primarily as bacon and hams.

The pig has sustained civilizations since it was domesticated. In recent years there has been a move to give it back its freedom, with as many as one in five now reared outside. Campaigners have, however, been concerned that some pigs have rings put through their noses, which stops their natural practice of rooting for tubers and other foods below ground. The trade and quality has become militarily uniform.

COOKING: Two countries have eradicated the disease-producing micro-organism *trichonella* from pork: the UK, since the late '70s; and Australia. The extended cooking times in most books can now be read as overly cautious, and pork cuts cooked merely to a point of pink-ness (but not undercooked, because there are other problems in rare pork to worry about) improve in flavour. Allow about 20 minutes to the 450 g (1 lb) for roasting.

Way with Pork

Flavours that go well with pork include that of many fruits, such as apples, prunes, apricots and pineapple; also acidic and demanding flavours, like gherkins, mustards and soy; and, when cold, the more tart pickled vegetables.

RARE BREEDS OF PIG

A t the end of the 18th century there was a large importation of Asian pigs, either directly into the UK or via Italy, where the influence is still seen in the Neapolitan pig. European pigs were long and lean; Asian pigs were short and fat – and prick-eared. For 150 years afterwards the British pig meant one of seven breeds.

The Middle White, was the original pork pig. It was fat and compact, a beer barrel on legs with a sergeant major's snub nose. The Japanese had particularly admired it and raised a statue in honour of its physique. The Berkshire was not so rounded and needed feeding up to reach any size. The British Lop came from Devon and Cornwall and was a quiet old grazing pig, as was the Large Black which was also from Cornwall but found in Norfolk. The Gloucester Old Spots (yes spots) was the orchard pig let out to graze on the apples and feed on the whey from cheese-making. British Saddleback was found in Wessex: a docile forest pig, it was good for both pork and bacon, and an important breeding stock because of its docility. The red Tamworth was mostly a bacon pig, wanted for its lard.

The Ministry of Food ended the era of small pig farming. During rationing, farms were only allowed to kill two pigs a year – with a policeman in attendance to verify. After the war, there was enormous government encouragement for pig farmers to change from the smaller native breeds and go over to the placid Norwegian Landrace. In Denmark all other breeds of pig were taken out of production. Danish bacon had a reputation for quality and uniformity. It looked the part as whole sides when it was fashionable for butchers to hang the carcasses outside their shops (the colouring of native breeds was deemed unattractive). Crossed with a faster-growing Large White, this became the bacon pig of the '50s and '60s.

The political pressure against the native breeds was twofold: to stem the tide of imports; and to satisfy larger factory processors who wanted uniformity and larger cuts off larger animals. The docile Landrace was also happy to be moved indoors while other breeds resented the confinement.

Research for the Rare Breeds Survival Trust has shown that the water loss in cooking from the rare breeds can be to up to one-quarter less than from Landrace, Large White and the equivalent American breeds, Hampshire and Duroc.

PORK CUTS

BATH CHAPS are the bottom half of the jaw, cut in half. Usually boiled and sold skin on, they are fatty and sold as a cheap salad meat. SHOULDER breaks down into the HAND, a bony cut with 675 g (1½ lb) of meat and the same of bone. Lean and good value, it is often overlooked, though it tends to be sinewy and the meat is caramel-coloured rather than white. 'Too ordinary for anything other than the family table', said Escoffier, but it is flavoursome and good value for stuffing and for long slow roasting. Boned and salted, it is found in soups and *potées* across French regional cooking. HAND AND SPRING, weighing 1.35-2.7 kg (3-6 lb), may be only one-fifth bone but is fattier than the hand and makes a good roast. There is more – and sweeter – meat than on a hand, so it is even better value. It also presents a good expanse of crackling. Because the SPRING is fatty, smaller butchers will tend to use it in sausages. SPARE RIB JOINT is the shoulder with the hand and spring taken out (ie the blade and the neck) and usually boned and sold as a joint, but it is inclined to fall apart on cooking. With sweet meat it is fair value, preferred by people who like a fatty cut. When the bone is left in it is called SPARE RIB CHOPS (ie the neck, but never called as such). This has a good meat-to-bone ratio when cut across as chops. It is good for casseroling or roasting and serving with strong sauces, such as the traditional Oriental sweet-and-sour. Cubed meat taken from the spare ribs and the hand are good for casseroles, etc. BLADE BONE is awkward to carve. Weighing about 1.35 kg (3 lb), it is lean, but has sweet meat and is good value. NECK BONES are good for stews at around 40p per 450 g (1 lb).

LOIN is primarily used for chops, but is a

Ensuring good crackling

Scoring the skin allows the added salt and oils to seep into the fat under the skin and also helps to make it more manageable after cooking. The fat dries out and creates the crackling. One trick, not infallible, for failed crackling is to put it under a tea towel in a microwave for 60–90 seconds.

prime cut with a high percentage of good-quality meat. The BEST END, next to the spare rib, has one eye of meat and nothing under the bone. It is good for grilling or a joint roast. LOIN PORK CHOPS are best as a joint or chops. TENDERLOIN is the best-value cut, including the kidney underneath the bone, and has no fat and the best flavour. Weighing 225-350 g (8-12 oz), it is usually taken off bacon pigs and put into the pork trade because of its value.

A LOIN OF PORK FILLET END, complete with the tenderloin and the kidney, is the best roasting joint. Score it finely for the crackling.

PORK STEAK is the hip bone, and is equivalent to a rump steak. A good alternative to tenderloin, it is low in fat and is good marinated or in casseroles.

LEG OF PORK is *the* roasting and crackling cut, but is not as good value as loin. Weighing 3.5-6.8 kg (8-15 lb) complete, it is usually cut into joints. With the bone in, these should be at least 1.8 kg (4 lb) or they will fall apart.

KNUCKLE, sometimes called HOCK, is good value. It is sold on the bone, though it can be stuffed if the butcher will bone it. It usually goes into sausages, or is sold ready-cooked, often at appreciably larger mark-ups.

BELLY can be used as a roast. Usually the flank end, nearest the legs, goes for sausages. It has good crackling and is sometimes sold as slices for baking or grilling. It is also useful in terrines or cut into 2.5 cm (1 in) wedges as an extra source of fat in a casserole, where it lends sweetness and richness.

CHINESE-STYLE SPARE RIBS is the end of the belly and used to go for sausages but is now cut the length of the rib to give a meatier chop. These used to be thrown away, but somehow supermarkets and butchers have succeeded in raising the price to £1.59 per lb or more, disguised with dubious flavours.

SUCKLING PIG

Most independent butchers can find young pigs on request. Roast them for between 90-120 minutes, basting with oil not fat. The tradition was to stuff them with onion, breadcrumbs and beef kidney mixed with sage and eggs and seasoned with nutmeg. Raymond Blanc roasts his suckling pig with marjoram and, unusually, makes a sauce from the bones for stock.

Ways with Trotters

Butcher's recipe: boiled for 30 minutes, then roast with sugar and treacle.

They cook well with lentils.

Pierre Koffmann: stuffed with truffles, sweetbreads and morels.

PORK OFFAL

Offal from pigs tends to be among the least expensive items in most butchers' shops. They reward careful cooking.

HEAD mainly goes for processing: for pies, salamis, luncheon meat; or, occasionally, it will be made into brawn (see opposite) or what the French call *fromage de tête*. Traditionally the whole head was served at banquets or at a Christmas table.

TONGUES are rare, but can be cooked like calves' tongues.

EARS were esteemed in Middle-European cooking – singed, boiled in salt water with vegetables and then breadcrumbed.

KIDNEYS are stronger and firmer than those of lamb. They weigh 115-170 g (4-6 oz) and are rarely larger. The core and pipes should have been removed. Cut them in half length-wise and grill or fry.

LIVER weighs 900g-1.8 kg (2-4 lb) and is usually sold sliced. Stronger and firmer than lambs' liver, it becomes cardboardy if cooked too long. It is, however, better for a casserole than lambs' liver because it retains its shape. Cook for 45 minutes maximum. It goes well with potatoes, onions and bacon.

HEART is sold whole and is larger than a lamb's heart, but leaner. It is a cheap old-fashioned cut, which now often goes as pet food but can make good meals. Try stuffing it with bacon, bread, herbs, egg or vegetables and rice, and bake for 40 minutes. It is also good cold, sliced with ravigote sauce.

CHITTERLINGS are the intestines, stripped and boiled. Popular in Wiltshire and Lancashire as a snack with salt and malt vinegar; they are served fried in America. The intestine skin goes as sausage skins, although these are increasingly artificial in origin. Chitterlings on sale in a small butcher should be a sign of home-made sausages.

TROTTERS are the feet and are sold at a give-away price. They do not have much meat, but are highly gelatinous and very versatile for casseroles or extended recipes. Usually poached and then breadcrumbed and grilled or roasted, they can also be stuffed.

CAUL is the transparent cobweb of fat lining the stomach, widely used to wrap dry mixes that need extra fat during cooking like terrines, but can also be used for sausages or even wrapping fish for baking.

PIGS' OFFAL PRODUCTS

BRAWN is the head and trotters (and sometimes beef shin) boiled together. Currently out of vogue, it can be excellent when well done.

A traditional recipe from Wiltshire: saw the head into quarters, remove the ears and eyes, add 3 whole peeled onions, parsley, thyme, bay, salt and pepper. Cover with water in a large pan and simmer for 3 hours, or until the meat is falling away. Allow to cool, then take out the meat and chop coarsely. Reserve the liquid and add a handful of chopped parsley and salt to it. Add just enough of the liquid to give the mixture a thick sloppy consistency and pour into a mould. Cover, weight down and cool for a day. Turn out and slice.

FAGGOTS are the lights (the lungs, liver and heart), fat and breadcrumbs, minced and fashioned into balls and then baked wrapped in caul. Small butchers' shops will omit the lungs. A traditional recipe: Chop or mince 450 g (1 lb) liver, 85 g (3 oz) streaky smoked bacon, 85 g (3 oz) pork fat with 450 g (1 lb) of breadcrumbs (soaked in milk and rung out), 3 onions, a teaspoon of freshly grated nutmeg, 1 teaspoon of chopped parsley and 1 teaspoon of sage. Make into balls the size of a tangerine. Lay out on the caul fat and wrap completely. Bake in milk for 30 minutes. Add

575 ml (1 pt) of brown stock and bake for a further 10 minutes to make the gravy.

BLACK PUDDING, or BLOOD PUDDING, in English versions uses pork blood, fat and barley, often in an ox stomach lining as a casing as pig's is too small. The use of rice is also credited to English butchery, brown sugar, currants and sultanas to Flemish. The fat is properly the suet from around the kidney, and is often disguised in the mincing. French versions, principally from Normandy and Brittany, tend to be smoother, omitting the barley. As follows: mix 500 g (1 lb 2 oz) of pork fat with 400 ml (14 fl oz) of pig's blood, 100 ml (3½ fl oz) of cream, 200 g (7 oz) of softened onions, mixed spices and fill a casing. Poach at 95°C (203°F) for 20 minutes, then allow to cool. Grill lightly to serve with mashed potatoes. French BOUDIN BLANC or WHITE PUDDING is made using 2 parts pork fat to 1 part lean pork, though it may also be veal or chicken, pounded and mixed, in classical cooking at least, with foie gras, eggs, onion, cream and seasoned with nutmeg. The traditional British version is based mostly around oatmeal and pork fat.

ZAMPONE is the stuffed shank, a speciality of Italian butchers, and usually sold here pre-cooked to be served warm with cabbage, pulses and purées or served cold and cut thinly as a starter.

SAUSAGES

Sausages are arguably the most popular food in the country and the last surviving artisan craft of the butcher, although the craft has been allowed to diminish considerably without protection for decades. The usual contents are now 65% belly, shoulder or trimmings; the rest will be water, rusks etc.

The smoother, emulsified texture of modern

sausages disguises what might have gone into the mix. In law, even skin can count as 'meat'. Good sausages have a coarser texture, a mark of the maker's self confidence. The best cuts of meat for sausages are probably the more labour-intensive cheek and shoulder.

Natural skins were often taken from sheep, rather than pigs. Since the '60s, most casings are made of collagen taken from cow hides – an accidental discovery by medical researchers working for Johnson & Johnson, the US Health-care conglomerate in their factory outside Glasgow in 1962. Now collagen skins are used for 75% of all sausages. The collagen has the advantage of being a regular size, which suits factory production. Sausages tend to burst because the water in the rusk content expands and cannot escape in an artificial casing. Sausages in natural casings do not need pricking, because the skins already have minute openings. They can be spiked three-quarters of the way through cooking to drain off any excess fat.

The best sausages were always attributed to Cambridge and Newmarket. The rusk was made with freshly baked bread which was toasted for two hours and then ground (most breads today have too much yeast to achieve this), and the sausage enriched with egg.

Sausage names are applied loosely and carry less and less weight. *Cumberland* is sold in coils; *Lincolnshire* will contain sage, but even these are often overlooked; and an *Oxford* used to be veal with lemon. Despite the tomes written and the many competitions to find the best sausage, the essential difference is between hand-made and factory-made. Many are just gristle, bone, slush and slurry. However, supermarkets – led originally by **Tesco** – have broken away, with impressive mass-produced versions under tradi-

Vegetarian Sausages
CAERPHILLY SAUSAGE is traditionally made using the eponymous cheese and leeks. These are now often aggrandized using spinach and herbs.

HASLET is sausagemeat wrapped in caul fat, then steamed and roasted. It is usually sold pre-cooked and sliced.

FOOD *watch*

Sausage prices tend to be governed by the level of pork content, ranging in most supermarkets from 65% to 85% for top grade premium. Generally the differences are infinitesimal and hardly allow for prices to vary from £1.15 to £1.90 per lb. Even a 20% difference in pork does not equate to 75p per lb. At **Waitrose**, premium chipolatas sold inoffensively at 95p for 8 oz were, in fact, more expensive than their very good traditional range at £1.79 per lb, with the same 85% of pork. Downmarket **Gateways** are only a few pennies cheaper. Some brands – notably last year's so-called 'sausage of the year', **Porkinsons** – are packed incomprehensibly in 398 g bundles which make quick price comparison almost impossible. At £1.69 in **Gateway,** they were in practice as expensive as those from a nominally upmarket supermarket like **Waitrose**.

tional labels. London has seen a small revival of sausage-making led by the brilliant ****Bill O'Hagan** in Greenwich, and followed by a small central chain **Simply Sausages** originally in Farringdon Road and Brewer Street, which has also spawned a rival offshoot in Bath, **The Sausage Shop.**

Matthew Fort of the *Guardian*, who hosted a series of tastings of more than 1,500 sausages nation-wide in the search for a sausage of the year, is unequivocal, 'Good sausages are about two things, the quality of the meat and the higher quantity of meat'. Common-sense says they will likely be from a shop selling about five different types in weekly batches. They should be kept for 24 hours to settle into their skins after stuffing.

FRANKFURTERS were originally lightly smoked sausages made from pork mixed with salted bacon fat. The kosher influence added beef. They have become up-market variations on HOT DOGS, which are further extended with cheaper chicken, even potato starch and numerous additives, from 'natural' smoke flavour to liberal dashes of water-retaining phosphates.

Most tins of frankfurters claim percentages of meat which hover around 50% meat, but **Sainsbury** offers 58% in packets, 67% for premium hot dogs in cans against 70% for its canned frankfurters. The price difference between frankfurters and hot dogs can be as great as 43p, which is hardly a true reflection of the relative costs of ingredients.

The big brand names for hot dogs are disturbingly tasteless: **Plumrose** are dark, almost purple-skinned and vapid; **Kingsford** are quite mealy; **Ye Olde Oake** are nastily vapoured; **Princes** are very wobbly and anaemic. They all reflect very little of the traditional virtues. **Sainsbury** tinned premium frankfurters have some vestige of flavour to the skin and stand out, but its ordinary range returns – not untypically for **Sainsbury,** who specialize in selling top and bottom of many meat ranges – to being dry, creamy and as near to tasting of nothing as is possible.

Sainsbury Original German frankfurters in brine, resplendent with Gothic lettering on the tin, are two-thirds of the size of their own-label, which also has two more sausages per can (for 5% more meat). They are barely worth the premium over the salty own-label.

*Danish Sausage Co Giant skinless frankfurters are much closer to the traditional juicy (if fatty) ally for sauerkraut. The skinless notion is spurious as they split. As do ***Herta Skinless Continental** frankfurters, which have enough skin to split but are reasonably solid, with a distinct Middle European flavour.

Beni Foods Frankfurter-Traditional (pork and beef) German sausages have a stale sour unattractive flavour.

The general quality is so poor that, for the most part, one suspects collusion with the mustard manufacturers to save the day.

BACON

Before 1940, the Berkshire pig supplied much of London and South Wales bacon. The Tamworth provided for Birmingham, where it was wanted not only for its meat but also for its lard, used as a cheap substitute for butter on bread. Pig farms had to be around the cities for safety.

To be bacon or ham the meat must be cured. A whole romance has been built up around the different cures for bacon and ham. The reality is disappointingly mundane and standard. The cure is injected and many of the old cures may have been sources of food poisoning in themselves. Hams, usually the back legs though sometimes (and less good) the shoulder, will be cured longer than the conventional 4-5 days for bacon.

The nitrates in the cure react with the haemoglobin in the tissue and turn to nitrites, causing the pinkness. The use of saltpetre was one means of achieving this, but its use is restricted not just because it is an explosive, but because the potentially unpredictable levels of nitrites can be carcinogenic. 200 parts to a million, or a combined 500 parts per million with nitrates, is the legal maximum, considerably higher in this country than in Italy, for example – one gram can be lethal.

Wiltshire Cure was used for whole sides and was more to do with the cut rather than the cure, which is simply 26% salt; 0.1% sodium nitrite; 0.32% sodium nitrate (E251). Other cures reduce the level of salt to as low as 15% and add up to 3% polyphosphate. The phosphates allow the meat to absorb up to 15% of the brine water, double the amount of a traditional Wiltshire cure.

Ayrshire Cure means only that the meat has been skinned and boned. The basic recipe on which most regional hams are based still favours a dry cure rather than the wet brine baths of the bacon factories. It mixes 2.7 kg (6 lb) of salt with 1.35 kg (3 lb) brown sugar and 115 g (4 oz) potassium nitrate. For every 450 g (1 lb) meat, 45 g (1½ oz) of this salt-and-sugar mix is rubbed in. Middles and backs are left for four days, gammons for five. Wash them off before use, but do not soak.

BACON CUTS

GAMMON is the back legs, weighing 6.8-11.3 kg (15-25 lb). Sold whole, as halves or as boneless joints it tends to be very lean and as a result increasingly dry. Roast or boil.

SLIPPER is a joint cut off the gammon, weighing 900 g-1.35 kg (2-3 lb). Very lean, it is the equivalent of rump steak.

Ways with Gammon

A butcher's recipe: boil for 45 minutes. Using kitchen gloves (not to scald yourself), cut off the skin with a sharp knife leaving the fat on. Score the fat in criss–crossing diagonal lines to make a lattice pattern. Stud the cloves into the intersections. Mix brown sugar, honey and treacle and cover the fat well with this mix. Bake for 20 minutes to the 450 g (1 lb), basting occasionally.

BACON PRICES

Bedlam... variations in breed, feed and age of most bacon are minimal and cures vary in only slight degrees. Yet there is a massive, incomprehensible spectrum of pricing. Take a few examples at random. **Sainsbury** charges 10p more for smoked; **Waitrose** 74p less. **Sainsburys'** has been selling a low–salt extra–trimmed unsmoked bacon, a minimum of extra work and ingredients, for 80p more per lb than its normal range. **Waitrose** sell Dutch back bacon £1 cheaper than English back, **Sainsburys'** 15p cheaper on the deli counter than at the chill cabinet. **Sainsburys'** add a premium of 10p for cutting off the rind, **Waitrose** 50p for slicing it. **Tesco's** 'extra trimmed for leanness' suddenly prices itself in inconvenient sizes of 255 g, as against the lb for everything else, and is the most expensive bacon of all, topping even **Sainsburys'** 'traditional oak–smoked' by almost 20p. **Tesco** in the same week had a sensibly restrained window of pricing from £1.99 to £2.19 per lb for back cuts, compared to **Sainsburys'** of from £1.79 to £3.38. **Safeway** complicate matters further by pricing in bands of 5 oz, 9 oz and 15 oz. Brands like **Danepak**, alongside, are in 184 g packages.

BELLY is streaky bacon, half the price of back. With a high fat content, it is good for pâtés and stuffings.

BACK is the traditional breakfast cut and is always sold sliced. It includes the loin and the chump and is lean. It is more popular unsmoked. Sainsbury is claiming a breakthrough in dry-cured bacon 'without the use of water' and with lower salt levels. The process is said to be much quicker and therefore cheaper.

FORE-HOCK is the equivalent to the hand and spring of the pork or shoulder. Good value, it is fattier than the gammon and is sold on the joint or boned and rolled. It makes an excellent mid-week joint.

*COLLAR is the spare rib. Boned and sliced as bacon, it is cheaper than back, with larger slices though it tends to fall apart without the bone. It is also sold as joints. Fattier than gammon, it is therefore more moist and usually £1 per lb cheaper. It is good for roasting or boiling.

*KNUCKLE, or GAMMON HOCK, is usually very cheap in independent butchers. If smoked, soak or boil it for 15 minutes and throw way the very salty water. Simmer for 2 hours with vegetables. It is traditional in pea and ham soup.

BACON RIBS are the spare ribs and are cheap. Parboil and glaze like ham, or simply glaze and roast.

HAM

English ham is the long cut of the back leg. It was necessarily produced in areas where the Wiltshire sides of bacon were not. Most were called York hams, though they were produced everywhere.

YORK HAMS were salted and turned every three days for a month. They were then hung in calico bags to mature for several months. In the south, they were smoked; but not in the north. Escoffier declared these as the best hams for serving cold. When he was writing in 1905, however, the breeds would have been very different and significantly fattier. A small amount of York ham is still cured in the traditional way, notably **George Scott's** in York and more interestingly because it is matured longer at **Radford's** at Sleights near Whitby, both of whom do mail order.

BRADENHAM HAMS from Chippenham in Wiltshire are cured as for York ham and then pickled in molasses for a month, which gives the distinctive black skin and supports the sweetness of the meat. DEVON HAMS were centred on Plymouth but seem to have disappeared.

PRAGUE HAMS and WESTPHALIAN HAMS,

smoked over juniper and beech-wood, and the more highly smoked BLACK FOREST HAM can be stunning, but are harder to find. AIR-DRIED HAMS are found across Europe, each valley claiming for itself a distinction derived from the smells hanging in the wind. Some of these are wonderfully outrageous. Parma claims its winds sweep over 'olive groves, pine and chestnut trees, before reaching Parma and infusing the hams with their scents'.

ITALY

**SAN DANIELLE has been a protected name for dried hams since 1970. Production is limited to the area around the village of San Danielle del Friulli in Udine. The trotter is left on and the hams are beaten into a guitar shape. It will be matured for at least nine months, in which time it loses a quarter of its weight. Production is now centred on 26 plants in the foothills of the Alps, producing 1.8 million hams a year. Each carries the 'SD' seal. The flavour is more pronounced than Parma, but is its equal. The flesh is dark and reddish, tending to be like a leather hide. The taste is sweet, with hints of nuts and an intense saltiness, 'like being at the seaside, but with bite and a great length of flavour, the sourness edged with salt and a shade of sweet'.

**PARMA hams were made in the hills around Parma from before the Roman era and have been famous for as long. The name has been protected under the same legislation as San Danielle since 1970. The pigs must spend the last four months grazing in Emilia, Veneto, Lombardy and Piedmont. The legs are salted (in sea salt) and left in drying chambers for 70-100 days. They are washed, dried and beaten into the familiar chicken-leg shape. The airing houses must

> **Suffolk Sugar-cured Ham**
>
> This particular cure was found around Ipswich: Mix 285 g (10 oz) salt, 30 g (1 oz) saltpetre, 1.1 litres (2 pt) of old brown ale, 300 ml (½ pt) of malt vinegar, 450 g (1 lb) black treacle and 225 g (8 oz) of brown sugar. Pour this mixture over the ham in a crock and turn the ham twice a day for a week, then daily for 30 days. The temperature should remain below 4.5˚C (40˚F).

be in Parma province in specified valleys up to an altitude of 900 metres. Hams of 7-9 kg must be hung for 10 months, larger ones for a year. They are then branded with the ducal seal. The flesh tends to be an opaquely pink-brown, the taste dry and meaty, not unduly salty, 'a lovely deep delicate flavour with a sweet finish... more feminine than San Danielle'.

Another consortium has been set up to link the 12 producers in the hills between Padua and Vicenza. Their products carry a lion's head seal and the words 'Veneto'.

PANCETTA is the Italian version of bacon, usually using both back and flank rolled into a round. Although it looks like streaky bacon, because the pigs are older there is a different dimension of flavour. It is salty and sweet, with an intense distinctive aniseedy taste 'eau-de-vie of sea breeze'.

SPECK is from northern Italy, mostly the German-speaking parts. It is made from the legs, which are opened up, salted, smoked and matured for a few months. ROSSEN-SPECK COTTO is cooked to an opaque pink-hued beige and usually sold sliced, the flavour 'goes from sour to sweet and disappears into sour nuts and peas'.

FRANCE

BAYONNE ham is lightly smoked. Whereas the San Danielle and Parma hams are aristo-crats that demand to be eaten alone, amber-hued Bayonne is subtler and more fragrant. Different ages of ham are sold: firstly around 7-months-old, when the hams are quite light; by 12-months-old they take on more character and in the dryness become more leatherine. Bayonne ham doesn't have the subtlety of others. The taste tends to be of the cure rather than of the meat. It needs accompani-ments to bring out its more lyrical flavours and suits well the traditions of serving it with melon or figs.

SPAIN

**JAMON DE JABUGO is arguably the finest and most expensive of all hams. Sold at around £13.75 per 115 g (¼ lb), only a small amount ever comes out of Spain. It is sold with the hoof on to show its origins. Attempts to industrialize the process or to introduce different breeds of pig to the area around Huelva have failed. The oak forests are still populated by small farmers each of whom lets out his black Iberian pigs to roam wild on the mountains and feed on the acorns. There are as many curers as there are farms and the result is an astonishingly rare and brilliant ham. Bright orange with deep scarlets running to black, it has the taste of the forest. The flavour of the acorn diet comes through, with overtones of lychees, chocolate and treacle, and it is sweet like a pâté. The cure seems to create an effect as if the ham were cooked.

SERRANO comes from the mountains of Caceres, Granada and Salamanca and, like other Spanish hams, tend to be rougher. Quite a meaty product, it has unfashionable visible layers of fat. It tastes leathery and is a big chew, with saltiness that ebbs and flows.

BRITAIN

Air-dried hams may well have been a feature of the diet before the 18th century, but they have dropped out of circulation. The best examples are from **Woodall's** of Waberthwaite in Cumbria, but even with these the maturation period is a quarter that of Parma. The result is completely different. **Denhay Air-Dried Ham** from whey-fed pigs raised near Bridport, Dorset, uses apple juice and honey in the cure and is oak-smoked for several months. Closer to a fresh Bayonne, it goes well with fruit as it is juicy, citrusy and fresh-tasting. Much small production is now being done by smokers rather than the curers themselves, which may be another obstacle to pursuing the Parma tradition.

SALAMI ETC

The warmer climate of southern Europe favoured cured pork over the bacon and fresh meat of the north. The art of charcuterie began in Italy and spread north and west. Today 217 different varieties of Salami are still claimed to be made in Italy.

The Italians say their salami is better than that of the French or Spanish. Their agriculture is set up primarily to produce charcuterie rather than bacon or fresh pork. The pigs have been bred from English Large Whites and are allowed to get much larger than in England – up to 180 kg (400 lb).

ITALY

The best salamis come from the Po Valley, with its strong dairy heritage, and feed on the whey from the cheese-making. There are four styles of salami: fine cut, coarse cut, pure pork and pork and beef. Beef is added to give an element of hardness that pork rarely achieves.

A good salami smells fresh and pure. Held up to the light, it is possible to see the coarseness of the mincing. Poorer meats will still have hairs and edges. In the best, the tastes will evoke white truffles or bacon. In the dry cures, the flavours usually go from sweet to sour; but in the cooked products, like the specks from the north or the smoked products, this is reversed.

MILAN SALAMI was originally just from around Milan, but is now made all across Italy.

Salami Colour Codes
Now owned by **Kraft**, **Negroni** grade their salami as follows: the best and most expensive is blue label, down through blue and white, then red and finally green.

The recipe was for one-third pork (usually shoulder), one-third beef (again forequarter) and one-third pork fat (the fat should be taken from the back and the belly, while the soft fat from around the kidney goes for lard – back fat is supposedly lower in cholesterol). These are then mixed with 3% salt, a gram of pepper for each kilo, some garlic and wine. The salami is matured for a minimum 40 days. Some will be aged for eight months, in which time they can lose 45% of their weight.

CACCIATORI salamis are only cured for 20-60 days and are almost always sold whole, and Veronese is lightly smoked.

CREMONA salami is similar to Milan, but more loosely packed. It has survived because Cremona was the home town of **Negroni**. The sausage is only made in winter when it is snowing, to 'create the adhesion' they claim.

FELINO, made around Felino near Parma, is often held to be one of the best salamis. Pure pork is mixed with peppers, wine and garlic, and then matured 30-60 days. It is lean and delicately flavoured. **Fini** is a good example.

VARZI used to be made in the town of that name, but the trade has dwindled, and it is now mostly made in the north. Conspicuously low in fat, it uses 75% pork from the forequarter and 20% fat from the throat, and is matured variously for 1-8 months.

NAPOLI is distinctly bright red and sometimes flavoured with chilli. It has twice the pepper content of a Milan. The mix is pork and beef, and it is lightly smoked during the drying and matured for 2-3 months.

SPIANATA ROMAGNA is distinctive because it is flattened out, a practice typical of the area around Rome, with large visible cubes of fat and often strongly peppered.

FABRIANO from Marchese, Umbria, Latium, has pronounced higher levels of pepper (1½ grams per kilo) and garlic, but uses lean cuts of pork or beef.

FINOCCHIONA from Tuscany, is distinctive in being flavoured with fennel and very salty – possibly because Tuscan bread is unsalted, unlike that of the rest of Italy.

MORTADELLA is the original sausage from Bologna, hence 'baloney' for American imitations. The name probably comes from the pounding of meats in a mortar or, more fancifully, from using up the dead horses after battle. In Medieval times, it cost four times more than ham. As with bacon, the bright pink colour comes from the action of the nitrites and nitrates. The longer cooking time for larger sausages (18-24 hours) draws out more flavour. Pork neck, shoulder and hand are the main cuts used – usually from hogs not sows – and 10% is tripe. Beef is not used in the best mortadellas, though the casing will often be from cows rather than pigs. The fat is the harder fat from the back and cheeks. Seasoning is salt, pepper and sugar. The flavourings used are garlic, wine, pistachios and milk powder. Sometimes polyphosphates are added to enhance the water retention. The resulting mass is often now frozen to make it easier to work. The fats are added later to create the distinct pink and white checks seen on the slices. These giant sausages are cooked in special ovens at 80°C (176°F), then cooled in cold water straight after to gel and left to stand for 24 hours.

COPPA from Emilia, is widely made from the neck of pork. The meat is not minced but trimmed of fat, salted and seasoned with garlic, pepper and rosemary, then rolled out in a natural casing it is matured for 4-5 months. It has no protection in its trade name.

ZAMPONE, from Emilia, is traditionally a Christmas or mid-winter dish. A medium mince of pork (equal parts lean and fat) and spices is stuffed into the skin of the trotter and dried for several days at above room temperature and then boiled for 5-7 hours. It is usually sold here pre-cooked.

FRANCE

A great many French *saucissons* are made, but few rival the sweetness of the Italian. The best known styles are ROSETTE which has a white crinkled rind and large visible knobs of fat set in a deep pink-rose flesh. It has the smell of hung bacon and is sweet and acrid in flavour, 'noticeably sour with a peppery finish'. JESUS (DE LYON) has a white rind, and distinctive oyster-shaped ridging, from a deep meaty red to beige flesh, with the sweetness of chestnuts, high *umami*, and an intense finish of pepper.

POLAND

Polish salamis have increasingly become available and offer interesting new dimensions. The long crenellated thin sticks of KABANOS offer a very true salami flavour; sweet in the centre, the taste develops in the mouth. The rust-skinned, ham-coloured MYSLIWSKA has a hint of truffles but a short finish. The bacon-rasher-shaped SOPOCKA is sweet. The mild KRAKOWSKA is also sold in a dry version, where it picks up a tough leathery texture and develops an accentuated sourness. The black-skinned KOLSKA is soft and sweet in taste, with a vegetable hint ending in sourness and spices. The highly concentrated TUCHOWSKA is intense in flavour. These are all worth experimenting with ahead of any German or Danish competition, which are mostly mass-produced (stripped of its pepper overcoat, the widely available GERMAN PEPPER is tasteless meat, while DANISH SALAMI is simply fat, coloured with beetroot juice).

SPAIN

Spanish salami tends to be rough and ready, lacking subtlety if not taste. The most famous is the CHORIZO, with bright red rusty skin and a pronounced fat content in the meat. The flavour has an immediate edge of chilli, with a following taste of chilli sours. It is striking but primitive and often very hot. The SALCHI-CHON, from Catalonia, uses gammon and strips of salted belly and is matured for 6 months. It looks like the French Rosette and is visibly fatty. It has a good dry texture and a sour taste on the edge.

POULTRY

The battery farm was introduced from America in the '40s to provide for the needs of the supermarkets. Before then egg production was seasonal, the hens laying fewer eggs as the days shortened. The best eggs were said to be laid in May or June. By controlling the light, the battery farms deceived the chicken into laying all year. Most are culled at age three, but can go on laying until well into their fourth and fifth years. Henri IV's proud ambition that every French family should have a chicken for the pot on Sundays has been subverted. The healthy image of the meat is at odds with the intensity of the production.

Chicken
Eggs
Duck
Emu
Goose
Guinea Fowl
Ostrich
Turkey

CHICKEN

No animal has so comprehensively established its relationship with the kitchen. There are more recipes in more cuisines across the world for chicken, let alone eggs, than any other food. It may have paid a high price in crossing from the farmyard to the battery, but protagonists might argue that so have we in moving from the countryside to high-rise cities. As ever, the chicken has just moved with us. Its versatility and adaptability are outstanding.

A good chicken will have a plump breast and no bruising or marks on the chest. Glassy skin is usually a sign of age or mistreatment in the cold store. The bird should be cleanly plucked with no tears in the skin. The best value birds will be 1.8 kg (4 lb) plus, where the ratio of meat to bone is better. As it will be an older bird, the flavour will have developed more. Previously these were always boilers who had finished their stint of egg laying, but these now tend to go for processing.

Whatever Happened to Giblets?

The EC has ruled against chickens being sold with their livers on the grounds of hygiene. Sadly this has consigned a prime cut to frozen tubs and to the processing industry – and allowed another ratchet on the pricing.

There are five classifications of chickens sold in this country: CORN-FED will have been fed on a diet that is 70% corn, maize or cereal, but will probably have been raised in a barn. The yellowing of the flesh is distinctive, but whether it improves the flavour of the meat on the breeds used here (unlike in France) is debatable. EXTENSIVE REARING means the chickens have been kept in a controlled environment in large houses, and fed on a high-protein (meat and fish) diet. FREE-RANGE BARN is tautologous, the birds are free to roam in a barn, but have no access to open ground.

Most chickens sold will reach 1.35 kg (3 lb) in 42 days, before reaching sexual maturity. What are called cockerels are fed on a super enzyme diet that can give them a weight of 5.4 kg (13 lb) before maturity. Free-range birds are often allowed to live longer. TRADITIONAL FREE-RANGE must be at least 81 days old and must have access to grass. TOTAL FREE-RANGE are birds which have been reared in an environment which allows a maximum of 13 birds per square metre and gives them access to pens at night, and they will be at least 56 days old. The move to free-range flocks has brought with it attendant concerns of stressed animals living in unnaturally large flocks. Mass agriculture remains in conflict with the traditional image of the cockerel and his hens in the farmyard. Often genuine free-range will be more emaciated because they have worked harder and therefore are not so plump – not the Barbie dolls of intensive breeding. The skin is sometimes rougher and the meat can be tougher and darker, but the compensation is in the flavour, or at least the genuine taste of chicken. The most famous and distinctive are the POULET DE BRESSE, from north of Lyons, where whole tracts of the *départment* are given over to freedom for chickens.

CAPONIZATION was made illegal in 1988: this practice implanted male hormones in the neck of male birds to postpone sexual maturity and allow the birds to put on huge weights. In the last century around Dorking in Surrey, farms specialized in rearing capons on milk diets for nine months for the Christmas market.

EGGS

FREE-RANGE EGGS must come from farms with not more than 404 birds to an acre. The requirements to test eggs for salmonella have made small production uneconomic.

The official advice is not to eat eggs unless they are hard-boiled or the equivalent. It is probably preferable not to eat eggs at all as a protest against the state of the industry than to give in to such fey blackmail. Pasteurized egg mixes are now being widely adopted by the catering trade. However, the same zealousness has not infected the supermarkets where they are not stocked. Some alternatives are found in health food shops, such as a non-dairy mayonnaise using an emulsion of sunflower oil, vinegar and apple emulsions.

Freshness is the main issue in eggs. Although eggs will keep for two weeks and longer in good condition, the packing stations still tend to date the boxes with the date of packing – not laying – and some packers may only collect twice a week. **Tesco** insist its eggs be dated with the laying day and claim to have eggs within 24 hours. In an old egg, the white will be loose and flaccid, the yoke will not sit up on the white in frying, and the air space at the tip will be more than 6 mm (¼ in). Textbooks suggest it is possible to see this with a candle, but it is quite tricky to do at home, let alone in a supermarket aisle. There

---

Chicken Jargon

Broilers: the term used to be used for all birds.

Boilers: used to describe pensioned-off egg-laying birds, but is sometimes now used for cheaper birds damaged in the killing.

Spring chicken: is no longer a relevant term, but it used to be used for the first birds of the year, sold around 900 g (2 lb) in weight.

Poussin: baby chicken, weighing under 450 g (1 lb); usually too young to have much flavour.

Suprême: breast with first bone of the wing left on.

Label rouge: French quality grading scheme, not as rigorous as *appellation contrôlée.*

THE SALMONELLA SAGA

The aftermath of the Gummer-Currie fiasco – thousands of birds needlessly slaughtered, farmers inadequately compensated, small producers put out of business, half the nation terrified to eat breakfast, imports of inferior (older) foreign eggs, another tier of testing bureaucracy – dwarves the original concern. On the other hand, practices have been cleaned up: for instance, the disgusting habit of feeding chickens on the feathers of other poultry – and even chicken meal – has been stopped.

FOOD *watch*

Salmonella enteriditis seemingly occurs at random. A chicken may lay 50 unaffected eggs and then one that is affected. The numbers of eggs discovered containing salmonella have been minuscule, but the risk is inherent. Egg shells are porous, so can absorb infection. Current thinking is that salmonella is a danger that we have to learn to live with. Short of keeping chickens yourself there is little opportunity genuinely to compare the quality of eggs from a bird that has happily strutted freely around a farmyard to the products of the commercial breeders.

is no essential difference in colour either in the shell (brown or white depends on breed) or the yolk, often coloured from the feed. Larger eggs come from larger birds.

FOURGRAIN eggs from chickens fed on a diet of wheat, barley, maize and corn have shown relatively well in tastings. **Eggs from Speckeldy Hens** claim to be a move back to pure breeds, but the emphasis is probably more about marketing than quality. FREE-RANGE, as sold in supermarkets, now suffer from new problems of hens being kept in enormous flocks, which stresses them and affects the quality. Moreover, as John Gummer effectively stopped small flocks, the era of the fresh quality egg may have passed completely for anyone without the space for a chicken coop.

The smallest egg is grade 7, at 45 g or less, then in gradations of 5 g to the biggest, grade 1 at 70 g or more. Grade 3, at 60-65g, is the most popular and the most used in recipes.

DEEP LITTER allows for seven birds per square metre of floor space and enough straw/sawdust to ensure the top layer is not damp. PERCHERY or BARN is the 3D version of deep litter with 25 birds per square metre, each with at least 15 cm of perch space. BATTERY is not a word that appears on the packaging any more, for obvious reasons.

DUCK

Britain's most famous duck, the Aylesbury, became extinct some 20 or so years ago in a flurry of cross-breeding and centralization. Nearly all the ducks sold now come from one firm, **Cherry Valley** in Lincolnshire. Fresh will always be better than frozen, as the freezing affects the fat and defrosting allows the flavour to leach out. The fat was insulation for living in water, but levels seem to have fallen back with domestication.

AYLESBURY – or what passes for it – is now rather a large duck, about 25 cm (10 in) long, and pallid white in colour with blue patches. They are usually packed tightly in boxes on top of each other, which does them no favours, misshaping their long, otherwise elegant, limbs. Now a hybrid crossed with Peking and rarely the 4.5 kg (10 lb) they used to make, they need considerably longer cooking than other ducks – right at the edge of maximum cooking times, 2 hours or even more, to burn off the levels of fat and get the skin crisp. Succulent but fatty, it carves with difficulty, falling apart from the breast, but crisp skin is achievable. It is disappointing for the national duck. Expect two cups of fat from a bird. The WALESBURY is a cross with a Welsh Harlequin, bred for eggs and meat, and raised to be at table-weight within 16 weeks.

GRESSINGHAM was developed in Cumbria by Peter Dodds as a cross with a wild mallard. It was originally a strongly meaty bird. However, success has led the business into franchising, with disappointing collapse in their bone structures and a falling off of the meat-to-bone ratio. Nevertheless it is a good duck, if not the mega-star originally perceived. About 20 cm (8 in) long, with neat military configuration, it has dark meat with a good flavour and skin that crisps. The fat content is about half a cup per bird.

**BARBARY from the South of France, has a sallow yellow skin, usually with signs of hand-picking of the feathers. Often the innards retain large pieces of fat and are poorly cleaned out. They have an excellent ratio of dark flavoursome meat to bone. They are best well cooked (about 2 hours) to let the skin crisp up. Done like this, one bird is really only enough for two, so they are expensive. The fat content is about half a cup. KHAKI CAMPBELL are bred for egg laying only.

EMU

Farmed in western Australia, some of these exotic birds have started to be imported frozen. The virtually fat-free red meat is not dissimilar to ostrich and tastes and looks like prime fillet. Some goes for charcuterie, designed as a low-fat salami for Germany, but it is best briefly cooked in the pan. The Aborigines used the oil as a lubricant, but government sponsorship has created farms in the last 20 years for meat production.

GOOSE

Geese were an important part of the economy of the Middle Ages, the feathers used for arrows and the down for pillows.

The main breeds are EMBLEM and TOULOUSE, sometimes crossed together, or DANISH LARGARTH. Now very much a small-scale, free-range or barn business, the young are hatched between March and July for Christmas. GREEN GOOSE or GOSLING were the first young geese which were killed in spring or at Michaelmas (September 29) for the Harvest Festival, but are almost impossible to find now.

'Long-legged' or 'New York' means weighed with the guts in. You lose one-third to one-quarter of the weight, which makes it more expensive than it appears. Most of the meat is on the breast, and one bird should do five people. Goose is nearly always roasted with fruity stuffings like prune and Armagnac. Some wild geese, usually Canadian, are also shot. These will have less fat after their arduous flight and need extra basting; they are usually cooked with stock or cider, plums, apples or oranges.

Goose fat used to be used as medicine, especially for bronchial complaints, while long-distance swimmers used it for insulation. Reserve it to use for sautéing potatoes and flavouring casseroles. The low instance of heart disease in South-west France has led some nutritionists to the seemingly unlikely suggestion that the fat may have some positively healthy properties.

GUINEA FOWL

Native to the Guinea coast of West Africa, the purple grey plumage dotted with white of the guinea fowl has found them favour as far back as Roman and Greek times. One theory is that they were the original bird meant by references to turkey, before being usurped by the American bird. Traditionally they were sold between February and June when other game was out of season and considered akin to pheasant. They used to be mainly available frozen from France, but fresh are now increasingly available. It used to be said that guinea fowl was an expensive tasteless chicken, but given what has happened to chicken the roles are probably now reversed. There is a 'Label Rouge' scheme for them to be raised on grain. Smaller than a chicken, one will only just stretch to four people, but they are more flavoursome – even if, at first sight, they look unpromisingly grey and not

---

Foie Gras

The production of *foie gras* (goose liver swollen from force-feeding) is not permitted on UK farms. A small amount is imported fresh for the restaurant trade, and this is infinitely superior to most of the tins of ready-made pâté found here. The price fluctuates through the year, from £15 to £90 per lb, hitting a peak at Christmas. The big white bready lobes need careful handling: slice them with a hot knife and pan-fry or bake in an oven which is not so hot you cannot put your hand in. The best is from Alsace and around Toulouse, but most comes from Hungary and Poland. Some very inferior examples have come out of Spain, from **Markiko of Navarra**, they are presented in deceptively beautiful sleek packaging. Duck *foie gras* is arguably better than goose. Guard the leftover juices for cooking.

as voluptuous as a modern chicken. They do tend to dry in cooking, so benefit from barding and delicate saucing. They are likely to become more fashionable and widely available, and are worth seeking out.

OSTRICH

Farms are being set up to breed ostrich meat in Britain, although the trade is mostly in eggs for breeding. Some is imported to Europe from Africa, where it has a long history as a culinary animal, especially in South Africa. Californian restaurants have also begun to sell it. The meat tends to 'look like lamb and taste like steak, with a hint of chicken', but its nutritional advantages are low calories, low cholesterol and one-third of the fat of chicken.

TURKEY

At one time considered one of the most difficult birds to rear in captivity, the turkey's popularity the length of America was down to wild birds. They were first brought here from the Americas at the time of Henry VIII. The Americans established the association with Thanksgiving and Christmas, while here it was traditional to serve roast beef and – right up to the '50s – often chicken.

Out of the Christmas season, a good turkey is hard to find. Most of the smaller birds, weighing 2.3-3.2 kg (5-7 lb) at around 11 weeks, go for processing or the larger 'stags' at 16 kg (35 lb) go directly to the catering market. Most are raised in three-sided poll barns (ie with space to jump around) or broiler-like sheds, but breeding has reached such a point that they are too fat to fend for themselves so have to be artificially inseminated, and some larger birds have difficulty moving around. One of the most economical birds to rear,

FOOD *watch*

Turkey Prices
Supermarkets sell four kinds of birds at Christmas, ranging last year from £1.99 per lb for the top-of-the-range Bronze Grade-A free-range to 98p for normal grade-A. Free-range at **Safeway** was £1.65, **Waitrose** £1.79.

converting 450 g (1 lb) of meat from 1.25 kg (2½ lb) of feed. 'New York' dress means they are sold with the guts in. At 20 weeks the difference between the sexes is negligible, though hens will be slightly smaller. Traditionally they should be hung for 10-12 days, but supermarkets rarely do this now. Independent butchers will and so increasingly do abattoirs. The seeming bargains of the large legs sold in cut-price supermarkets may not have had their sinews drawn and will be tough as a result.

Most turkeys now are hybrids, based on the BROAD BREASTED BRONZE derived from the American breed BELTSVILLE WHITE. The English bird until the '50s was a NORFOLK BLACK or a CAMBRIDGE. They lost favour for their smaller breast and grey speckling. FARM-FRESH TURKEY, identifiable by a black triangle on the packaging, should have been fed on a diet of 70% grain and 30% milk powders. A good turkey will be white, not pink or purple, with a layer of fat all round, dry and with large breast and plump legs.

Some argue that stuffing a turkey restricts the flow of hot air needed to cook the insides properly, and an apple in the chest is the only thing it needs. Cook them breast-side down and turn them over for the last half an hour.

> **Ways with Turkey**
>
> **A butcher's recipe**: 'My mother put a pint of double cream in the pan for the whole roasting time and it made wonderful gravy.' The liver, which is rather stronger and more ungainly than that of the chicken, often goes for pâté.

GAME

Duck (wild)
Grouse
Hare
Partridge
Pheasant
Pigeon
Quail
Rabbit
Snipe
Venison
Woodcock

The fate of wild game mirrors the ravaging of the countryside and the rise of pesticides. What was once a poor-man's food has become a luxury.

Some animals, like rabbit and pigeon, are cheap, abundant and overlooked. Pheasant, quail and venison are extensively farmed and increasingly widely available. Yet some of the most famous game birds, notably grouse but also snipe and woodcock, are endangered – and will go on being so until their habitats are protected.

DUCK (WILD)

Ducks have survived the onslaught of mass farming rather better than other game. The ** MALLARD is the prime wild duck for table. One duck should feed two and it should be hung for 4-5 days then simply roasted for 45 minutes. With small legs and mostly dark good quality fatless breast, it has a gamier, richer flavour – sometimes said to be fishier – than domestic ducks.

Old books suggested the breast being roasted separately (it 'should only fly through the hot kitchen before being sent to table') and the legs braised. Now mallard are often hand-reared, not as intensively as pheasant, but then released for the shoot.

TEAL are small birds shot in smaller numbers than mallard, mostly in the north. In season from October to February, but at their best after the frost has set in, allow one per person.

WIDGEON, of which even fewer are shot, are larger than teal and smaller than mallard. In season from October to February, they are at their best earlier in the year.

GROUSE

Of the 16 species of grouse in the world, four are found here; including the finest of all, the red grouse. The ptarmigan you will not find and the capercaillie was almost lost to us.

Hunted to extinction by 1770 and only reintroduced 60 years later in Perthshire, again as a sporting bird, CAPERCAILLIE reached their peak at the turn of the century. The spoilage of their preferred woodland habitat and increasing exposure to rising numbers of predators, especially foxes, has pushed their territory back to North-west Scotland, and once again extinction is possibly looming. Three years ago it was estimated there were only 2,000 left in the wild. Moves from the Secretary of State for Scotland to ban the shooting were, however, stopped on the grounds that estates might never be persuaded to re-plant the forests of Caledonian pine, their natural habitat, if there were was no prospect of revenue from shooting. Currently a voluntary ban remains in force and numbers are estimated by the Game Conservancy Council to be around 3,500.

Their dark plumage is enlivened with a metallic green breast. They are shot from October 3 to December 10, and usually now are stuffed as trophies. Young birds in autumn feed on bilberries and other plants, which is one reason the shooting season is later. As the year wears on they eat the pine needles which give an unattractive turpentine flavour to their flesh.

Unique to Britain and in need of protection, the **RED GROUSE is the king of British game, but is now in serious – if not terminal – decline from the encroachment on its moorlands. Famously, the shooting season opens on August 12 and goes on to December 10. The Yorkshire moors still have the same density of bird as decades ago, but the moorland

Ways with Grouse

The dish for which grouse are renowned is a well-hung bird, roasted and served on croutons with game chips and bread sauce. The older birds (more than a year) are only good for casseroling, which helps counteract the bitterness in the legs. Modern recipes for serving just the breast are rarely so successful. Game dealers will pluck, draw and hang the birds. Although expensive, they are a unique treat.

itself has shrunk. Many of the birds go to Germany. Most grouse sold here are from northern Scotland where the numbers have been in decline. This may be down to foxes. Before myxomatosis, estates employed keepers to keep rabbit numbers down, but they were laid off in the '70s and '80s and the return of the rabbit has brought back foxes in large numbers, large enough also to interest themselves in the grouse.

Some 500,000 are shot a year, which represents about 30% of the breeding population in August. Despite its culinary reputation, the commercial reason for grouse-rearing is shooting. Guns pay £75-80 to shoot a brace, against £3 when sold to a game dealer. Unlike pheasant and partridge, estates have shied away from farming to preserve the sport.

A healthy bird can weigh 350 g (12 oz). They usually arrive within 24 hours and the butcher can then hang them. Peter Hudson of the Game Conservancy Council explains: 'Hanging was designed for older birds and is really a Highland tradition. London restaurants would not dare to serve traditionally hung grouse. The taste is in the guts, which are unusually long and needed for a digestive system to cope with the fibrous heather. It is this where the flavour comes from.' The perennial debate about whether grouse can be eaten fresh or needs hanging is based in snobbishness. The only unhung grouse available are at shoots or the few that expensively arrive at London hotels for the first day of shooting. The real debate is about how long, not if.

The BLACK GROUSE is larger than a red grouse. The female is grey and the cock is black. Found on the edges of moors, they are in serious decline – there are perhaps only about 15,000 birds left. One hundred years ago they were found on heathland across

Britain; as recently as the '50s they were abundant in the Highlands, Devon, Somerset and the New Forest. They are now very rare south of the Border and are mostly found in Tayside. The season is a week after the main grouse season, starting on August 20 and ending on December 10. It must be well hung or it is dry and flavourless. It is as good as red grouse, but it is not necessarily as expensive because there is no proper trade. Attempts to introduce the bird into Ireland have failed.

HARE

Under the 1880 Game Act, farmers can shoot hare all year round except Sundays and Christmas, but they can only be sold from August to February. Hares used to be commonly as big as 5.4 kg (12 lb) and sometimes as much as 9 kg (20 lb). There are two kinds: the BROWN HARE, probably introduced by the Romans, which thrives in cereal-growing areas; and the MOUNTAIN HARE, which is probably indigenous and shares the same moors as the grouse. In the last century there were so many of them, they roamed the fields in flocks. Brown hare numbers have dropped markedly in the past twenty years.

Unlike rabbit, they should be hung – with the entrails in and by the legs not the head – for up to a week, and sold with the blood, liver, heart and kidneys. The brown hare is larger than the mountain hare, and opinions divide as to which is the best. Nicola Cox in her *Game Cookery* sides firmly with the brown. The flesh is rich, but good value at around £1 per lb. The best cuts are the hind legs and the loin, which are sometimes cut as one piece to make a baron. Hare does not overcook easily and should never be served

Ways with Hare

Casseroling Hare

First marinate the hare joints overnight in a mixture of red wine and wine vinegar, with bay and orange. Make a stock from the trimmings. Put the hare and the marinade in a covered casserole, add the stock, some onions, bacon and herbs. Stand the casserole in a larger pot. Fill that with boiling water, so the casserole is completely surrounded, and bake for 3 hours in a medium to slow oven. Take out the meat, reduce the sauce to thicken it and sweeten with redcurrant jelly and Port. Add the blood to thicken it, but do not bring the sauce back to the boil.

rare. They are traditionally roasted or 'jugged', using the blood for the sauce. Ideally you need a young animal, preferably a leveret being under a year – ideally only six months, otherwise the cooking time may prove excessively long. The blood should be mixed with a little vinegar to stop it curdling.

PARTRIDGE

The devastating decline in the indigenous GREY PARTRIDGE (*Perdix perdix*) in the '50s coincided with the collapse of estate management and the introduction of herbicides, insecticides and artificial fertilizers on the land. Nor was this confined to this country: the impact was world-wide. Organized game shooting began with drives on English estates for the partridge in the 19th century and it became highly fashionable across the south. Now the concentrations of the birds are nearly all to be found in Lincolnshire and East Anglia.

The FRENCH PARTRIDGE (*Alectoris rufa*) have red legs and were introduced here 200 years ago from the south of France, expressly for shooting. They thrived in the open marshland of East Anglia. They are hardier than the grey, and less susceptible to herbicides. Since the '60s, they have been cross-bred for hand-rearing and shooting like pheasants. Numbers have risen sharply and has led to the wide introduction of new shoots across the whole country, but mostly in Norfolk, Essex and Hampshire.

Shot from September 1 to February 1, the birds are at their best early in the year. The English are more expensive and the flesh sweeter. They should be hung for 3-4 days. The French confusingly also differentiate between young birds: *perdreau*, which need brief cooking, and the older, *perdrix*, which should be casseroled.

PLUCKING FEATHERED GAME

Put a polythene bag between your legs (be out of the wind or draughts), put the bird's head down and pluck carefully against the lie of the feathers. Don't snap, just pull gently, taking extra care around the breast and parson's nose. Gut after plucking.

PHEASANT

The most beautifully feathered of all game birds, the pheasant was originally brought here from China. The Romans may have brought pheasants here; the Normans certainly did, and there was much cross-breeding of different species in the 19th century. They are now bred so prolifically for shooting – 20 million are reared a year – they have become a more common sight in country lanes than rabbits or pigeons. The season is from September to the end of January. The first birds are often last year's. They are at their best after October, reaching their prime in November.

Check that the spurs, 5 cm (2 in) up the leg, are not long and sharp. On a new season's bird they will be short and rounded. The cock is larger than a hen, weighing up to 1.35 kg (3 lb), but the hen is considered better meat even if two-thirds of the size. They can be hung by the neck up to seven days, and in the old days longer for a green (high) bird, they waited until the head fell away. Make sure they are not badly shot. They should have plump breasts and needs a line of fat (to the side) to help keep it moist in the cooking.

A large bird will feed three. Near domestication may not have helped their flavour, as they potter about the fields like country vicars certain of their next tea, but it has brought the price out of the realms of luxury – at around £6 per brace. The science of rearing pheasant is borrowed from the poultry industry in the early '50s. The chicks are released into pens at six weeks and are fed regularly for the first year. Woodlands managed for pheasants have recorded notable rises in the variety and numbers of other wildlife, notably butterflies.

Ways with Pheasant

Traditionally pheasants are roasted, but sealing either in a roasting bag or pot compensates for the innate dryness which may also account for their often eccentric and wayward pairings with almost every fruit, liquor and cream sauce in many recipe books. One envisages long dark nights in baronial Northern castles with solitary cooks over-endowed with pheasants desperately thinking up new ways with pheasant. 'Is that Drambuie over there, Macduff?'

PIGEON

The number of pigeon shot bears little relation to the few that arrive at market... an unholy waste of life. In the middle ages, the pigeon loft was an important source of food for both the farm and the estate. They are sold whole or as breasts, the difficulty is judging the quality before cooking. In the feather, young birds will be slightly paler grey; otherwise, there are few tell-tale signs. Older birds will be fatter and age translates as toughness. Marinate pigeons and cook them slowly. Young birds can be excellent, especially if they have grazed near corn crops. Imported French pigeons, or SQUABS, from Anjou are found in top-class restaurants and are worth the enormous expense.

QUAIL

The name quail used to be used of any small bird and was associated with many miracles: they may have been the manna from heaven, falling out of the sky exhausted after a long migration over sea. In Egypt, they were caught with huge nets on the shore and shipped via Marseilles to Europe in the '20s as return cargo on the ships taking cars to Africa, until the cruelty of the trade led to it being stopped in the '30s. These were the *Coturnix coturnix*, which are still shot in Continental Europe but not here in Britain, where the Japanese quail *Coturnix japonica* is farmed. The tiny birds have to be contained in confined spaces or they fly off like sidewinder missiles and crash into the meshing or the walls of a barn. Farming seems needless and cruel. At £1 per bird they are also expensive. Traditionally they are roasted, and said to have an affinity with vine leaves and grapes. Some recipes suggest over 21 other ingredients, a sure sign of meekness of flavour.

QUAILS' EGGS

These pretty small eggs with brown speckled shells should be simmered them for 1-2 minutes only and then shelled. Serve with celery salt and sesame seeds. Most of the charm is in the size.

RABBIT

Probably introduced by the Normans in the 11th century, rabbits were an important part of the economy until the start of the 18th century. They were kept in enclosed warrens on estates to provide meat and fur (for hats) and only ran wild after their place was taken by developments in the breeding of other animals and imports (especially from Australia) began.

They bred in prolific numbers until the epidemic of myxomatosis started in Edenbridge in Kent in October 1953 – probably from infected imported animals – and wiped out 99.9% of all rabbits. Myxomatosis is spread from animal to animal by the rabbit flea. Some argue that its impact was the most significant event in modern agriculture, allowing huge areas to be put over to crops and cereals which previously the rabbits might have destroyed. It is not, in fact, harmful to humans, though the epidemic also destroyed all the trade in the meat. Although myxomatosis is still found, the numbers of rabbits has grown steadily and in Scotland they are found again in force. The Ministry of Agriculture is piloting a scheme to put a contraceptive in the feed.

They are shot all year round. Good value at £1-1.50 each, they provide a good proportion of lean meat. Most of the trade is from rifle to butcher's door, and a good butcher should be able to help revive its reputation. LEGS and the LOIN (SADDLE) are the best cuts; roast or casserole them. Rabbit is sometimes (or was, I have never encountered it) used as substitute for chicken in the catering trade. Look for an animal around 900 g (2 lb), with clean pale-pink flesh which is not emaciated.

Chinese rabbit is mass-produced and sold frozen, but has little flavour and is often more expensive than fresh.

SNIPE

There are two types of snipe: the COMMON SNIPE and the rarer and protected JACK SNIPE. Both migrate here, preferring the westerly wet reedy flatlands and moving north in spring to breed. There is some hope that the move to set aside farmland and less intense agriculture will see their numbers start to rise again. Shooting is from August 12 to January 31. They were once regarded as one of the finest of all game, and are usually roasted like woodcock, with the guts still in.

VENISON

The word venison used to cover all kinds of furred game, but has come to be used solely for deer meat. The native is the RED DEER, found mostly in Scotland where it has migrated further and further north to avoid civilization. It is the strongest-tasting meat. Older textbooks favoured it above other breeds, especially if well-hung. Young meat, say 12-18 months, is rarely hung and is distinctly different. More recently, other writers have advanced the cause of the SIKA, imported from Japan originally to graze parklands but some have escaped and are interbreeding with the red deer in the wild. There are also the woodland FALLOW DEER, again originally the deer of parkland and large estates, and the smaller ROE DEER.

Venison is a modern meat, almost fatless and freezes well. Except for that of young roe deer, the meat invariably benefits from marinating for at least 4-5 days (if the aim is to tenderize) in oil, red wine, vinegar and aromatics. Traditionally it is paired with sweet fruity sauces: redcurrant jelly, baked pears, cherries, apricots etc. Venison is always served on very hot plates to stop the fat congealing unattractively (traditionally in

Scotland, spare plates were kept hot for the second helpings).

HAUNCH, LOIN and BEST END are best roasted and served rare, when they will still be juicy. STEAKS and CHOPS can be pan- or wok-fried, but need more fat than other meats. The less expensive cuts, such as NECK, SHOULDER and SHIN, need marinating and then long slow braising. The LIVER was always a hunter's perk; it is highly valued and should be fried lightly and served pink.

WOODCOCK

The numbers of woodcock have been kept up because they like the same open forest as pheasants, but they are very fast and difficult to shoot and therefore prized trophies. They are nocturnal and secretive, with long beaks and matronly expressions. Many migrate here, especially in colder winters. They must be fat, and are at their best in October and November. They are not hung and are, unusually, cooked complete with their giblets and the neck folded back around the wing. Roast them for 20 minutes, covering the breast (which should be rare) but not the legs, and place on a crouton to collect the juices. 'There is more art in roasting a woodcock, than any other bird,' argues '30s food writer Henry Smith. He says the oven should not be hotter than 230°C (450°F/gas 8).

'Scotch woodcock' is nothing to do with the bird, but a savoury of anchovies and capers in scrambled eggs on toast.

DAIRY PRODUCE

I n 1950, an Italian company boasted that it performed the complete cycle of 49 industrial processes for milk-creating products as diverse as whey-milk posset, albumen and pharmaceutical lactates. Add the variety of different cheeses made across Europe and milk products extend to perhaps 10,000 different foods – even more if we count all the flavoured variations of fromage frais and ice-cream. This diversity is both an amazing testimony to our ingenuity and also a measure of how important dairy products must have been to earlier civilizations as well as our own.

The expansion accelerates. Chill cabinets burst with new innovations – from low-fat ice-creams and non-dairy substitutes, to the sublime examples of crème fraîche from Normandy and the extremely gunky quasi-desserts like double cream adulterated with Cointreau and sugar. The EC's huge 'lake' of milk, the new quota restrictions and the supermarket chains' quest for novelty have all forced man to invent and innovate even further.

From the replacement of the milk-maid at the turn of the century, no other foodstuff has so accurately encapsulated the effect of Man on the food chain with all its political chicanery, impact on the countryside, massive subsidies and debate over its role in a balanced diet.

MILK

It is only in this century – and mostly in this country – that fresh milk has come to the fore. Before, the difficulty of moving fresh milk around the country prohibited its mass sale and cow sheds in and around Victorian cities were reviled as dirty places selling potentially dangerous, disease-carrying liquids.

To the British nutritional movement, milk has provided two great *causes célèbres*. The nutritional importance of milk is its calcium, riboflavin, protein and zinc content, as the vitamins – A, D and E – are mostly in the cream and are skimmed off. For this reason babies and children under two – recently revised down from five – should be given whole milk. In the '20s and '30s, milk was seen as one cornerstone of a diet that could nourish the malnourished. In the '80s, the fat in this same milk was depicted as a dietary villain, a harbinger of heart disease. In just a few years, sales of skimmed and semi-skimmed milk have risen to equal those of full-cream milk. However, unlike other dairy products, whatever the health message the saving in the fat is not passed on – skimmed and full-cream milk cost the same.

Friesian cattle, first introduced from Holland in 1922, undermined the standing of the traditional dual-purpose 'meat and milk' cow, especially the Hereford, by producing more milk than any other breed. The growing universality of pasteurization – which destroys the differences in flavour between milks from one breed of cattle to another, and from one area to another – means Friesian cattle now supply eight out of every 10 pints of milk sold nation-wide.

From the late '20s, this country inexorably adopted policies which meant that fresh milk

Skimmed milk
Semi-skimmed milk
Whole or full-fat milk
High-fat milk
Pasteurized milk
Raw or unpasteurized milk
Homogenized milk
UHT milk
Evaporated milk
Condensed milk
Other milks

MILK MARQUE
is the organization newly designated to take over from the now-defunct **Milk Marketing Board**. Its prime – even sole – objective is to buy and sell milk and then share back the profits to the farms.

was favoured over other milk products. The creation of the Milk Marketing Board, initially on a government subsidy in 1933 to provide milk in schools, centralized our milk policy. In 1940, the Ministry of Food extended the policy to ensure all under-fives and their mothers had cheap or free milk. The production of cheese and butter withered under these decrees and the supremacy of the Friesian – neither have ever properly recovered.

Jersey and Guernsey cows survived the move to the one-cow policy because of the higher fat levels of their milk and cream and, to a lesser extent, because the male calves went for veal. Jersey cows were originally called Alderneys, after the Alderney Packets, or steamboats, which brought them from the Channel Islands. The first herd was established on the mainland in 1811 to decorate the park-lands of the Audley End estate in Essex. Guernsey cows are descended from two French breeds originally taken to the island around the 11th century.

MILK GRADES

SKIMMED MILK has 0.3 % fat or less; SEMI-SKIMMED MILK has 1.5-1.7% fat; FULL-CREAM MILK has at least 4% fat; HIGH-FAT MILK (from South Devon, Jersey and Guernsey cattle) has 4.8% fat or more.

PASTEURIZATION

From as early as 1768, it was known heat pre-served foods. Milk was heated and canned by Nicholas Appert in 1795. Louis Pasteur's experiments in the 1850s and '60s explained why bacteria multiplied to sour milk, wine etc.

Pasteurized milk is nowadays heated to 71.7°C (160°F) for 15 seconds to kill bacteria, principally tuberculosis. Farms with accredited bacteria-free herds still sell unpasteurized or 'raw' milk but, as our diets have become more

---

MILK BOTTLE TOP COLOUR-CODING

Bottled milk is colour-graded: **BLUE** for skimmed; **RED-AND-SILVER** for semi-skimmed; **RED** for homogenized; **SILVER** for full cream; **GOLD** for high-fat milks from South Devon, Jersey and Guernsey cattle; **GREEN** is unpasteurized.

sanitized, so the risk of our not being able to cope with the kind of bacteria found in unpasteurized milk has risen. Writing, in 1943, in *The Living Soil* Elizabeth Balfour was unequivocal about the pros and cons of pasteurized and unpasteurized milk: 'Nutritionally there is a world of difference between the two. Pasteurization, and of course cooking, injure both the vitamin and calcium content of milk, and the beneficial lactic acid bacteria, which attack disease organisms (and in the process cause souring) are killed by heat, leaving pasteurized milk as a perfect breeding ground for subsequent contamination.'

HOMOGENIZATION
This process spins the fat molecules through a narrow tube which evenly distributes them through the milk, creating a smoother, more consistent texture. Homogenized milk is usually therefore whiter.

UHT MILK
LONGLIFE is the most widely available UHT, or ultra-high temperature milk. The milk is heated to above 132°C (270°F) and held there for a few seconds. This process was developed in the '40s and milk thus treated first sold in 1965. Heating to such a high temperature creates off flavours (usually said to be caramel), but it extends shelf-life to up to six months when sealed (but no more than fresh milk once opened) and there is minimum nutrient loss. MILK CANS contain milk processed using a new form of UHT technology that heats the milk more swiftly and cools it instantly to minimize off flavours. **Halo** is a milk alternative launched by **Express Dairies**. It is 97% milk but only 0.2% fat, and the use of sunflower oil to replace natural fat reduces cholesterol to zero compared to 7% for ordinary semi-skimmed milk.

Lactose Intolerance

Some people have an intolerance to the lactose in milk. SOYA MILK is often used as a basis for an alternative, the hulls mixed with water. In the unsweetened version it is fairly puritanical and the effect in real (not instant) coffee is cosmetic – coffee meeting soya beans is an unusual head-on collision. The sweetened version, built up with apple juice and calcium, tastes pleasantly of what it is and has potential as a genuine alternative drink rather than a substitute.
LACTOLITE is cows' milk in which the lactose has been reduced by adding an enzyme that transforms it into glucose and galactose. Conspicuously sweet, despite its fat level of 4 g per 100 ml, it has the thinness of poor skimmed products.

EVAPORATED MILK

This is milk which has had its water content reduced by about 45% (and must contain 7.8% fat) and is then canned.

CONDENSED MILK

This has been reduced to under 33% of its original volume and has added sugar as a preservative.

OTHER MILKS

HORSES' MILK contains the least fat – at 1.2% – of all animal milk, while GUINEA PIG MILK contains the most, at 45.8%. HUMAN MILK is close to cows' milk, at 3.7%.

SHEEP'S MILK is hard to find and usually frozen. It will keep for three days once open. GOATS' MILK contains less folic acid, but is otherwise similar in composition to cows', but there have been cases of anaemia in babies fed solely on boiled goat's milk.

CREAM

Traditionally, cream in this country was always sold fresh, not ripened as for butter or the French crème fraîche. The advent of pasteurization further rendered this idea obsolete as it destroyed the bacteria that create the sourness.

The fat content determines what cream is called, and usually this is indicated now by coloured tops to the cartons (see right).

Half cream
Single cream
Diet extra-thick cream
Whipping cream
Double cream
Clotted cream
Sour cream
Crème fraîche

HALF CREAM
At 12% fat, this is designed for pouring and for coffee. Of limited use, it is irritatingly packed in half-pint cartons rather than quarter-pints like other creams.

SINGLE CREAM
At 18% fat, this is around 15p cheaper per 150 ml (¼ pt) than double. It is useful for pouring or in cooking where there is a lot of liquid (soups, casseroles or quiches). Mix in a little of the hot liquid first to blend it evenly. It will not whip or freeze.

DIET EXTRA-THICK CREAM
Containing 23.5% fat, this name must be the ultimate in marketing tautology. In fact, it has more fat than ordinary cream and costs slightly more than whipping cream. (Also misleadingly priced in millilitres not pints.)

WHIPPING CREAM
The 35% fat in the cream absorbs the air for whipping (under 35% fat and there would not be enough to absorb the air properly).

DOUBLE CREAM
With 48% fat, this is supremely versatile in cooking as it withstands higher temperatures.

CREAM CARTON COLOUR-CODING
BROWN for half cream; **RED** for single; **GREEN** for whipping; **BLUE** for cream; **ORANGE** for clotted cream; **PURPLE** for sour cream.

FOOD *watch*

The labelling of types of cream is strict but confusing. Nutritional labelling weighs cream in grams, but cartons are sold in mls or pints. Easy translation in the supermarket is about as difficult as it could be. Price goes up with fat level, roughly ½ p per g. Double cream is almost £2 per 600 ml (1 pt), compared to milk at 30p.

Whipping Cream

Whipping by hand you are unlikely to create more than a 70% air to fat ratio with either whipped or double cream, but machines can now achieve ratios close to 100% for commercial sweets. Whipping cream was pioneered as a cheaper alternative to double cream – usually about 5p per 150 ml (¼ pint). It will double its own size on whipping, and when lightly whipped will keep frozen for up to two months. It can be used to give bulk to soufflés and mousses. It can have added sugar, clotted or canned cream, or emulsifiers and stabilizers (nisin is a common preservative, usually found in ready-made cream dishes rather than straight whipping cream).

To whip it, first thin it down with a little milk to increase the volume – this is probably marginally less expensive than buying whipping cream. It should whip to 1½ times its volume and will keep frozen for up to two months.

CLOTTED CREAM

This has 55-60% fat and, unlike the rest of the English dairy tradition, was ripened and heated in huge wide pans, either for cream or for what seems to have been a very fine – but now extinct – butter. It produces unpredictable results in cooking, but will keep frozen for up to a month. Its sweet unctuousness is at the heart of the traditional Devon cream tea. **Hobb's** clotted cream is sold in **Asda**, and **Tesco** have begun to sell an own-label.

SOUR CREAM

With 18% fat, this has a starter added and has been ripened. This adds outrageously to the price – which can be as much as 20p more per 150 ml (¼ pt), or on a par with crème fraîche. It is, however, still cheaper – and fattier – than Greek yoghurt.

CREME FRAICHE

Where British cream is traditionally as fresh as possible, the French allow a natural sour nuttiness to develop the character of their cream, as if making butter. Good crème fraîche is thick enough to hold its shape in the pot if turned upside down. The high fat content (30-47 %) make crème fraîche versatile in cooking, especially in sauces and casseroles. Like double cream, it is multi-purpose. As the fat levels descend, so the cooking applications become more restrictive. The best examples are sealed in foil-topped tubs and unopened will keep up to three weeks in the fridge, but will not freeze.

Some rather pointless low-fat crème

fraîches have insinuated their way into the market, but tend to be vanilla-ish sludges that lack the distinction of the original article and acquire severe graininess from the bulking agents. The list of ingredients used to stabilize them tell their own story. A full-fat Greek yoghurt is possibly a better alternative.

Sainsbury led the way in introducing crème fraîche to the British mainstream, other supermarkets have followed. We are unusually fortunate in getting nearly all our crème fraîche from Isigny in Normandy, which produces the best in the world and holds an *appellation contrôlée* for it. There is a premium of about 20p against double cream, but **Sainsbury** has held its advantage by undercutting its rivals.

****Isigny** from Sainte-Mère in Normandy has an *appellation contrôlée* as for its butter and its crème fraîche. Found in clean red-and-blue-lettered pots, sealed with foil, fat levels are higher than own-brands, around 40%. Solid and immovable, you can hold the pot upside down without fear of it dropping out. Creamy in colour, with a sublime silky texture, it has a long-lasting flavour edged with flowers and nuts, and the sourness works as a flavour rather than being all-pervasive. **Sainsbury** sell it for 69p per 200 ml (7 fl oz) as own-label, against £1.39 for the same quantity in delis. **Marks & Spencer**, **Safeway** and **Tesco** also stock it.

***Waitrose** own-label has reduced the fat content to 30% without destroying the quality. Thick and immovable, it is very good, with an immediate flavour of lovely sour lemons and edges of almonds.

****Neal's Yard** rightly calls its version 'slightly soured cream'. The fat content is a swaggering 47% (still 1% off double cream). With a beautiful thick texture devoid of wateriness, it again has hints nuts and lemons. The price, though, is nearly three times **Sainsbury's.**

Yoplait is made in France for Dairy Crest, with 30% fat and a culture added to speed up the ripening. It has a pronounced accent of sourness, lemons with nuts, and a texture that tends towards graininess rather than smoothness. **Yoplait Light**, as well as containing a starter culture, has added skimmed milk in order to reduce the fat by half, plus starch, gelatine and pectin to stabilize, and potassium sorbate to preserve. The effect is looser and creamier in texture, the sourness is muted, more of a diluted version of the real thing with some unattractive grainy after-tastes. **Yoplait Épaisse**, with 30% fat, is for cooking and is more solid than the ordinary crème fraîche, with a resulting concentration of its sours. **Yoplait Gastronomique**, with 40% fat, is designed for hot cooking and is very solid, very rich and has a defined accent of sour lemons, but is somewhat dull and one-dimensional.

YOGHURT

Yoghurt is the right-on product for the forward-looking dairy trade. The mark-ups are restrained and health benefits well tabulated. As a viable low-fat alternative to other dairy ingredients, yoghurt makes sense – even the new generation of frozen yoghurt ice-cream alternatives are outstandingly successful.

Before 1960, there seems to be hardly any evidence that yoghurt was ever made in this country. Yet it is one of the oldest foods, found widely around the Mediterranean rim, certainly used by the Egyptians and Israelites and taken east to India by Arab traders. Its first arrival in mainland Europe is thought to have been around 1600, but it was then mostly confined to monasteries and Bulgaria where it has been held, rightly or wrongly, as contributing to amazing local longevity. Unfortunately, common-sense suggests there is quite a distance between the Bulgarian monk and his sheep's-milk yoghurt on the one hand and a diet bio raspberry flavour with added sugar and 'fruit' on the other.

Yoghurt-making is distinct from cheese-making in that the curds and whey are not separated. It remains a milk product, but not a natural one. Milk needs the bacilli *Lactobacillus bulgaricus* and *Streptococcus thermophilus* to turn it into yoghurt. First scientifically identified at the start of the century in the Pasteur Institute, these bacilli feed off the milk and detrimental bacteria it contains which might otherwise cause decay and so help postpone the break down. The first commercial factory making yoghurt was opened in Barcelona in 1925 for **Danone**.

The explosion in the yoghurt market has perversely knocked ordinary yoghurt out of the ring. Most supermarkets stock Greek

Set yoghurt
Stirred yoghurt
Strained yoghurt
Bio or live yoghurt
Whole-milk yoghurt
Low-fat yoghurt
Flavoured yoghurt
Greek yoghurt
Sheep's-milk yoghurt

yoghurt at one end of the spectrum, low-fat at the other. Ordinary yoghurt is now out of the ordinary. Supermarkets classify yoghurt and fromage frais as part of the dessert aisle rather than the dairy, which has led to a head-long rush into novelty flavours and 'fun-packs'. Prices are, however, reassuringly consistent and **Safeway** has been undercutting most of the supermarkets by a few pence. Added flavours are only charged at one or two pence more, compared to the practice in fromage frais, where mark-ups are much greater.

SET YOGHURT

In this, the yoghurt is poured straight into the pots in which they are sold. For this reason they are, arguably, more natural.

STIRRED YOGHURT

The yoghurt is poured into a large tub, mixed and then poured into the individual pots, possibly with some additions like milk or whey powders to extend them. The general effect is to make it more cream-like.

STRAINED YOGHURT

In this, the liquid (ie water content) is drained off to concentrate the fats and give creaminess.

BIO OR LIVE YOGHURT

These are sold on the benefits of the bacteria, reputedly in cleaning out the gut. The lettering BA to be found on most of this type of yoghurt stands for *bifidus* and *acidophilus*. These bacilli can be beneficial to people whose natural resources of these bacteria may be run down or depleted and their addition also supposedly creates a less acid taste.

WHOLE-MILK YOGHURT

This is currently out of vogue. Farmers can

sell on the cream and therefore have been happy to follow the trend to skimmed-milk products. Occasionally it is possible to find organics like **Dairy Farm**, a thick set yoghurt at 69p for 340 g. **Sainsbury** do a bio, allegedly with active cultures, and an 'extra mild' with 5% fat. **Little Swallow Bio** is 3.5% fat, has a loose double-cream texture and a piercing good cool flavour. Compare that to **Onken**, often said to be the main market influence at 45p for 150 g, which has a clean, strong, attractive impact and a distinctively creamy aftertaste.

LOW-FAT YOGHURT

This type has become the standard. They are made from skimmed milk and the fat levels fluctuate from about 5% to only 1% as in VIRTUALLY FAT-FREE, or DIET. Ironically, many adjust the health balance by adding sugar. Prices are consistent at around 20p per 100 g and the saving from not using the cream is passed on in this case, unlike the prevailing practice with milk.

There is a middle ground with odd names: **Sainsbury** and **Müller** do **Thick and Creamy**, **Waitrose** call it **Custard-style Yoghurt**, **Safeway Rich and Creamy**. The fat level is 3% and the price nudged up another 3p as a result.

FLAVOURED YOGHURT

The cost of flavours is consistent, whether it be strawberry or blackberry. Straight flavoured yoghurts hover around 30p for 125 g to disguise the small mark-up from whole milk, with savings of about 1p for buying cartons or multiples thereof. **Müller's Fruit Corner** pioneered the idea of the yoghurt and fruit being separate in the same carton, selling for 37p per 175 g, at 5% fat. **Safeway** followed with **Double Treat**, and **Sainsbury** with **Duet**.

GREEK YOGHURT

This was first introduced by **Total** as recently as 1985. It is thick and creamy, with a relatively high fat content of around 10% (compared to 18% for single cream). It bears favourable comparison with other mainstream dairy products, both in terms of price, honesty of the marketplace, quality and interest.

GREEK-STYLE YOGHURT is made here in the same manner, although some examples have higher levels of sugar and are not as thick.

SHEEP'S-MILK YOGHURT

This would presumably have been the original yoghurt, but sheep's-milk yoghurts are now rare. Fat levels are lower, at around 5-6%. One example is **Live**, with 5.8% fat, available for 68p for 227 g in delis. **Robert Acidophilus**, a natural live goats'-milk from Anchor End Farm, Brandon Bank, Norfolk, is £1.39 for 500 g; it is soft and slidy in texture, with a tart lemon milk flavour. **Sussex High Weald Dairy** sheep's-milk yoghurt from Duddleswell is 99p for 225 g; it is distinctly more solid in texture and less alternative than other versions. Henrietta Green in her *Food Lovers' Guide to Britain* recommends the hard-to-find **Yan-tan-tethera**, made on Llugwy Farm, Powys, from a herd of Frieslands, whose milk in spring can give a fat content as high as 8%.

ICE-CREAM

Farmers originally sold ice-cream on market days in summer, often employing strings of boys on bicycles to peddle it around the towns. The Ministry of Food banned all ice-cream containing cream in 1940 and even after the war it could only be made with skimmed milk powder. Originally ice-cream was literally frozen cream, but custard-style recipes were also used. The health risks of old ice-cream were well known and it was a frequent source of food poisoning.

The duopoly of **Walls** and **Lyons** in the '60s persisted in keeping the cream out of ice-cream. By infiltrating corner shops with their own chillers, they strangled the market and invented a new generation of ice-cream in which the dairy qualities were devalued to save money. The health arguments for using non-dairy ice-creams are somewhat spurious – even the highest fat contents are lower than single cream. Although regarded here for many decades as a children's food, in Sweden, Russia and America ice-cream is aimed at adults. This trend really only began to be evident here in the mid '70s with the opening of the **Dayville** ice-cream parlours.

Two things have rejuvenated ice-cream: the arrival of the American giant **Häagen-Dazs** – blatantly exploiting the fact that the big dairy companies had abandoned cream – and the imposition of milk quotas which have forced farmers to find other outlets for their cream (not least because of the rising sales of skimmed milk). Proper ice-cream is based on a custard made from eggs, sugar and a cream-enriched milk and, generally, the higher the fat content the better the product. Air is added in the whipping and the trade term for this is 'overrun'. Something very

A PRE-WAR GROCER'S RECIPE FOR ICE-CREAM: 'Whisk 4 eggs, ¼ lb sugar and 1 oz fresh butter in a quart of new milk; place the mixture in a pan on the fire and stir well until it nearly boils. Then empty into the freezer, adding a little essence... As the mixture freezes, it should be worked down from the sides of the freezer with a wooden spoon or spatula, so as to make the mass of uniform consistency.'

foamy – like a **Mr Whippy** – has a high over-run: quality ice-cream has a low overrun. The other key factor is the quality of the flavouring agents used. Few companies are consistent across the range in this respect.

Ben & Jerry's ice-cream is a fable of the business pages: how two hippy-looking drop-outs went into ice-cream and finally raised enough equity from Vermont farmers to go world-wide. The ice-cream itself is smooth and sugary but lent some individuality by the quality of the vanilla, It is more of an iced milk product than an ice-cream. There are also lots of interesting flavours beyond the vanilla,

****Bowman's** farm near St Albans in Hertfordshire began making ice-cream in 1989, and it is available from the farm-shop, run by Bruce Luffman at junction 22 off the M25. The ice-cream has one of the highest fat contents, at 18%, and an overrun of 40%, with the resulting benefit of silky smoothness.

****Godiva**, the Belgian chocolate company has diversified into a range of superb ice-creams made with crème fraîche, whole milk, egg yolks and a great range of high-quality flavours: vanilla, praline, chocolate, passion fruit, apricot and raisin, fruits of the forest. The fat content is 20-22% and it is sold in original and sensible hexagonal polystyrene tubs, designed to keep the ice-cream frozen for up to four hours.

****Häagen-Dazs**, created by Reuben Mattus in 1961, redefined the American market-place. The fat content is 16% and the overrun about 30%. It is inclined to egginess and sweetness, but has brilliantly selected flavours. The boxed choc-ice on a stick is covered in Belgian chocolate and was the forerunner to **Walls'** best-selling but (marginally) inferior **Magnum**.

***Hingston's** ice-cream is most notable for its inventive range of high-quality flavours. Made by Andrew Hingston, an ex-Wall-Street

---

Ice-cream Alternatives

Some of the ice-cream alternatives introduced in the last two years have been surprisingly successful. Two stand out and, interestingly, both use very different techniques. Neither seem to taste of what they are. ****Häagen-Dazs's** range of fruit frozen yoghurts are widely found, even in **Gateway.**

Swedish Glace are completely non-dairy, using organic soya milk which transforms miraculously into a superb imitation of ice-cream. Three flavours are available: vanilla, strawberry and chocolate.

lawyer who settled in Dunmow, Essex, the fat content is sometimes as high as 17.5% and the overrun under 30%.

Norfolk County ice-cream is made near Norwich. It is very sweet, with the vanilla only used to underpin the honeyed creaminess rather than to dominate. It could, however, allow more cream to come through.

Rocombe Farm ice-cream, from Newton Abbot in Devon, is made not just with Jersey milk but using organic eggs and milk powder. The result is very richly creamy, almost inviting comparison with malt drinks, while the texture is classic English brick.

Steve's is the other big new American player of last summer. Using raw cane sugar, it is not as smooth as **Ben & Jerry's**. In effect, the flavour is very close to that of the cream on top of coffee.

Other good names that have shown well in comparisons of vanilla ice-creams have been **Loseley**, **New England**, **Criterion** and **Marks & Spencer.**

BUTTER

In the 19th century, good butter was deemed to be yellow – supposedly because the cows had grazed on grass, though usually it was coloured – in this country with carrot juice or anatto dissolved in hemp or sesame oil; in Holland, America and Australia with coal-tar yellow. It was also highly salted, often as much as 7%.

Butter from fresh milk has little flavour and a poorer yield, so the milk was always ripened to allow the bacteria in the dairy to influence the flavour. In Scotland the milk was sometimes left for as long as a week. All this was a bit haphazard: in the dairy there were good and bad bacteria; sometimes the butter was fine, sometimes it wasn't. Part of every grocer's duty was to check his consignment after two weeks to see if it had gone rancid – if it had, it was sent to the bakers.

In 1891, the bacteriologist C. O. Jensen discovered a maverick bacteria in the dairy and cow sheds at the Dueland Estate Dairy in Denmark. He could kill it if the milk was heated to 70˚C (160˚F). Following the principles of cheese-making, he added a small quantity of good butter or yesterday's ripened milk from another – clean – dairy and produced excellent butter. If Jensen did not invent pasteurization, he had found its commercial application and his idea was to change dairy-farming forever.

The new pasteurized butters won every show medal. Within six years of his report, 97% of Danish dairies had gone over to pasteurizing all milk for butter. In 1906 it became Danish law to pasteurize all milk, and all butter had to be marked with the national **Lurbrand** and dated.

Jensen's discovery coincided with R. S.

Woodwell's invention of a centrifugal cream separator in Orange County, New York (it was first shown here at the Royal Agricultural Society Show in Kilburn in 1879). The separator increased the yield by 10-20%. This was the end for the dairy-maid. The centrifuge was more efficient in extracting the water from the butter – where lingered many of the impurities which would otherwise cause the butter to go off – and this made it possible for the creamery to take milk from surrounding farms and mass-produce butter. Co-operative farming became possible. The first European creamery was set up in Denmark in 1882, three years later there were 84, and in the next five years another 595. The Danes and the French sent huge exports to Britain.

British farmers were reluctant to form co-operatives. They sold their butter piecemeal to blenders who would batch the lot and package it for market. It was only with the creation of the **Milk Marketing Board** in 1933 (see page 116), that we moved over to the Danish system of collecting the milk directly from the farm and delivering it to larger creameries. In Normandy, by contrast, farmers sold their butters to factors who graded the best to be sent Paris and London and only blended the lesser butters. The difference in the trade has meant that many more individual butters have survived in France than here.

Devon and Somerset produced what was recognized as some of the best butter in the world. Even at the start of the century, however, they were being blended with other butters outside of the counties to meet the demand. The fresh milk was poured into wide shallow pans and left for 24 hours to let the cream rise to the top. It was then heated until the first bubble appeared, the heat then turned off and left to stand for a further 12 hours. The cream formed a dense, clotted

FOOD *watch*

Blending butter was known to produce a lesser product. W A. Robinson writing in 1928 declared: 'If butter is worked after the first manufacture, such working or blending tends to weaken the texture and destroy that smooth silkiness of touch that is so pleasing.'

FOOD *watch*

The nutritional labelling
on the butter packets
suggests 100 g (3½
oz) per day supplies an
adult's vitamin A
requirements and one-
third of the necessary
vitamin D. However,
anyone eating that
amount of butter in a
day would have a
serious dietary debility
in the first place.
Manufacturers only
have to comply with
nutritional labelling if
they are making health
claims.

layer on the surface which was collected in a crock, either for use as cream on the farm or stirred by hand into butter. A Devon dairy-maid was always said to need cool hands to do this well. One explanation for this practice has it that the Phoenicians may have traded tin with the Cornish and introduced this way of making cream and butter which was otherwise unique in Europe.

Butter must be at least 80% fat. Farmhouse butters often reach levels of 85-87%. The colour comes from the grazing pastures and the level of fat in the milk: the higher the fat, the more yellow the colour. Butter from Friesian herbs will be paler than Guernsey or Jersey, because of the lower fat content.

Butter has become so standardized that the main differences are in the packaging not the product. A few are still highly salted. British, Irish and Commonwealth butters are made without a starter culture.

FRESHLY CHURNED BUTTER
This means that the milk has come directly to the creamery after milking. Butters without this label tend to be blends of different milks which may have been stored and possibly frozen.

˚ CHANNEL ISLANDS BUTTER
This benefits from the Jersey and Guernsey herds, with their higher fat yields and the lush pastures on which they graze. It is usually sold as a log, a habit previously used in Normandy after the co-operatives were set up to mark out butters of distinction. Of all the mass-market butters this stands out. Marigold-yellow in colour, it has the taste of buttercups.

COUNTY BUTTERS
These have reputations which are more mar-ginal. Cornish retains some individuality:

FOOD *watch*

Supermarket blends
tend to be the
cheapest butters at
around 63p per 250 g
(8 oz), followed by
generic English at 69p
and Danish at another
4p more, then
Normandy at a
minimum of 20p more.

mostly sold in round pats and usually freshly churned, it is a beige-yellow in colour, with 1-2% salt and a mild good clean flavour. **Kerrygold** matches it for colour, if not flavour. As you travel east, even as soon as Somerset, the bland hand of uniformity takes over: the butter from this county is the colour of Brie, and is discernibly inferior to that from Cornwall. More spurious geographical claims, such as the vapid **Scottish** butter sold by **Somerfield** is more of an exercise in marketing imagination than flavour or quality.

WELSH BUTTER

This is a throwback to feeding the miners, and is famously high in salt; starkly out of step with the rest of Europe, it has salt levels as high as 7%, which outstrips even some specialist salt products. *Rachel's Diary, Brynllys, Dyfed is a solitary UK entry in the specialist butter market. Its organic farmhouse salted butter is made in the lactic style (see overleaf) but is churned in a wooden churn, using milk from a Guernsey herd. Deep saffron-yellow in colour, the salt disguises the texture and the flavour is mild and mainstream.

WHEY BUTTER

These are a by-product of cheese-making. The whey will be taken off after the starter culture for the cheese has been added and there is, therefore, a distinct cheesy edge to the flavour. Little is actually made, but examples can sometimes be found in specialist cheese shops. The best examples are from:
**Quicke's, who are better known for their Cheddar cheese;
**Appleby's of Hawkstone, Shropshire, who are better known for their Cheshire cheese;
**Duckett's, of Wedmore, Somerset, known for their Caerphilly cheese.

FOOD *watch*

Spreadable Butters

These were first introduced by **Anchor** in late '91 and sales have been spectacular. Others have followed, noticeably Danish giant **Lurpak** and **Tesco. St Ivel** tested the market but withdrew. Different techniques are used: **Anchor** extracts the hard fats from the butter, using a technology borrowed from other parts of the fat industry. The butter is treated in New Zealand and then shipped. An alternative approach, employed by **Tesco** and others, is to use early summer milk, when the concentration of hard fats in the butter is at its lowest. The butter is then frozen and worked to improve its spreadability. The difference in flavour compared to other mass-market butters is marginal, but the spreadability is significantly improved by both processes.

Also good is that from **Mrs Montgomery** of Manor Farm near Yeovil, Somerset, who also makes Cheddar.

LACTIC BUTTER

The big Danish creameries introduced pure lactic cultures to start their milk ripening more swiftly. In a few years the butters – which previously had been subject to the diet of the cow, the light and bacteria in the individual dairy, and the diligence of the milk-maid – had become a blank canvas on which the creameries could paint any flavour they desired. The flavour is more uniform and predictable. The best of these butters taste of reduced cream, which is what they really are. French sauce cooking is based on lactic butters, so they should be used for French recipes, especially for sauces. The European custom is not to add salt. Only **Sainsbury**, perversely, charge more for salted than unsalted. Most Danish generic butters hold to a single uniformity of flavour which is only marginally diverted from in brands like **Lurpak**. Slightly more lush still is **Wheelbarrow** and, even more so, **Cornflower** organic.

FRENCH BUTTER

Round the coast from Holland to Normandy, the sense of the pastures in the flavour becomes more pronounced and the best individual butters tend to come from France.

Beurre au Sel de Mer de Noirmoutier is more of a promotion for the island of Noirmoutier and its salt industry. It is not a brilliant butter and the saltiness is less marked than ordinary Welsh.

**Échiré from Deux Sèvres is sold in distinctive blue-lined wrappers or small wooden tubs. Widely used in top-class restaurants in the UK and often put up as a candidate for *appellation contrôlée*, its flavour is resonant with elements of sea breezes.

****Isigny** in Normandy has been recognised as the premier butter-making district of France since early this century. The butter from here was the first to hold *appellation contrôlée* status. It is rarely found over here, where **Échiré** has made a determined bid for the quality market, although **Harrods** and selected branches of **Sainsbury** do stock it. There is an unpasteurized version in a gold wrapper which does not carry *AOC* status, but still bears a hefty premium. It is lushly creamy, like unctuous clotted cream. The **Extra Fin** is pasteurized, cheaper at £1.80 per 250 g (8 oz), and lighter and more delicate. It has a lovely lactic edge to the flavour, with hints of flowers and ending in echoes of Camembert. Novelty butters from the area, impregnated with caviar and sea salt, are beginning to be sold.

Lescure is a *grand cru* butter from Charentes. The legend of the butters of the last century survives here. Charentes claimed its butters were superior to those of Normandy because Norman butter was a by-product of cheese-making. Sold in a long gold log with a white label bearing blue lettering, this good solid, above-average butter has a deep creamy taste and the best is said to taste of hazelnuts.

***President,** in its gold and white wrapper, is only sold by **Waitrose** at a premium price. Of those widely available, it is an outstanding example of a French supermarket butter, with a deep, intense lactic creaminess.

***Surgères**, from Charentes, has been made since 1889, albeit not quite in the same way. Its flavour is intense and long-lasting with hints of nuts. A good surviving example of the style of Charentes butter, it is hard to find here but it is widely available in France.

Other French butters worth looking for

include: **Pampile** from Deux Sèvres, with a cheesy edge and muted butteriness; clear-tasting **Paysan Breton** from Brittany; and **Paquette Normande** from Normandy, with a deep sweet-cream lactic mix of richness.

ITALIAN BUTTERS

These rarely surface here. The cows tend to be kept indoors and fed on hay, and produce an almost lard-white butter. One example is **Buro Montanaro**, which is white, sweet, milky and very different.

BUTTER ALTERNATIVES

The quest for purity in butter opened the door to other fats and spreads. Many of these are simply fats diluted with water, so less goes further. The invention in 1911 of the process of hydrogenation – which turns liquid fats like vegetable or fish oils into hard, workable substances for industry – meant that butter could be widely and cheaply imitated. Hydrogenation also meant that other oils could replace butter in biscuits and cakes and this led to the industrialization of the bakery. The disadvantage from a health point of view is that hydrogenation turns unsaturated fats into saturated ones.

Alternatively, by buying more interesting bread you could dispense with spreads altogether. The real fatless dairy product is, in fact, not a butter or a spread but low-fat fromage frais.

FROMAGE FRAIS

This was originally fresh, low-fat unripened cheese potted and eaten within a week. The fat content is graded into three categories: ordinary at 6.8%, low-fat at 3% and diet at 0.1% or even less. Low-fat varieties lack the flavour of full-fat versions. The taste goes granular and unattractive, so it is usually disguised with flavours. Larger, 500 g (1 lb 2 oz) pots are cheaper all round. Premium prices – as much as 20p – tend to attach themselves to brands and to organic.

Factory versions take off some of the water, which produces a glossy 'pot of emulsion' effect. The sense of creative adventure in the trade has created a spectrum of innovative fromage frais, very few of which anyone might guess to be cheese at all: **Munch Bunch**, **Pot Shots** and **Hippopots** for children; **Shape** and **Delight** for slimmers; **Quark** in Germany is eaten with fruit for breakfast; **Chambourcy** in France; **Valfrais** for dips. The dairy industry has discovered a product that has no fat, no taste and can do with it what it likes.

Craft versions tend to be creamy, firm but gloopy, coarse and structured unlike yoghurt. **Neal's Yard** unpasteurized fromage frais is a fine example of its historical origins. **Sainsbury** import fromage frais from France which is very distinctive; denser and stickier, it has a yoghurt-like flavour and a resounding sweet mild vanilla finish, very imitative of cream. Also, there is **Sainsbury's La Faisselle**, billed as a French country-style natural fromage frais. The differences are marked: La Faisselle being intrinsically white, more cheesily granulated than the smoothness of the own-label, and discernibly with an ancestry in cheese-making. The low-fat ver-

MULTIPACK CONFUSION

As the fat content drops, the games begin. Flavours are introduced and the pop-art packaging comes on line. Sizes of pot vary from 60 g to 400 g. Multiply the confusion by multipack offers, x 6, x 12, x 18 etc, and by any reasonable standards, the pricing structure is mesmerizingly incomprehensible. This is food sold as a TV game show. Ordinary fromage frais is 25p for 100 g. Compare that to the prices per 100 g from the same week from different packaging shown in the table below. Safeway seem intent on hiding their best buy by putting it in 41 g pots. **Onken at 25p for 100 g, sold in 500 g cartons, not only tastes the best but is nearly the cheapest.

Sainsbury:	30p
Petit Fromage Frais (in packs of 6 x 360 g)	18p
Petit Fromage Frais (in packs of 18 x 60 g)	21p
St Ivel	31p
Ski	31p
Yoplait (in packs of 6 x 60 g)	38p
Country Love (in 150 g pots)	16p
Petit Danone (in packs of 12 x 60 g)	26p
Safeway	23p
*Safeway (in packs of 6 x 41 g)	15p
Tesco	30p

sion, however, is a eunuch by comparison to either. Some good sheep's-milk versions, notably **Sussex High Weald Farm**, are sold through health shops.

CHEESE

Supermarkets have begun to move cheese out of the dairy section and into the novelty and dessert aisles. We are perhaps witnessing the end of an era and the new dawn is one that promises 'pick'n'mix' cheeses or Cheddar flavoured with Christmas pudding.

Possibly the traditional craft of cheese-making is just too onerous for the modern world. There are signs, however, of a revival in proper cheese-making and of interest in it. This must be seen against the backdrop of decline of indigenous quality cheese, replaced by fatty bland protein for the masses. In no other industry is the hand of government so obvious in its machinations and in no other industry, it might be argued, has the consumers' preference been so thoroughly ignored.

Three out of four cheeses sold in supermarkets are called Cheddar. The rest just make up the weight – providing a mere veneer of choice, suggesting more than there is and more likely a device to divert farmers' subsidies to supermarket bottom lines. The great abundance is a mirage. Great names like Cheddar ad Camembert are prostituted.

It is academic to compare factory-made cheeses. More pride seems to be taken in getting them to taste inoffensively uniform than to create anything individual or of distinction. **Lymeswold** should have proved the epitaph for that way of thinking, but it probably has not. The closure of the **Milk Marketing Board** may open the door for new thinking, but the past 50 years suggests the industry is too introverted to change.

Meanwhile, buying good cheese means looking out carefully for good individual names and supporting those shops that keep cheeses properly – before both vanish completely.

CHEESEBOARDS

Cheesophiles argue that a proper cheeseboard should contain examples of all seven different styles of cheese: fresh (Ricotta, Feta); natural rinds (goats'); bloomy rinds (Camembert); wash rinds (Milleens, Langres); semi-soft (Gubbeen, Reblochon); hard (Cheddar) and blue (Stilton). At the Paris restaurant of the great cheese factor Androuët, a whole meal is constructed around the seven styles, with two or three trays of different cheese for each type offered in ascending order, from fresh right through to blue – with Roquefort, symbolically, offered on its own at the end. The plasticization of cheese has encouraged people to serve a great number of different cheeses. A proper farmhouse cheese deserves to be taken more seriously and given a course of its own, with fresh bread and perhaps a salad. The British habit of taking cheese to finish a meal may have contributed to this latent gluttony as the port is passed. The French custom of having the sweet after cheese provides a better grammar for the end of the meal.

TRADITIONAL ENGLISH

Caerphilly
Cheddar
Cheshire
Derby
Gloucester
Lancashire
Red Leicester
Wensleydale
Stilton

The nine English territorial farmhouse cheeses represent some of the last links with the foods that people have eaten on this island for hundreds of years. Records of Cheshire cheese go back to the Domesday Book, Cheddar was revered by the Elizabethans and others can trace their roots back to at least the 1700s. Abused, imitated and adulterated, these nine cheeses can at least claim to be our heritage. They are some of the finest hard cheeses found anywhere in the world, though what is normally found in plastic wrappers in supermarkets bears little relation to the original article. Even if the flavour is not dissimilar, in terms of texture and subtlety they are invarairably miserable failures.

Many factors undermined farmhouse cheese-making. In 1940, the Ministry of Food unilaterally declared fresh milk was to have priority over cheese-making and this war-time edict was never properly repealed. The post-war Labour government preferred or understood industrialized production better and was in no mood to favour the traditionally Conservative farmers. The pasteurization of all milk robbed the cheese-maker of the individuality that raw milk offered. The supermarkets were happy to preside over the plasticization of cheese in neat vacuum packs and, more recently, to encourage the growth of novelty lines. The now defunct **Milk Marketing Board** unashamedly tried to pass off factory cheeses as if they were farmhouse; trying to give these some claim to regionality or tradition when they transparently did not was to the detriment of anything that did.

The current revival in British cheese-making has come about despite these successive acts of genocide.

CAERPHILLY

This was the miner's cheese, only made west of the Usk. Now the best is made in Somerset and some new farms in Dyfed. Good Caerphilly is magnolia-white.

Caerphilly is a simple cheese. Morning milk is mixed with some from the night before and then warmed, and the whey from the day before's cheese used as a starter. Before salting, the curd should be soft enough to retain the imprint of a hand. It is moulded for 30 minutes, salted again, pressed and then washed in brine. Factories have tended to go for higher acidities, which is safer and quicker, usually by increasing the level of starter.

It can be eaten after a week, but becomes smoother and sharper with age. It is best taken out of its vacuum pack, wiped dry and left to breathe and recover. It is a cheese that loses most of its character in mass-production. Unpasteurized versions are much closer to the character of the original.

****Duckett's Caerphilly** made by Chris Duckett at Walnut Tree Farm, Wedmore, Somerset, has a whole cellar given over to it exclusively at **Neal's Yard Dairy** in Covent Garden. Aged properly, Caerphilly alters its complexion quickly. The fresh cheese is bready, pliable, fresh and pleasant; by four weeks it will have acquired that distinctive effervescence and hints of primrose; by six weeks the acidity mellows dramatically; after 8-12 weeks, the crust will go peachy grey and then it behaves more like a Brie, losing its magnolia whiteness, going a deep cream with orange hues and developing an intense creaminess, like a French cheese. Other typical tasting notes on a fresh Caerphilly are: 'friable lemons, crushed with bracken, hints of stone walls'. Duckett's also make a **Wedmore**, with band of chives through the centre, and an intense **Torville**, matured for

RENNET, taken from the (fourth) stomach of a suckling calf, contains an enzyme, *chymosin.*

It is used to clot milk: the mildest is junket rennet, and cheese rennet may be five times more concentrated.

VEGETARIAN RENNET was originally anything of vegetable origin that would acidulate – from nettle extract to lemon juice – and more recently it was taken from a mushroom mould, but these all produced a softer curd. Now there is a genetic imprint developed for a vegetarian version of genuine rennet.

six weeks and washed in cider.

Other good examples from Dyfed include the smooth wax unpasteurized rounds from **Caws Cenarth** of Pontseli (there is also a smoked version); **Glynhynod Caerphilly**, unpasteurized and organic from John and Patrice Savage-Onstwedder; and **Welsh Farmhouse Caerphilly**, made by Peter Sayer with pasteurized milk, to be eaten young. He also smokes a variation and the **St Ishmael** is with laver bread.

CHEDDAR

Cheddar was almost certainly first made with sheep's milk. By early Tudor times, however, co-operatives were making gigantic 90-120 lb Cheddars from cows' milk. These were probably taller than they were wider. The use of common land meant that each family put its cows' milk into the co-operative and was paid back in cheese. Although most of Somerset made Cheddar cheese (as did East Devon, Dorset and, later, Wiltshire), the parish of Cheddar and nearby Mere produced outstanding cheeses. The cattle used were probably Dairy Shorthorn.

In Elizabethan times, Cheddar was rare and fetched high prices; it was regarded both here and in Europe as one of the finest cheeses in the world. In 1724 Daniel Defoe visited Cheddar: '(on the large common) in which the whole herd of the cows, belonging to the town, do feed; the ground is exceedingly rich, and as the whole village are cow keepers, they take care to keep up the goodness of the soil, by agreeing to lay on large quantities of dung for manuring and enriching the land.' Ironically it was to be 150 years before such ideas on improving the pastures took hold for the dairy industry at large. Defoe said these Cheddars were 'the best cheese that England affords, if not, that the whole world affords'.

In the middle of the 19th century, the expansion of farmhouse cheese-making was further limited by a cattle plague combined with the growing demand from the new cities for fresh milk and, by 1870, further by imports from new cheese factories in Denmark, Holland, France and America. In 1939, the last year before the Ministry of Food centralized production, 513 farms in the South-west were registered as makers of cheese, of which 333 were making Cheddar. By 1948 there were only 57. By 1974 there were 33. By 1988, only 11 farms were making Cheddar in the traditional way and only four were still using unpasteurized milk. In Cheddar itself no Cheddar is made any more, although there is a touristy farm-shop museum nearby. Residents even raised a petition against the setting up of a creamery in the '80s.

Cheddar takes its name from 'cheddaring', the traditional hand turning and stacking of the curds to release the whey. In the traditional recipe, the rennet is added to the milk and starter at 29˚C (84˚F). The curds are cut, placed in a vat, the whey expressed out and the curds heated to 32-38˚C (90-100˚F) for 40 minutes. (The two scaldings of the milk are distinctive: overcooked, it goes rubbery.) The whey is drawn off again; the curds cut and stacked in 8-12 inch blocks, and turned by hand to work out more whey (cheddaring). This smooths the rubbery, spongy curds. These are broken again, salted, milled for uniformity, moulded and pressed. It is then kept at 13˚C (55˚F) – the ideal storage temperature for the cheese.

Cheddar today is made across the world in massive machines with names like Cheddarmaster or the Bell-Siro system that takes the milk at one end and produces 18 kg

STORING CHEESE

'Sell-by' or 'consume-by' dates on cheeses need to be read with caution as many cheeses will not have reached full maturity by the date given. Chilling regulations mean most cheeses are sold in more stabilized conditions, but these will not help them ripen. Store cheeses in the salad compartment of the fridge, ideally in a plastic container, and take them out two hours before serving. Soft farmhouse cheeses can be ripened swiftly by keeping them at room temperatures for a few days.

(40 lb) blocks at the other. Sealed in plastic rather than the traditional cloth (in which it could breathe), these will be matured for 5-12 months depending on the strength of flavour required. The technology was the result of the collusion between big dairies and supermarkets in the '50s that led to mass uniformity. Another factor was that to make bulk cheese, the starter culture had to be used in ever greater concentrations. Professor Barry Law at the Institute of Food Research at Reading has pointed out that the modern cultures are very efficient but have produced bland cheeses.

Nevertheless, Cheddar is the biggest-selling supermarket cheese. Its success lies in its robustness: better than other cheeses it can withstand the industrial mauling.

Safeway and **Tesco** have introduced different grading levels to encourage Cheddar buyers to experiment with other cheeses of similar strengths. Canadian cheddar is **Safeway's** strongest at 5, where a mature **Davidstow** from Somerset is a middling 3.

Where the precise taste is reminiscent of proper Cheddar, the lack of texture and variety in these vacuum-packed slabs places them nearer to the confectionery counter. The zeal for something novel has seen two separate generations of sub-Cheddars sold in the past few years. First there were the plastic, Technicolor derivatives invoking quasi-historical names – ALBANY with cumin; APPLEWOOD, smoked and rolled in paprika; CHARNWOOD smoked; CHEVIOT with chives; ILCHESTER with beer; NUTWOOD with raisins and nuts; RUTLAND with garlic, beer and parsley; and, most vivid of all, WINDSOR RED following the old practice of adding elderberry wine. The flavours have no significant interaction with the cheese and are purely cosmetic.

Last Christmas, a second generation arrived which bends the mind further: Cheddar with smoked garlic; Cheddar with Marmite; Cheddar with Christmas pudding in neat little triangles. A bizarre marriage with pineapple pushes the price up to £2.55 per lb. As outrageous as these may be, they are not horrible – they are intriguing. What they have very little to do with at all is Cheddar.

The word 'farmhouse' has also been devalued. Proper Cheddars made on a farm with milk from specific herds and grazed on specific fields change by the season and the maker: sweet or sharp, moist or hard. Put these cheeses into factory production with uniform milk and machinery and it is a different product. Factory cheeses still win prizes at cheese shows, but often these are judged by factory graders, or they are often special cheeses made solely for the occasion. They will be sold to specialist cheese shops or to supermarkets as premium brands. They are the exceptions which are supposed to delude the market place into believing such artisan practices are still the rule. Traditional Cheddar was round. Factory cheese was oblong, to suit the cutting mechanism for the supermarkets, but even this dividing line is being eroded. To protect themselves from this corruption, many of the new generation of cheese-makers using Cheddar techniques are calling their cheeses by other names, for example Llanboidy or Gospel Green (see New British cheeses, page 157).

The following seven examples – all but the last made in Somerset – are possibly the only surviving, genuinely traditional Cheddar cheeses. Some of the unpasteurized versions lean towards what are deemed today as faults – most commonly an eggy sulphurousness – but nonetheless underline their supreme individuality and potency. A specialist cheese shop or factor will mature the cheeses for more than a year to bring them to maturity. It is this art, as much as anything else, that the culture of the supermarket has destroyed – to the detriment of us all.

*Chewton Cheddar is made by Nigel Pooley at Chewton Dairy Farms, Chewton Mendip, in 4, 6 and 56 lb rounds, using vegetarian rennet.

*Cricket Cheddar is made by Derek Butler of Cricket Malherbie Farms, in 36 lb rounds using only local milk and vegetarian rennet.

**Green's is made by H.G. Green at Newton Farm, third-generation Cheddar-makers. Richly buttery, it has extraordinary depth of flavour and composed intensity.

Unpasteurized **Keen's Cheddar is made by George and Stephen Keen of Moorhayes Farm, in smaller 3-7 lb or 60 lb cloth-bound rounds. Sometimes stocked by Waitrose, it is dry, intense, full-bodied, nutty and sweet, with hints of liquorice and green grass.

Unpasteurized **Montgomery's Cheddar is made by J. A. & E. Montgomery at Manor Farm, North Cadbury, using milk from their own Friesian/Holstein cows. Known as a wet 'gummy, clammy, chewy' cheese, it is superbly rich, explosive, complex, with an almost curried acidity.

Unpasteurized **Quicke's is made by Mary Quicke and partners in Devon from milk of a single herd. Intense and tangy, with hints of almonds to hazelnuts, it has a searing acidity. They also do a pasteurized version.

CHESHIRE

Fans of Cheshire claim it to be one of the oldest identifiable cheeses, thanks to its mention in the Domesday Book. Properly, it should come from within a 20-mile radius of Whitchurch; and for centuries it was the major industry of the area. The cheese's saltiness

---

Milk for cheese

Gloucester were probably the only cattle raised exclusively for making cheese. Ayrshire, still an active dairy breed, was known until the 17th century as the Dunlop and esteemed for its good cheese-making qualities, which contributed to the now extinct Dunlop cheese. One of the new revivalist Cheddar-style cheeses, Llanboidy, is made exclusively from the milk of Red Poll, an East-Anglian cow.

came from the ground: Cheshire is, and was, also the centre of the salt industry. Ironically the Nantwich Cheese Show, now a Mecca each July for makers and admirers of myriad cheese concoctions, was originally just for the local Cheshire cheese.

The recipe is a variation on Cheddar (or the other way round), but the temperature at which the curds are set is lower and the cheese is not pressed. This makes it a more difficult cheese to keep (it needs turning daily) and it was usually sold young – creameries are inclined to make raw wet cheeses to get extra weight.

Two types of Cheshire are made: the original white, and an orange version dyed with annatto. It is sold young, from about 2-3 weeks. The crumbliness has worked against it in the supermarket, where a denser product survives better in vacuum packs.

The traditional ways of making Cheshire have been maintained by two women: Christine Appleby, and Mrs Bourne of Bank Farm, Malpass who sadly died last spring. Today there are only perhaps 10 farms making traditional Cheshire, where 20 years ago there were 50 or 60 and in 1939 there were 400. Cheshire cheese is an endangered species.

Appleby from Hawkstone Abbey Farm, Weston, Shropshire, is handmade, unpasteurized, bound in calico, and uses annatto for a deep salmon colour. The milk is from their own herd of Friesian and Holsteins, and they use a minimum amount of starter which slows the process. The cheese is kept on the farm for 6-10 weeks, but some factors will mature it much longer – for up to a year.

Bourne from Bank Farm, Malpass, first won the Cheshire Show prize in 1933 and repeated the victory in 1993. It is not as well distributed as Appleby's, but just as good.

JUDGING CHESHIRE

Tom Hassal, who runs the cheese section of the Cheshire Show gives these instructions to judges on looking for a winning cheese. 'Use all the senses: first, sight: the colour should be clean throughout, a buttery waxy, cream to yellow. It should fill the iron without breaking at the edges. The back of the iron should be clean. Second, touch: break a piece off in your fingers and it will become friable – but should not be so sticky that it would stick to the ceiling. Third, listen: hold the iron to the ear and squeeze the sample and you can hear how moist it is. Fourth, taste: it should be silky, rich, warm, with a little bitterness/ sourness, chewy and grassy'. Professional cheese tasters will often use Cheshire to cleanse the palate after tasting other cheeses.

What exactly will happen now that Mrs Bourne has gone is an open question.

Other good names are **Windsor** of Whitchurch; **Hares** of Whitchurch; and **Overton Hall** from Mr and Mrs Barnett at Overton Hall, Cheshire.

DERBY

One of the great cheeses that distinguished itself, like Cheshire, early on from the wealth of Midlands cheese-making. The original cheese was 35-40 cm (14-16 inches) across and 10-15 cm (4-6 inches) high, weighing nearly 13.5 kg (30 lb), the best wrapped in calico, though some were kept in paste and flour. This cheese died out around 1925, partly due to the excessive secrecy among makers. The traditional recipe was similar to Cheddar and Cheshire, very akin to the Scottish Dunlop, and made in Gouda-like rounds with the salt added to the outside after moulding. A variation lived on because Derby was also the pioneer of large-scale factory dairies set up in the town and at Longford. Following a grant in 1862, the first cheese factory was set up in Siddals Road, Derby, using the steam from next door's silk mill. By 1876 there were 10 factories devoted to cheese, serving five counties. Even this softer version, however, has declined into oblivion.

More familiar to look at – if not similar in taste – is SAGE DERBY, which is about half the size but vividly green. Traditionally these were the spring cheeses, mixing the curd with the strained juice of sage leaves (quite brown) and young spinach or potato tops (for greening). The moulds were filled with alternating layers of the green cheese and the white to produce a spectacular combination which was brought out for the harvest workers at the end of summer. The vivid emerald waxed rounds sold as traditional in supermarkets are just poor processed sweaty cheeses, with odd bits of stalk and leaf inside, which brings out the worst of the sage in its 'dirty-football-socks' mode.

GLOUCESTER

A mild cheese that lends itself to abuse, Gloucester is relatively easy to make – and easy to make poorly and often sold too young. Sometimes called 'the orphan' because it was made with the milk from Gloucester cows which are now a rare breed. Proper production came to a halt in 1983 with the closing of Watercombe Creamery in Somerset. It is usually made with the skimmed evening milk added to the morning, as with Cheddar, but washed in beer after a month to give it colour (though now it is achieved by adding annatto).

A good Gloucester should be more solid than Cheshire, less flaky and more waxy than Cheddar. SINGLE GLOUCESTER was made with the skimmed milk from the farms, with the cream going for butter and for the farmer's table. DOUBLE GLOUCESTER, made with whole milk, was the premium cheese for selling at market and its reputation grew as the barges took it north to Birmingham and south to London. Some is still made out of a sense of tradition by other cheese-makers. Charles Martell still has a herd of Gloucester cows.

Like Cheddar, Gloucester has spawned a number of gimmicky children of dubious parentage: ABBEYDALE with onions and chives; COTSWOLD with chives; the popular HUNTSMAN, layered with Stilton; and SHERWOOD with sweet pickle.

** **Appleby's** of Hawkstone Abbey Farm, Shropshire, are as well-known for their Cheshire, but also make this lightweight cheese (compared to Cheddar). They do a beautifully orange version of double.

* **Martell's** by Charles Martell, of Laurel

Farm, Dymock, is made from the milk of one of the only surviving Gloucester herds (his first love). He no longer makes the Double Gloucester, only the single – 'a good cooker', sometimes bound with nettles.

Quicke's by Mary Quicke of Devon, who is famous for her Cheddar, but also makes 'enigmatic toffee-like versions of both single and double Gloucester', underlining the link between the two processes.

Smart's by Diana Smart of Old Ley Farm, Gloucestershire, is made using milk from their own herd. The double is matured for seven months, 'like double fudge with citrus zest'; the single is paler, made with the full-cream milk of the previous day added to the day's skimmed milk, to give a flavour of double cream and scorched caramel.

LANCASHIRE

This was a kitchen cheese, first differentiated from Cheshire around 1700. The best was said to come from the south of the county and two kinds were made – acid and fatty. The acid, like a Cheshire, uses one-day-old curd and was made for a fast sale. The fatty uses the curd from two days' milkings and matures into a softer, stickier, creamier cheese. This was the prime cheese for cooking as it falls away under the heat and does not go stringy like Cheddar. Today the farmhouse label should apply to fatty cheese.

In the old recipe the milk was left overnight to let the acidity rise, then heated and the rennet added. The curd forms in an hour, is cut and the whey drained off after another 30 minutes. It is then cut again (cheddared) to remove more whey. This fresh curd is then mixed with the day before's curd (with its higher acidity), ground, salted, moulded and pressed to extract the last drops of whey. It is bandaged after 24 hours and pressed again for 6 hours. It is eaten from 1-6 months old. Until the '60s, the rind of most Lancashire was buttered, but now they are waxed. As a result they have become wetter. **Neal's Yard Dairy** is the only factor currently buttering its Lancashires.

Unlike Cheshire, a good Lancashire should be moist enough to stick to your fingers. Good Lancashire should be dry, crumbly, soft, fatty and mellow: tasting notes include 'lemons, acid body, buttery, tons of grapefruit'. Most is now factory-produced.

It is argued that the more acid cheeses were encouraged as an expedient by the Ministry of Food in the war and this led to the decline of sales in the '70s. There has also been a trend to build up the levels of starter to make them faster-ripening. Few supermarkets sell more than one variety. **Nuttal's** initiative in packing crumbly cheeses more appropriately (see below) marks a major breakthrough.

****Kirkham's** from Goosnargh, Lancashire, uniquely use the unpasteurized milk from three days' milkings to produce a lighter buttery cheese with more complex flavours and peppery overtones.

***J.M. Nuttal**, a brand of **Dairy Crest**, has introduced a new form of brown paper packaging backed with cellophane, that allows the cheese to breathe more happily and retain its 'sense of crumbly lemons'.

Other good names to look for include: **Sandham's** of Preston, which is very sweet, fruity and supple; **Butler's**, which is soft and buttery with hints of grapefruit; **Centurion**, which is buttery and excellent for cooking; and **Dewlay**, which is often a classic cheese 'wetter, yeasty and pungent'.

RED LEICESTER

LEICESTER used to be made alongside Stilton, using up the leftover milk. It was widely established and acclaimed in the 1700s. The first factory opened in 1875 and farmhouse production died out by the 1920s. The lavish use of annatto actually indicated attempts to conceal faults in the cheese, but these faults also contributed to the flavour. The addition of annatto was stopped as an economy in the war and hence the coloured cheese became known as RED LEICESTER to differentiate it from the more anaemic version.

The traditional recipe is as follows: the rennet is added at 23-24°C (74-76°F) and the curds are cheddared smaller than for Cheddar, which makes it flakier. It is packed in the widest hoops of any English cheese, 50 cm (20 in) across, and left to ripen until a blue mould develops. It is normally kept for three months, but is better after six when it develops a nuttiness.

It is a widely abused cheese, but some good versions are still made by **Tuxford and Tebbutt** at Melton Mowbray after a valiant rearguard action to preserve it by Patrick Rance and Elizabeth David in 1983. Cheddar-specialists **Quicke's** make some in Devon, as do Cheshire specialists **Overton Hall** in Cheshire.

WENSLEYDALE

Wensleydale, or cheeses like it – possibly made with goats' milk – are mentioned in the Domesday Book. The recipe was well adapted to making cheese from small amounts of milk. In that sense it was true farmhouse cheese, which accounts for its longevity. It is a simple cheese, dependent on the quality of the raw milk. Its decline is traceable precisely to the arrival of bulk milks by train to the Dales and, later, the impact of pasteurization.

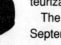

The original cheese, made from spring and September milk was round and flat, 30x10 cm

(12x4 in). Summer cheese was tubby, like Stilton (and, in some cases, naturally allowed to develop a blue), designed for the Christmas market. The rennet is added at 36˚C (97˚F) and the curds form within 15 minutes. They are cut and then heated again, pressed and salted. The taste should be of wet curds, milk and grass. 'Once tasted by epicures, Wensleydale is not likely soon to be forgotten,' said *Law's Grocer's Manual* in 1950.

Alas it was already being forgotten. **Dairy Crest** stopped production of Wensleydale at Coverham and Kirkby Malzead in 1983. A management buyout of the dairy at Hawes is possibly a last lifeline, but so far there has been more hype than evidence of a determination to re-establish the virtues of true Wensleydale.

Mark Robertson at **Redesdale Dairy**, Northumberland, still makes an unusual variation, mixing cows' and sheep's milk. A more accurate reincarnation of traditional Wensleydale may well be another Dales cheese, **Swaledale**.

STILTON

Stilton is the only British cheese to have protected its name – by court judgement in 1969, affirming the Stilton-makers' definition laid down in 1910 that Stilton has to be made in the district of Melton Mowbray and surrounding areas within the counties of Leicestershire, Derbyshire and Nottinghamshire. It was never made in Stilton itself. A local cheese, known as QUENBY, was sold at the Bell Inn (now restored) at Stilton and its reputation and name spread with the coaching parties that passed through.

Patrick Rance attributes its parentage possibly to Lady Beaumont's cheese at Quenby Hall, Hungarton, just outside Leicester. It was certainly made around 1722 and its development was probably down to Elizabeth Scarbrow, a housekeeper at the hall. She married a farmer called Paulet who gave her the milk. They had two daughters, one who helped her make the cheese and one who married Cowper Thornhill, the landlord of the Bell. As late as 1756, Stilton still seems to have been sustained by this family link. By the end of the century, however, Stiltons were being made across the district.

These would have been potent creamy cheeses, often called 'English Parmesan', which suggests they were kept much longer than the fresh-faced creamy versions now sold. Defoe gorily points out in his *Travels Around England* (and this was the origin of scooping) that two spoons were given to eat a Stilton, one to dig out the centre and one to eat the maggots and mites that lived in the crust (this was deemed the point of ripeness). Sometimes the rind was washed in beer, or wine was added to the curds – hence the tradition of pouring port into a Stilton. The tradition of serving Stilton at Christmas stemmed from making the best cheeses from September milk.

WHITE STILTON, originally preferred by Nottinghamshire miners, is still made in the same way, but without the added mould or *Penicillium roqueforti*. The rennet is added at 29-30°C (84-86°F) and the curds set in about an hour. It is then sliced, drained for an hour, lightly squeezed and left 12 hours. The curd is then broken and salted and is ready for the mould.

Good Stilton looks like shattered porcelain and should never have a brown rim inside the crust. The streaking of the needle marks for the blueing can be seen like spoke scorches going from the outside in. The cheeses are not pressed and as the whey drains it leaves cavities where the air can penetrate and create the blueing. Good Stilton is hard and buttery, with streaks of salt and a smell of flowers. It is matured for 3-4 months. Factors point out that the pasteurized versions are ripening quicker than unpasteurized versions. Fifteen weeks' keeping is generally regarded as a peak. To keep a Stilton, the surface should be covered with cling film or a damp cloth.

The enthusiasm of the past year has been to sell white stilton with dates and pecans or apricots, which underlines the trend to move cheese out of the dairy and into the novelty area. The king has been put into pantomime.

SHROPSHIRE BLUE, the same cheese only with added annatto, is marked up often by £1 more again. However, in its different clothes it is a reminder of the aristocracy of the genre. The annatto, as with some Gloucesters, serves to eke out different elements.

There are six Stilton makers, all of whom might claim to produce excellent cheese. The protection of the name and the weight of the cheese's reputation have allowed them to uphold the principles. Cheeses from the same day, the same dairy, and the same milk can still vary noticeably. Good Stilton will become buttery and explosive; under-ripe, a common criticism, it will be just cream and blue, unseparated.

****Colston Bassett** has been made by Mr Wagstaff in Nottingham for the last 25 years. It is the last of the dairies to give up unpasteurized milk, but seemingly with only a marginal difference in quality. The broadest cheeses measure 26 cm (10½ in) across and have an intense flavour of herbs and white wine. They also make a definitive Shropshire Blue.

Long Clawson, in Melton Mowbray, began

as a co-operative for local farmers. Its cheeses are not quite so broad as Colston Basset and are inclined to firmness.

J. M. Nuttal of Hartington, although owned by **Dairy Crest**, is still capable of producing brilliant cheese, which can be golden-crusted, with a wide variation in textures.

Tuxford and Tebbutt, of Thorpe End, Melton Mowbray, is the dairy closest to Stilton's birthplace, eight miles north of Quenby. Although it comes under the umbrella of a large concern (**Express Foods**), the quality and notable creaminess of their Stiltons survives.

Milway Foods of Melton Mowbray supply much own-label supermarket Stilton.

Cropwell Bishop is made at the Somerset Creamery, in fact in Nottinghamshire. They also do a credible Shropshire Blue.

NEW BRITISH CHEESES

The revival in farmhouse cheese-making over the last ten years has been encouraging. The quality of many of these new cheeses is as good as anything that has been seen before. However, the cheese-makers remain an individualistic and private band of people, and only very rarely will any one shop sell more than a few varieties.

The Specialist Cheese-makers' Association lists around 250 new cheeses, though many are variations on the same themes. They are all individually made, using traditional craft techniques. It is no coincidence that the same maker is responsible for a number of the cheeses.

Beenleigh Blue
Bosworth
Cornish Yarg
Duddleswell
Emlett
Golden Cross
Gospel Green
Lanark Blue
Little Rydings
Llangloffan
Spenwood
Tymsboro'
Waterloo
Wellington
Yorkshire Blue

**BEENLEIGH BLUE

First made 11 years ago by Robin Congdon in the Dart Estuary, Devon, but only in May and June because after that the character of the sheep's milk changes. About 1,500 cheeses are made a year. They are turned six times and kept at 22°C (72°F) for the first day to encourage the bacteria to develop. They are then spiked – to allow the air in for the blueing – and salted. The cheese are matured for four months, though the flavour will improve for eight or nine. The new year's cheeses are first sold in September. They are steely blue, tangy, rich and – unusually – slightly sweet. Congdon also makes HARBOURNE BLUE from goats' milk.

**BOSWORTH

Hugh Lillingstone makes this series of equally outstanding pocket-sized goats' cheeses, 9 cm (3½ in) across, in Staffordshire. Superbly packaged with leaves from the estate, they are firm and dry when young, but develop a sensational burnt caramel flavour with a won-

derful subtle citrus finish as they age. They
are very intense, so only a little is required for
the full effect. Lillingstone also makes a fresh
BUTTON and CLIFTON, a smaller version of
Bosworth.

CORNISH YARG

This is made in Liskeard, Cornwall and named
after Mr Gray (spelt backwards) who discovered the old recipe. Now made by Mike
Horrell in 3.2 kg (7 lb) rounds, it is wrapped in
nettles which begin to turn pink and crinkle
with age. Young Yarg resembles Caerphilly.
After 4-6 weeks it develops into a softer,
creamier cheese. Often said to be one of the
best cheeses to go with wine, it is now widely
available in supermarkets. It has a subtle
blandness, with edges of sooty grey from the
rind which is also eaten.

DUDDLESWELL

Started in the early '80s by the Hardy family at
the Sussex High Weal Dairy, who also make a
very good Haloumi, Feta and soft sheep's-
milk cheeses. Made from local ewes' milk, the
small truckles are 20 cm (8 in) tall. The skin is
mottled pale orange, the paste parchment yellow. Sweeter than Spenwood, it has an
intense dryness with walnut edges and verdant tones.

EMLETT

Made by Mary Holbrook in Timsbury, Avon,
this is a round craggy cheese, 7x3.5 cm
(2¾x2 in), with white flecks on pallid shades
of cream. When it is young it stands out
white and pure and firm, but when properly
matured it wrinkles and the orangey-pink pigment comes through as the curd softens.
Tasting notes include, 'burnt cream, very
strong, very spiky, a concentrated sensation
of burning'.

GOLDEN CROSS

A goats'-cheese log made by Kevin and Alison Blunt of Lewes, East Sussex. Notable as it is, it is not widely available.

GOSPEL GREEN

James and Cathy Lane started making cheese in Petworth, Sussex, in the early '80s. Gospel Green is one of the most admired of the new cheeses, 'because it tastes as if it might have been around for 400 years'. It is a small production, using local unpasteurized milk, made in 18x14 cm (7x6 in) truckles. A cross between Cheshire and Cheddar, it is cloth bound (which leaves an imprint), a deep buttery yellow, and quite springy when young. Tasting notes include 'supple, smooth, grasses, lemons, even grapefruit'.

LANARK BLUE

Made by Humphrey Errington in, predictably, Lanarkshire from a single flock of sheep that graze on the moorland heather, this cheese is herbaceous in flavour and at its best when young and creamy rather than flaky.

**LITTLE RYDINGS

A sheep's-milk cheese also made by the outstanding Mary Holbrook in Timsbury. It is sour rather than bitter and has much of the unctuousness of a Camembert. The rind is floral and the taste is very long.

LLANGNOFFAN

Leon and Joan Downey make this unpasteurized Cheddar-style cheese from Jersey milk at Castle Morris, Haverfordwest, Dyfed, between March and December. They sell it mail order or from the farm gate. Fine and crumbly in texture, it is also at the same time dense and creamy, and grassy in flavour with a touch of English mustard.

SPENWOOD

Made in Reading, Berkshire, by Anne Wigmore, the production of this ewes'-milk cheese alternates with Wellington (below). The mould is white-brown with clouds of red, the hard paste is pale lemon. Vegetarian rennet is used. It has a beautiful nutty grapefruit flavour; it is not as tart as Wellington, but still makes the eyes water.

**TYMSBORO

Mary Holbrook's third cheese is an outstanding goats' cheese. The ashed white pyramid grows a Camembert-style mould on top. With age it dries out and an orange pigmentation appears in the rivulets. The flavour concentrates to a unique and magnificent creamy sharpness. It just tastes of flowers. You would be hard pressed to think of another goats' cheese in Europe to match this.

**WATERLOO

Ann Wigmore in Reading washes the rind of this cheese to take off the rancidity. Made at 6.5x5 cm (3x2 in), it has a grey smoky skin and buttery paste. Soft, crumbly and tart, it is an outstanding cheese. She also makes a WIGMORE, with washed sheep's curd.

WELLINGTON

The Guernsey cattle on the Duke of Wellington's estate provide the milk for this cheese made again by Anne Wigmore. The rough skin is pink to orange, while the paste is a smooth clean orange. The colour derives from the richness of the milk and vegetarian rennet is used. It is a dry cheese, with creamy and nutty overtones.

YORKSHIRE BLUE

Made by Judy Bell of Shepherd's Purse, North Yorkshire, she also does a good Feta.

IRISH CHEESES

Three exceptional Irish cheeses are sold in this country. As with the new revivalist British cheeses, they are individual and hand-made.

Cashel Blue
Gubbeen
Milleens

**CASHEL BLUE
Made by Louis Grubb in Cashel, County Tipperary, this is unusually creamy for a blue cheese. The rind is eaten. It is at its peak in a state of semi-collapse, when it explodes like a blueing sunset and brings water to the eyes.

**GUBBEEN
Gin Ferguson in County Cork makes this semi-soft washed-rind cheese using pasteurized milk in 1-3 lb lots. Somewhat akin to Pont l'Évêque (see page 170), it has a loose dog-skin-like rind, which is pinkish-orange, very supple and bouncy. The flavour has a dense earthy vegetal finish.

**MILLEENS
Made by Norman and Veronica Steel in Beara, County Cork, this washed-rind cheese is quite firm when young. The moon crater crust is eaten. Pink to white, it has a sweet farmyard taste.

FRENCH AOC CHEESES

Abondance
Beaufort
Bleu d'Auvergne
Bleu de Causses
Bleu de Gex-Haut-Jura
Brie
Camembert
Cantal
Chaource
Crottin de Chavignol
Fourme d'Ambert
Laguiole
Langres
Livarot
Munster
Neufchâtel
Pont-l'Évêque
Reblochon
Roquefort
Sainte-Maure
Sainte-Nectaire
Salers
Selles-sur-Cher
Vacherin

The French system of *appellation contrôlée* developed for wine was extended to more than 30 cheeses from the end of the '70s. The point of *AOC* (*Appellation d'Origine Contrôlée*) is that it recognizes the tradition and the craft of making a food on a specific and identified piece of land or region in a particular way. Age and progeny may not, however, be a complete guarantee of quality in themselves. *AOC* for cheese is more advanced than that for other foods and – despite criticisms that in some cases the boundaries have been enforced elastically to include large commercial creameries or that pasteurized milk is allowed to the detriment of some cheeses – they remain as fine examples of crafts that may go back a millennium.

The making of the cheese itself is only one part of the creation of a great cheese. The French trade of the *affineur* is different to that of the English factor. An *affineur* is not just a trader, but a maturer of cheese. They will buy direct from the farm and allow the cheeses to ripen, often in specifically designed cellars, so they are sold in different stages. Some shops – like **Jeroboam's** and **Neal's Yard** for English cheeses – may follow the practice if they have the space, but to a more limited degree. Supermarkets do not, which is one reason why great soft cheeses are so rarely found in larger retailers.

ABONDANCE

This is a fine cheese, but whether it deserves recognition over other fine mountain cheeses is a moot point. It needs to age to develop its distinction. Large, at 20x6 cm (8x2½ in), with a hide-pink skin and the occasional pock mark, it has a pure and deep creaminess unusual in a hard cheese, as if processed.

BEAUFORT

Among the oldest recorded cheeses, dating back to pre-Roman times, these are huge cheeses co-operatively made, with the farms receiving scaled payments according to the quality of their milk. The cattle graze above 2,000 metres (6,500 ft) in the south of the Savoie. The BEAUFORT HAUTE MONTAGNE will be marked with a green oval plaque. Milder and more delicate than the other big mountain cheese, Comté, unless allowed to mature, it melts well in cooking and would have been one of the original cheeses for fondue (half and half with Emmental or Comté) and is also used in raclette. *Al dente* in texture and floral in flavour, it has hints of freshly crushed nuts.

BLEU D'AUVERGNE

This cheese was badly hit by the rise of the new blues from Bresse and also the move to pasteurization allowed by the *AOC* in 1976. Kept in caves for three months, the blueing is more olive-to-green. Dusty of rind, with squarish crenellations, it is sold in gold paper and is creamy, sour and softish. A good second to Roquefort, it is more reliable than distinguished.

BLEU DE CAUSSES

From Rouerque, these are blued in separate caves to Roquefort. Made from cows' milk, with 45% fat, 25x10 cm (10x4 in) in size, large injection marks under the wrapping indicate where the veining marks were made. It is the most immediate of all blues: beautiful, sea surf salt on the first taste; creamy and vanilla as the taste ebbs away slowly like a tide.

BLEU DE GEX-HAUT-JURA

Unusually light, someone described this cheese as 'like a Cézanne portrait of a southern Pyrenean skyline'. With its clouds of small pocking, this cheese is probably more than 700 years old. Tasting notes include, 'digs deep into the wells of the creaminess to pull out the blues, gains sharpness and intensity, cheek puckering, violent, later bitterness'.

BRIE

Brie was not known to the Romans, but Charlemagne certainly knew of a famous cheese from the same area around AD744. Brie was served at the French court right up to the revolution. Although its reputation survives, it is probably not as important a cheese now as it was 250 years ago. Nevertheless, Magritte once painted its label for **Dinkla**. *Appellation contrôlée* was given to both Brie de Melun and Brie de Meaux in 1980, Although the Melun is less common, it was probably the original Brie.

**BRIE DE MELUN is sharper than the Brie de Meaux and deeper, consequently it always has a fine slightly chalked centre and never softens as much. The texture is more grainy, though it becomes runny next to the rind.

**BRIE DE MEAUX is brilliant. The skin white with terracotta streaks, the paste smooth, gold and swelling, like solid seaside sunshine. Tasting notes include, 'white skin, traces of orange, the paste going fluid and smooth on the outsides, but still a line of pock marks, chalky inside, the smell is of mushrooms, tart, long finish'.

In both cases, the unpasteurized version is infinitely more complex and rewarding. Occasionally there are interesting combinations of cows' and goats' milk, sold as Brie-style, the skin is usually more ashen grey white and goat-like, with a flavour of herbs and primroses, but the inside is soft and surprising.

Marks & Spencer's pasteurized Brie is probably the pick of the supermarket crop.

CAMEMBERT

The creation of modern Camembert is credited to Marie Harel, née Marie Fontaine. In 1789, she took in a priest Abbé Gobert who was fleeing the Terror. He told her what he knew of how Brie was made – patience with the curd and leaving it unbroken before going into the mould – and she adapted the recipe from there. She sold her cheeses at Vimoutiers market, where they went so well that she enlarged the mould size to its modern size of 11 cm (4½ in) across. Its meteoric rise to fame coincided with the advent of the railways and also the neat wooden boxes which allowed it to travel.

Camembert became high fashion; the round boxes took labels that were art: in the early part of this century there was 'King Kong Camembert', 'Mini Mouse Camembert', 'Cowboy Camembert', 'Charleston Camembert'... even, later, 'Sputnik Camembert' and 'War Veteran Camembert'.

Like Cheddar in Britain, it was widely imitated and manufactured in factories across France and abroad. The *AOC* protection since 1983 extends only to CAMEMBERT DE NORMANDIE as the last vestiges of what real Camembert was about. The high fat content of the milk from the Normandy cattle is critical.

With 45% fat, it is ready to eat when all traces of white disappear from centre – though some say a few shafts are good – it should never be chalky. It is at its best between the two consistencies of white and liquid, usually in summer. In 1910 *Penicillium candidum* was introduced to replace natural surface blue *P. glaucum*, which must have fundamentally altered the cheese. As with Brie, unpasteurized versions have much more developed flavours.

The art of the *affineur* is well demonstrated by Henry Pannec with his **Camembert**

In a blind tasting for the Covent Garden delicatessen **Mortimer & Bennett**, an independent panel of food writers and experts rated unpasteurized cheeses against their pasteurized counterparts. Unpasteurized outscored pasteurized by 75-25% for goats' cheese; 82-18% for Pont l'Évêque 53-47% for St-Augur; 57-43% for Petite Munster; 67-33% for mountain ewe; 73-23% for St-Paulin and 56-44% for triple cream.

Voluptueuse Aphrodite, which he macerates in cider and sells with a cork embedded in the skin into which is poured Calvados as a variation on the *trou Normande*. It is a brutally strong cheese, like a ripe Livarot, but matched with the softness of the Camembert.

*La Petite Normande, Moule a la Louche**, is unpasteurized and twice the price of a supermarket version. One from **Selfridges** was a sizeable £3.50, whereas a comparable cheese in a French supermarket might be the equivalent of £2.00. The full blooming smell of clean citrus and flowers comes through immediately. There are also elements of the cellar, as if you could smell the room itself. All of which gives way to a crystal-clear, almost caramel flavour, rather than the nuttiness of pasteurized versions.

Sainsbury Camembert is sold in halves. As with other pasteurized Camemberts, the elements of nuts seem to be more pronounced. This is quite bouncy and mild, just a deep sticky hint of what it might be. Tasting notes: 'That socks and smoky railway carriages taste is in the rind, the paste is like springy butter with elements of oily richness. There is a big uplift in flavour at the end'.

Sainsbury Traditional Camembert is made with unpasteurized milk. It promises more than it delivers, being fairly nondescript and milky with the accent on the acids and the sours. Very much a dairy flavour, it is quite different from the pasteurized version, lacking a sense of aristocracy.

St Michael Camembert is pungent, and smoothly soft. One sampled was without any traces of chalkiness, and distinctly nutty if a bit mild and polite.

CANTAL

Probably one of the oldest of all cheeses, Cantal is often produced by the same makers as Salers. The *AOC* does not insist on raw milk and there has been a tendency to blandness and commercialism. The best remain unpasteurized and dry with age, though it is sold at different degrees of maturity. The paste is smooth, ivory in colour and gets nuttier after six months (*vieux*). It is a warm rich cheese, with a slight metallic taste from the volcanic soil of the Auvergne.

CHAOURCE

Records go back to Louis X eating Burgundian Chaource. It is bright and creamy, with a white chalky exterior, running fresh rich inside. A light-hearted richness like no other cheese in the world, it needs to be ripe and this is difficult because of the deep coat and broad drum-like shape. The cheeses are made to different shapes, but smaller versions tend to be more reliable for an even ripeness. If it is too young, the texture is Caerphilly-like and chalky: but it turns into a Brie-like creaminess after four weeks. It should be unpasteurized, but *AOC* permits the use of pasteurized milk and there are a number of factory versions which lack the true potential of a great Chaource. The milk is ripened before renneting, and the Chaource matured for 14 days on rye straw. Good Chaource tastes of 'lemon essences of double cream, long tang' and has 'the puckering bite of mature Parmesan or Cheddar'.

CROTTIN DE CHAVIGNOL

Goats' cheeses were first mentioned in the area in 1573, but Berry probably had goats' cheese even before then. Crottin (meaning 'dung', which they resemble as they age) was adapted from the Franks around 1500, and first officially adopted as the cheese's name in 1829. It was awarded the *AOC* in 1976, but this allows frozen curd, some of which can be imported from the UK. If they are left to age, as is the French practice, they go from a soft creamy white rind to bluish grey to dark grey to black.

FOURME D'AMBERT

Fourme is the old word for a mould for cheese. A kind of Fourme d'Ambert was certainly made prior to the Romans. The Auvergne caves where they ripen for three months are naturally infected with *Penicillium glaucum*. The *AOC* allows pasteurized milk to be used, so the old nutty flavour has given way to standardization closer to Gorgonzola. With 45% fat, it has pock marks of yellow, a drift of penicillin across marble. A good Fourme will have a lovely intense creamy flowery taste, sweet not overly strong blue, like a blue soup. Poor examples tend to be one-dimensional, with a wet, sour texture and a very salty taste with hints of nettles.

LAGUIOLE

Pronounced 'la yole', this is a very old hard cheese, though records are not specific. Made from the milk of fabled Aubrac cattle (which some say produce the best meat in France), which is well suited to cheese-making, it was brought into *appellation contrôlée* in 1976.

LANGRES

Made on the highland plateau on the Burgundy borders, this unpasteurized washed-rind cheese is made to be eaten within six weeks. The flavour is immense, and not for the faint-hearted when it goes over the top. Creamy when young, it quickly goes soft – sometimes even liquid – in the centre. The flavour is also mild when young, but later gives way to a smooth, rampant cream, tasting of concentrated oranges. It is stronger than Livarot, but not as strong as Munster, and stands out in the cheese shop as a bright orange chef's hat with a sunken head. Some are washed in Mirabelle and acquire a sweet pungency. Tasting notes include, 'The rind smells of pussy-cat fur. Smoky acorns, chestnuts, woody clothes around and intense centre of milky cream'.

**LIVAROT

Despite its reputation as one of the strongest cheeses, it is quite mild when young and much of the pungency comes from the skin rather than the flesh. Related to, but possibly not exactly the same as, the ancient Norman cheese ANGELON (or ANGELOT), it is first mentioned around 1693.

Inside the round box, a proper Livarot will have five orange bands of sedge grass, designed originally to hold softer cheeses in shape. Hence the French nickname, 'le Colonel'. With a firmer and stronger paste than Camembert, it is a plump, rosy big drum of a cheese, twice the height of a Camembert.

Livarot is made from two days' milking, lightly skimmed, to give 40% fat, and then washed in brine three times during 48 days maturing. The *AOC* was given in 1976 for cheeses from the Pays D'Auge, between the rivers Touques and Dives. A good version will have a marbled, rust-and-white crust, the flesh will be creamy golden and smooth with tiny pock marks. Softly sweet in flavour, it is in fact milder than Langres, although the smell of the skin is deceptively strong. **Graindorge** is a good example. Tasting notes include, 'Going to old hay and bitterness. Intense, distinct earthy farmyard, full-bodied'.

*MUNSTER

One of the strongest of all French cheeses, the name derives from the word for monastery, where similar cheeses were probably made from the 6th century. The *AOC* has lumped it together with the second cheese of the area in Alsace, the larger, GÉROMÉ. Géromé traditionally comes from the western slopes of the Vosges mountains, and Munster from the east. Most of the milk will be organic as the cattle graze above the vines. The orange rind is neatly lined, like a tiled roof, and sometimes turns shades of pink (historically this was from drying in the sun). Morning and evening milk are used and the cheese fashioned by hand. The smell is inherent in the crust, taking on the bacterium linens from the maturing caves. It goes well with Alsace wines.

NEUFCHATEL

This cheese from Normandy comes in a variety of different shapes, including hearts, loaves and discs. The new cheese is kneaded with older, riper cheese before moulding. The skin is brilliant white, the paste golden and the fat content 45%. Cream-enriched variations include PETIT-SUISSE.

PONT-L'EVEQUE

Another Norman cheese which was first thought to have been made around the 12th century. It may originally have been round and possibly changed its shape to differentiate itself from the other local cheese, Angelon. Originally the crust was just brushed and washing was only adopted in the last century. Washed, the crust is smoother and more russet; brushed, it is more granular and pale fawn. It is now made from milk in all five Normandy *départements* and the Maine *département* of Mayenne –'stretching the Vallée d'Auge beyond reason and inexcusably allowing pasteurized milk' accuses Patrick Rance. It should weigh 350-400 g (12-14 oz)

and be 10.5-11.5 cm (4¼-4¾ in) square. Unlike Brie or Camembert, the curd is broken. When young it is almost Brie-like; allowed to mature at room temperature it will get progressively stronger. The most interesting will be unpasteurized. The paste will be soft, golden, not runny until in the mouth. The flavour is rich but not sharp, with a wide edge of citrus. Usually sold in a box, it also keeps surprisingly well after cutting.

** REBLOCHON

From the Savoie, Reblochon was originally known as *fromage de devotion* as the farmers asked the local monks for their blessings on their mountain huts. The rent for the huts was paid in a percentage of the value of the milk, and the farmers came to hold back some of the milk from inspection and used the (rich) milk from a second illicit milking to make Reblochon for themselves. Until the Revolution, the cheeses were never sold. The warmth and humidity of the caves in which the cheeses are ripened were historically provided by a sheep penned in there for the winter. The milk is from the Abondance cow. Good Reblochon is golden-pink and weighs around 500 g (1 lb 2 oz). The smaller PETIT REBLOCHON or REBLOCHONNET is regarded as inferior because it does not ripen so consistently. It has a mild, soft, voluptuous flavour and creamy but springy texture.

** ROQUEFORT

The fame of one of the world's great blue cheeses – arguably the greatest – rests with the calcareous (limestone) caves above the River Soulzon. The romantic story is that a shepherd left his cheese and bread in one of the caves when he went off to seduce a shepherdess. Coming back some weeks later, he discovered the miraculous effects of the blueing. The 23 natural caves were known to the Romans as places to store cheese. The caves now go down 11 stories and the subterranean village is twice the size of the one on the surface.

To create the blueing, loaves of barley and rye are left in the caves for three months until they have developed furry coats. These are then dried and powdered and added to the cheese. Blueing is also further encouraged by the puncturing of each cheese with 38 needles to allow the air in.

The first month-old Lacaune lambs are weaned in December and then the numbers of cheeses rise through to April to peak and fall off again as the sheep mate. One litre (1¾ pints) of milk produces nearly 115 g (¼ lb) of Roquefort, which is 45% fat. Some milk is now imported from Spain and there has been an influx in the region of British Milk Sheep. There is fierce discussion over which cheeses still use Lacaune milk. *AOC* states the milk must be unpasteurized.

Good Roquefort is firm with large holes. The intensity of the blue (or aquamarine green) is electric, giving the cheese a taste of the caves. It is best eaten with sweet wine or even sweet ale. The most commonly found Roquefort in Britain is from the **Société** co-operative. **Papillon** claims to be one of only two or three using local milk. It has pale aquamarine to dusty blue-green cratering, and has a good mild flavour and creamy texture. Other good examples are from **Constans Crouzat** and **Gabriel Coulet.**

SAINTE-MAURE

This mild goats' cheese from the Touraine is long, ashen and orange tinted, staked through its axis with a wooden axle. Quite subtle when young, it is creamy, with edges of Roquefort and hints of primroses.

*SAINT–NECTAIRE

Related to the better-known Auvergne cheese, Cantal, and just as ancient, it is made in 12 cm (4¾ in) discs, 3.5 cm (1½ in) deep. White or grey-red and mimosa-like, sometimes even jade or blue in colour, it is made with milk from Salers and Ferrandaises cows and ripened 2-4 months. Awarded *AOC* in 1979, the best use unpasteurized milk, have an oval green plaque on the face of the cheese and the word *fermier* on the label. The cheeses with pale pink rinds tend not to be farmhouse.

SALERS

One of the oldest French cheeses, Salers takes its name from the Auvergne cattle who supply the milk. It is similar to Cantal, but is less liable to short-cuts. In summer the cattle graze at over 800 metres on volcanic pastures, both of which factors contribute to the flavour. They are also moved from pasture to pasture to maintain an organic approach. The full cheese is made from the milk of at least 40 cows, weighs 35-55 kg and carries an aluminium plaque. The golden crust turns red and marbled and the paste is yellow and giving. The flavour improves wonderfully with age.

**SELLES–SUR–CHER

The traditional cheese of the Loire, it is sprinkled with a mix of charcoal and salt to preserve it. It can be eaten very young, when it is mild and lemony. As it ages it develops a bluish-grey rind and dries out, concentrating the flavour. Good examples can be strong and long-lasting, with a gummy vanilla spikiness and hints of spring flowers and nuts.

VACHERIN

Following the 1987 outbreak of listeria in Switzerland associated with Vacherin, the French government stopped exports of their own versions of the cheese made in Savoie and the Franche-Comté, while the Swiss went on happily selling theirs. The Swiss version is pasteurized (as it was at the time of the outbreak) and called MONT-D'OR DE JOUX. Both cheeses are made in the same mountains and the difference is political not natural, though the French cheeses are by general consent superior, due to the quality of the cheese-makers. To differentiate them, these French versions are now called LE MONT D'OR or VACHERIN DU HAUT-DOOBS. The Swiss version is also more expensive because it attracts a levy on being imported into EC countries.

Vacherin is made from August 15 to March 31, when the Montbeliarde and Pie-rouges de l'Est cattle are brought inside. Sold in distinctive round, wobbly, thin wooden boxes, the crust is pink, swollen and undulating as if indicating the potent forces underneath. When ripe, the paste looks like mayonnaise and the skin smells of the cobwebs in the cellar. The bark around the outside is from the mountain spruces and needs to be cut with a serrated knife. An enthusiastic Patrick Rance declares: 'If you are not in stuffy company, lick your bark after each mouthful of cheese, and do not waste what is left; put it on the fire to die in a scent of glory'.

Tasting notes on an unspecified unpasteurized French example includes, 'smells of football socks, very vegetal, unctuous, clean taste ending in flowers, powerful, lovely texture. **Badoz** is a good maker. Swiss **Le Pelerin** has an intense creaminess, but lacks the depth of other good cheeses.

L'Edel de Cleron is a commercially made copy of Vacherin. If properly looked after, so the insides starts to run, it can be a sensational alternative at half the price – if a shade one-dimensional. Tasting notes include, 'the smell of bitter almonds, woody lovely cream, in fact quite a gentle smoky flavour of casseroled lemons'.

OTHER TRADITIONAL FRENCH CHEESES

The *AOC* is not definitive. A number of other excellent traditional cheeses find their way over here and often provide better value for not being *AOC*.

BANON
Made in Provence from 90% cows' milk, but with some goat's milk added, these 7x2.5 cm (2¾ x1 in) cheeses are wrapped in chestnut leaves. With a delicate greyish-blue mould, they are either matured to softness or dried to concentrate them. They may now be found in supermarkets. Good examples are firm, grainy and potent, with a sour milk and dairy-yards flavour and hints of lemons.

CABÉCOU
From Quercy, the name of this cheese means 'little goat', which it is. It can be eaten fresh within 48 hours of making (as an aperitif), kept in the caves for 15 days to dry out (good in salads) or it may be even macerated in eau-de-vie de prune, when it is known as CABÉCOU TRUFFÉ.

CARRÉ DE L'EST
This square, pale orange cheese from Champagne is underrated and good value among the stronger cheeses. Unlike Époisses and Livarot, the aroma is in the cheese itself. It ripens quickly and is known as the 'Champagne of Brie'. Good names include **Saulxurois**. There is a white Camembert-rinded Carré on the market, which is unwashed and lacks the flavour and character of the original.

COMTÉ

The French version of Gruyère from the Comté (sometimes called 'Gruyère de Comté') is creamy beige, with a firm rind and should have a few small holes in it. The unpasteurized versions are superior and nearly all production is still farmhouse. This was a pioneering area for cheese-making in the 12th century. It is made in the summer using milk from the same cows that provide Vacherin in winter. About 530 litres, or the yield from 30 cows, goes into a single cheese. The crust should have bells and the name 'Comté' engraved in it. If not, it will have been downgraded at inspection. It should always be sold with the crust on (a device that prevented it being sold pre-packed in supermarkets, as happened to Cheddar). The nutty flavour is often used in fondues.

COULOMMIERS

Although in practice this is a Brie, it is sold as a different cheese. It was first recorded around the end of the 10th century and although it does not have the *appellation contrôlée* is as good as many cheeses which do. The fat content is higher, at 50%, which has led to accusations of adultery, but the milk from the Coulommiers cattle has a naturally high fat content.

**COULOMMIERS LE SAINT-JACQUES, from the Île de France, is round, 15 cm (6 in) across, with a chalky white rind (it can have a blue bloom on it which is just wiped off without any adverse effect). Tasting notes include, 'soft, voluptuous, dry meadows, hay and lemons, long finish into citrus'.

ÉPOISSES

This classic washed-rind cheese from Burgundy comes in round wooden boxes and the cheese inside is sometimes wrapped in vine leaves. The pale orange skin is washed with *marc* or wine to encourage the strong aromatic smell. Inferior versions will have just been washed in brine. It is the rind that smells and gets quite sticky. The inside is soft and white and not quite so pungent. Kept at room temperature for 2-3 days, it ripens dramatically. Some say it is the strongest of all cheeses, outdoing even Munster. Better examples are from unpasteurized milk.

**FLEUR DE MAQUIS

A fresh sheep's-milk cheese from Corsica, it is coated in rosemary, chilli and juniper – the *maquis* or scrubby bush of Corsica on which the sheep graze. One of the few cheeses with herbs on the outside which really suit. Soft in texture, it is a stunning cheese, with the taste of roast lamb from the rosemary.

GAPERON

A distinctive cheese from the Auvergne, it is hand-moulded in deep white half-ovals and flavoured with crushed garlic and peppercorns. A buttery deep yellow with grey flecks, it is really an excuse to use up the garlic of the region.

MORBIER

A mountain cheese, properly made with the milk of the morning and the evening, top and bottom separated by a thin filling of ash – though sometimes other vegetable fillings have now crept in. Akin to Comté, the 30 cm (12 in) rounds are off-white, solid and milder and softer than you expect. Available all year, it has a pink to orange rind, and a smooth paste with the odd hole and the fleck of ash through the middle. Soft, pungent and spongy it does have a good elastic texture and the mild hint of farmyard.

PALET DE BOURGOGNE

When older, this cheese from Burgundy is reputedly as strong as any French cheese. A pale beige round, 10x3 cm (4x1¼ in), which is washed in *marc*, it should change from dry chalkiness to a golden paste. Tasting notes include, 'skin has a silage-like smell, but inside is a slug of cream, sharp at the back of the throat.'

RACLETTE

This unpasteurized cheese, 12 cm (4¾ in) high by 30 cm (12 in) across, has a dusty beige rind, tinged with reds and yellows. The flesh is yellow and smooth with pockets of air. It is an individual cheese, with a gamy flavour of chestnuts and long high notes and finish as in Cheddar and Parmesan. Usually used in cooking.

SAINT–FÉLICIEN

Made near Lyons around the Beaujolais region, this 45%-fat fresh cheese is eaten within two weeks of making. It is unattractively packed in clear children's-party-style jelly moulds and marked like soft butter. Lightly washed, it begins very curdy but becomes more alcoholic with age. It is an excellent cheese with Beaujolais, but is at its best in winter.

TOMME DE SAVOIE

Tomme means a 'big round'. Usually sold quite young here, older variations of this cheese can be found in France. Usually unpasteurized, this was *the* mountain cheese, alongside Comté and Emmental. Grey-cream in colour, with a distinct mild taste enhanced by the mustiness of the rind, it will be at its best around September and October when the milk is from the richest grazing in June.

MODERN FRENCH CHEESES

The new generation of French factory cheeses can be impressive, despite their industrial parentage. A few, like BOURS-AULT, GRATTE-PAILLE, PAVÉ D'AFFINOIS and ST-AUGUR are capable of being miraculously improved by affinage. Others remain themselves whatever. Also worth looking for are BRILLAT-SAVARIN (invented between the Wars by Androuët's father), PONT MOUTIER, VIEUX PANÉE and ROULÉ.

Boursault
Chaumes
Explorateur
Pavé d'Affinois
Port-Salut
Saint-André
Tourrée de l'Auber
Vignotte

BOURSAULT
This big brother of BOURSIN has triple cream added to the milk for a high-fat content. The cheese is usually sold in a box and its deep yellow sticky rind wrapped in paper. It tastes like clotted cream, running soft with hints of lemons. Go for those near and after their sell-by dates.

Invented in 1953 by Henri Boursault at Le Perreux sur Marne, the creamery was later bought by Boursin. The unpasteurized is sold as 'gold label'; the 'silver label' denotes the less interesting pasteurized. Patrick Rance says to take it out of its box and paper and keep it on straw in a cool place, turning daily three times a week to let the pink coat develop – maybe 7-10 days.

CHAUMES
This popular mass-produced cheese is well made and well marketed. The rind is waxy and a vivid orange, the paste stable but it will ripen like Brie. First made in Jurançon in 1971, based on what was an Alpine cheese, the original seems to have died out. About 20 cm (8 in) across, the modern version is wrapped in orange paper with an egotistically

large logo and fattening curves bulging out the sides like a spare tyre. The paste is silky cream with pocks of air, the flavour clean with hints of vanilla.

EXPLORATEUR

Invented in the '60s by M. Duquesne of La Fromagerie du Petit Morin at La Tretoire and named to honour the then mayor of Coulommiers – and explorer – Bertrand Flornoy. The rocket on the logo is said to be France's only rocket. It is a triple-cream cheese – therefore 75% fat.

*PAVÉ D'AFFINOIS

Small white cubes of cheese which, if allowed to ripen, will become liquid in the centre. Cut them across the centre and spoon out the insides, which are like melted butter. Now sold in supermarkets, it is quite dry with a velvety skin and has a Brie-like chalky texture when unripe.

PORT–SALUT

Until 1988 Port-Salut was made by the monks of the Notre Dame du Port-du-Salut, probably since around 1830. The name was registered in 1874 and commercial imitators forced to use the name SAINT-PAULIN. The monks' hold on the cheese has been eroded since the '50s, when the marketing was put outside the abbey, and finally finished by the Swiss Vacherin-associated listeria outbreak – the monks refused to pay for their raw milk to be tested each month. With a bright orange rind, and about 15x4 cm (6x1½ in), fattening out at the edges, it has a parchment-yellow paste and warm waxy smell. The taste is quite homely, fireside, with some hints of nuts and a nice short sweet finish.

*SAINT–ANDRÉ

A triple-cream cheese close to a Vignotte, it is made in rounds about 20 cm (8 in) across and 8 cm (3¼ in) deep. With a 75% fat content, it has a clear white rind and a luscious, very thick buttercream paste with a long-lasting flavour that hints of meadows and acid lemons.

TOURRÉE DE L'AUBER

This cheese from Isère is another modern copy of Vacherin. About 20 cm (8 in) across and 8 cm (3¼ in) deep, its orange-to-brown rind, neatly lined on surface with crevices filled with white, is ringed with conifer bark to constrain it, corset-like, the creamy white paste is bursting at the sides. Not as brilliant as Vacherin, but interesting in itself with a mildly sour, flowery flavour.

VIGNOTTE

This highly popular cheese with 72% fat, 7x8 cm (2¾x3¼ in) in size, is Camembert-white. Smaller ones are sold in red boxes. Double-cream with an edge of lime and lemons, it is almost like double cream by another name.

ITALIAN CHEESES

Italian cheese-making has gravitated from the farm to the factory. Unlike here, however, there has been no rush to diversification. The big names still dominate, often monitored by consortia applying strict rules for size, shape, ripening and labelling.

BEL PAESE

Created by Galbani in the '20s, this is one of the best-known cheese brand-names, but not to be overlooked for that. It is supple, mild and slightly sweet.

CACIOCAVALLO

One of the original Italian cheeses, and the similarities with the way cheeses were kept on the backs of horses in sheep- and goat-skin bags in the Caucasus and Central Asia suggests there may have been a very early trade with the east. Caciocavallo is father to Mozzarella and the *filata* process – the curds placed in hot whey and heated to 45°C (113°F), then cut into strips, put back in warm whey and finally kneaded. Caciocavallo is moulded into 3-4 kg (6½-9 lb) rounds and hung for 3-6 months, or even kept for a hard grating cheese. With a 44% fat content, its flavour is mild and delicate.

**CROTIN

This cheese from Piedmont is made from half cows' milk and half ewes' milk cheese. It is kept in – and named after – the cellar in which the white truffles are kept and these imbue the cheese with their flavour. Aged for a month, it can be hard enough to shave over Bresaola, or it is served with Mascarpone.

DOLCELATTE

Meaning 'sweet milk', this modern imitation of Gorgonzola is made in Pavia with pasteurized milk and matured for 45 days before the *Penicillium* is introduced. Notwithstanding, **Waitrose** claim a mountain Dolcelatte, which is smooth and dry, 'with just a hint of blueness and is very mild for a blue cheese'. A good version should be nutty and defined, with a developing character that is sweeter and creamier than Gorgonzola. DOLCELATTE TORTE is layered into a 'cake' with Mascarpone.

FONTINA

This is designed for fondues, but is a good cheese in its own right eaten from the block, especially when made in summer after the cattle have grazed on the mountainous pastures of the Val d'Aosta. FONTAL is the second-grade cheese. It is the basis for the Turin dish of *fonduta*, warmed to a sweet creamy mess. The cheese has a pleasant, lactic, nutty flavour.

GORGONZOLA

Named after the town in Lombardy, north of Milan, this cheese has probably been made in the area for more than 1,000 years. The cattle drovers stopped here, bringing the cattle down from the mountains after their summer grazing. The cheeses are matured for two months before the *Penicillium* is injected. The cylindrical cheeses, 25 x 20 cm (10x8 in), with a 48% fat content are usually wrapped in silver paper marked with the brand.

Tasting notes on an example from **Waitrose**: 'smooth, bouncy white through which violent circular and serrated crevices of blue have run rampantly, as if ravaged by an alien force that has since departed. The

visual aggression is in contrast to the mildness of the cheese itself. Creamy. The blue is
nutty, not sharp, and develops a relationship
with the creaminess that gives an aftertaste of
mellow meadows'; on an example from
Sainsbury: 'dense, creamy, compact, sharply
herbaceous, tarragon tang'.

GRANA PADANO

Grana is the generic name for all hard cheeses,
invariably made with semi-skimmed milk, while
the cream will often go for Mascarpone. This
cheese was originally made in the Padana valley but now is made across Italy, regulated by
its consortium. Unlike Parmesan, it uses an
assortment of skimmed milks. The cheese may
be matured from 1-2 years and can weigh as
much as 40 kg (90 lb). Made all the year, with a
fat content of 32%, they are cheaper than
Parmesan, but not necessarily inferior. The
best can grace a cheeseboard or be served
with fruit as a starter.

MASCARPONE

Made in Lombardy in the winter and sold in
pots, this is a by-product of the *grana* cheeses
(see above). This soft cream cheese can have
a fat content as high as 70%. It is similar to
crème fraîche, but has had a starter culture
added, so it is a cheese not a milk product. It
is eaten with fruit and cognac. Those with long
shelf-lives tend to develop an off tone. The
Sainsbury version is dramatically sweet and
sticky, triple-cream with very little element of
cheese at all. A little would go a long way.
Mascarpone is the main ingredient of *Tiramisu*
(meaning 'pick-me-up), in which it is flavoured
with coffee and alcohol.

MOZZARELLA

This cheese takes its name from the cutting,
mozzare. The curd is drawn by hand into

rope-like strands and spun into concentric circles to creates its elasticity. The best is made from the milk of buffalo introduced into Lazio and Campania in the 16th century to work the rice fields, but it is now widely made with cows' milk (even in Wembley and Ireland), though much of this will go for commercial pizzas. MOZZARELLA DI BUFALO is slightly fattier at 50% to 45%. Good mozzarella will be subtle, nutty and sweet, the traditional foil for raw tomato.

PARMESAN

Responsibility for this great cheese is claimed both by Tuscany in 11th century and Parma in the 13th. Cheese made in the areas around Parma, Bologna and Mantua has been protected since 1954. The cows' milk is skimmed, unpasteurized and the cheeses pressed and matured for a year or more. In Italy, they are sold in different stages of ripeness, the young designed to go with fruit. Reggiano is only made north of the Po, in Mantua, where the pastures are deemed to be more lush and have more clover. About 16 litres (28 pts) of milk makes 1 kg (2¼ lb) of Parmesan and the fat content is 32%.

The cheese in the ready-grated tubs of Parmesan is, for most part, stale and poor. The best argument for grating it at home is that it will be fresher and less will go further.

There is an English Parmesan, **Avanti**, made in Sussex; often sold too young and wet to grate properly, but regarded as a distinctive cheese of merit in its own right.

PECORINO

Made in Lazio from November to June, using sheep's milk and rennet, this cheese is dried for a month and matured for eight, though some examples can be matured as long 10 years. The 36% fat cheese is sold in big cylinders, weighing 8-22 kg (18-50 lb). The younger cheeses are supple, distinctly sheepy and clean-tasting. Older cheeses, known as SARDO, are designed for grating. They are very salty and good for pasta, soups and other hot dishes. Nutty, with a sweet caramel flavour, the cheese needs a strong country wine when served on a cheeseboard. It can be found selling for less than Grana or Parmesan in some supermarkets. A similar cheese is also made in Sicily.

PROVOLONE

Another spun-curd cheese, but using rennet from goats rather than cows, and allowed to mature. Poor examples are rubbery; the best are harder, fruity and *piccante*.

RICOTTA

Strictly speaking, this not a cheese, but made from the whey which is then cooked (*ricotta*, 'to re-cook'). The whey is often left over from the making of other well-known cheeses, notably Fontina. In the south it is often made from sheep's-milk whey, which is stronger. The practice of making Ricotta is ancient and varies from region to region. With a 30% fat content, it is eaten fresh, though salted versions will keep two months. It is essentially a cooking cheese, for sweets and pasta.

TALEGGIO

Like Gorgonzola, this cheese is named after a town in Lombardy where the drovers rested overnight when bringing the cattle down from the mountains after the summer grazing. It probably dates back to the 9th century and is matured for 40 days. With a fat content of 48%, the large flat square orange blocks, 20x4 cm (8x1½ in), with a pinkish brown gritty rind have a superb texture, like spring Brie or undulating Vacherin.

SPANISH CHEESES

Cheeses from Spain have increasingly been brought over here since her entry into the EC. Some are strikingly individual and artisanal. Under three month's old, soft Spanish cheeses must by law be pasteurized, but hard cheeses can be unpasteurized.

Cassoleta
Etorki
Garrotxa
Iberico
Idiazábal
Mahón
Manchego
Montenebro
Picos Blue
Queso de Murcia
Rey Cabra
Sierra de Zucheros
Tetilla

CASSOLETA

Typical of many Mediterranean coastal cheeses using goats' and sheep's milk, it is coagulated using thistle juice and the curds are moulded into volcano shapes. These are then pressed and sold in brine within a week. Often fried with peppers in Valencia, it is also used in salads in the same way as Mozzarella or Haloumi. TRONCHON is a similar cheese, but larger and usually older.

ETORKI

This Basque cheese, made from ewes' milk, is 20 cm (8 in) across by 10 cm (4 in) deep. The dappled rind is straw-yellow or rusty, the paste a shiny grey white. It is a mild dry cheese, with a strong accent of nuts and chestnuts. It can be lightly grilled.

GARROTXA

A compact goats' cheese from Catalonia with a blue-grey velvet bloom, the flavour is infused with crushed acorns, rye grass and wild flowers. It can be fried and served with olive paste and toast.

IBERICO

This variation on Manchego from central Castile (although now made across Spain) looks much the same but is made using a mix of sheep's and cows' milk. It is sold in four stages of maturity: after 20 days, vacuum-packed, when it will be white; after 30 days, when the outside is painted black; fully cured after three months, with a natural brown rind; and (not often found here) fully matured at six months, marked 'Anejo'.

IDIAZABAL

Highly expensive and revered in the Basque country, this hard-pressed sheep's-milk cheese is unlike other smoked cheeses in that the smoking is a traditional variation based on the shepherd's hut where it was hung in the chimney over the fire. It has a distinctive long flavour, 'subtle with three or four waves of hues'. It is usually only sold here in restaurants. Production of the cheese is now restricted to North-west Spain, under the EC Denomination of Origin.

MAHON

Eighteenth-century invaders brought the Friesian cow to Menorca and insisted the milk was used instead of sheep's milk to make a Cheddar-like cheese. Known as 'the Brit', it is flat, square, with rounded edges, it has a bright orange rind. It is unusual in that it is sold at different stages of ripeness: from 10 days, when it can eaten sliced with oil and peppers; semi-cured it becomes herbaceous and salty with a firm texture; later as it dries out it becomes hard and Gouda-like. The cheese has an EC Denomination of Origin, for island production.

MANCHEGO

A hard sheep's-milk cheese made only from the milk of the Mandega sheep, 20x10 cm (8x4 in), is brown with pretty latticework from where it has stood. Older Manchegos will be matured for up to 12 months, when they achieve an intense sourness and velvety taste. Younger, they tend to be buttery with a slightly chewy texture and a taste of apples and crushed walnuts. Such cheeses are served thinly sliced to allow to them to breathe, often with sherry. It makes a good alternative to Cheddar and Parmesan for people with an allergy to cows' milk. The cheese has an EC Denomination of Origin for the Castile La Mancha region.

** MONTENEBRO

Obscure but brilliant, only 40 of these goats' cheeses are exported here each month. The 7x10 cm (2¾x4 in) log is virgin white and smooth. Strongly creamy, it has sour verdant seaside notes.

PICOS BLUE

This round leaf-wrapped cheese, 9 cm (3½ in) across with well-spread mottled fleck, is possibly the strongest of all blues, 'all bluntness and no cream. Interesting but foot-soldierly'. An older version was creamy but with enormous blueing.

QUESO DE MURCIA

A goats' cheese weighing about 1 kg (450 lb), it is patterned top and bottom from the olive wood mould. It is sometimes made unsalted for desserts, in which it is usually mixed with cinnamon, nutmeg and honey.

** REY CABRA

From the Ronda, Malaga, this is the king of the goats' cheeses and arguably among the finest cheeses in Europe. Hard and about 25x35 cm (10x14 in) in size, it has an outstanding and perfectly delineated taste of nuts and purified lemons and salt, not even immediately recognizable as a goat's cheese.

SIERRA DE ZUCHEROS

Andalusian semi-soft round, 7 cm (2¾ in) across, goats' cheese which is firmly pressed and drained, then rubbed with salt and paprika. It has a brilliant orange rind with a straw lattice. It is crumbly, goaty, with a hint of smoky bacon, and is usually served at home with dried pressed fruit cake. An example had an intense flavour hinting mildly of oranges.

TETILLA

Expressively meaning 'a little breast' – more politely, known as PERILLA, or 'little pear' – this Galician cows'-milk cheese is sold with or without the rind. It is creamy, mild, elastic and full-fat. Production is controlled under EC Denomination of Origin.

VEGETABLES

E urope has been a collecting house for the world's vegetables. The first introductions came from China and Asia, probably with the Persian traders who sold them to the Greeks and Romans. The second generation arrived in the Dark Ages with the Moors, who brought aubergines, cauliflowers and other exotics from Africa to Spain.

The discovery of the New World was as much about finding new kinds of vegetables and fruits as it was about gold and silver. The mid-16th century sees the first mention of many vegetables, though this may be related as much to the rise of the first textbooks as to the vegetables themselves. Many still had to wait until the 19th century before there was any serious cultivation, certainly in this country.

How far the older varieties resemble what we now see is a matter for conjecture. Potatoes and cabbages as just two examples of vegetables that we know were very different. Gregor Mendel, a Czech, is credited with much of the early work on the genetics of vegetables and selective breeding, although much of his thinking was not generally accepted until after his death in 1884.

We might be said currently to be enjoying the fourth great age of the vegetable, with the development of new varieties — and even new vegetables — that can be moved across the globe to markets. Some of this is obvious — aubergines, courgettes, bell peppers, even mushrooms were unheard of in Britain as recently as the '50s, but are now a common feature of the supermarket shelf. Other changes have been more clandestine: for instance, potato varieties changed radically in the late '80s and commercial canners and freezers bought up exclusive rights on old varieties of peas.

All this change has brought vegetables to the front of food fashion after centuries when they were often generally mistrusted and their nutritional virtues overlooked, or they were cultivated purely for their perceived medicinal value. With this resurgence have come new ideas about cooking vegetables that have broken down traditional boundaries and introduced strategies from other parts of the globe. The vegetable is, in many ways, the great triumph of the global food economy.

LEAF VEGETABLES

The brassicas – cabbage, Brussels sprout, cauliflower, etc - have been somewhat unrecognized, possibly because they spent so much of this century sitting around in boiled water or smothered in a white sauce. They are cheap, nutritious and deserve rediscovery, combining well with the new flavourings like garlic and ginger.

The hothouse culture that has delivered fresh leaves to supermarkets throughout the year is one of the great triumphs of the past decade – even if we pay excessively for them compared to more traditional winter leaves. The mixed leaf combinations tend to be poorly understood by supermarkets and need careful sorting out. **Waitrose** now sells salad leaves still in the soil for extra freshness.

BROCCOLI

Nowadays the main property of broccoli – also known as SPROUTING BROCCOLI or CALABRESE – is the texture. Any other merits it once possessed have been bred out of almost all varieties, purple or green. Where great lengths are gone to with other vegetables, say asparagus, to point out the different cooking times needed for the tips and the stalks, with broccoli the consumer is handed two almost separate and quite distinct vegetables on the same stalk and expected to cope. These mini umbrellas are too old and too big for any serious cooking. Anything bigger than a thumb is past its culinary prime.

By contrast the relatively unexploited PURPLE SPROUTING BROCCOLI, available in early spring, shows the potential for flavour from the stalk, the leaves and the florets. Cook and serve it as asparagus.

Ways With Sprouts

Apart from boiling, they can be grated and then stir-fried, sautéed or puréed. The inherent nuttiness is reinforced in pairings with chestnut, hazelnuts and nut oils; or more traditionally, with cream and butter.

This is often mixed up with the PURPLE CALABRESE which arrives at the same time from the New World, most of whose colour is lost in an inky stain in the cooking water.

BRUSSELS SPROUT

The Belgians claim the Romans introduced these relatives of the Savoy cabbage, but they may be confusing it with broccoli. There was certainly serious cultivation there by the 13th century, which did not follow in England for another 600 years. Compact and tightly furled green – not yellowing – leaves are the best. Buy sprouts of a uniform size for consistency of cooking.

CABBAGE

The motherly cabbage is one of Europe's oldest vegetables. The Romans saw it poetically as a cure for melancholy and it was a staple to the Celts and Saxons. The French expression *petit choux* is more endearing than the colloquial English use of cabbage for a vegetating person – perhaps familiarity bred contempt... or over-cooking. In the kitchen it has the ability to surpass nearly all other vegetables and it has infiltrated the diet in ways which are often overlooked, like coleslaw, bubble and squeak, and sauerkraut.

The season of the cabbage starts in April with the first SPRING GREENS, which are all leaf and no heart, then follows leafy SPRING CABBAGE, and by July there is pointy-headed HISPI and PRIMO, with their tight bright, rugby ball shapes peaking out of stubby leaves. The first SAVOY starts in September, with the deep green SAVOY KING and the resplendent JANUARY KING beginning in November. The tight-leaved WHITE CABBAGE was originally from

Holland, but the wild cabbage may well have been native to our coastline.

CAVOLO NERO is the black Tuscan cabbage, in season in November to coincide with the new pressing of the olive oil. Some can be grown here, but is not produced on a commercial scale; some importing has begun recently.

Good cabbages are heavy, richly coloured and should squeak when squeezed. RED CABBAGES should have a grey blush on the outside, but rarely seem to. They need vinegar in the cooking to stop the colour fading. Very fresh cabbage leaves will actually weep.

CAULIFLOWER

This relative of the cabbage was first grown by the Syrians, Turks and Egyptians and only brought to Spain in the 12th century and to England in the 16th, possibly from Cyprus. Mark Twain famously said cauliflower was nothing but cabbage with a college education. He may have had a point.

New varieties have emerged with differently coloured florets. The so-called CAPE BROCCOLI, from South Africa, needs to be bought young and small; the turreted florets of ROMANESCO are disappointingly vapid compared to the traditional white curds – eaten raw there is some redemption.

CHINESE LEAVES

Chinese vegetables have begun to emerge out of Chinatown supermarkets into mainline shopping. Most just need simple steaming.

PAK-CHOI grows amazingly quickly – from seed to plant in six weeks, thus providing two crops per season. There is a lot of white for the money and it tends to need the

Ways With Cabbage

A cabbage needs either short cooking or long slow cooking, though some dietitians favour cooking it twice: first blanching it and then braising or sautéing it to make it more digestible. Soups, casseroles with bacon or chestnuts, and stuffed cabbage are found across Europe. More modern approaches, like wilting and stir-frying with smoked haddock, grating it and dressing it with hot vinegar or pairing it with singular strong flavourings like juniper or cider, show it to better advantage. To counter the sulphurous smell produced when boiling cabbage, add a corner of stale bread to the water.

Ways With Cauliflower

Cauliflower cheese was a highly fashionable and very rare dish in London at the start of the 19th century. Cauliflower has great potential for vegetarian dishes: with watercress sauce, with coriander, or with hollandaise.

kind of strong oyster sauces that Chinese restaurants use on it. It is sold both as a vegetable and young as an extra for salad. The leaves are warming, spicy, moist and sour, with a good texture. Raw it leans instinctively towards dressings with Oriental spices or soy in them, and can be rather dominating in leaf mixtures. There is a green variety; in both this and the white the brilliance of the colour is a mark of their freshness.

More interesting is CHOY-SIM, which has to be grown quickly to stop it going stringy. Like spinach, it should have decidedly more leaf than stalk. CHINESE MUSTARD GREENS are more large-scale, with stalk and leaf. KAI-LAN looks similar to Choy-sim, but has more stalk than leaf.

Although both these were both solely the province of Chinese restaurants and supermarkets until recently, they are now being planted under polypropylene on a commercial scale in Lincolnshire and are likely to become more widely available. Huge plantations around Valencia begin to send to Chinese supermarkets from April.

DANDELION

Forgotten in the hedgerows and rarely making the market, this is one of the oldest native foods still running wild. The young leaves were among the 'bitter herbs' of the Old Testament and go for the regional French dish of *salade de pissenlits au lard* – with crisp bacon and the fat poured over. The *pissenlit* refers to its diuretic qualities. Related to wild chicory, the plant's roots are also used as a coffee substitute sold in health-food shops. The flowers make a retsina-ish wine. In the American south they go for 'poke salad'. Older leaves need to be blanched and treated like spinach.

LETTUCES

The cost of designer salads is now on a par with wild mushrooms and fillet steak. The mark-ups on a whole lettuce are in the region of 1,000%. The only work involved is separating the leaves from four different lettuces and putting them in a bag. This is convenience at an astronomic price.

BATAVIA, with its large handsome crenellated leaf, has a strong flavour, bordering on the sour with traces of acidity and metal. Characterful and dominating, it has been said to be a 'very male' leaf.

BUTTERHEAD is a good but undervalued lettuce, with lolloping large soft pale green leaves about 20 cm (8 in) across when compressed. The outside leaves are bitter and sour with hints of grass; the heart on the other hand is white and sweet. This lovely interplay produces an interestingly varied flavour that shows off dressings and other herbs well.

COS, sometimes called ROMAINE, is increasingly out of fashion, but the staple for Caesar Salad. The long leaves have a crisp texture, but not much flavour.

ESCAROLE is the primary braising lettuce. A thicker-leafed version of frisée, with thick white stalks and green leaves, it is rough, bitter and chewy, with a interesting – slightly meaty – flavour and bitterness in the stalk.

FRISÉE is sometimes called ENDIVE. Like dandelion, this was one of the original 'bitter herbs' of the Bible. With thin stalks and wispish brackenish leaves which are yellow at the stalk becoming green at the edge, it is sweet and crunchy – only bitter at the stalk bases. Good, grassy and clean-tasting, it is cleansing, although its content of vitamins A and C is slightly down on other lettuces. The singular flavour is good with a blue cheese dressing, and it can also be blanched and served as a vegetable.

ICEBERG is the classic crisp and crunch lettuce: clean and wet, it is mostly texture and bite and the flavour is elusive, if at all apparent. It is also not as effective a palate-cleanser as frisée.

LAMB'S LETTUCE, sometimes called CORN SALAD, has small curly leaves with a mild peppery, floral – almost a pot-pourri – aroma. Not dissimilar to a gentler version of watercress but nearly twice the price, they are used to season other salads. **Waitrose** sells corn salad at an astonishing £6.75 per lb. **Marshall's** sell packets of seeds for 75p.

LITTLE GEM is the gardener's favourite. Deep green going to yellow at the centre, it is small and bullet-shaped. Soft-textured, it has a real lusciousness from the thickness of the leaf. The taste is almost floral and slow to assert itself. This is a good lettuce for braising. SWEETHEART GEM, developed by **Tesco**, is a gem lettuce in which the strains of sweetness have been bred on so the leaves are distinctly sugary with minimum bitterness.

LOLLO ROSSO is originally from Italy, but is now widely grown in the UK. Frilly and attractive, with a deep red fringe going to green in the centre, it has a good texture and is mildly bitter. Its popularity is more a matter of looks than flavour.

LOLLO BIONDO is the frilly light-green-leaved variation of Lollo Rosso. It has a neutral, rather sour taste, but a good texture.

*OAK LEAF, or FEUILLE DE CHÊNE, owes its name to the beautiful large oak-leaf-shaped leaves, deep red at the rim going to green deep inside. It is a very glamourous leaf, a queen to the Batavia's king'. The outside of the leaf is soft and smooth, verging on the sweet, but with bite. It is bitter and assertive by the stalk; so there are almost two tastes.

RADICCHIO

Related to chicory, these resplendently vermilion fused leaves paling to pure white have a beautifully crisp texture. In its native Italy it is often grilled, which does not help the colour, nor that distinctive gentle bitterness it gets from its cousin. It does not need overpowering with strong flavours, although it can handle them well enough.

ROCKET

Also known more pretentiously as ROQUETTE, the small 10 cm (4 in) long leaves are the most distinctive of all the salad leaves – indeed they are often listed as a herb when sold in pots – with a potent very sweet pepper taste and a texture that is strong and characterful, but still delicate enough to combine with other, milder leaves.

SORREL

Brought by the Romans from North Africa to Northern Europe, these arrow-shaped deep green leaves have a pronounced lemon sour, or vinegar, flavour. Used as vegetable in the Middle Ages, it may be cooked as spinach; alternatively, use it in salads, in soup or to flavour fish sauces (only the briefest heating is needed). It is high in vitamin C and was used against scurvy, but it also contains oxalic acid which may inhibit nutrient absorption. The commonest form is FRENCH SORREL, but BUCKLER SORREL is smaller-leafed and better for salad.

SPINACH

Younger spinach leaves can cost twice as much as older, which is proper testimony to their worth. Having endured the worst

---

Edible flowers

NASTURTIUMS were brought here from Central and South America, but are named after the old battle habit of piling defeated enemies weapons in a heap, the leaves look like shields and the flowers like blood-stained helmets. Known to the Romans as *tropaeum* (trophy) hence *Tropaeolum majus.* Easily grown from seed, they are now widely sold in supermarkets. The leaves, buds and flowers are all edible. The leaves are peppery, the flowers are very pretty in salads; the pickled buds are akin to capers. It is said chewing leaves will ease sore throats and the juice will clear pimples.

Ways With Spinach

The leaves should be washed and placed in a covered pan without any extra water over a moderate heat, squeezed dry when they have shrunk and then married off with cream, butter and sometimes a very little nutmeg. There is a famously unhealthy recipe from the great Fernand Point of Le Pyramide in Vienne in the '30s in which 900 g (2 lb) of spinach are cooked with ham and bread along with 170 g (6 oz) of butter, 300 ml (½ pt) of béchamel sauce, 6 tablespoons of double cream and 3 egg yolks.

excesses of over-boiling, zealous nannies giving children cups of spinach water and the bizarre inanity of Popeye, the rehabilitation of spinach is long overdue. The Arabs brought it to Europe, and it has been esteemed across the southern Mediterranean for centuries; used in tarts, with eggs, in salads, and also for its medicinal properties as the 'broom of the stomach'. It is a prime source of iron, calcium and vitamin A, although some say its high oxalic acid content works against their full benefit.

The summer leaves are round and in winter they are prickly seeded. Older spinach might have been designed for butter – it will absorb vast amounts.

WATERCRESS

Nasturtium officinale from the Latin *nasi tortium*, 'nose twisting' (from its pepperiness), as watercress is known horticulturally, grows in lazy running rivers and springs in sandy soil, almost exclusively now around Arlesford in Hampshire and in Dorset. It is a particularly good source of vitamins A and C and deserves rescuing from its ubiquitous fate as a garnish. Packets are usually poor value, containing the smaller (less developed) leaves and more stalk, and quickly going sour in their airless environment. Bunches tend to have good percentages of the better wider leaves. The pepperiness is concentrated in the stalks, which can be diverted for soups while the leaves go for saucing, salads and anything with eggs.

PODS & SEEDS

Pods and seeds are among the few types of vegetables with which freezing and canning really come into their own. Historically, corn, beans and peas were grown mostly for drying as winter staples. Massive plantings in Kenya have brought fresh vegetables to market all year round, but often the shelf-lives are too prolonged, and they are sold well past their superb best.

Beans
Beansprouts
Okra
Pea
Sweetcorn

BEANS

Green beans are a modern development. Even country people would have been inclined to keep most of their crop for drying and storing as food for winter or to grind to a flour (see Pulses, page 246). There are many varieties and variations, BROAD BEANS alone are known as SHELL BEANS in America or WINDSOR BEANS, FIELD BEANS and HORSE BEANS, which all pass in Latin as *Vicia faba*, with a parentage somewhere in South-east Asia.

Young BROAD BEANS, the size of a finger nail, are as fine a vegetable as young peas and maintain their allure even flown across the globe – unlike imported strawberries, even in February. Most broad beans now tend to come from Kenya, Egypt, Spain and Cyprus; while most of the UK crop goes for processing and PYO, where they are surprisingly early and usually finished before the full flush of strawberries begin.

Broad beans should be cooked or, as in the Mediterranean region where it is now heredi-tary, a condition called favism results in which the pollen from the plant creates anaemia and blood clotting. Dried broad beans are not widely stocked any more, but the price is linked to age and the cheaper usually the longer the cooking.

It was these that sustained the old world before Columbus brought back not just the potato but the RUNNER BEAN, the GREEN BEAN and the FRENCH BEAN from Central America.

RUNNER BEANS were initially grown for decorative use on the walls of kitchen gardens as they were known for their scarlet flowers, but they helped establish a culture of greenness as against a mealy brown. The strings that bedevilled the early plants, especially the red flowering rather than the white, have been largely bred out of modern strains. As ever, however, youth is a virtue and there is little indication of varieties in markets or supermarkets so comparison is difficult.

FRENCH BEANS are so-called for their popularity in France after being introduced from America. They are the immature bean that would otherwise produce an haricot. The home-grown beans are harvested from June. Kenya supplies all year, but the quality seems to be getting increasingly slack.

Beans should snap when they are broken open and not limp around like impotent drunks. All three freeze after being blanched.

BEANSPROUTS

These are usually from MUNG BEANS. Immigrant Chinese families brought the culture with them growing in small dustbins in their back rooms for family restaurants. They are a prolific crop, going from seed to sprout in four days. This has spawned a factory industry with warehouses able to produce 50 tonnes a day. Much is made of the nutritional advantages of sprouts, which seems in inverse proportion to their cost.

OKRA

Also known as GUMBO or LADY'S FINGERS, okra is the young seed pod of the *Hibiscus esculentus*. Okra came from West Africa with the slave trade and was adopted by the Caribbean and the American South.

It is one of the mallow family, related to cotton. Its fibrous mucilaginous juices are principally used as a thickener in soups and stews, most famously in Creole gumbos or stewed with pork in the Caribbean. It has also been accepted into other cuisines; in India it is steamed as a vegetable – *bindi* – and in the Middle East it is pickled.

Originally it was imported into this country only in tins, but it has surfaced in supermarkets and ethnic grocers. The pods should be perfectly green, not brown, and not more than 10 cm (4 in) long. They can be salted like aubergines to reduce the stickiness. Cook the pods whole or sliced lengthwise to show the beautiful spokes. The seeds can be roasted and ground to make a coffee substitute.

PEA

The large commercial freezers and packers of peas have taken the copyright in their strains of pea and bought out the best seeds. What is left is found in gardeners catalogues or the few stragglers that manage to get to market. The *Yorkshire blue* was a highlight of the year but seems to have disappeared. Greengrocers tend to buy according to grower rather than variety. The pea has a schizophrenic history. In French and Italian courts they were eaten by hand as little snacks. The Romans reputedly ate them like popcorn as they watched the gladiators. Before potatoes, they provided the poor with a basic staple: the basis for soups such as Scotch Broth.

PETITS POIS are literally young – therefore sweeter, riper – peas than those which go for splitting and drying. In practice, though, the

Price comparisons between fresh, frozen and tinned peas are complicated by the packaging which splits brands into sizes as various as 907 g, 410 g, 340 g and 145 g – not to mention **Bird's Eye's** commitment to 1 lbs, and other devices that seem to offer 20% more or less. The big difference is between cans and bottles on the one hand, and frozen on the other. **Sainsbury** makes some attempt to indicate the difference by saying 'Continental'. In frozen peas, the gradation to 'garden peas' is essentially as much about size – they are probably the equal in flavour across the board. **Bird's Eye** has some justification in claiming to pick only the smallest and the sweetest. **Lindsey Manor** is most uniform. The difference between **Sainsbury's** 'Garden', 'Economy' and 'Peas' is so subtle as to be irrelevant.

In tins, **Green Giant** 'Small peas', with added sugar and salt, are closer to the French-style petits pois, while **Morton's** look sensationally green thanks to the colouring and the use of added flavours. **Sainsbury** cans are indistinct and vapid, and a poor buy compared to frozen. Processed and marrowfat peas seem to acquire more liquid in the can possibly on the argument that – because they are mealier and more distinct in flavour – fewer go further. The big brands like **Farrows** and **Batchelors** are bravely slimy and ooze gently out of their skins in a manner much closer to that of the historic pea, betraying a cousinage to something like a chickpea. **Safeway** colours its processed peas. *Sainsbury does not, but then adds sugar to what it terms its 'marrow fats'

trade glosses over the difference between young peas and the much mealier beige French varieties which just took the name. Very old pre-war varieties like *Onward* and *Kelvedon Wonder* are still widely available for amateur gardeners, who can get crops through to October – but few get to market after August. SUGAR PEAS and MANGE-TOUT PEAS are pea pods that are picked even younger, before the peas themselves have developed; the imports from Kenya and the new world have been massively successful. (See also Pulses, page 246.)

SWEETCORN

Whereas maize is one of the most important staple crops of middle-America, supplying all needs from liquor to cattle to grits, here it remains rather daintily in the realms of the etiquette of how to eat a corn on the cob. In Italy (as polenta) and in Africa, corn is and has been an essential – the last crop before starvation, what the broad bean was to early Europe. In other countries corn is red, purple, black, brown. Here it is steadfastly yellow. Until the '40s, sweetcorn was only grown for fodder. GIs stationed here are credited with introducing it to this country.

Freshness is absolute, the more so with the older varieties. An old expression in the American South says to take the pot to the field and not pick it until the water has boiled. New varieties have, however, improved the keeping qualities. The old advice about only buying creamy coloured kernels is only relevant to older varieties (not that they are named in the shops) and new varieties can colour to golden. Fresh corn will ooze a milk if you nick the kernel with a fingernail, but as quite a few people know this trick it is worth checking that you are not buying a well-thumbed cob. Sweetcorn is invariably boiled, but it also bakes and roasts well.

Tinned sweetcorn, sold either as creamed or whole kernel, is arguably superior to fresh because of the steep decline that corn goes into when picked. There is really no contest between tinned and frozen, but unlike peas it is the tins that win hands down. New 'light' versions have been introduced although in the case of **Green Giant** there is no clue as to why one is 'light' and the other not, because neither adds sugar and the label just infers that one variety is naturally sweeter. Light versions are more insipid and super-market own-labels boost the impact with doses of sugar and salt. **Sainsbury** own-label borders closely on the overly sweet. The best is probably the ordinary **Green Giant** and the **Safeway** usweetened. **Citation** from France are vacuum-sealed without water, but are sadly dry as a result. To achieve the creamed consistency **Green Giant** uses cornstarch and sugar, which makes the contents very soupy and sweet.

Ways With Tinned Sweetcorn

For a tinned sweetcorn salad: hard-boil 2 eggs, shell and quarter them. Quarter 2 tomatoes. Mix together with a 500 g (1 lb 2 oz) tin of sweetcorn, using the juices for the dressing. Season with a generous amount of freshly ground black pepper.

ROOTS, TUBERS & BULBS

Root vegetables have sustained populations all over the world for millennia. Attempts at different varieties in supermarkets seem half-hearted excuses for increasing mark-ups. Often the differences between varieties seem poorly understood, with the prime being sold cheaper than the everyday. Large differences in price attach to packaging – loose, in boxes, or washed. In mitigation, root vegetables start from very low price points. It is hard to understand the economics of bringing something across Europe to sell it for less than 20p per lb.

BEETROOT

Beetroot originates from the southern Mediterranean region, possibly North Africa. The Greeks and Romans used it for its leaves, but it was brought on by German gardeners in the Middle Ages.

There are other beets in the family, notably SUGAR BEET, developed in the 17th century and taken on by Napoleon when his supplies of cane sugar were threatened, as well as SWISS CHARD and the fodder MANGEL WURZEL. The Victorians were enthusiastic about beetroot and reputedly even sold the juice as a hair pomade. Although the red is standard, there are occasional white, yellow (unfortunately named *Burpees*) and pink varieties found in seed catalogues – as well as a cylindrical variety.

Young beets are sold with the leaves from June, the main crop following six weeks later. A deeper colour indicates a longer, unforced growth cycle; too large and they become fibrous. Its public image is rather that of a throwback to a vegetable Stone Age, a yobbish and unruly vegetable that stains the kitchen and the grocer's bench and has to be constrained by tight plastic bonding before being allowed into the sanitized glare of the supermarket. It is maligned as a lost cause. Many are cooked at the farm and drenched in acetic acid which may account for their poor standing. The ready-cooked vacuum-packed long shelf-life types are at best 'emaciated' (**Safeway**) and at worst 'disgusting' (**Sainsbury**).

Beetroots need more cooking than one suspects, and are best baked slowly in foil until the skin comes away easily. If they are pronged, they leach messily. Stains can be removed with lemon juice, but the betanine compounds invariably stain the digestive tract. Like artichoke, beetroot is best served tepid. An inexpensive vegetable, properly cooked it can be sublime.

> **Ways With Beetroot**
>
> They combine well with grown-up assertive flavours like oranges, apples, capers, anchovies, nut oils and horseradish. The way they sustain all the variations of the Russian classic beetroot soup, *borscht*, stresses their adaptability. For the colour, do not over-cook or just add it at the end of cooking.

CARROT

The carrot was found wild across most of Europe, though early varieties tended to be yellow or purple rather than the more familiar red – which reportedly came from Afghanistan. The idea that carrots help you see in the dark was first put about by the Ministry of Defence in 1940 anxious to ensure that their vitamin A content was used to counter deficiencies that might lead to night blindness. Their vitamin C content is almost as high. Most of the nutrients lie near the surface, so carrots should only be peeled if it is really necessary. The pale central stalks are worthless and tasteless, and best removed.

Carrots have become a slothful somnolent giant occupying acres of shelf space with seemingly little enterprise behind them, content to be seen as everyday bulking agents. In 1987 **Safeway** moved towards identifying different varieties: the small, sweet *Parisienne*; the tapered, tangy *Chantenay*; the sweet, crisp *Mokum*; and the prime juicer *Zino*. This enthusiasm seems to have waned lately. The round carrots featured in gardening catalogues are rarities. The old trade practice of differentiating the new season's carrots by selling them with their leaves is two-edged as the leaves suck out moisture quickly. Improvements in packaging with micro-perforations has compensated. UK growers claim to have their carrots in the shops within 24 hours, against imports at a week.

The legacy of carrot jams, cakes and wines is a reminder of their dexterity and role as a source of sweetness for all cooking, as well as their endless friendliness towards flavourings like orange, lemon and lime, herbs like thyme and marjoram and coriander, and even stronger influences like Pernod and nut oils.

CELERIAC

The other name for celeriac, TURNIP-ROOTED CELERY, explains its ancestry more accurately. It was developed in Europe by Renaissance gardeners and brought here in 1723. It is a winter root available from October. The best are younger – about 450 g (1 lb) in weight, with smoother skin so there is less waste. The leaves are sometimes used to flavour soups, but are rarely sold now. The root should be firm with no signs of softness or mushiness. Once peeled of its hairy brown skin, the flesh discolours quickly and needs to be kept in acidulated water. It is an assertive and powerful vegetable that pairs well with other strong flavours that can take advantage of its fennel/aniseed tones. It is usually cheap so represents very good value.

GARLIC

The properties of this potent bulb are all about where it is grown. It is a cultivar and the shapes and characteristics come from the preferences of the growers in different regions. In Lautrec they favour a strong, leek-like spike in the centre. In Venice the whiteness of the skin is paramount. The heat of the flavour, it is said, derives from the length of the days. Longer growing times and colder nights mixed with hot days, as in Portugal, Turkey and Hungary, produce the most fiery .

The potency lies in a compound, alicin, which comes about when the garlic is cut, mixing the naturally present chemicals allinin and allinase. For the same reason, the way garlic is cut, crushed or squashed affects its virulence. Cooking actually arrests the process; as it cooks it loses its bitterness and becomes sweet, with hints of artichoke and potato, or in the rose variety, chestnut.

Early books concentrated on garlic's medicinal virtues; it was a poor man's cure-all. It was used against leprosy and the plague and was left in saucers at times of cholera to dispel evil spirits – which may be linked to its role in tales of vampires. Right up to the First World War it was mixed with sphagnum moss as an antiseptic.

Coincidentally or not, it is associated with diets where there is a low instance of heart disease – even accommodating some of the more unexplained areas that the fashionable Mediterranean diet does not, South-west France and Korea in particular.

For centuries cookery writers rejected it: John Evelyn, Mrs Beeton, Escoffier – even, quite recently, Tom Stobart – were against it. The cult of garlic is strictly a modern-day phenomenon. The festival in Gilroy, California – which produces 90% of American garlic – started in the '60s now attracts tens of thou-

ELEPHANT GARLIC is a cross between an onion and garlic. Grown in Chile, the giant bulbs are sold ceremonially boxed and are very mild, like an oversized shallot, with a slightly sour smell that becomes like sticky vanillas. It is overpriced for what it is, at five times the price of ordinary garlic.

SMOKED GARLIC is an increasingly fashionable trick. The smoke overpowers the garlic but some say that it 'adds the smell of smoking bonfires to a casserole'. Others hold that it 'smells out the shopping basket with stale farts'.

sands of participants each year. The Isle of Wight Festival in August attracts 30,000. Across France each region has its own excuse for a fair.

The garlic season begins with the first trimmings and wild garlic arrives from France in May. The tiny purple bulbils are as potent as whole cloves. Fresh garlic is briefly available in June and July, but rarely found here. The peak is at the end of August, when the two big French growing areas – Lautrec (for *rosé*, or pink) and Beaumont – have had enough time to dry on the *grappe* (plaited string) and these begin to come to market and then slowly the more northerly areas follow.

The best garlics are the pink from **LAUTREC – especially **Lucien Cadayon** – and the white from **BEAUMONT. The Lautrec tends to keep its potency beyond November. Other areas produce good garlics, but most of what is sold in this country is poorly graded by comparison. Italian garlic can be as good: the **VENETIAN-STYLE is brilliantly white-skinned, heavy, strong and keeps well. NAPLES-STYLE is rounder and flatter and does not keep so long. CALIFORNIAN GARLIC is derived from Italian. SPANISH is particularly valuable early in the summer, when the supermarkets are filled with very poor and brutal examples from Mexico and USA. English garlic, from the ISLE OF WIGHT, is not to be instantly dismissed; based on cultivars from the Auvergne, it suffers from peaking at the same time as everyone else. EGYPTIAN tends to be small-cloved and does not cook well, but is chilli hot – if briefly so. There are persistent rumours that the Chinese are about dump vast quantities on the world market.

The trade buys on the size of the cloves, because restaurants do not want to pay to peel smaller ones. Solid bulbs are what are wanted. Out of season, a big bulb may not correspond to bigger cloves, especially in early summer when there is a lot of rubbish about. The age of garlic can be told from the size of the kernel and the growth of the sprout in the centre. It keeps better on the *grappe* than singularly.

JAPANESE ARTICHOKE

Also known as the CHINESE ARTICHOKE or, sometimes, CROSNE, these pretty and unusual tiny rootoid ringlets, not more than 6.5 cm (2¾ in) long, are originally from central and northern China, though the French village of Crosne adopted them in the last century. Available from October to March, they have no skin and are used raw or lightly baked or stir-fried.

JERUSALEM ARTICHOKE

A variety of sunflower (*Helianthus tuberosis*) native to north America, this was first identified in 1605 and brought to the Netherlands two years later to be cultivated. The association with the flavour of artichokes was the reason for that part of the name, and the other is a corruption of the word *girasole*, French for sunflower.

The wasteful knobbliness of early varieties and their justified reputation as a flatulent, made them unfashionable. Old textbooks harshly denigrated them as 'sweet but soapy', but they do have a commercial use as a source of alcohol fructose which has sustained them.

They are easy winter vegetables to grow and available from October to March. Imported varieties take Russian-sounding names, like early, very white *Bianka* and attractive *Topianka*; while UK plantsmen favour *Fuseau*, which is almost nodule-free.

Peel and keep in acidulated water; then steam, bake or microwave, or roast in their skins. They go well with potatoes and asparagus, but their strong flavour needs to star in any combination.

KOHLRABI

Introduced from Germany around 1558, for centuries kohlrabi was regarded primarily as fodder for sheep. More tender than other root vegetables, because it grows on top of the soil, it is part of the cabbage family and most often likened to turnip. The leaves can be eaten but do not store well; nor do the roots freeze well, except when very small. They are an excellent buy in early summer.

GREEN KOHLRABI has a thick lime-green skin and a bowling-ball shape about 8 cm (3¼ in) across, with spooky tendrils. It is an underrated vegetable. Raw it has a mild celery-to-turnip taste and some of the texture of good potatoes; steamed the turnip flavour develops and the texture is arguably better.

PURPLE KOHLRABI is slightly larger and nuttier, with peppery overtones. Raw, it has a flavour akin to an apple/potato; but when cooked it seems more of a marrow/turnip. A good buy.

LEEK

There are different theories as to the origins of the leek. Some texts say Europe, even more precisely Switzerland, and others think points further east. They have been cultivated for a very long time, and leeks were often a second crop in southern Mediterranean vineyards.

Most of the leeks here are home-grown, with first samples coming as early as July, grown under polythene, or from France. Most of the work on the breeding of varieties has concentrated on the keeping qualities so that leeks pulled in March can hang on in over the spring.

Good leeks are young and erect, with a good percentage of white. New washing techniques have cut out the perennial problem of flushing out the dirt trapped between the leaves. The huge allotment award-winning leeks are inedibly bitter.

ONION

Onions are the most universal of foods eaten in every country, almost it seems as far back as the Persians. Quite what happened to *Danver's Yellow, Nuneham Park, Blood Red* and *Giant Rocca* is not a matter of culinary record. Ailsa Craig survives in some seed catalogues, as does *Bedfordshire Champion*. However, the varieties that dominate postwar allotments have disappeared for the most part, to be replaced with shovelfuls of unidentified Spanish or obscure Japanese varieties that can over-winter. Warmer climates mean larger and sweeter bulbs.

The new season's crop is usually available by September, but the sophisticated storage methods used for onions can obscure the differences between the new and the not-so-new. In fresh onions there will be no sign of sprouting in the central core. Good onions will also be firm and well-coloured.

The skin lends colour to stocks and casseroles. Once cut, they lose their potency. Keeping them in the fridge cuts down their ability to make you cry as you peel, as will peeling and cutting under water.

The beautiful RED ONIONS seem more different than they are: the exquisite purple casing around a deep white inside offer higher notes and a sharp cleansing juiciness. As

Ways With Onions

Onions were always poor man's food and there is a great repository of hearty recipes for stuffing them. An old peasant recipe from Provence blanches whole onions and garlic, removes the central core of the onion, pounds this with the garlic and some olive oil and puts this back into the onion to bake coated in breadcrumbs. A white sauce with onion was traditional with lamb. These ideas have been overtaken by more fashionable dishes like French onion marmalade or glazed onions.

they cook, however, the true differences between onions are in levels of sweetness: the red being much higher pitched – a trumpet to a Spanish onion's bassoon – but with sufficient complexity to be served raw.

PICKLING ONIONS: the gleamingly white *Paris Silverskin*, about the size of a marble, survives as a variety for gardeners and professional growers. There is also the darker-skinned and larger *Giant Zittau*.

The SHALLOT is a small clustering variation of the common onion, cultivated originally around Bordeaux. They are stronger than onions, but have less smell. There are different varieties: grey brown, blush pink and – most common – bronze, which are known for their longer keeping. Unlike onions, they should not be browned or they will become bitter: braise them slowly. They are preferred by restaurant cooks as a more subtle variation on onions, with more of the positive notes of garlic without the smell,

SPRING ONIONS are merely young onions forced for their stalks. The long-standing *White Lisbon* first established itself as an early crop and remains defiant in the face of competition from Japanese hybrids. WELSH ONIONS are not Welsh at all, but from Siberia; they are coarser and longer-lasting, because the bulb does not form.

PARSNIP

As with many indigenous vegetables, parsnips were always said to be at their best after the first frost of the year. Native to Britain, it has been cultivated here since Roman times, although often despised as food for cattle or as overly sweet compared to other roots, like carrots. They respond well to other flavours, especially seeds like sesame or pine nuts, and the stronger spices like turmeric and ginger, and butter – as in the saying 'soft words butter no parsnips.

POTATO

The potato season was officially opened with the delivery of the first Jersey Royals to the Queen on April 26. Now the ceremony is gate-crashed by earlier Egyptians and Sirema from Noirmoutier followed by an unholy rush from Cornwall, Pembroke and all points south.

Potatoes were discovered in the high Peruvian Andes between 1531 and 1536. The high plateau remains a huge and largely untapped resource of black, blue and mis-shapen specimens that might yet again source the world for another 500 years. These first specimens brought back by the Conquistadors may well have been sweet potatoes. Walter Raleigh was the real enthusiast and planted some on his estate in County Cork. At first they were reviled and treated with suspicion, and it remains unclear just what happened to turn them into one of the world's most essential crops.

By the time of the famines of 1845 Ireland had become a one-crop nation, and when that crop failed hundreds of thousands died. It was also the Irish who are credited with taking the potato back to North America, where they were called 'Murphys'. The cultivation of potatoes began seriously in England in the 1750s, when they started to appear in large numbers on the London markets. By 1836, no less than 136 different varieties were being grown commercially. This was not a healthy and forgotten seed bank, rather it is a list of species that have evolved against blight, scab, disease and viral infections. The potato is a fickle and fragile plant.

The height of the potato's popularity was in

1870, when it occupied almost twice the acreage it does today. The potato was a common man's food and was the first expression of the allotment. The country gardener grew for himself; the commercial grower grew for the cities.

The test of an early potato is the skin, if still soft and pliable then the potato is still young.

ARRAN COMET is one of the large Arran family developed by the great Scottish grower Donald Mackelvie. The COMET was introduced in 1956 after his death and for two decades was a major potato from Cornwall. They bulk up quickly and tend to be sold either as small new or large. The younger versions are long, yellowy brown with darker pocks; the dense white flesh with a starburst of sweetness. Growers now see it as a rather dated crop.

*BELLE DE FONTENAY is one of the oldest potatoes still in circulation, dating back to 1885. Although posing growers difficulty, particularly in dry years, they have been continually esteemed at the table, especially in salads. Larger and fatter than La Ratte, they are also darker with a silken smooth egg-shell skin. Soft on first bite, the flavour builds into butteriness and goes well with oils and vinaigrettes.

CARA is a highly fashionable potato among growers. Originally from Ireland, it responds well to growing conditions in Cyprus and Egypt. One of the better baking potatoes widely found, it is not quite as good as the King Edward which it is replacing.

*CARLINGFORD was introduced from Ireland in 1982, with a very classic old-fashioned sense about it. Well favoured by **Marks & Spencer**, the light brown skin turns grey/beige. The white flesh smells a little of socks, but is creamy and distinctive. It is good boiled, steamed or microwaved.

**CHARLOTTE is a new French variety first introduced in 1981 and now starting to be grown here. Pear-shaped and often slightly larger than the smallest new or salad potatoes, it is the rising star of the potato world. They are brilliant boiled, or baked they taste of pure chestnuts. Use either in salads or as a main vegetable.

CLEOPATRA is a new early variety introduced in 1981. Red, like Désirée, and speckled and blemished, they have firm, dense flesh that has high flavour notes. It promises more than it delivers and is only suitable for boiling.

CORNISH used to enjoy a similar standing to Jersey Royals, which they have sought to exploit; though much of the acreage has gone over to a new variety, COLMO, first introduced in 1979. It is small round dark-skinned and white-fleshed and inclined to wateriness in the cooking. Missing the classic dry chestnutty finish, it is a side-show rather than a main event.

DÉSIRÉE is a red variety introduced from Holland in 1961 and widely grown around the world. It is liked by the trade as it is a heavy cropper and is a familiar sight at many farm shops. The flavour is pronounced and it is best used for roasting.

DIAMANT are brought in as new potatoes in January. The small examples from Egypt tend to be underdeveloped and inoffensive, with tones of chestnuts in the background – but also that 'Smashy' flavour.

DUNBAR was one of the great potatoes of the '30s, with varieties like CAVALIER, ROVER and YEOMAN. A long wide potato, it has slightly greying skin which is cracked like that of an old man. Tending to absorb a lot of water, it seems poor in today's company.

ESTIMA is much liked by the trade because it is high yielding; the tubers bulk up early, but can stay happily in the ground afterwards. First introduced in 1973, it has established itself as an everyday potato. It is a classic example of a trade that ignores flavour. Mashed, they taste very white and institutional; they tend to break up as a roast; baking pronounces its vapid cardboard taste. A lot of very poor samples are found in spring and early summer, dumped on the market and quick to sprout.

JERSEY ROYALS were first introduced to Jersey around 1879 by Hugh de La Haye and swiftly became the main agricultural preoccupation on the island, until eventually the Jersey States department ruled that no other potato should be grown. It is now only grown on Jersey, where the soil seems uniquely adapted. Although prohibitively expensive in early May, by June they become widely affordable. Despite the growing competition, this is still a wonderful and unique potato. Brown and kidney-shaped, with a fragile skin, it has a strong body and a distinctive chestnut flavour.

KING EDWARD enjoys a legendary reputation which has been encroached on in recent decades. It was developed originally from a seed stock called *Fellside Hero* in Northumberland in 1902 and within four years was already well-known. For the first half of the century it was the most popular potato in Britain, second only in planting to the *Majestic* (eventually to fall victim of skin russeting and bad cracking). The King Edward was vigorous and a good cropper, but inclined to be erratic in dry seasons.

It is as a roasting and baking potato that it is primarily known, though it boils well enough. Although it does not enjoy the same status as it once did in previous decades, it remains a good benchmark against which to judge new breeds.

**LA RATTE is another very old variety, dating back to 1872. For many years it was disliked by English gardeners, who found the small tubular growths proliferating everywhere in their beds. New seeds have come over from France and imports are being revived. Outstanding and justly famous, it has milky brown, innocent-looking skin which is slightly marked; the cream flesh has notes of chestnuts and sour greens, rising to a second taste of sweetness.

LINZER DELIKATESS, introduced from Austria in 1976, was designed as a salad potato to rival La Ratte – which it does not. Tubular, going to pear shape when larger, it has a creamy soft yellow nutty skin, with a smell of bitter honey. It is a good minor potato.

MALAGA is large and clumsy. Usually sold washed, it is a good potato but not in the company of other new varieties.

MARFONA was introduced in 1977 and mainly now comes from Cyprus. A beige yellow, lightly marked, it has a sour nutty flavour. Better than Estima, but...

MARIS PIPER, the favourite of chip shops, was introduced in 1963 and took up the position vacated by the Majestic, though its merits as a mainline potato are increasingly being brought into question by foreign imports. It remains the biggest planted potato here, but breaks up easily on boiling and prefers the tougher treatment of baking, roasting and chipping. It needs the right soil to be grown in gardens – neither too light nor too heavy.

MONA LISA was introduced in 1984 and comes mostly from Portugal. They tend to be large for new potatoes, fat square ovoids, beige/yellow on the outside; waxy inside with a floury texture. A good mainstream new potato, but not special, it has a well-rounded flavour of sour chestnuts.

NADINE was only introduced in 1987, is now widely found in supermarkets, and often organic. White to yellow, with a smell of chestnuts, the deathly white flesh has a cloying acrid aftertaste and breaks up easily.

NICOLA, derived from German stock, was introduced in 1973 and is now a popular potato from Cyprus, Egypt and Morocco. It is said to be a stronger version of a Wilja, which is hardly a compliment. It is best boiled as an everyday potato, and not really worth paying a premium price for it.

NOIRMOUTIER is from the island of the same name, which – like Jersey – is one of the fabled isles south of Nantes where the sandy soil and the algae produce a special potato. The island is all oysters and potatoes. The first, *Charlottes*, are highly prized and arrive about the first week of June and run through to September. Before that is the *Sirtema*, which is a little fragile to be said to be in the same class, but is neatly rounded and with good skin and texture.

**PINK FIR APPLES are the oldest potato still commonly sold in supermarkets and are enjoying a revival 144 years after they were first introduced. Distinctively elongated and shaded a pink that turns to a mellow beige-yellow on cooking, it is meant for salads and serving cold in the skin. With an excellent mealy, soft texture – like condensed clouds of potato – it also has a shrill nose and slight sourness, turning to an overwhelming sweet surge, with a long-lasting taste of clear chestnuts. A very good potato, it keeps quite well without losing its 'new potato' flavour.

ROMANO has an attractive red skin which pales in cooking into pastel shades of either mahogany in baking or mauve in boiling. The flesh is cloudy: baked it is inoffensive and weedy; boiled it has a nutty-neutral mildness. The skin is quite edible and the texture holds up, but the flavour is slightly reminiscent of dirty socks. The quality is very variable from area to area.

**ROSEVAL looks spectacular on the supermarket shelf, with its deep red – almost purple – skin. First developed in 1950, it was until recently quite rare, but is now increasingly common as an import from France. A mild version of La Ratte, the distinctive pinky to deep red/chestnut small kidney-shaped ovals, contain parchment flesh which is tinged yellow and has an alcoholic perfume, redolent of warm chestnuts. This good, well-balanced mix of flavours and skin is a good match for salmon.

SANTÉ is a new main-crop variety introduced in 1985. It is a good roasting potato, especially brushed with olive oil. Baked or boiled, it is innocuous and needs peeling. It has a good texture and a slightly sour grassy taste.

SIEGLINDE, although listed in textbooks as rare, is a 1930s variety which provided the parentage for Linzer Delikatess and was being sold in supermarkets in some volume this year from Cyprus. The long ovals with yellow skin have a chestnut smell and nutty taste; quite soft, they break up in mouth.

VIOLET, sometimes called TRUFFE DE CHINE, is brought over from France either for the restaurant trade or for upmarket **Sainsbury** stores. They are deep purple ovoids, sometimes with eyes, a rough skin and bleeding violet. We have had two examples in the last year: the one direct from Rungis in September was floury and had a superb mild taste of chestnuts; another later in the year from **Sainsbury**, apparently a snip at 99p per lb was blue-skinned, with a rough outside and a watery texture. Unattractive and unappealing, it had the looks of a drowned body and a vapid flavour... a bit of an off-putting silly novelty.

WILJA may have peaked after 15 successful years; it is now being replaced by new varieties. Developed in 1972, within eight years it had occupied 11% of UK fields, overcoming the perceived problem of the yellowness of its flesh. It is best known for its boiling qualities.

Although not even distantly related (they are actually members of the *convolvulus* family), SWEET POTATOES are native to tropical America and remain an important subsistence crop. They were almost certainly the first potatoes Columbus brought back, pre-dating the common potato by some decades, possibly even by a century. The potatoes Shakespeare mentions were certainly sweet potatoes, and were used in pies.

There are two kinds: the white-skinned and the red-skinned, both with yellow waxy flesh. The white are drier, not so rich and less dense. Both cook in the same time as ordinary potatoes, but do not keep as well. Their rich sweetness responds to tropical flavourings like brown sugar and cinnamon.

RADISH

The family relationship with turnip and horseradish describes them well. Radishes are an ancient food, cultivated in China and Japan for millennia for their freshness and looks. Here they have become the province of the gardener, with seed catalogues offering different kinds: from the perfectly formed deep crimson globes of *Cherry Belle* to the elongated white-tipped *French Breakfast 3*. In the shops they are still just plain old radishes.

In France and Italy they are eaten with sea salt as a starter. They are rich in vitamin C. Medium-sized ones are the best; any larger and they become woody. They are overlooked as a cooked vegetable, and can make attractive gratins with cream or glazed with sugar or

honey as a vegetable to accompany meat.
They lose their crispness within 48 hours with
the leaf on. Packets tend to be cheaper (they
don't have the weight of the leaf) and are
longer-lasting but less pretty.

The almost 1 m (3 ft) long MOOLI or
JAPANESE RADISH is from the same family,
but is a less attractive creamy white without
the sharp peppery heat.

SALSIFY

This has enjoyed bouts of fashionability
across Europe at different times, though outside of country areas it has rarely established
itself as part of the dietary currency in this
country. It used to be called the 'vegetable
oyster', because the taste was said to be similar. It appears from October through the winter and the slender beige roots are surprisingly delicate; they bleed easily and discolour
quickly once the skin is off and need keeping
in acidulated water. They are easier to peel if
first soaked overnight. Raw, they go in salads; cooked they are usually boiled or
steamed and then finished with a stronger
medium, like butter or chicken stock.

SCORZONERA is from the same family,
but has a black skin and so is sometimes
called BLACK SALSIFY. Its survival has been
as much to do with its supposed medicinal
qualities – against snake bites and leprosy in
particular.

SWEDE

A varietal form of the turnip (as is rape),
known in America as RUTABAGA, it was
introduced here in 1781 via Sweden from
Bohemia and usurped the place of the turnip
in much of northern cooking – which is why
recipes confuse them. They are a true winter

vegetable and should be firm and strongly yellow to orange in colour. They are best in mashes with violent flavourings, like pepper and horseradish; or roasted or consigned to stews and casseroles, where they can make their presence felt. Most famously, mashed swede or 'neeps' is traditional with haggis.

TURNIP

The swede arrived much later and replaced the turnip in northern cooking. Today the distinction is plain: turnip is a spring vegetable when young; swede a winter stalwart. The turnip has history on its side. The Romans cultivated them – the name comes from the Latin *napus* and it was a staple before the potato and used as cattle fodder.

However, it was looked down on. The French for a cock-up is a *navet*. Their poor standing comes from being too old and too big. The best are small, the smaller the better, and should be cooked with flavourings that emphasise their sweetness, like honey or orange. Very young, they can be served raw with just a vinaigrette containing some herbs.

The tops used to be sold separately; peppery leaves that can provide different dimensions to spinach recipes. While this practice is still common in Europe and the southern states of America, it has died out here.

Many recipe books suggest recipes for turnip and swede are interchangeable, but that mis-states the case for both. Any turnip that can do the job of a swede is too old.

SQUASHES

The replacement of the huge tasteless watery marrow by the petitely perfumed courgette symbolizes the transition of food shopping from one era to another. The arrival of squashes possibly heralds yet another. They provide challenging new frontiers for the cook.

Courgette
Cucumber
Marrow
Pumpkin
Squash

COURGETTE

Elizabeth David is credited with the arrival of courgettes here, where their larger brothers the marrow had previously dominated. Seed catalogues are now expansive, with yellow and even striped variations, some of which occasionally arrive in the shops.

On a good courgette the skin will still be tough enough to resist a fingernail. The best are small, cigar-shaped and need to be eaten swiftly. They will keep in the salad drawer though their flavour becomes elusive. They can absorb other flavours in casseroles, most famously in *ratatouille*, but are versatile enough to accommodate strong herbs like fennel or rosemary and will soak up oil like aubergines if they are not salted first. In restaurants, they are served decoratively with the flower still on, often stuffed with a light mousse or shallow-fried.

CUCUMBER

The cucumber originated in the Himalayan foothills, and found its way to ancient Egypt. It used to be colourfully graded as 'Fine', 'Bastards' (misshapen), 'Chumps' (big), 'Double Chumps' (seedy) and 'Spotted' (marked). There are two kinds: the familiar long thin HOTHOUSE or FRAME CUCUM-

FOOD *watch*

MINI VEGETABLES

These are ordinary vegetables picked young using conventional seeds that favour good looks at an early stage of development. They are mostly grown under plastic, sown tightly together, with the first pickings in March and the full season available from May. Such vegetables were first grown in this country in 1988 by Ron Smith at Colchester in Essex.

BER (developed by the Romans) and the shorter stubbier RIDGED CUCUMBER, which is grown outside and usually goes for gherkins. They are at their best in late summer, when the sun has been on them. Most of their best combinations combine them with hot summer dishes. They have a refreshing sympathy for strawberries and salmon. In Europe they are often paired with cream or yoghurt, as in the Greek *tzatziki*, or tomatoes, as in *gazpacho*. Earlier in the year, imports are frustratingly erratic, with high densities of pips and tough skins, especially those from southern countries. If they are to be cooked, they need salting like aubergines or courgettes.

MARROW

The marrow comes from America where it was assiduously cultivated by the Indians, and did not arrive here until the 16th century. The huge marrow beloved of the garden show and the harvest festival possibly says a great deal about our national attitude to food in past eras. Size is not everything: a good marrow is not more than 25 cm (10 in) long, before the seeds have matured and the flesh becomes coarse and stringy. They should be cooked in a minimum of added water as, after all, they are 90% water.

PUMPKIN

Pumpkin is also native to the Americas, the Pilgrim Fathers' first Thanksgiving dinner was turkey, cranberry and pumpkin. A bland vegetable, it needs saucing. There is a lot it can do – breads, jams or bulking stews – but a soup with strong flavourings, like saffron or cinnamon, or a pie illustrate its true worth. Pumpkins will keep for a few months, which allows time to plot a strategy of recipes – the vegetarian homesteader's equivalent of killing the pig.

SQUASH

Squash look more spectacular than they taste. They belong to the same notoriously watery family as melon and marrow and need marrying off with rich flavours – but they do repay the work. The recipe repertoire is still in its infancy, although American books are far more advanced, where the focus of Halloween has given the whole field the same emphasis that turkeys get at Thanksgiving. The larger squash can be hollowed out and the shell used as soup containers.

Younger examples in summer, like the pretty little PATTY PAN in shades of green and cream with crenellated edges, respond to light cooking with herbs and butter.

BUTTERNUT is the bulbous pale beige formation most widely available, about 20 cm (8 in) or more high. Inside the firm flesh is fragrant and vivid orange, with only a small amount of seed. Cooked, it comes somewhere between swede and carrot; slightly more delicate and a little floral, it mixes well with other root vegetables and is distinctive enough to avoid the usual blandness label. Microwave or roast in oil.

GEM, a neat round deep green, the size of an orange with hard skin, is also widely found. Boil for about 25 minutes, then halve, seed, and serve with butter (quite a lot).

STEMS & STALKS

Artichoke
Asparagus
Cardoon
Celery
Chicory
Fennel

The horticultural classification of vegetables shows how far the languages of the gardener and the cook have grown apart. Celery, chicory or fennel might as happily be listed with the salad leaves. Their unusual availability and good value – at least of the first two – contrasts with the aristocratic prices of asparagus and artichoke, both of which oddly seem to have lost ground in the English garden while their culinary fame has spread.

ARTICHOKE

Essentially a Mediterranean plant (*Cynara scolymus*) that flowers from July to November, its name comes from the Armenian *ardis-chauki*. There are two main strains: the stubby milky-green-leaved artichoke of which the best known is the CAMUS DE BRETAGNE (or more colloquially GLOBE ARTICHOKE), a tall plant growing to 2 m (6 ft), with a violet edge to the leaves as it gets older and deep purple silken core; and the VIOLET, which is earlier, has spikier leaves, a narrow deep heart (so is less good value), is inclined to bitterness as it ages as well as becoming progressively more purple in coloration.

The artichoke is a perennial root that flowers annually. The smaller heads found in Mediterranean markets are from the same plants, but have not been pruned in spring and so send out many smaller branches which produce youthful heads. The crop in Britain is marginal, the climate mitigating against producing the size of heads that most supermarkets now demand. However, they have been cultivated here from the 1500s. Usually they will be Camus de Bretagne.

Woodiness and stalkiness are signs of

Ways With Artichokes

Boil them for 30-40 minutes, then turn them upside down to drain; or microwave. The lower leaves should pull away gently and the hairy choke removed. They are best served tepid, rather than hot, with a sweet herby vinaigrette. Remember that artichokes clash badly with red wine.

either an overly long growth cycle, without enough sun, or that the artichokes have been stored too long. Italian examples have tended to be the best-looking. The season starts properly in July and trade price is around 25p.

ASPARAGUS

Originating from eastern Europe, asparagus was known to the Greeks and also here, especially as a wild plant. The Arabs introduced it to Spain, where it still flourishes. Modern varieties trace their ancestry back to around the 1100s. It is part of the lily family, but contains an odorous chemical, methyl mercaptan, which scents the urine and has encouraged the idea that it is a diuretic.

Beds will last 20 years in most gardens, though professional growers replant after 10. The crowns start to bear shoots from the third year and then give their best in years four and five. Quality is supremely about freshness. The asparagus year starts on April 21, with the first English from the Isle of Wight, the main crop following through May and June, supplemented with fine examples from France and then a succession of lesser imports. These start with California, Washington and Virginia in later summer; Peru in October; New Zealand, Zimbabwe and South Africa for December; and moving slowly north to Mexico by January and California again in February; with the first earlies from Egypt and Spain in March.

The development of the New-World cultivation in the last 20 years has brought a uniformity to varieties that previously invoked all manner of descriptive allusions – the Danish fairy-tale goblin names like the large *Backlim*, the grooved *Boomlin, Gijnlim* and the fat, widely grown and ascendant *Franklym*, or else ostentatiously classical, the old French *Argenteuil* or the other English favourite, the first all-male variety, *Lucullus*. At other points growers gave up and turned to the expedience of *Connover's Colossus*, still widely grown by gardeners, or the scientific *University of California 140*. The Americans opt for the tweeness of *Mary Washington*, the forerunner of *Mary Grand* and *Mary Green*. The varieties are dominated now by Franklym and its derivations, an all-male variety (females dissipate their energy in flowering) with lime-green stems, and mauve epaulets and spears.

As important as the variety are the soil, the climate and the speed with which they get to market. In the 19th century, England grew more asparagus than any other country, mostly in the London suburbs of Battersea, Fulham, Deptford, Mortlake and Chiswick, where it was known as 'sparrow grass'. The best came from the Vale of Evesham.

Evesham has a micro-climate – an otherwise 'horrible' soil of heavy clay is topped up with river silt from the Avon when it floods, as it still does in winter. The Vale is surrounded like a horseshoe on three sides by the Malvern, Cotswold and Clent hills, which protect it from the north and easterly weather, but opens up across the river to the south-westerly. As a result, here are produced the first crops – some 11 days before, say, Derby. The height of Evesham asparagus was in the '20s, but production has fallen back to half that amount, and other areas – notably Lincolnshire – have come on line.

Cito is grown along with *Franklym* on the Isle of Wight. A cousin breed, with similar outside markings, the core is more substantial. It replaced *Colossal* and *Mammoth* for commercial growing on the island. It is not quite so sweet, and has a tendency to flatten out in the larger stems.

*EXTRA FINE ASPARAGUS, from Thailand, is available most of the year. It is small, about 8 cm (3¼ in) long, and pistachio green with pink to white epaulets and spears. They have a good texture but not much flavour cooked; raw in salads, they are pea-like and nutty with a good crunch. Out of mainline UK and French seasons, these make a good buy, and are not horrendously expensive by designer salad prices.

**EVESHAM ASPARAGUS is the *Franklym* variety. One reason for Evesham's reputation is that it produces slender green spears – straight, neat, about 1 cm (½ in) across and well trimmed, with a sweet taste, especially at the white core. Although delicate, it has a good crunch. UK growers argue that the cooler climate allows the flavour to develop more slowly. Other growers claim that the optimum is a short fast spurt. For flavour, indisputably the smaller and more slender are the best; the macho virile varieties have already shot their bolt.

FRANKLYM, from Cambord in the Loire, is usually bigger than UK examples, being nearly 1.5 cm (2/3 in) across and slightly woodier as a result. Mild to start, but with a strong developing taste right up to a mild arti-choke flavour.

*SPRUE arrive early in the growing season only, often from France. The tiny lime-white young shoots hang across the hand like a necklace. Pliant, succulent and gentle, they are very nutty raw in salads and have a superb texture when cooked as a vegetable, with no trace of woodiness.

UNIVERSITY OF CALIFORNIA 140 is an imi-tation of the Franklym. An example from Lincolnshire was a slightly redder mauve on the epaulets and spears, but with a similar shape and difficult to tell apart. They were

Ways With Asparagus

When cooking green asparagus, the simple approaches are the best: lightly trimmed, the woody end of the stalks cut off (and reserved for soup), they are best steamed or microwaved and served with butter when hot or olive oil and Parmesan, or hollandaise sauce when cold. Asparagus also has an affinity with egg yolks, and good salt and individual flavourings like paprika, hazelnut oil in a vinaigrette, or herbs. To avoid asparagus soups becoming sourly sludgy, add a blend of green herbs or celery tops to give texture and colour. Use the tips as garnish. White asparagus will take more robust extenuated cooking, such as gratins.

FOOD *watch*

Tinned asparagus

This might be another species – overcooked to the point of mushiness, no stalkiness and the brine infiltrates and sogs everything that seems to draw out all the worst characteristics. White examples bear up better than green, but they are wet through from the brine, their sense of regality drowned... a taste familiar at wedding receptions.

curled rather than straight, and were less sweet than Franklym, tending to be green all the way through and missing out on the lack of the core.

WHITE ASPARAGUS is grown differently, with the earth ridged up on all sides to protect them from the light. White is favoured ahead of green in France, Belgium and Germany (there is also a violet), but essentially the different approach creates a different vegetable with a bitterness closer to chicory and a meatiness that deserves marriage with other flavours, like meat. Very little is imported. Some unidentified species sampled from the Loire were dirty on the outside and needed scraping; woody and cracked horizontally, the spears were more heart-shaped than ears. Really more of a vegetable, they were succulent if stalky and bitter like chicory. Good for cooking in gratins and as a vegetable. Other competitors are more critical, 'like chewing iron bars'.

CARDOON

Related to the artichoke (*Cynara carduncu-lus*), this tasty vegetable is rarely found these days. It is invariably earthed up to blanch the leaves and keep them white, and is mostly used in salads.

CELERY

Sometimes called SMALLAGE or WILD CELERY, this is native to the south-east Mediterranean region and the Roman and the Greeks held it as a symbol of grief. It arrived here in Tudor times and was initially seen as a medicine and for eating raw. The ground seeds are used with lemon verbena as an alternative to salt and are used in pickling or as a sedative tea. The pale green varieties are now predominant. Self-blanching, the leaves are trimmed and neatly packed. The white varieties, often still with soil attached, are the older trenched celery and can be found in specialist greengrocers, especially in the North. On market days, there were celery men and celery washers as recently as the '50s. The cliche of serving it with cheese has little merit other than providing a refreshing end to the meal. Celery's main role is is an essential ingredient in most stocks and it is also good in braises and gratins.

CHICORY

Meaning now the WITLOOF, developed in the Brussels Botanical Gardens in 1850 as a forced and blanched vegetable grown in the dark, like mushrooms. There are earlier references of similar techniques being used on ships to supply fresh leaves. Before then it was a winter vegetable only, which accounts for the recipe list of warming braises. Its more modern role as a salad vegetable is botanically more appropriate. It is related to radicchio, both originally from succory.

Its infamous use as an adulterant in coffee began in Holland in 1830 and was banned here two years later. This was later relented on the grounds that some people liked it for what it was. The chicory used, however, was a different strain, sometimes called MAGDEBURG, where the roots are cut, dried in a kiln, crushed and roasted.

Much of the white chicory, with its beautiful yellow edging and precise bitterness, is grown here. As it wilts badly in cooking, it is better value as a raw vegetable than in the traditional braises with strong flavours like garlic, orange and mushrooms, or serving it with gamy meat or scallops for a texture contrast.

Equally pretty and novel is the development of the red-tinged chicory which is sweet at first bite, but becoming stronger and more bitter than the yellow. Chicory makes an excellent gratin with breadcrumbs, bacon and a little cream added two-thirds of the way through cooking.

FENNEL

Sometimes called FLORENCE FENNEL, this is a bulbous aniseed-tasting root vegetable as well as a herb. For the Egyptians, Greeks and Romans it was primarily a medicine and the Italians are only said to have started cooking it in times of severe famine. Smaller bulbs tend to be better than large, and they should be white rather than green, and tightly configurated. They may be grated raw for salads, or steamed, sautéed or even made into gratins. The flavour is pervasive and needs strong companions, like tomato and basil and olive oil – or judicious portion control.

VEGETABLE FRUITS

The vegetable fruits are among the miracles of the story of food in the 20th century. Taken from their tropical jungles and happily transplanted into new climates, they have become ubiquitous. For the most part inexpensive, they lend some fascinating new dimensions to our diet.

Aubergine
Avocado
Chilli pepper
Sweet pepper
Tomato

AUBERGINE

The aubergine has more names than a vegetable ought to have, EGGPLANT, EGGFRUIT and GUINEA SQUASH; in America it was sometimes called JEW'S APPLE or MAD APPLE, though the name probably derives from the Sanskrit, *vatimigana* – it still an important part of Indian cooking. Its first appearance was in China in the 5th century and it seems to have arrived in Europe after the Greeks, strangely because aubergines are one of the cornerstones of modern Greek cookery. They probably came via Africa with the Moors into Spain and reached here in 1597, initially as beautifully decorative plants.

Its popularity here has mainly developed in the last decade. The UK crop is grown under glass and first go on sale in July. However, sun and water are what an aubergine needs, so imports generally have more flavour. Mostly we see the purple-to-black-skinned varieties, but there are mauve, white and striped versions – some with fanciful names like the graphically evocative *Monstreuse de New York*. The bitterness associated with older varieties seems to have been largely bred out. The skin of the aubergine is nutritious and wherever possible should not be peeled and discarded.

Ways with Aubergines

To roast them, they should be pricked to let the air escape and stop them bursting. Alternatively, slice them in half, brush them with oil and roast for 30 minutes, until soft. Mix the flesh with basil, garlic and oil and replace in the skins to eat with a teaspoon. The same trick works well with the Japanese sweet *mirin* and *miso* as flavourings.

A good aubergine will be spongy; as it ages, it goes soft and the calyx turns brown. It is sensitive to ethylene and should be kept away from tomatoes and apples in a fridge or it will ripen too quickly. There are different opinions on the value of salting – either slice and soak them in salted water for 30 minutes, then squeeze out the brown juices and drain for another 30 minutes; or slice and cover with salt for up to three hours. Some say they absorb more oil after salting, others less.

Requirements for recipes tend to be influenced more by shape than variety: long and thin for stuffing, round for slicing. Above all other vegetables, the aubergine is in sympathy with the Mediterranean flavours of lemon, parsley, tomato, garlic, courgette, oregano, onions and olive oil. All of which appear in their main-event dishes, such as *ratatouille, moussaka, imam bayildi* (aubergine caviar, sometimes just with lemon juice, garlic and olive oil, but in other variations also using tomatoes).

AVOCADO

The avocado has been known in Central America for more than 7,000 years. The Aztec word for the plant meant 'the testicle tree', from the way the pods hang off the slender laurel-like leaved branches. In the Amazon they are eaten at the end of a meal with cream and sugar. Over the centuries it has acquired names that tell their own stories – 'poor man's butter', 'mountain pear', 'midshipman's butter', or 'alligator pear'. It was first taken to Jamaica around 1650 and arrived in England about 1895. An inhibiting agent in the leaves prevents it ripening on the tree and, like the banana, it is ripened en route – or, only too often, is sold totally unripe and as a result rock-hard.

To ripen an avocado, wrap it in foil or in a polythene bag and leave in a warm place. Unlike melons, the sides should be pliable; squeezing the tip you will damage the end. They do not freeze well. Out of the skin they discolour swiftly, which is one reason for the supremacy of recipes that use acidic dressings, like vinaigrette, or the Mexican dip *guacamole*, in which it is mixed with onions, tomatoes, chilli, garlic, coriander, parsley and lime juice. They are high in fat and the B vitamins. In producing countries they are given to babies as their first solid. Israel and South Africa supply most of the winter avocados; Mexico the summer.

There are four main varieties of which the usually (though no longer exclusively) black-skinned hass is very much in vogue, though South Africa has been developing other strains which may appear soon.

ETTINGER, shiny and with a brighter green skin than the Fuerte, is almost exclusively from Israel in winter.

FUERTE was once the most commonly found, green, with slightly pear.

content and for the best. The though some in resolutely

shiny green co through

neless avocado, VOCADO, quite a small AN GIANT is, sadly, most

CHILLI PEPPER

Chillies are always credited to Bolivia, but the profusion of varieties further south, in India, in Thailand and also in China suggests that that area may not have had a monopoly on the smallest of the capsicum family. Chillies are a sub-culture of their own, with countless variations. Recipes are prescribed for individual varieties in cuisines as different as Mexican and Indian. Their brutal heat was a poor-man's spice, making the unpalatable palatable; but they have developed their own cachet and cult status, and exotic named chillies have begun to surface in **Sainsbury** and **Safeway** and in specialist stores.

The broad rules are confusing. GREEN should be hotter than RED, because the *red* is riper and therefore sweeter. But the hottest chilli of all, the HABANERO is red. What **Sainsbury** calls green chilli is actually a box half full of red ones. The seeds and membrane contain more of the heat-giving agent capsaicin than the flesh does, so these need to be handled and extracted with care – with gloves or under water. The heat is measured on a scale in Scoville units. A bell pepper will rate 0; a Habanero rates 300,000, though this is commonly now scaled down to 1-10. Without a prolonged period of building up heat tolerances, it is not possible to compare different varieties in the same way that it is for other foods. The less strong chillies invoke flavours of fruits but, as the heat rises over the midway point, smokes, liquorice, and Marmite begin to edge in.

The choice is further complicated by the market. India now claims to be the largest producer of chillies in the world, with a quite breathtaking range of undocumented styles. The very small multi-coloured chillies that come from Thailand often claim, rightly or wrongly, to produce some of the hottest recipes. The more organized information coming through Mexico suggests another scale of ratings, which is in turn compounded by a fourth, more colourful, jumble from the Caribbean. The result is that much of what reaches the market remains anonymous.

Sight is no indicator of heat. The only guide is a cook's instinct. Chilli is a culinary adventure playground. To counteract the heat, add sugar or drink some milk. The heat factor is something of a distraction from the flavour, but chillies also respond differently in cooking if they are cut, left whole or ground, and different parts of the same chilli taste different – this is part of their fascination. They freeze well.

ANAHEIM is a long fat finger, about 15x2 cm (6x¾ in), scarlet turning cricket-ball-red, sometimes sold younger when still green. Fat enough to slit open and stuff, they are relatively mild.

CARIBE is tapering at the end, 7x2.5 cm (2¾x1 in), ranging from lemony white to bright orange and deep red, going brown as it over-ripens. Quite sweet and mild, it is often used crushed or powdered in Mexico, or in *salsas* when fresh.

HABANERO is innocently pretty, a deep orange box-like lantern, 2.5x2 cm (12x¾ in), sometimes sold green, possibly a different species from other Mexican chillies. It is the intensity which marks it out at the top of the heat scale, but also for aficionados. Fruity and intense, it is widely used in *salsas*, stews, most often with fish and curries. In the dried form, they are a rusty red and look like small sun-dried tomatoes, and reconstitute into a fiery tropical fruit heat.

HOT BONNETS are reputedly the hottest of the Caribbean chillies. Small and squat, as if they have been sat on, they come in yellows, greens and reds.

DRIED CHILLIES

The Cool Chile Company has begun importing dried chillies from America, which have added a further dimension. The stalks and seeds are taken off and they are reconstituted in hot boiling water for 20 minutes and then puréed ready for use. They can also be lightly toasted before soaking, but must not burn. PASADO is light and smoky, with hints of citrus and dried apples, herbs and celery. It is used in soups and stews. PASILLA, known as little raisins – a parody on their enormous liquorice black pods nearly 20 cm (8 in) long – have a taste of berries, grapes and liquorice, and are mostly used in sauces and with seafood. CASCABEL is also called 'the little rattle'; beautifully decorative and round, 4x3 cm (1½x1¼ in), with black grape skin, the pips shake inside like maracas. The flavour is nutty and woody, with a rounded heat. It is best known in its own *salsa*, but also in slow-cooked casseroles. GUAJILLO continues the confusion over chillies with this large leathery red-skinned pepper. Tom Stobart writing in his *The Cook's Encyclopaedia* in 1980 called it 'exceedingly hot'. Dodie Miller of **Cool Chile** gives it a mild rating of 2-4/10. 'A sweet medium heat with tones of fruit, citrus, green tea and pine'. It is often used with fish. ANCHO is the dried variation of POBLANO, both widely used in Mexican cooking, often as constituents for cooking. Stobart says, 'rather mild and rich'. Frances Bissell says, 'hot'. Miller says, 'medium 3-5/10'. Red turning black with a crocodile skin texture and distinctive umbrella handle stalks, they are sweet and fruity, with hints of coffee, liquorice and tobacco. CHIPOLTE is the smoked version of the well known stubby JALAPEÑO that underscores much of Tex-Mex cooking. The smoke fundamentally alters its impact without undermining the heat, which remains above the average.

INDIAN CHILLIES: the green is used fresh, while the red is usually dried. The best-known is the KASHMIRI, but this is a name often invoked for other varieties. A true Kashmiri is bright red and neatly plum-shaped. Few go for export. It is more likely that the chillies here will be the more elongated GUNTUR, a bright red pepper that goes largely for curry powder because of its strong colour.

SWEET PEPPER

The rise of the sweet pepper has symbolized the supermarkets move into fresh vegetables, sometimes called a BELL PEPPER to distinguish it from the chilli pepper, to which it is related but does not share the heat. Peppers were brought to Europe by Columbus from the Americas, but have happily transplanted to green- and hot-house cultivation.

The GREEN PEPPER is the unripe version of the YELLOW or the *RED, which is probably the best example. Other colours, such as WHITE or PURPLE, tend to be cosmetic, with only marginal differences in flavour which are mostly down to ripeness not variety. Occasionally interesting, smaller red peppers are imported from America.

Peppers are good sources of vitamin C. The white seeds have to be taken out as they are violently hot. Depending on the recipe, the skin is stripped off – grill or roast in the oven to char the skin which can then be peeled off. Heat brings out their full motherly character. The red pepper can reinforce tomatoes, adding a deceptive warmth, and provide an interesting basis for soups or can be puréed for sauces. They also freeze well.

Ways with Peppers
Slice a red pepper in half and remove the seeds and the stalk. Place one anchovy fillet in each half, followed by a wedge of Mozzarella cheese, and a basil leaf. Add one tablespoon or more of olive oil to each and bake for 15 minutes.

TOMATO

Although usually classed as a vegetable, like melons and courgettes, tomatoes are on the botanical borderline. The berries are the fruit of the annual plant *Lycopersicon esculentum*. The range has become breathtaking, but for all the manipulation of the genes, growing cycles, and the feed, it has been the flavour that has suffered. Tomatoes may look the part, but they don't taste it.

*AILSA is an old variety, irregularly round, about 4 cm (1½ in), scarlet to deep red in colour, with salmon-pink flesh and a good

GROWN FOR FLAVOUR

The past few years has seen well-publicized attempts to recreate flavoursome tomatoes, with varying degrees of success. Only the named varieties are really worth pursuing, because others have had their virtues bred out of them and tend to be high in ratio of pip to flesh, with no acidity to speak of and part of a general move to mass-market blandness. By contrast, the little CHERRY TOMATOES show very well. Nevertheless, the market is cynically prepared to charge huge premiums – seemingly arbitrarily – on one type of tomato against another. And to add insult to injury, supermarkets confusingly price in both grams and lbs.

ratio of it to yellow pip. The seed pod breaks off easily, and it is good for cooking, particularly in sweet-and-sour combinations. An example from the UK had an oppressive resistant skin, and a sweetness mingled with classic sourness. At 89p per lb, it was worth its * rating for value in cooking.

BRITISH GOURMET has an orange blush, and is about 55 cm (2 in) across with 1 cm (½ in) of flesh. Handy to cook with, because the seeds slip out easily leaving a good rim of flesh for dicing, it has a sweet but vanishing flavour. Our sample from the UK were 75p per lb.

*CHERRY YELLOW: although the amount of development would suggest that cherry tomatoes are just a cosmetic affectation, in fact they show well for flavour against larger varieties. Pretty, deep yellow to orange and perfectly formed inside, it is mild and inoffensive, but good looking. SONGOLD from **Safeway** has shown consistently well.

CHERRY DELIGHT is round, about 3 cm (1¼ in), bright orange fused with deep red. Inside the pip jelly is translucent green, the pips white to yellow, with a good configuration (as in all cherries). Examples tend to have a sharp, quick taste of sourness mellowed with sugar. Sold as sweet, it is not really. There is

CONCENTRATED TOMATO PURÉES vary infinitesimally from brand to brand. The intensity and fidelity of flavour presents a very real alternative to using fresh tomatoes in cooking, where it would take a considerable length of time to achieve the same results. Only **Gerber** includes any additives: an acidity regulator, E330, which has the effect of making it taste not unlike ketchup. The lovely old-fashioned tins of **Petti** have discernible attractive acidity levels left in. **Cirio** is the one most obviously different, with the accent on the acidity and lightness. Tubes of **Napolina** and **Bella** fall somewhere between the two, obviously favouring sweeter tomatoes. On the other hand, **Menucci** in jars has an unmistakable sense of a tomato's sourness. *Valfrutta's purée of sieved tomatoes is not really comparable, because it is not a concentrate (though the French on the packaging call it a purée); more of a 'world-class tomato juice' and brilliant for Blood Marys – a star but in a different class.

a confusing price ratio alteration from lbs and grams between cherry and ordinary tomatoes.

DELICE is round verging on squareness, about 4.5x5.5 cm (1¾x2¼ in), bright red fused with yellow; with red flesh, red jelly and a small white seed. The flavour of an example from France was mild, forgiving, and sweet with no acidity. Soft and fulfilling, it cooked well.

FLAVIA is a small traditional tomato, about 5 cm (2.5 in) across. Sharp, with little acidity but a high ratio of pip to flesh, it is neutral but classic, and makes a fair benchmark. Exclusive to **Sainsbury**, they are reputedly left longer on the vine to mature.

FLAVOUR TOP, previously known as ELOISE until **Tesco** changed its name, is about 5 cm (2 in) across and a very mainline red, with classic contours and a summery taste. With firm skin, it had a very good interaction of textures between the skin, flesh and the juice of the pips, to produce a mildly

FOOD *watch*

Tinned Tomatoes
Miners asked for tinned tomatoes, believing the acidity to be an antidote to silicosis. The **San Marzano** was an aristocrat of canned tomato from Italy. Standards tend to be very up and down: consistently good brands over a number of years have been **Don Mario**, **Safeway**, **Dominic**, **San Remo**, **Epicure** and **Gerber Pride**. Price does not equate to quality, as low-grade tomatoes are often used for export.

TOMATO KETCHUP derives from the Chinese fish sauce *Koe-chiap*, which was first adapted to 'catsup' for a blend of mushrooms, walnuts, anchovies, eels or oysters. The first mention of tomatoes being added is in 1814. **Henry Heinz** introduced his tomato ketchup to **Fortnum & Masons** in 1886, a novelty without additives. The speed of pouring is graded by the American authorities. Grade A's top speed was reduced to 0.00148 mph during the Gulf War to accommodate **Heinz** which was too slow. Other brands don't really equate because **Heinz** has so defined the market by using its own variety of tomato.

FOOD *watch*

The ENGLISH tomato season starts in June followed by PLUM, sometimes called AROMA or OLIVADE, which are worth the price difference before the brilliant vine ripened tomatoes arrive. **Trust** is a **Safeway** label for its Dutch and Portuguese imports; the better ones from Provence go under the names of FERLINE and PRISCA. Look also in **Safeway** for CLEOPATRA. **Sainsbury** SLICING, PORTUGUESE and DUTCH tomatoes have been disappointing. Better are the PROVENCE. Dutch tomatoes on the vine smell the part but are not comparable to those from further south; Good reports about MAYFAIR from **Somerfield**.

acidic effect.

JERSEY OUTDOOR is a squat pale tomato, meaty red hued with orange; crimson inside with yellow veins and green pips, the thick flesh is good for cooking and dicing.

MANHATTAN is a classic Maserrati red, 3 cm (1¼ in) across, with a conventional configuration. It has green to orange pips, pink to white sweet flesh, and a strong skin: a good combination. Another example two months later in August from Jersey was sweet, sharp, mellow and juicy.

*MELROW is round, 3-4 cm (1¼-1½ in) across, with a red blush from translucent dark flesh inside streaked with white pith; inside is pretty configuration of deep green jelly, white to yellow pip, and blood red flesh. It is sweet, with little sourness or acidity, almost honeyed, with a lasting flavour. Good at £1.19 per lb.

MOMOTARA is large and deep cerise pink, with a good aroma and a small percentage of pip to flesh. Squattish to square, soft to cut, with a lovely smell, pale watermelon-pink flesh and yellow seed, it is juicy, with a delicate taste and low acidity. Ît was good, but at £1.58 per lb you pay for all this flavour.

ROYAL DELICIOUS, about 3-4 cm (1¼-1½ in), has an orange blush to a deep red that darkens as they ripen, and a circle of yellow on the root. Classically contoured, with a thick skin and 5 mm (¼ in) of flesh to yellow pip, and with a similar configuration and merits to Manhattan, it is a good juicy all-rounder, but not special.

**SICILIAN TOMATOES ON THE VINE are fat deep red tomatoes sold with their stems still attached. The internal division of textures is almost an equality of pip, pith and flesh. Juicy, succulent and very sweet, with low acidity but still some, these are excellent.

VANESSA is squat, about 3.5-6 cm (1½-2½ in), firm, watery crimson in colour, with a smooth skin, a useful measure of flesh around the rim for cooking and a pretty configuration, with the few pips held in firm jelly – a vegetable version of a watermelon, with slightly woody hues.

PULSES

Adzuki bean
Black-eyed bean
Butter bean
Cannellini bean
Chickpea
Flageolet
Haricot
Kidney bean
Lentil
Split pea

The dried ripe seeds of legumes are among the oldest cultivated foods and some of the most nutritious. They are good sources of both protein and fibre, and usually also of the vitamin B family. Before we began to harvest them young, most peas and broad beans were dried as staples for winter. Most pulses need soaking in water overnight before use. The exceptions are lentils and black-eyed beans, which can usually be cooked without any pre-soaking.

Most notoriously, red kidney beans and soya beans build up toxins which must be destroyed by fast boiling for 10 minutes. This water should also be replaced before cooking the beans on. Allow 1.1 litres (2 pt) of water for every 115-225 g (4-8 oz) of pulses. Salt only serves to toughen the skins, so add it after cooking.

There is some discussion over whether the haricot and other beans need soaking. While most textbooks and packets say they should be, Coenders argues in *The Chemistry of Cooking* that soaking could start enzyme changes and encourage micro-organisms to ferment. The compromise is that they need longer cooking of around 90 minutes plus. Times for cooking soaked beans vary according to how old they are.

Some beans are now being imported from Spain under the **Tormesina** label, from Sierra de Gredos in Avila. They carry an EC logo for specific denomination on the grounds of the well-aerated, low-calcium granite soils and the pureness of the water. These beans are quite outstanding: the butter beans, three times the size of those in supermarkets, thin-skinned and immensely creamy, are well worth the premium.

FOOD *watch*

Pulse Prices

Pulses are, of course, famously cheap. The better-known split peas, chickpeas and lentils are even less expensive than other beans. Most will fall into a price band of between 40-80p for 500 g (1 lb 2 oz), though few supermarkets carry the full range. **Sainsbury** usually has the widest choice; **Safeway** is the least expensive. Wholefood shops tend to be arbitrarily expensive, depending on their philosophy.

Pulse	Soaking	Hard-boiling (minutes)	Simmering (minutes)
Adzuki bean	overnight	10	50
Black-eyed bean	overnight		60
Butter bean	overnight	10	75
Cannellini bean	overnight	10	75
Chickpea	overnight	10	up to 3 hours
Flageolet	overnight	10	60-90
Haricot	overnight	10	60-90
Kidney bean	overnight	10	40-45
Lentil	None	None	20-40
Split pea	None	None	30-45

PULSE SOAKING AND COOKING TIMES

ADZUKI BEAN

Also known as the ADUKI, DADUKI or sometimes AZUKI or FEIJOA BEAN, it is identified
by the Latin *Phaseolus angularis*. Widely
used in Asia, especially China and Japan
where they are admired for pastes in sweet
rather than savoury dishes, or mixed with rice
in a ratio of 1:8, they are now grown across
South-east Asia. Eastern herbalists prescribe
them for kidney disorders. Usually sold dried
or sometimes in cans, they can be sprouted
or ground into flour. Their nutty flavour finds
extensive use in vegetarian dishes, and they
bind well in stuffings and loaves. **Sainsbury**
is currently the only supermarket to stock
adzuki beans, considerably cheaper (at 36p
for 250 g) than some wholefood shops which
sell their organic varieties at four times that
price.

BLACK-EYED BEAN

Sometimes called COWPEA or BLACK-
EYED PEA, this arrived in the Southern
states of America from Africa with the slavers

Ways with Cannellini Beans

Cannellini are the beans for minestrone or in Tuscany, *la ribollita* – literally 'the re-boiling' soak 250 g (8½ oz) cannellini beans overnight. In a heavy pan, sweat an onion in olive oil. Add 1 carrot, 1 celery stalk, 1 leek, 2 tomatoes, ½ a cabbage, chopped, 1 piece of dried chilli and 4 garlic cloves. Stir for 10 minutes. Add the beans, mix well, cover with 2 litres (3½ pt) of water and simmer slowly for 2 hours.

Take out half the beans, purée and return them to the soup. Sweat 4 garlic cloves with a sprig of thyme and pepper in oil and add to the soup. Leave for 24 hours.

The next day, slice an onion (preferably red) over the top of the soup and cook in a preheated medium oven, uncovered, for 30 minutes. To serve: cut a slice of country bread per person, rub each with garlic and place in the bottom of the soup bowl. Ladle over the hot soup and serve with extra virgin olive oil and salt.

in the 17th century. Now principally grown in California, the small creamy beans with a distinctive black or yellow smudge have an earthy flavour.

A staple of Creole cooking, notably in rice'n'peas, they combine well with other flavours and are good in soups and casseroles and with salads. They are, however, likely to lose texture and have a much more defined mealiness than soya for example. Usually cheaper bought loose in wholefood shops, they can be sprouted.

They are useful because the skins are thin and thus cook quickly. They are high in folic acid, and because they are not toxic they do not need long boiling.

BUTTER BEAN

Also known as the MADAGASCAR BEAN after the island from where most now come, *Vateria indica* was the main grocery bean before 1940. The similar LIMA BEAN is slightly smaller and sweeter, and often sold younger when still green. It is the bean from a tropical climber, *Phaseolus lunatus* or *limensis*, which is native to Central and South America.

The creamy butter bean is the largest of the pulses. The lozenge-shaped cream beans are best in individual casseroles in which they can star, and their seductive silky mealiness can be brought out – they are one of the most floury of all pulses. Some varieties contain markedly high levels of hydrocyanic acid and must be cooked before being eaten.

CANNELLINI BEAN

Also known as the FAZOLA BEAN, this is the prince of pulses. Longer and thinner than an haricot, it is a staple of cooking in Tuscany, where they arrived originally from Argentina. The cooking liquid makes one of the best cooking stocks for other dishes.

The beans themselves are best in salads, especially with virgin olive oil and herbs, and in casseroles in which the liquid takes on their creamy nutty qualities. Slowly becoming more widely available, **Sainsbury** and **Safeway** now sell dried as well as tinned cannellini beans. Strangely they have yet to be priced above other pulses, which their savoury flavour deserves. This is probably because the market is still young and their qualities remain largely undiscovered when they get lumped together with the considerably duller haricot. Some people argue that canned is as good as dried, because the flavour and texture survive.

CHICKPEA

Sometimes known as the GARBANZO BEAN or in India the BENGAL GRAM or CHANNA DAL, its Latin name is *Cicer arietinum*. They arrived from India and have become pivotal in the cooking of the Middle-East, notably Greece and the Lebanon. Chickpea flour is used for *chapatis*, breads and *bhajis*. Middle-Eastern varieties tend to be smaller and darker than the Mediterranean type. Their robust one-dimensional chestnutty texture combines well with the complicated spicings of the Near East. The plants grow to 40 cm (16 in) and exude a sticky form of oxalic acid and so have to be harvested with gloves. They are occasionally eaten fresh, but most chickpeas are dried. Best with vinaigrettes, in curries, vegetarian pâtés, and in dips, notably Greek *hummus,* they can also be used to thicken sauces.

After overnight soaking, rinsing and boiling for 10 minutes, they need simmering for

---

FOOD *watch*

Chickpea Prices

Supermarkets sell both cans and loose around 50p for 500 g (1 lb 2 oz), rising to 70p in wholefood shops – and even as much as £1.28 in one particular example. They are best bought loose.

Ways with Chickpeas

To make hummus:
liquidize 4 parts
chickpeas with cooking
water, 2 parts tahini (be
generous), 1 part
skinned garlic cloves, ½
part lemon juice, and a
drizzle of sesame oil.
Garnish with virgin olive
oil and pomegranate
seeds.

sometimes more than two hours – up to three (depending on age more than other pulses). They are best overcooked, so the skins burst allowing other flavours to mingle. The cooking liquid can make an earthy vegetarian stock.

FLAGEOLET

A variety of haricot, this distinctive attractive slender lime-green bean is an aristocrat among pulses. They are sometimes found fresh, which are excellent; but they are more usually sold dried, which deserve serving on their own, or traditionally with roast lamb – they are cooked separately, added to the pan juices as the lamb rests and served with the gravy.

The beans are harvested when still young, which accounts for the sweetness and also the higher content of positive nutrients. They are good in salads, terrines, in vinaigrette or dressed with the juices from a roast and some herbs. Supermarkets tend only to stock the cans, though **Sainsbury** has broken the trend with 250 g bags.

HARICOT

Sometimes known confusingly as the FRENCH BEAN, NAVY BEAN, BOSTON BEAN, NORTHERN BEAN or PEARL HARICOT BEAN, its many names reflect the size of its family. Though the name haricot was probably derived from the Aztec *ayecotl*, the Latin name is simply *Phaseolus vulgaris*. These neat cream oval beans tend to lack the flavour of the younger flageolet and need support in the cooking or dressing. They make a good mainline filler, lending body to soups, casseroles, cassoulets and – most famously – baked beans. **Heinz** first produced its baked beans in 1895 and brought them to England in

1912, although full production was only eventually established here in 1928.

The price of haricot beans fluctuates wildly from supermarket to wholefood shop. Their reputation for making people fart stems from the high levels of carbohydrate not being digested and being passed into the colon. Selective trials are trying to breed this out of commercial strains.

KIDNEY BEAN

Also known as the RED KIDNEY BEAN or FRIJOLE NEGRO, this black bean is part of the large family of beans Columbus originally discovered in South America and brought back to Europe. Now cultivated in Thailand and China but widely used in Creole cooking, it is valued for its bulk and mealiness. Chinese black bean sauce is not related, coming from fermented soy beans. The RED KIDNEY BEAN is often called the MEXICAN BEAN or CHILLI BEAN to point out its affinity to hot spicing. These kidney-shaped beans are grown in America and Africa, part of the same family as the black, and the colour can be anything from luridly dark maroon to pink. High in fibre, 115 g (4 oz) supplies the recommended daily intake for an adult.

Renowned for the toxin in the coarse skin, it must be boiled hard for 10 minutes and then the water thrown away before starting the proper cooking. They contain a protein which causes red blood cells to mass, so this must be destroyed in cooking.

Historically served with hot spicy dishes, it suits chilli well – as in *chilli con carne* – as it tends to need a lot of powerful flavour around it (the sugar in the tins seems to help in the same way) as the base flavour is nondescriptly mealy. Ironically and almost uniquely, brand names like **Princes** and **Don Mario**

can be cheaper in the can than supermarket own-labels.

LENTIL

The lentil is known in Latin as *Lens esculenta* because it is shaped like a lens; or, in other explanations, from the Latin *lentus* for slow, because the Romans said they bred indolence. Along with wheat and barley, the lentil is probably one of the oldest cultivated plants and is mentioned in *Genesis*. Many varieties are grown: mostly they are brown or green on the outside; cream, orange-yellow or red inside. BROWN *or* GREEN LENTILS are often called CONTINENTAL or GERMAN LENTILS and are the variety used in most European recipes. These are larger than the red because they retain their skin, and so tend to take longer cooking. RED LENTILS, sometimes called EGYPTIAN LENTILS and widely found in Indian cooking, tend to lose their shape quicker because they have been shelled.

Green or brown are usually more expensive, say 10p per 500 g (1 lb 2 oz) more than red, which are around 60p per 500 g. Organic can be three times the price. The best are PUY LENTILS: known as the caviar of Puy as the tiny slate-grey pods resemble caviar. **Sainsbury** have started to import these, not from France but from Canada – an interesting poser for the French *appellation contrôlée* authorities, who have approved Puy lentils on the basis of geography.

Ways with Lentils

Check over the lentils before cooking to make sure no pieces of grit have evaded detection. Lentils need to be cooked in well-flavoured stock, and are often at their best with something sweet. They take on the qualities and flavours around them and, left to themselves, can taste insipid.

The caviar of Puy: cook the 200g (7oz) lentils in a good stock for 20-30 minutes. Peel and dice a shallot. Make up a vinaigrette of 3 parts virgin olive oil to 1 part red wine vinegar and 1 part Dijon mustard and season generously with salt and pepper. Drain the lentils, toss them into the vinaigrette and mix in the shallot.

SPLIT PEA

Until the 16th century MARROWFAT PEAS were the indigenous peas in the British diet, of which mushy peas remains as a reminder. They need long soaking. Their sweetness is classically paired with salted meats – notably ham – for an old-fashioned but convincing strategy. SPLIT PEAS are slightly sweeter than marrowfat; the yellow grown in Britain and the green in Belgium. They are skinless, so quick to cook and do not need soaking. They do, however, tend to disintegrate and are best used as a thickener for soups and stews (for texture go for brown lentils instead). Traditionally, they are used in ham and pea soup and, of course, pease pudding or any vegetable soup. Supermarkets sell them for around 42p per 500 g (1 lb 2 oz), but health food shops can charge twice as much and the price of organic can be twice as much again.

FUNGI

Cultivated mushrooms
Chestnut mushroom
Oyster mushroom
Shiitake mushroom
Cep
Chanterelle
Hedgehog mushroom
Morel
Other wild mushrooms
Truffles

We have had a long dread of mushrooms in this country which has only recently eased with their reassuring arrival in supermarkets in neat blue boxes wrapped in cellophane. Perhaps the packaging placates our worst fears about things that grow at random in the dark. In most other European countries mushroom-hunting is a weekend enthusiasm and laws have been passed to protect the innocent from consuming the deadly, and the enthusiast from destroying his hobby.

There are more than 10,000 varieties of fungi, of which only a tiny fraction are eaten – not because most are poisonous, but simply because they taste of very little. The main culprit for wild mushrooms' fearful reputation is the DEATH CAP, *Amanita phalloides*, which accounts for a high percentage of fatalities. Others in the *Amanita* family can also cause poisoning, but some are eaten by experts.

Hunters claim that there are upwards of 90 edible mushrooms and other fungi found in Britain. For the most part, however, their reputation survives mostly on their rarity.

CULTIVATED MUSHROOMS

Mushrooms were first cultivated by the French in vast labyrinthine caves, dug out like mines, in the Seine region and around Paris, certainly by 1800. A cave at Mery in 1867 was 21 miles long and produced 1,350 kg (3,000 lb) of mushrooms a day. Another at Montrouge was 24 m (80 ft) below ground and 11 km (7 miles) long. 'Once more we plunge into a passage, dark as ink, and find ourselves between two lines of beds in full bearing, the beautiful white button-like mushrooms appearing everywhere in profusion,' wrote one visitor.

*BUTTON MUSHROOMS are the smallest and youngest; allowed to grow on they become CLOSED CAP, then OPEN CAP MUSHROOMS, with the pink to brown gills showing; and finally the large BREAKFAST MUSHROOM, which has fully opened up to 10 cm (4 in) across or more and the gills have turned black. They are the same common mushroom, *Agaricus*, as are found in the fields, though wild tend to be more strongly flavoured. The button mushroom's role in cooking is supportive, but it is a good example of mass agriculture at work and it is hard to say that it is worth four times less than the price of some exotic mushrooms. It keeps its shape well in cooking, the texture does not collapse (it remains *al dente* and bouncy in the mouth), and it takes in other flavours without losing its own. It will absorb roughly a tablespoon of butter to each 30 g (1 oz) of weight. In the larger open cups, the flavour has had time to unravel into sour grass and dusty roads, and is discernibly milkier and creamier, until eventually it becomes a bready sour inkiness reminiscent of its darkest, coldest, loneliest nights – in practice, too dominating for cooking with anything else.

CHESTNUT MUSHROOM

Sometimes called BROWN or BROWN CAP MUSHROOM or PARIS MUSHROOM, this is a bulbous variation on the common mushroom. The cap is a grey brown, the stalk fatter and the whole altogether firmer and less fragile. It tends to be more absorbent than the button, perhaps taking up only 1½ tablespoons of butter for each 30 g (1 oz) of weight. They keep their shape well in cooking and have a discernibly stronger flavour, which is sour when raw and stronger and more earthy and intense than the white.

OYSTER MUSHROOM

This is one of the more common finds in the wild, but it is also cultivated – albeit at twice the price of white mushrooms. They have the looks, with their silky beige-grey frills like swirling skirts; and they cook quickly but lose their shape too, retaining their sponginess, but are more resistant to taking on other flavours. They have their own delicious elusive taste. Raw they are sour, milky and bready; cooked they have some of the bounciness of white mushrooms and a sense of unacid lemons, which makes them good for bulking and providing extra dimensions of texture, especially in soups and eastern dishes. Apart from the most common white variety, there are also YELLOW and PINK OYSTER MUSHROOMS, which attract yet further premiums of up to £1 per 1 lb again. The taste is almost identical to that of the white, but the yellow keeps its attractive colour in cooking.

SHIITAKE MUSHROOM

Shiitake have very dark caps and thin stems. In the raw they are paper-dry and bready, with distinct hints of lemon; but in cooking they lose their firmness and some of the texture and become very sweet, rich, meaty and deliciously strong. Widely used in Chinese and Japanese cooking, they are good with meats and soups. Their main drawback is the price, at nearly four times that of white mushrooms.

The culture is ancient and was developed on the island of Shikoku in Japan. Oak trees aged 25-33 years old were felled, axe cuts were made at 10-15 cm (4-6 in) intervals and the logs left in the darkest part of the forest. 'The logs are steeped in water for a number of hours according to the dryness of the locality, and then struck with pommels to facilitate the growth of the mushroom,' wrote one observer.

Storing Mushrooms

Mushrooms do not like condensation or light. Either store them in a paper bag in the salad drawer of the fridge or take off the film from the prepacked box, if they have one, and cover with a cloth.

The growth appears in the ridges after the third year. They are now grown here.

CEP

Also known as the PENNY BUN, the botanical term for this highly prized wild mushroom is *Boletus edulis*. If one mushroom embodies the spirit and cause of mushroom-hunting, then it is the cep. It looks the part, with its shiny bun-shaped cap and swollen white stalk... only the gnome is missing. In fact, it looks so perfect it might have come straight from an antique shop by mistake. They like beech woods, but have been found in other woods. The flesh is meaty and substantial, tending to be slimy if they have been bottled.

> **Ways with CEPs**
>
> They make first-class soup, or the caps can be baked with butter. They also freeze well.

CHANTERELLE

Oh for a reputation like the chanterelle! How can such a wispy, stringy choir girl be sold for such a price? At £14 per lb, it is one of the most expensive of foods. They were once so plentiful they were harvested commercially around Chelmsford in Essex and some export still goes on from Scottish pine forests. These go mainly to France, where they are known as GIROLLES and have been over-hunted or their habitats chemically destroyed, if not quite to extinction certainly to serious decline. The earthiness and evocative nutty flavour – 'all moss and must' – imbues everything around it. The texture is a bit rubbery, but this makes it long-standing in casseroles.

HEDGEHOG MUSHROOM

Known to the French as PIED DE MOUTON, this is not actually a mushroom but a fungus found in broad-leaved woodlands from late summer. Pinky brown, it has a coarse spongy texture. It is bitter when raw, but when cooked tastes of chestnuts. Good in casseroles, they are woody and gutsy but also slightly granular. Probably because they are not as well known as other mushrooms, their price is less inflated. There is also a PIED DE MOUTON BLEU, in which the stems take on a moonscape blueness. The little frilly honeycomb inside the cap should be rubbed off before cooking.

MOREL

Possibly the finest of all wild mushrooms, this is found in open woodland in the south of England in late spring, though not in the same numbers as on mainland Europe. Those that squeeze into Nine Elms Market are usually from the Jura and the Vosges mountains, where hunting is a cottage industry. They should not be eaten raw, and retain much of their potency when dried.

OTHER WILD MUSHROOMS

The MOUSSERON is tiny, about 1 cm (½ in), with a dark brown cap. Often quite hard, they are 'expensive accoutrements'. Collectors can still find many species that were much more common until quite recently. The WOOD BLE-WIT was sold freely in Midlands markets before the advent of cultivated mushrooms. The blue tends to fade on the gills as it ages. The SHAGGY INK CAP or JUDGE'S WIG is edible while it is still in the shape of a torpedo, before its umbrella opens up. The gills should still be pink, not black as the ink starts to run. It is usually found under mown grass, often at roadsides. Most PUFFBALLS are edible and giant puffballs were served at the Freemason's Tavern in London at official occasions. They can be breadcrumbed and fried in butter or stuffed. Enthusiasts say the texture is like sweetbreads and the flavour mildly nutty. The HORN OF PLENTY is still abundant in patches, usually in beech woods in late summer, though they can be quite tough and are somewhat overrated. PARA-SOLS, both SHAGGY and FIELD, are related to the common mushroom and can substitute in most recipes. FAIRY RING CHAMPIGNON was common on lawns until the use of chemicals and was often used in steak and kidney pies. The ST GEORGE'S MUSHROOM is supposed to appear on its namesake's day, April 23, so is one of the first mushrooms of the year and is beautifully white and can have a particularly good texture.

TRUFFLES

Given the prohibitive price of truffles, this is a somewhat academic entry. Even most restaurants will only use shavings and trimmings, or more frequently something frozen. Another drawback is that with the BLACK TRUFFLE, you need quite a lot of fresh truffle to create an impression. To smell a box of fresh truffles from the Périgord is a magical and convincing explanation of their reputation, and possibly as close as most of us are likely to get. Périgord truffles must be used bravely and with abandon.

The advantage of the WHITE TRUFFLE from Alba (there is a market each October) is that less goes further. A few thin shavings transform an omelette, pasta, or even the whole room with their sexual pungency.

The SUMMER TRUFFLE is imported from Italy and there have been occasional finds here in Perth and in Avon, but it does not command the same respect. The skin is knobbly black, with pine kernel markings, and the flesh grey to black with a lighter taste that is less dramatic but not completely worthless. The vendors push their luck at £110 per kg.

FRUIT

The difficulty in buying good fruit is finding ripeness. Smell is always a good test. While the quality of most main-line fruits, like apples and oranges, is consistent, the more peripheral examples, such as exotics and softer fruits, are patently badly understood by supermarkets.

The supermarkets have a virtual monopoly on class-1 fruit. Street markets may appear to be the romantic way of buying from small producers. In practice, however, they are just picking up the leftovers cheaply. Any small farm production that might 40 years ago have supplied local or specialist produce of, say, apples, pears or cherries has long since been disappeared — to everyone's loss.

Sainsbury seems to have a particularly bad record for keeping fruit up to the mark. **Waitrose** is probably the best supermarket for fruit, possibly followed by better branches of **Safeway**, who tend to be rather better at their publicity in the area than they are in reality. **Tesco** appears to phasing out many exotic lines and varietal differences, which is surely a step in the wrong direction. **Marks & Spencer** has the quality, but usually a more limited selection and at a price.

The level of global standardization is frightening. Of all the grape varieties in the world, why is it that a mediocre seedless variety like Thompson can become so dominant?

BERRY FRUIT

Berry fruits are among summer's great gifts. However, their delicacy is often undermined by poor packaging. Across the board, growers have been so obsessed with yields and long-keeping that much of what gets to market is a shadow of its reputation. Looks and size have taken the place of flavour and diversity.

BLACKBERRY

The infinite — well, 2,000 plus — varieties of cultivated blackberries are credited to North America. This must, however, be a textbook aberration as, like the blackthorn, they must have constituted an important part of the early hedgerows in this country. In the wild they tend to be more sour, hence their ubiquitous fate as a part of blackberry and apple crumble. When perfectly ripe, there is no finer fruit. The first English cultivated varieties start in August; grown under cover they have a disappointing taste but look beautiful. *Sylvan*, with its long pod, is one of the better varieties. Browny purple to black and hairy, it is sweet to sour in a quick flush with an acid finish. In this it resembles imports like *South American Giant*, which is fat like a Homburg hat, with a juicy purple/black berry, about 3 cm (1¼ in) long but almost square, with a very big hull.

BLUEBERRY

The blueberry is part of the same richly named family as the huckleberry, whortleberry, bilberry and the cranberry — a branch of the heather fraternity, which at the other end of the spectrum extends to rhododendrons and azaleas. Blueberries are the pick of the family, developed in America and shipped here from Oregon, although cultivation has started in Dorset. They are usually available from July to September, with a few stragglers hanging on for the Christmas market.

BOYSENBERRY

Developed in France during the '20s, from the strawberry, raspberry, loganberry and dewberry — none of which it resembles, being mainly tart and juicy, this long berry, about 2.5 cm (1 in), is scarlet blue, with compact pods. It is sour, like an unripe cross between a raspberry and a blackberry.

CRANBERRY

The cranberry is often confused with its cousin the lingonberry. The cranberry grows in boggy ground from Cape Cod to Wisconsin, forming huge red lakes after the valleys are flooded from which they are harvested in nets. Cranberries were served at the first Thanksgiving Dinner in 1621. The name comes from the pink blossom which resembles a crane's neck. The berries first came here with the clippers to help sailors ward off scurvy, but it was only in 1974 that **Ocean Spray** took on the UK market seriously.

The European version which flourishes wild in Scandinavia is, in fact, a lingonberry. It is slightly smaller, richer and superior in flavour, though it is usually sold as a cranberry. **Ocean Spray** dominates the American market, but other good brands to look for are **Original Wild Swedish** lingonberries, **Wilkins & Son**, and **Sainsbury** own-label, Increasingly, they have become available fresh, which is a better option for classic variations with orange or port added at the end of cooking to make a sauce.

GOOSEBERRY

The gooseberry was first described by the invading Arabs in Spain around the 8th century, where it was probably used as a laxative medicine. They were well suited to our climate and were grown as hedges to medieval gardens. They are, however, martyrs to mildew and most go for processing. The best eaters are the red-berried *Whinham's Industry* and *Whitesmith*. The reputation of the gooseberry really hangs on one variety, **Levellers are round and fat, almost bursting the skin, with a colour going on amber from a veined lime. This is *the* eating gooseberry, with sour skin and a beautifully fleshy pippy sweetness that has lush high notes. Unfortunately, they are usually sold too unripe.

LOGANBERRY

Named after J.M. Logan, who developed it in California in 1900, this berry is inclined to go mushy quickly. The long purple dusky hairy pod is juicy and sour/sweet, with a similar impact to a strawberry.

RASPBERRY

Rarely sold by variety, the trade tends to buy raspberries by the grower. The Scottish Crop Research Institute at Invergowrie has 500 varieties, but commercially it really is a fruit that seems to have lost its way — which for something so prized is scandalous.

The most common is *Bliss* with a long pod, which is dry, tart and pippy. The pips are controversial, as is its hair. The demand of the multiples is for lipstick-pink, not the winy-hued purple berry. They are still picked by hand, another problem. The extending growing season, now up to eight weeks, has reawakened multiple interest at the expense

Ways with Raspberries

An old recipe for raspberry vinegar: Bruise 450 g (1 lb) of ripe raspberries in a large bowl and pour over 1.1 litres (1 qt) of white wine vinegar. Let stand for 24 hours. Strain liquid over a second bowl of fresh raspberries, let this stand for 24 hours and repeat the process yet again with more berries. Do not squeeze the fruit at any stage or it may ferment. Strain through canvass, measure and add 450 g (1 lb) of white sugar to each pint of juice. Stir well and pour into stone bottles.

of pick-your-own farms and small shops.

Supermarkets start to sell around June 15, but the first examples tend to be scabby and anaemic. The first varieties are *Glen Moy* and *Glen Prosen*, before *Autumn Bliss* which can go on to October. Among the Scottish raspberries, bravely flavoured shiny *Glen Lyon* compares against older neatly formed *Leo* from Kent, which has a grey blush on pink, with small white whiskers and a deep clean hollow for the hull. It is quite dry, with a classic tartness. Gardeners suggest *Malling Jewel* and *Malling Joy* are the most delicious mid-season varieties; *September* and *Zeva* for autumn fruit.

STRAWBERRY

The strawberry has become like a third-world country that has suddenly discovered some riches. New varieties spring up that are bigger, brighter and brasher; while everyone looks down on the old versions as smaller, misshapen and inferior — even if these possess the intrinsic charm of the interplay of the sours of the under-ripe contrasting against the sweet sugars of the ripe elements not found in many of the new generation. Possibly we have become blunted by artificial flavours, but to find such a strawberry these days is not easy.

Wild strawberries grow across the world, but most cultivated strawberries can trace their lineage back to the Chilean strawberry and the Virginian strawberry introduced in the 17th century and crossed successfully by French breeders 100 years later. It is a false fruit, the real fruit being the golden pips on the outside.

Pick-your-own farms usually start selling earlier than you expect, sometimes even on June 1, though more usually by June 15. The first through are *Hapil* and *Elsanta*, followed by *Cambridge Vigour* and *Cambridge Favourite* and then *Pegasus* and *Honeyoe* (good for jam). It is hard to resist the conclusion that many varieties are selected for their ability to deal with families of untrained fingers pulling them to pieces rather than for the flavour. Early commercial varieties in the shops, like *Chandler*, are quite poor in flavour and growers are moving towards *Ossogrande* for some reason. However, *Elsanta* is riding a crest of a reputation, possibly mostly due to its appearance. *Sovereign* is recognized as one of the best, but has less than a day's prime life after picking and so is really only the province of gardeners.

No other strawberries through the year really compare with open-air-grown English in a good summer. On poor varieties pairing with oranges or even a dash of Grand Marnier helps to reinforce the flavour; or try a salad of sliced cucumber and strawberries dressed with black pepper.

Cambridge Favourite is now somewhat out of vogue with the trade for its short keeping, but widely found on PYO farms. Annatto in colour, smaller than modern breeds, at around 4 cm (1½ in), it is bright pink and flat-topped, with yellow ears and pockets. The flavour is sweet, rounded, gentle and soft, with good body.

Cambridge Vigour is scarlet turning rare-beef red, softening on the darker parts, with a perfectly formed classic shape and about 2 cm (¾ in) in size 3 — any bigger and it starts to square up into body-builder's shoulders. The flesh is salmon-coloured and loose-textured; the taste dainty, sour and with hints of watermelon, sweetening as the berries get bigger into sugary water. An example in July was darker than the Cambridge Favourite, inclined to flatness, delicate, with less body and a good taste in the juice; it was a good strawberry but lost its virtues quickly.

Elsanta was developed in Holland 1985. All hues of red, firm and classically heart-shaped, at least 4 cm (1½ in) across, the flesh has a yellow-white hue to the salmon and the taste is very deliberate and distinctly honeyed with no sours, familiar from the sweet repertory of artificial flavours. It does not seem to have any of the virtues classically attributed to the great English strawberry, but it is prolific and does have a long season. This is a good variety for PYO farms, as the berries are firm and a good size as well as standing up well to being inexpertly hand-picked. An example in July had good looks, almost like a Pegasus, being a bright, deep ruby red. It had a good first bite, but faded quickly. Another example a week later had a short finish but a perfect first mouthful, although it lacked clarity and complexity afterwards. They do lack the taste of Cambridge and are all looks and texture, though their flavour can cut through the grease of a heavy meal. You can understand the universal enthusiasm even, if it is not fully justified.

Elvira is ovoid when small, with thin page-boy-hat-type fronds off the stalk, fattening into two halves like the torso of a busty waitress. The flesh has an orange cast to the salmon and the taste is an organized sourness, like crushed lemons, especially when small, but developing a honey sweetness in the larger fruit. An example in July was neat red, long and angular, with a deep long sweet taste of lemons and a little sharpness, but lacking all-round flavour.

Hapil is predominantly red to scarlet, broad-shouldered, tapering to a point — a lifeguard's figure — eventually bulking up into two sides. The texture is a bit woody, with a poor distribution of flesh to pip and of sour to sweet. It becomes softer and very sweet, and is a bit velvety and one-dimensional.

Pegasus is a good muscular berry, deep scarlet in colour, with page-boy looks again to the stalk, pointed and fat. It is inclined to wateriness, with a slight bite and not much acidity. It does look the part, however, and is possibly the most handsome of all strawberries.

Other named varieties worth mentioning include: *Selva* from Belgium in August, which is fat and wide, with a sweet first taste but going woody and having a short finish; *Rapella* is an interesting strawberry, but falling from favour because of mildew problems; *Evita* is a new variety bred in Kent to grow in tunnels for the Christmas market.

Cambridge Rival and *Cambridge Favourite* are relatively easy to grow in gardens. *Royal Sovereign* and the perpetual *Aromel* , with a second autumn crop, need careful husbandry.

TAYBERRY

The Tayberry is a cross between an Aurora blackberry grown in Oregon and a Scottish raspberry. First developed circa 1983, it is now also grown in France. It has the best qualities of both its parents. The long, 4 cm (1½ in), thin pendulous pale berry, has a tart raspberry-to-strawberry flavour. Again, it is usually sold too unripe.

CITRUS FRUIT

The wonderful array of citrus fruits reaches its peak when most needed, in the dark days of January and February − a fitting counterpoint to the berries of summer. An increasing monument to the successful marriage of diversity and the global market.

CLEMENTINE

An accidental cross between a mandarin and a sweet orange in the garden of Father Pierre Clement in Algeria in 1902, this survives where other mandarin crosses have not. Available from November to February, they come mostly from North Africa or from South Africa in early summer.

Smaller than a satsuma, at about 4 cm (1½ in) across, and round like an unformed orange, the thin tight skin is light orange speckled on a paler background which is almost completely hidden. The fruit has a lovely configuration, with no pips, and is firm and juicy. Fragrant juicy and long-lasting, it has more flavour than a satsuma, but is not quite as user-friendly.

They are usually eaten whole, as it is hard to separate the segments.

GRAPEFRUIT

The original grapefruit was probably a mutation of the exceedingly large SHADDOCK (named after the Captain who took it to the West Indies), found in Thailand, Malaysia and Indonesia and which can weigh up to 5 kg (11 lb). Since its discovery in the last century it has been intensively developed using strains of different sweetness.

The POMELO is known as 'the mother of

grapefruits', in fact a cross between a shaddock and a devolved grapefruit: much larger,
thick-skinned and with bitter pith. Some trials
have started to develop a pink version.

Another variation — or the next generation
— is the **SWEETIE from Israel: about 9x7
cm (3½x2¾ in), lemon to lime in colour, with
a very bitter skin and sour thick white pith, it
has an intense sour scent but a lovely sweet
flavour, like an ugli fruit (see below).

The white-fleshed grapefruits have tended
to be bred sweeter and to have few, if any,
pips. Much of the character has moved from
the fruit to the pith and they have been out-
performed by the enthusiastic revival of pink-
fleshed varieties. A high proportion of ordinary grapefruit were off the mark, and well-
known examples from **Jaffa** were poor and
acidic with a high ratio of pith. *Marsh
Seedless*, sometimes just called *Marsh*, turns
a deeper colour — almost a pink flush — as it
ripens. Widely grown and available, it is
mostly notable for its juiciness and thin mem-
branes.

By general consent, the best *PINK
GRAPEFRUIT comes from Florida, although
the best American variety, *Duncan*, is not
seen here or if it is then it is not labelled as
such. There are different grades: 'ruby'
means deeply red; then there is 'burgundy';
and 'pink' is paler still, but sweeter than both.
Florida Pink has a yellow skin and, although
called pink, the flesh has a rich opalescence.
The long segments are very sweet, with a little sour and the texture is strong.
Indian River has yellow skin, and orange
blush to yellow flesh. It has no acidity and is
sweet enough to be eaten like an orange,
having good tangs of citrus.
Star Ruby was developed in the '70s and is
extensively grown in Cyprus. It could be mis-
taken for a squat orange from the skin,

although the flesh is a corpuscular red. The pith is thin, so there is lots of juicy flesh; it is more sour than other reds, with a taste closer to lemon. Often called *Sunrise*, it was conspicuously more impressive from **Jaffa** in the tastings than its white-fleshed counterpart.

KUMQUAT

Originally from China, this thumb-sized fruit with edible, slightly bitter, skin is now grown around the world. Gimmicky, cocktail-party food, the flavour is quite sharp — actually the worst of most worlds, with a poor ratio of flesh to pith and skin – its single redeeming characteristic is its size.

LEMON

Lemons may not actually have reached this country until the 13th century. Only rarely do lemons carry their name, even if the difference between varieties in terms of acidity, sourness, pith levels and pip count are fundamental. **Safeway** has made some concession, importing thick-skinned Amalfi lemons in autumn and judiciously using cyrovac packaging to give its unwaxed lemons the semblance of a sheen. Price is a consistent guideline for quality, though unwaxed remain more expensive than waxed — a bizarre anomaly, as less is done. Otherwise, one suspects the British market is probably largely a dumping ground for the undiscerning, with precious few clues available for us to discover the true values of different fruits.

LIME

Originally from Malaysia, limes have proliferated in most warm climates where lemons also grow. A relative newcomer to this country, they were only planted seriously in the

West Indies around 1850 and almost completely unknown in our markets until 1890. The distinctions between limes from different varieties and regions are blurred and information scant. The round limes of the Caribbean and Southern Europe tend to be thinner-skinned, and are likely to turn yellow and be bitter. Indian limes tend to be sweeter. Occasionally *WILD LIMES can be found — brought in via Rungis, usually for the restaurant trade. Knobbly and deep green, scratch their skin and the potency is obvious.

MANDARIN

This is a hard fruit to find these days. They were also called the NARCHEY ORANGE or the CLOVE ORANGE or NOBLE ORANGE, being distinctively flatter than taller and more perfumed. They have been widely used to cross-breed with other species. A good mandarin will be larger and darker than a tangerine, with a thin manageable skin and full fleshy segments with pips. The taste is watery and acid, but with lovely scented high notes of the kind to which commercial orange drinks aspire. The European season starts in December, although the rather charming practice of wrapping each fruit in coloured paper or tin foil has fallen out of fashion.

MINNEOLA

A cross between a tangerine and a grapefruit, this is sometimes called a TANGELO or ORLANDO. Most come from Israel. They have a distinctive bulbous nib and are easy to peel, with only a small amount of pith and the occasional pip — the segments amply filling the globe. The mild tart juiciness has hints of mandarin, verging on the sour – 'actually it is the taste of Grand Marnier'.

ORANGE

The orange was first imported from Spain in 1290, but it was Sir Walter Raleigh who reintroduced them in the 16th century. By the 19th century there were warehouses devoted to the orange trade at Hunstrete in London and at Liverpool. The first oranges were bitter, SEVILLE or BIGARADE oranges, for marmalade-making. For oranges to flourish, the winter temperature must not drop below 4°C (40°F). Citrus fruit from the more tropical climates tends to have dirty skins, but this does not necessarily have a bearing on the quality. Pips in oranges and orange variations are becoming rare. The luminescent purple, red and green string bags in which they are sold tend to hide blemishes.

FORTUNA is squat and bowling-ball-shaped. Smooth and thin-skinned, it has one pip per segment and is juicy, with tones of mandarin but gentler and duller. It is a very safe flavour, with high acid.

MANDORA is squat, with a smooth tight bitter skin that is hard to peel; the coarse and deeply orange flesh is juicy, fragrant and tart, but a bit clumsy and unrewarding. An example tried from Cyprus, about 8x7 cm (3¼x2¾ in), with three pips per section, was very poor and unattractive.

NAVELINA is an early version of the WASHINGTON NAVEL, beginning around November. Our example from Spain was about 8x9 cm (3¼x3½ in), a perfect deep bright orange in colour and round but tending to point at the peak, hence the name. The thick tight skin is relatively easy to peel and there is little pith. The 10 neat segments have a lovely sharp well-pitched flavour, not overly sweet to start with, but building up a great balance of acidity and sweetness. Also related, but slightly later in the season starting around January, is the *Navellate*, which is very juicy, round and pipless.

RUBY RED, available from Spain in January to March, is sometimes called the BLOOD ORANGE or the MALTA ORANGE. Originally grafted from a pomegranate tree crossed with an orange, the blood-red colour of the flesh develops as it ripens and eventually colours even the skin. Round and small, at about 8 cm (3¼ in), it has a dusky, pock-marked thin skin. There are blood-red veins around the edges of the segments, which give the orange a bloody hue becoming more pronounced as they ripen. Unripe, they tend to be tart and one-dimensional in flavour. They are good in drinks, but apart from the colour have little appeal.

SALUSTIANA is sold as a juicing orange here, but also justifies its place as a sweet eating orange. Popular with growers in North Africa and Spain, they are about 7 cm (2¾ in) in size, with a thin tight pale skin which is easily peeled. The fresh neat segments have soft flesh and instant juice and fragrance. A bit underrated for juice, these are attractive and refreshing, and have no pips.

SANGUINE is spindly with a mottled orange skin flecked with red. About 7.5-8 cm (3-3¼ in) in size, it has ample skin and pith and small thin neatly formed segments. The flavour is sharp, sweet, tart, precise and to the point. They do not have the lusciousness of fruit earlier in the year, but are on the dry side, feeling more like a stored orange, a half-time football orange.

SEVILLE, usually from Spain, is almost round, about 6 cm (2½ in) across, with viciously bitter skin and pith on which its reputation for marmalade is based. It contains a small clustering of pale segments, each with 3 or 4 pips each, and a grapefruit-sour flavour which is quite arresting. The Sevillians must have been overjoyed to discover the idea of marmalade. The oranges do need vats of sugar to make them at all palatable — twice the weight of sugar to orange.

SHAMOUTI from Israel is tall and distinctively flat-topped and takes over from the Navel as the mainstream orange in March. With deep coloured, slightly wrinkled skin and thick pith, it is tricky to peel. Inside are neat segments, which are sweet, juicy and slightly tart.

SUNTINA is about 6.5 cm (3¼ in) in size and inclined to be oblong, with a deep — almost artificial-looking — orange spicy skin. Almost pithless, but perfectly formed clean segments are without pips and very sweet; like sucking a sugar cube out of an orange. Although interesting, the sugar level is way off the scale and the flavour is just a bit one-dimensional.

VALENCIA is a late orange and the handsome luminescent deep-orange ovoid is slightly deformed at the stalk. The thick-looking, pock-marked and cratered skin is easy to peel, revealing perfectly formed thin segments. An Israeli example was sweet and juicy, with a single pip to each segment or less, it was slightly pithy with a strong taste leading to sours. The less impressive examples tend to the taste of boiled sweets, but are at their best from Valencia: a round example, 8 cm (3¼ in) across, was luminescent, thin-skinned and strong-tasting leading to sours, chunky with no pips and quite long segments.

ORTALINE

Another of the family of tangerine/grapefruit crosses, this arrives in Spring from Spain. It has a flat, sat-upon configuration and a beautifully clean orange skin, quite tightly wrapped around healthy segments. Very sweet on the first bite, it is quite fragrant and tart, with a gentle and interesting flavour.

ORTANIQUE

The flat, squashed appearance of this fruit belies its superb quality. An example from Jamaica was about 7.5-8 cm (3-3" in) with a bitter thin skin, smooth-fleshed, flecked with black spots and occasional pips, the soft-fleshed segments filling the interior. It had a lovely texture and a beautifully perfumed intensity, building in its sweetness. Another from Morocco was more like a squat orange with a thin skin: juicy and tart with no pips. It was sweet to sticky and fragrant.

SATSUMA

A pipless variation of the Mandarin orange, originating from Japan and named after the province where it was first grown, it is typically the easiest citrus to peel. Organic examples can be twice the price of ordinary. Early varieties from Uruguay arrive in April with very pale tight skin and fat segments. Quite scented, they are sharp and juicy with a refreshing flavour not far removed from grapefruit. Early summer varieties from Uruguay can be thick-skinned and lemony green, very juicy but low on taste and quite tart.

An example tried from Argentina was ragged, with a mottled appearance; soft and pliable in the mouth, it was juicy with a lovely distinctive texture — better than the other, even if the flavour is muted. A third from Spain in December had a floppy skin which was deep orange, imbued with hues of green and lemon, and easy to peel: the 10 segments were juicy, with a mild tang, like a squash drink, although inclined to wateriness and with a short finish.

TANGERINE

Along with the mandarin, one of the mothers of the new generation of citrus crosses. It is quite rare and tends to look like a rejected small orange. The tightly knit skin is speckled and a bit dirty, but easily peeled; the segments fill the pith and have two pips each. Soft, juicy, mild and not overly tart, it is like an immature orange.

UGLI

This is a cross between a grapefruit, orange and a tangerine first bred in Jamaica and the name was patented by **Jamaica Produce**. A dirty soft-skinned grapefruit in smudged yellows and greens, it is full-fleshed inside the skin, which peels away from its white pith. The flesh is floppy in the mouth and juicy, like an unsour grapefruit, and with an intriguing soft texture. One from **Waitrose** was a vivid British racing green and a massive 12x10 cm (4¾x4 in), with cactus-like indentations — almost plastic looking. It was possibly under-ripe, but the orange-blushed segments sent an immediate tart zest of lemons and melons.

UNIQ has caused some controversy among some grocers as some say it is just another form of ugli, while **Safeway — the supermarket who first adopted it — claim it is a wild variation. It is as big, with a floppy thick soft skin, opening up to reveal whole segments. A sort of relaxed grapefruit, it has a lemony smell and a beautifully fresh first mild and fragrant taste, with a brief finish. Available from January to May, it is outstanding among all citrus fruits.

EXOTIC FRUIT

The arrival of exotic fruits has symbolized the pioneering nature of the supermarkets, although in the last two years some — noticeably **Tesco** — have cooled considerably. They have all experienced some difficulty with them in maintaining ripeness.

BANANA

Until the turn of the century, botanists still referred to the banana as *Musa sapientum paradisiaca*, as tradition had it that it was a banana — not an apple — that Eve gave to Adam. Hence its other name of 'Paradise figs', often still used for dried bananas in the trade. There is some confusion over the difference between the PLANTAIN and the banana, though the shorthand explanation has come to be that plantains are for cooking and bananas for eating raw. The confusion arises because all the bananas on a whole bunch are never fully ripe at the same time. The skill exercised on the plantations is to cut the cluster at the right time so they can be ripened on the boats.

The much smaller Canary Island banana was the first commercially traded banana in the London markets until, in 1902, the first boats docked in Bristol from Jamaica. The banana industry is sustained by international agreement, with different countries paying premiums to take bananas from underdeveloped regions. Nearly all the bananas sold here are from the Caribbean, supplemented occasionally when stocks are down by some from Central America. Although the traditional preference here — dating back to Canary bananas — has been for small fruit, Central American bananas are larger and, many hold, better-tasting, smelling more of fruit, even apricots. The Central American trade is better organized into plantations, compared to the dependent shanty industries of the Windward Islands and Jamaica. Not surprisingly, bananas do not like the cold and should not be stored in the fridge.

The best bananas in tastings in the past year has consistently been *COSTA RICA, usually around 10p more expensive. The RED BANANA, usually from Cuba or India, is rarely found. Left to ripen so the claret skin has streaks of black, the flesh will be salmon pink, perfumed and creamy. The APPLE BANANA is a finger-sized miniature, perfect for neat little recipes, like fritters.

CACTUS FRUIT

The spines of this fruit are usually nicked off; if not, handle them with extreme caution and peel them on the end of a knife. The softly smooth skin is a blushing red-orange and the flesh is a brilliant vermilion, tasting like a cross between a tomato and passion fruit. There is little waste, save the tough, shot-style pips. The flesh has an attractive soft sweet mealy texture and a versatile flavour that carries over well into cooked dishes.

COQUITO

These tiny coconuts from Chile, also known as BABY COCONUTS, are the size of marbles and are sold ready peeled. Although hollow, they are too young to have any milk. With a milky hazelnut flavour, serve these addictive fruits just as they are, like nuts.

DATE

According to an old Arab saying, dates need their feet in the water and their heads in the fire. The trees grow to about 15 m (50 ft) and open out into a cluster of 40 to 80 feather-shaped leaves, about 2.5-3 m (8-10 ft) long. From this cluster hang 180-230 kg (400-500 lb) of fruit in bunches of 9-13.5 kg (20-30 lb). They will not bear fruit until they are 8–10 years old and need temperatures of more than 38°C (100°F) and must be at least 25 miles from the sea as they can't bear any trace of salt.

The date palm can sustain a complete village, as they have done in the deserts around Tunis for centuries, where estates are handed down as dowries. The trunk supplies timber for houses, fencing and fuel; the leaves go to make baskets, bags, mats, fans, brushes, walking sticks, ropes, cords, roofs and walls; spirits like *arrak*, sugars and vinegars are made from the fruit; the young unfurled shoots and leaves are eaten as a vegetable, and the stones made into a kind of coffee or fed to the animals.

As with Camembert cheese, the long boat-shaped boxes for dates have been among the finest examples of packaging art, though the dates themselves — usually the fabled DEGLET NOIR — are drenched in a glucose syrup. The original North-African trade in these is now rivalled by that of California.

GOLDEN from Israel is a small kumquat-sized oval, 2 cm (¾ in) tall, with a colour of burnt ochre. The skin is sweet and the white flesh is sugary sweet and crunchy, as you might imagine sugar cane to be. These are even more expensive than Medjoul, at about £4.50 per lb.

HAYANI from Israel are large smooth brown lozenges, with a long stone and a sweet straw texture. Mealy and indistinct, they are pleasantly comforting with an interesting mix of textures.

**MEDJOUL, from the Jordan River in Israel, are large, nearly 5x2 cm (2x¾ in), morel-shaped, and translucent purple with a burgundy blush. They are dry, meaty and sticky sweet, but naturally sugared — some say they have a buttery voluptuousness. They have a small stone so make a big mouthful, but they are expensive at nearly £4 per lb.

BRANCH DATES from Tunisia will keep for a year. The beige to chestnut-brown flesh has a distinct gentle nuttiness which produces sweetness, but without the cloying levels of sugar in boxed dates. STONED DATES from **Whitworth's** are pressed into blocks, and may be the produce of more than one country. Granulated but not over-syruped, they are useful in recipes.

FIG

Figs are so redolent of the images of sexuality — male and female — and of dreams of power that they assume a mythical significance that surpasses their more mundane fate of being battered into cellophane blocks of dense sweet stickiness or of being the butt of laxative jokes. They are frequently mentioned in the Bible, beyond Adam and Eve reaching for the leaves to protect their modesty. It was also the flavour of Athens figs that reputedly tempted Xerxes to conquer Greece in 480BC.

The tree is native to Palestine and its cultivation has spread to encompass the whole of the Mediterranean. The finest were held to be the SMYRNA, being fatter and with softer skin after drying. The fruit from the male tree is inedible, but becomes home to a wasp which fertilizes the female. Traditionally, the female trees were wreathed in garlands of male figs from June 5-15. Smyrna figs go for drying and were also the rootstock taken to California.

The COMMON FIG does not have such a romantic aura, growing from seed and propagated by cuttings. The flavours vary from region to region, rather than by variety or colour of the skin. There can be two harvests in the year, the first to be eaten fresh and the second, much sweeter, usually used for drying, where the sugars can constitute more than half the bulk.

A ripe fig will be heavy in the hand and soft to the touch, as if it is filled with its own juice like a water bag. Cooking in water emaciates them, though they combine well other ingredients, especially Mediterranean flavours like anise and nuts.

*BURSA figs from Turkey arrive in late autumn to a chorus of enthusiasm: 'large pear-shaped, sweet and pungent'. Traditionally, these might have been served with cured hams or stuffed with sweetmeats. The best Italian figs are *KADOTA, familiar in shape from tins. Other varieties arrive from the Mediterranean through the summer in different hues of lime-green to almost purple or jet-black, but each contain dramatic crimson tendrils sometimes touched with lemon. These are the flowers, sometimes left in figs for drying, or allowed to grow on to seed.

> At the turn of the century figs were always eaten on Mothering and Palm Sundays. Fig pie or fig puddings were a tradition in the Home Counties, though in other parts of the country the figs were replaced with currants – and indeed currants are still called figs by many.

GRENADILLO

This speckled orange lantern from Colombia has a hard cardboard-like skin and white bready pith with a good volume of translucent grey pistules inside easily removable sacks. Related to the passion fruit, but not as tart, it has a better ratio of flesh and pip to skin, but is somewhat less intense in flavour.

GUAVA

When ripe, the smell of this fruit from Brazil can fill the room. Cooking brings out the flavour inherent in the sandy and deep-pipped flesh. An example tasted when the skin was still very green (on ripe fruit the skin should have yellowed) had a musky smell of elderflowers. Use in ice-cream, puddings, jellies, salads or to support more conventional fruits, such as apple or pears in cooking.

KIWANO

An orange oval from Colombia, it has small spikes like a tiny dinosaur. Inside it is obviously one of the passion fruit family, the pips held in a gel; but this is a refreshing lime version, with the flavour veering towards melon.

KIWI FRUIT

Sometimes called the CHINESE GOOSE-BERRY, before it leapt to universal acceptance on the back of mass cultivation in New Zealand. Most sold in this country now come from Italy. They have unseen virtues, not least their enormous vitamin C content which is 10 times that of a lemon, and they can tenderize meat in a marinade. The biggest problem is finding a ripe one: test the hairy khaki skin as for an avocado (see page 236). The ratio of brilliant emerald flesh to skin is excellent, and it is best eaten with a teaspoon. Although advocates would pair it off with anything, the high level of acidity mitigates against universal use as it will curdle cream and dissolve a gelatine-set mousse.

LOQUAT

This Israeli fruit looks like an exotic apricot and is available from late spring to early summer. Creamy orange and speckled as it gets riper, it has a tough, inedible skin. Inside, it has a smooth lychee-style pip and the flesh is juicy and refreshingly sour.

LYCHEE

This Thai fruit is hardly a new exotic, but it has still to establish itself properly. It is small, slightly larger than a grape at 2x4 cm (¾x1½ in), and the horned thin pastel-scarlet skin coats a translucent, purple-hued silky smooth flesh around the smoothest of pips. Perfumed and delicious, the flavour is refreshingly chill and sweet, one of the world's great luxuries. Like mangoes, however, the stickiness lingers more than it might. The juiciness is lost quickly and they are best bought in small quantities at a time. Paler varieties tend to have a fuller flavour.

MANGO

This fruit takes its name from the Malay *mang*, meaning a tree. Perhaps surprisingly, mangoes are from the same family as cashew and pistachio nuts. The dark shiny-leafed trees can grow to as much as 35 m (115 ft) in span and have transplanted from their native India to most hot climates. The fruits vary from the tiny egg-shaped wild varieties that taste like turpentine to the larger sweeter straw orange with which we are more familiar. There are more than 2,500 varieties in all. 'No fruit possess so wide a range from absolute vileness to the most delicious lusciousness,' declared an early writer. In India, they are picked before they are ripe to make tarts and preserves. Here they have invariably been ripened *en route*. A good

(see left)

Ways with Mango

Slice down both sides either side of the flat of the stone, cut the flesh in a criss-cross pattern into squares and turn the skin inside out to allow the knife to cut underneath. Shave the remaining flesh off the stone and cut into sections.

mango has a neon-orange flesh, oozes juice and should not be stringy or fibrous.

By necessity it will be messy to eat or to carve (see left). One easier solution is the new suckable varieties from the Gambia, arriving in July and August. Some of the sense of the many differences between mangoes has started to appear in supermarkets. Most are air-freighted, but the price comes down considerably if they are sent by ship.

Bombay has been highly regarded for many years as among the finest of mangoes. A golden sunset-yellow, this plump oval fruit is found only during May. The succulent flesh is even deeper yellow — almost saffron — and can stain. Expensive at nearly £2 a piece.

Haden from the Gambia are squat, elongated to 11 cm (4¾ in). Khaki going on red in colour, the flesh is bright yellow, smooth and rimmed light green. It has a distinctive flavour of sweet lemons with something floral, and is not fibrous.

Mangop from Brazil is tropical green into verdant orange and smooth reds, about 11x9 cm (4¾x3½ in). The smooth deep peach-ochre flesh is fibrous to eat and slightly shreddy, but fragrant with a tart sweetness.

Ruby from the Gambia is only available in July and August. It is unusual in that the top can be cut across and the flesh sucked out. Yellow to dusty apple-red in colour with a bright yellow flush and about 11 cm (4¾ in), it has a pure excellent taste and is very juicy.

Tommy Atkins from Puerto Rico is a flattish smooth ovoid, apple green going on red in colour. Inside the flesh is vivid orange, fibrous and apricot-like with a hint of pineapple.

MANGOSTEEN

Again from Thailand, the imposingly impressive outer casing of this fruit is like a well-worn cricket ball encrusted with hard green leaf and stalk. Inside is a lychee-like fruit in sections which is deliciously impressive. It is available from April. Tinned examples tend to be poor.

PAPAYA

Also known as the PAW PAW, this Jamaican fruit is ripe when the skin turns yellow, with just a hint of green hue. The flesh should be an intense pink that responds to lemon or lime. Slice it lengthwise and scoop out the black seeds which are also said to be a laxative. The fruit contains the enzyme papain, so it cannot be used to form jellies or mousses; it can, however, be effective in a marinade.

PASSION FRUIT

The passion in question is religious rather than sexual, christened by missionaries in South America who thought the cluster of the flower and stalk resembled the crucifixion. The round fruit, about 4-5 cm (1½-2 in), has a wrinkled rhino skin which breaks up like parchment to reveal the generous filling of yellow black pods. The flavour is tart and direct, but the sweet aftertaste is the attraction. Now mostly from Zambia, they are considerably cheaper than most other exotics.

PERSIMMON

Examples of persimmons are usually quite small in supermarkets here, but Italian and Spanish top-grade fruit can be as large as a beef tomato. The persimmon has such a high tannin content that it is virtually inedible unripe. The SHARON FRUIT is a variety of persimmon developed in Israel which is tannin-free and can be eaten like an apple, before it has matured. The smooth shiny skin is slightly fragile and bursting when ripe, with a distinct shade of dirty orange, and the stalk decoratively encrusted with its leaves. The flesh is beautifully and uniformly streaked in shades of deep orange; if it is apricot-pale then it is not ripe. It has a delicate, quite elusive, honey-sweet flavour, in a silky smooth and richly fibrous texture which is its great attraction. However, the skin is viciously bitter.

PHYSALIS FRUIT

Artistically wrapped inside its own resilient paper-like leaf, this small golden berry the size of a small cherry, is tart, sweet and custardy. Also known as the CAPE GOOSE-BERRY, its tiny pips are edible. Very decorative and now mostly imported from Colombia, it has a distinctive taste, like a sour cherry or the first taste of a strawberry.

PINEAPPLE

This is a 'false fruit' like the strawberry, ie made up of lots of little fruits which form the scales and eyes on the skin. The Spanish discovered the pineapple in the 15th century in Paraguay, where the Guarani Indians had already developed a considerable trade in the 'beautiful fruit'. As early as the beginning of the 1700s, pineapples were being grown in European greenhouses to sell to the rich. The French in the late '40s encouraged the cultivation across Africa. A pineapple does not travel well once picked and only air freight has made its reputation as a fresh fruit.

Pineapples contains an enzyme, bromelin, which breaks down protein and is useful in marinades, but for the same reason will not allow the setting of gelatine. Those fruit still with the long leafy stalks are easier to judge for ripeness — the smaller inner leaves will come away if the pineapple is lifted by them.

Fully ripe, the stalk will give and move around. Yellow pineapples tends to eat sweeter, but are twice the price. Smell the bottom of a pineapple and you will gauge almost precisely how fresh it is. QUEEN PINES, from South Africa, are smaller at about 8 cm (3¼ in) square, with deep blistered orange skin and are very sweet. They have a fragrant smell and are intensely rich, but quite dry.

RAMBUTAN

The most spectacular of the lychee family, with its mad monstrous tendrils, the fruit is ripe when the skin is bouncy and turns a violent crimson and the tendrils are fused red, not brown. The flesh is drier than a lychee.

TAMARILLO

This elegant deep red, heart-shaped fruit with a woody stalk, opens to reveal a stunning inside of black-to-purple seeds set in deep orange flesh and translucent juice. The flavour is tart, almost savoury, somewhere between tomato and plum. The skin is very bitter indeed and the seeds small like passion fruit. An example from **Sainsbury** was perfectly formed, like a tomato/passion fruit cross, with no acidity and luscious flesh around a central jelly pod with black pips.

ZALACCA

Another in the lychee family, this fruit is very rarely found here. Looking like a bauble-sized armadillo, it has inedible pips and sharp tart juice which is quickly lost as they get older.

STONE FRUIT

Apricot
Cherry
Nectarine
Peach
Plum

The beauty of stone fruit lies in it being perfectly ripe. Too often it is sold hard and ungiving. The supermarkets' problem with it is that what looks good does not necessarily have much flavour.

APRICOT

The old English word for this fruit was 'apricock' from the Latin *praecox*, meaning early ripening. By June, they are one of the heralds of summer proper. Apricots have been grown in kitchen gardens since 1542, but they do need the sun and any frost at flowering time and there will be no fruit.

Most apricots come from France and Spain, though they originally came from Armenia and China and are widely grown around the Mediterranean rim, as well as in America, Australia and South Africa — much of this only surfacing here in tins. There is currently great enthusiasm among growers in France for giant apricots, twice the normal size. Known as *Jumbocot, Lambertin, Hargrand and Orange Red*, they began to be grown around Nîmes in 1989. The biggest apricot growers, centred in the Rhône valley, used to grow mainly the Polonaise variety until 1989 and have now switched to the Bergeron, and this has been said to account for the increase in sales in the UK.

Jane Grigson accepted defeat in her *Fruit Book* over fresh apricots, 'As things are in this country, you will probably be wise to regard apricots as a fruit for the kitchen, then you will not be disappointed'. Tarts, fillings, jams, glazes, bakes and puddings were their destiny in English cooking. On their travels around the globe, however, apricots have been assimilated into an extraordinary number of different preparations, from meat stews to low-fat baking substitutes.

Things may be improving, although a great many apricots are still sold without reference to their variety. If the celebrated English *Moor Park* is still grown commercially, it is being passed off under a pseudonym — though saplings are still sold in garden centres. Good apricots will be warmly coloured and rosy-cheeked, but will only keep a few days before wizening. Store them in a bag in the salad drawer of the fridge.

Castelbrite from Spain, is about 4x6 cm (1½x2½) with a rosy blush to the soft orange, light fur, and a stone that is less than one quarter of the fruit. It has a bright pleasant sunny taste and a good texture, although it tends to be uneven for ripeness rather than quality.

Orange Red from France, is one of the new larger breeds at 5x5.5 cm (2x2¼ in). Apricot-orange to mauve pink in colour, it is long and thin, like a half-egg shape. The sweet flesh is mango-yellow, soft, luscious and juicy, but can have threads of woody filament. With an elusive flavour, it tends to dry up in the mouth, and although generally good, they are nearly 40p each.

Peach Apricot from New Zealand is large — almost the size of a small orange — with an orange flush to the pink fur. The crevice is about as accurate a representation of the human bottom as the fruit world possesses. Very dry and grainy, it is missing the subtle elements of a good apricot, it is possibly tired out from the journey.

Red Royal from France is about 4x6 cm (1½x2½ in), with a white to yellow sheen and peach/mauve blush. The flesh is an even-coloured orange, sweet, juicy, with a good mellow flavour.

FOOD *watch*

Preserved Apricots

It is often said that some of the world's best apricots go for drying. Some of the brighter and seemingly attractive replicas of fresh fruit have, in fact, been doused in sulphur dioxide or glossed with oils and glucose to extend their shelf-life. Left to dry naturally, they will go fig-like brown.

The best are HUNZA, which look more like soft walnuts, dried on the roof tops of Kashmir and Afghanistan. They need soaking or poaching for five minutes with a little lemon juice. Other varieties from Persia are often mentioned as well, although the trade is spasmodic.

The kernels of apricots are worth the labour of cracking and adding to a salad. The culture of glacé and crystallized apricots comes from the south of France.

CHERRY

Lucullus, the Roman general and *bon viveur*, brought the cherry tree from the city of Cerasus, hence also the French *cerise* from the Latin *Prunus cerasus*. These would have been sour cherries and the sweet *P. avium* developed later. Cherries are prolific across Europe, especially in France, and date here back to Henry VIII. The orchards were centred around Sittingbourne, but have almost disappeared in the last 40 years. They have dwindled from more than 3,000 acres in the '50s to less than 2,000 today, and now most cherries are imported. As a trade, it just seems all to have been too much trouble. Cherry picking was an unwieldy industry: the tall trees susceptible to the climate, badly hit by rain damage in poor summers and wasps and birds in good weather.

For all the 200, or perhaps more, varieties of cherry there are only two basic types: the sweet, heart-shaped black, white or red *Géans* or *Guignes*; and the round or oblate, more acid, *Griottes*, which includes most of the famous cooking varieties like *Morello* or *Reine Hortense*, the latter usually going for eau-de-vie and for drying. The Géans are very much in the ascendancy.

Bing is a term for a hard-style sweet cherry commonly used for catch-all labelling, rather than more specific variety names like *Burlat* or *Washington*. The best are flown from America and can last up to a week, which accounts for the premium prices — usually double that of the same cherries from Italy. Washington State is largest producer of cherries. They start picking on June 25 and the season lasts until mid-August. American varieties are susceptible to having the shoulders of American footballers and the taste of tap water. Of the European varieties *Van, Bing, Burlat* and *Napoleon* will dominate in the next few years, because that is the way plantings have gone. Consistently, the French have been producing the best cherries for the market. A good cherry is told by its stalk, which should still be green and pliant; as it ages, the stalk dries and withers.

Bing, from the USA, is mostly looks and little substance. With lockets of pink to purple and juicy, it is short on taste. An example, called *Extra* was big, at 4 cm (1½ in) across, fat and expensive. Saffron-coloured with bright red cherub cheeks, it was almost box-shaped and the white flesh was very juicy with a gentle flavour.

Early Burlat, in season in November, is about 3x2 cm (1¼x¾ in) and deep cerise going on brown. The flesh is soft purple with a small stone and a short juicy cheeriness, although slightly watery. Not a special variety.

Ferrovia from, Italy, is fat, at about 3 cm (1¼ in) across, heart-shaped, and a shiny evenly coloured purple-brown. Inside, the flesh is a vivid red, and is juicy and sweet with a lingering tastiness.

Gaucher, from Britain, is lantern-shaped and cerise to purple in colour, with mauve flesh. It is soft and sweet to sour. A good variety, but unpopular with the trade as they do not keep.

Larium, from France, has perfect medallion contours. Long and about 2 cm (¾ in) across, it is dusk-red to mahogany and sold with its stalks on. An all-round good quality variety, it is slightly sour, even-textured, with a bouncy texture and large stone (helpful in a cherry).

Little Gem, from Sittingbourne in mid-July, is a quarter the size of an ordinary cherry. Black and juicy, with a large stone, the flesh is red and has a good flavour.

Napoleon, from Britain, is traffic-light yellow to red and beyond. Round, with yellow flesh, it is tart and sharp.

Ranier is a luxurious orange-gold, scarlet and

cream cherry, which is packed by hand. The season lasts until mid-August.

Stella is a new variety developed from Canadian rootstock. Crimson-pink to mahogany in colour, it is almost square and about 3 cm (1¼ in). The white flesh is juicy, with a pure flavour that is rather neutral — nice but noncommittal.

Van is another new variety, like Stella, from Canadian rootstock. Red-mahogany to chestnut-brown, or even deeper, it consists of two buttocks. The flesh is sweet, with a pink hue and a distinct, gentle flavour — 'a lullaby'.

NECTARINE

A strain of peach, akin to the almond and apricot, the nectarine differs mainly in the skin which is smooth. Many are frustratingly out of condition and only hint at what pleasures they may have to offer. As a rule-of-thumb, the French varieties are better looked after, but the Italians and Spanish have more sun and the silken red and yellow skins now seem an increasingly familiar sight through late summer. Varieties are remarkably uniform in size, invariably between 6.5-7.5 cm (2¾-3 in).

Fire King, from Spain, is coloured deep orange-red to black flecked with yellow. The flesh is deep apricot with red marks by the pip: juicy, fleshy, with a short taste and hints of sourness, it is a pure example of the mainline nectarine.

*Honeygold, from France, has a smooth lemon skin with odd pink clusters; the flesh is rich and buttery sweet, very honeyed with no acidity.

Independence, from Italy, is coloured golden sunset into a deep delicious red.

*Silvery, from Spain, is yellow-lime going on scarlet to deep purple; white-fleshed, the flavour is soft, floral, herbaceous and luscious like soft apples. Very good, but they are

expensive at nearly 80p each.

Snow Queen, from Spain, is deep red, almost apple-like colour, with hints of orange sunsets and streaks of lime, like pictures of the cosmos: it has a good sweet floral, apple-like scent and the flesh is white hinting at lime.

Tasty Free, from France, is coloured an orange, honey-yellow to a broken veined red, looking like a moonscape. The example tried was dry, woody and off.

Venus, from Italy, is cherubic red with yellow streaks, like sunsets and freckles; the creamy beige flesh was tough although sold as ready to eat. Meaty, and juicy when ripe, they have little flavour and are mostly texture.

PEACH

Once called 'Persian apples', after their Latin name *Prunus persica*, they probably originated in China and Japan. They need so much daylight to flower, they are grown only between latitudes ranging from northern France to southern Europe, though much is also grown in America and the equivalent latitudes in the southern hemisphere across South Africa and Australia. In France, there were many small orchards mainly centred around Montreuil which sent peaches across Europe.

The common peach tree grows to around 6 m (20 ft) and flowers in pink blossom, like the almond, which it resembles closely. The way to judge a good peach is by smell — brush the fur and if it smells good then it will taste good. On a ripe peach the skin should peel easily and the pip should rattle freely in the centre. As with much skinned fruit, the colour of the flesh will be the same as that of the palest colour on the skin. The supermarket problem is that what tends to look good on the shelf is not necessarily fully ripe.

Cling Stone, from Italy, about 6.5-7.5 cm (2¾-

FOOD *watch*

Italy is now the biggest
European producer, but
where such peaches look
resiliently firmly beautiful
in the shops, they can
shrivel up on the
windowsill the next day.
They will have been
picked too early — a
perennial problem.
French peaches are
picked later and tend
therefore to be better, if
not cheaper. For a brief
fortnight at the start of
September, **Tesco** has
been selling late-ripened
French peaches
delivered in 48 hours,
which are of a different
calibre to much of what
comes before.

3 in), is marked with ruddy red veins opening
to a deepening yellow. They have a perfumed,
eau-de-cologne smell and distinctive flavour.

Fayette, from Italy, about 6.5-7.5 cm (2¾-3
in), has a creamy yellow, soft downy skin, with
patches of purple; the yellow flesh is dry,
fibrous and disappointing.

May Crest, from Italy, ranges in colour from
dirty yellow (under-ripe) to an almost black
purple, with fiery-furnace markings on the
sides and a clean yellow cleavage; the yellow
flesh has a floral orange flavour. It has a better flavour than Spring Crest, but is less juicy.

Redhaven, from Italy and about 6-6.5 cm (2½-
2¾ in), was developed in America, but is now
grown world-wide. With a yellow to purple
blush and clean yellow flesh, it is crunchy
when unripe, but clean — 'probably good
when ripe'.

Red Top, from France, about 7-8 cm (2¾-
3¼in), has good fat looks, coloured with deep
scarlet clouds on yellow. The white-orange
flesh is woody in texture, juicy, sweet to sour
and low on flavour — sweet on first bite, but
the flavour disappears quickly.

Spring Crest is round, 5 cm (2 in) across, and
was developed in Spain as an early crop starting in May. With deep yellow-to-red colouring,
its velvet skin is dappled purple and orange.
An example tried from Italy had a mild, juicy
taste which was not fully developed, but full of
brilliant textures and a good ratio of pip to
flesh. Another example from **Safeway** was
firm and unripe when bought, softening up —
even wrinkling — after a day on the windowsill. It was larger, at about 6 cm (2½ in),
with creamy, buttery yellow skin, speckled
with red sunset colours going to deep fiery
purple; the flesh was bright yellow to ochre,
fibrous and with sharp notes and edges of citrus — OK, but not really very brilliant.

Spring Lady, from Italy, about 6.5-7.5 cm (2¾-

3 in), is butter yellow streaked with orange and purple; the yellow flesh is soft and juicy, with good sour notes and caramel tones.

Yellow Cling, from California, has an apricot blush and the flesh is a faithful mango yellow. It is used in tins because it is hard and doesn't go soft with ripeness. It is a lovely individual peach when eaten fresh — not dissimilar to the canned varieties (which is a tribute to the canning industry).

PLUM

These are the northerly cousins of the family that also includes peaches, apricots and almonds. They are supposed to have first been cultivated from the sloes, wild plum and blackthorn of hedging and woodland, though there is a view that they were brought here from around the Caspian or possibly even China. At their peak they are lush and juicy, one day off their summit and they remain a closed world. The old saying was that a plum was ripe if the fruit could be picked from its stalk, but this is only partly true.

BELL, shorthand for BELLE DE LOUVAIN, is an old Belgian variety now grown here. It is tall, 6x3 cm (2½x1¼ in), coloured green to deep purple mahogany, with a crease down one side. Dry, tart and coarse, fibrous and pippy, it is somewhat insipid according to some texts.

BLACK DIAMOND, from Israel, is buttock-shaped, about 5x5.5 cm (2x2¼ in), with a smoky blue sheen over a deep brown to purple; bright watermelon-red flesh goes orange near the stone and cuts cleanly; crunchy and solid, it has a good distribution of juice and a precise delicate flavour.

CASSELMAN, from the USA, at about 5 cm (2 in), are favoured by **M&S**. With bright crimson skin and orange flesh, they have lots of texture, but small flavour. More expensive are

PRUNE

Prunes, which are of course dried plums, take their name literally from the Latin *Prunus*. Those from Agen in France have been the best known for centuries, supplying most of the Californian stock. Their high sugar content makes them better suited to drying. They are sun-dried and then stoved gently for six hours at temperatures under 93°C (200°F), allowed to cool and then warmed again.

the Israeli versions, which are smoky blushed grey/blue and generally riper, the gentle juicy sweetness going to lushness.

CZAR is half the size of a normal plum. Blushing pink to dark red black, they are mostly grown in northern Europe for cooking and available from August. The flesh is lime-coloured, with a feathery texture, and juicy, neat and pleasant.

DAMSON is a cultivated form of the wild plum, named after the city of Damascus, and used exclusively for jams, jellies and cheese. Like Seville oranges, it owes its place in cooking to its bitterness. Intensely flavoured, but short on juice, they are available from August.

FRIAR, from the USA, is fat, about 6 cm (2½ in) square, and almost black all over. A product of the 'big is beautiful' philosophy, the blood-rose flesh has little flavour — all looks and no character.

GAVIOTA, originally from Italy but now adopted by the New World, is shaped like a square apple, about 5 cm (2 in), translucent yellow to deep red in colour; the flesh is yellow to white, fibrous, soft and sweet, with a lasting taste and melon flavours, getting stronger round the pip. With a good ratio of flesh to stone, it is good for stewing. Available from America from June and from South Africa from January.

GOLDEN JAPAN is widely grown but most on sale here are from Spain. About 4 cm (1½ in), it is golden, primrose yellow and bell-shaped; the yellow flesh is soft and loses out to the bitterness in the skin eventually vanishing. It is an unhappy combination, which is a pity as it is so pretty. Available from Europe from June, from the New World from January.

GREENGAGE is properly the REINE CLAUDE, dating back to the 16th century and said to be named after the consort of François I. There are varieties, like the larger, reddish-brown *Reine-Claude d'Althan*, developed in the 19th century in Czechoslovakia, or the still larger *Reine-Claude d'Oullins*, which is a bright green that turns brown. In markets the inferior GAGE plums sometimes will be passed off as greengages. The proper greengage should be going mauve, with the flesh a deep yellow and tart. The season is from August, but of all plums the fruit must be ripe and then it becomes honey sweet.

*MARJORIE SEEDLING is green to purple, about 7x5 cm (2¾x2 in), with grape-yellow flesh that is sour with a sweet edge. An example from **Marks & Spencer** was oval, purple with a smoky hue and scratch lines on the skin, about 4x5 cm (1½x2 in); the lime-green, translucent white-veined flesh was juicy and mellow, with a very pure plum taste.

OPAL, like the Czar, grown mostly in northern Éurope, but increasing in its appeal, Small and green to yellow red, it has yellow flesh with a good clean taste.

POLISH SWITZEN is purple, almost black, about 3x4 cm (1¼x1½ in), it has soft yellow vapid flesh.

RED BEAUT is an early variety available from Spain in June. About 2.5x4 cm (1¼x1½ in) and deep red to purple in colour, it has a smooth firm texture and a small stone. Although sour and refreshing, it is fairly one-dimensional.

ROYSTON is bell-shaped, about 4 cm (1½ in), and coloured red to purple to black; the juicy flesh is a lovely purple to orange and sweet — with the sour skin, a classic interaction. Available in June.

*RUBY NELL, from South Africa, is fat and dark mauve plum in colour, 6x8 cm (2½x3¼ in), The lurid luminescent orange flesh, has a soft texture, little moisture like soft straw, but is sweet with elements of melons. It is a good plum, with a high ratio of flesh to stone.

**SANTA ROSA, originally from America,

now mostly come from Israel. Bell-shaped and about 5x5.5 cm (2x2¼ in), they are coloured a tawny speckled red to mahogany-blue, with a smoky blush. The flesh is unevenly coloured, red rim to yellow-white interior, purple in places. Soft, juicy and delicate, they have a good clear taste, very sweet and wet, but not long-lasting. An example later in August was lantern-shaped, deep reddy black, with sweet pink juicy flesh, tart around the pip. Another example was sweet, gentle, attractive, with a good lasting flavour, not cloying. Available June to September from Europe, but from South Africa in December and January.

SONGOLD are deep yellow in mid-winter, plum-coloured in early spring. The pale yellow flesh is juicy, with a good ratio of flesh to stone, and an attractive mild but lightly soured flavour.

**VICTORIA has a reputation as one of the great plums of the world, possibly as a result of its scarcity value due to its very short storage time. The season starts halfway through August and lasts just four weeks. Bronze, orange, opaque rust in colour, about 5x3 cm (2x1¼ in), it has pale yellow flesh which is sweet, the perfect mix of juice and texture.

TOP FRUIT

From a nation that prided itself on its apple heritage, we seem to have accepted complete surrender. The supermarkets, initially **Safeway** and more recently **Sainsbury**, have capitalized on the publicity to be had in bringing back old varieties. However, this is mere lip service to an idea. **Safeway** last year hoped to move 1,000 tons of old varieties of apples. To put that into context, that represents 1/145th of the market still existing for the last main-line surviving English apple, the Cox.

Orchards are not being replanted and a few bijou packets with olde-worlde labels do not represent a realistic attempt to reverse the decline, just a cynical exercise in exploiting an emotional response. It was the multiples' desire for uniformity, for colour above all other virtues, and for mass standardization that undermined the British apple market in the first place. It was the supermarkets that created the catwalk for the ambitions of apple growers in other countries which now parade themselves monthly in all their glory along the first aisles of the supermarket.

Apple
Pear
Quince

APPLE

There were 1,545 different varieties of apple shown at the Apple Congress held in the Royal Horticultural Gardens in 1883. By 1950 only 22 English varieties had established themselves as 'commercially viable' mainstream crops. What happened to *Gladstone, Miller's Seedlings* or *Devonshire Quarrenden* and most of the others in this list of 22 is clear. They were grubbed up and replaced by foreign trees as huge imports washed across the supermarket shelves. Why they should

FOOD *watch*

Apple Prices

Price differences on apples between loose and packs are small: Gala 59p and 60p; Cox 64p and 67p. Organic varieties carry high premiums at 89.9p a lb, or 25p more — as much as double for Golden Delicious.

have been forsaken so readily is less clear.

Were these old varieties of English apple of any value at all? Who, now, knows? It is not unreasonable to suppose that this country had the climate, the culture, the seed stock, the knowledge and the producers to grow great apples. We threw it away. Even what we are now tempted to believe is a traditional British apple, the first of the new season on August 10, the wide shouldered lime-to-vivid-red *Discovery* is itself a modern apple, developed only in 1949 and its name changed in 1962 to fit some marketing whim. The first genuinely old English apple is in fact the *Worcester* which arrives in September.

BEAUTY OF HAMPSHIRE is credited to Mrs Eyre Crabbe, before 1850 at Colston, Southampton. Big and ovoid, it has a lovely contrast of orange-red cheeks and pistachio green, with good crunch, and intensely acid white flesh.

BERTANNE is a small russet from France said to be nutty in flavour. Arriving in March, it has rough olive skin and white juicy sweet flesh with a clean bite. Without the acidity of an Egremont, it is an inoffensive apple which is good with cheese.

*BRAEBURN, from New Zealand, is one of the brightest stars of the New World. Well liked by the trade for its long keeping qualities, it is nevertheless a good apple in low seasons. About 6 cm (2¾ in), it is squat to ovoid — as if someone sat on the flat side. The skin is lime green, pistachio to orangey-red with yellow flecks, and the flesh creamy white to pistachio. They are crisp, Cox-like, juicy, with a good hard texture and a flavour of melon.

BRAMLEY'S SEEDLING, stands supreme in this country as *the* cooking apple, a triumphant vindication of the quality of English apples and a monolithic symbol of mono-culture. What became of *Annie Elizabeth, Bismarck, Crimson Bramley, Grenadier, Lord*

Derby, Lord Grosvenor, Lord Suffield, Monarch, Newton Wonder, Sterling Castle, Warner's King, Emmeth Early, Pott's Seedling, Gascoyne's Scarlet, Edward VII, all of which were freely available as recently as the '50s? Bramley's were raised by Mary Anne Brailsford at Southwell in Nottinghamshire around 1809, and were introduced commercially around 1865, but rose to fame at the 1883 Apple Congress. Their acidity is a seemingly well-established part of English cooking, though modern cooks have tended to favour the French Reinette family, especially Clochard, or Golden Delicious.

CALVILLE, from France, has a ribbed quince-like shape, lime green skin and hard pistachio-coloured flesh. It has a distinct russety, aristocratic flavour with hints of grapefruit. The finest can be as expensive as £1.40 each.

**COX, originally the Cox's Orange Pippin, was bred by Richard Cox in Slough around 1825. Difficult to grow and notoriously erratic from year to year, they are picked around September and peak at Christmas. Round, with a sat-upon configuration, about 6.5 cm (2¾ in), they shade from lime to mahogany-red like a Constable landscape. A late-picked example was crisp, lime-fresh, with a brilliant impact and excellent balance of acidity and flavour. Compare that to notes on a New Zealand import early in the summer, 'sour, lemony, fleshy, soft'.

EGREMONT RUSSET was first recorded in England in 1872. There have been recent signs of a revival in russet apples, which has encouraged new planting. Khaki in colour, with rough unshaven skin, the crisp white flesh has a distinct smell of pears and butter, with a rich and nutty sweetness that builds up, like the taste of cooked apple.

ELLISON'S ORANGE RED is originally from Lincolnshire around 1900. About 6.5-7 cm (2¾-2¾ in), its colour varies from pistachio-green to bright mottled sunset red. It is softer to bite than Cox, the crumbly flesh having a creamy melon flavour, with hints of orange.

ELSTAR was first bred in Holland in 1955. A cross between Golden Delicious and Ingrid Marie, it is now widely planted in the Netherlands. Heavy in yield, it is larger and redder than a Cox, but less interesting.

FIESTA There are different versions of the story about the breeding of the Fiesta, the most authoritative credit it to Kent in 1972. A cross between a Cox and the heavy cropper Idared (see below), it is held by many to be the most interesting variety bred in the UK in recent years. With red and yellow coloration, a soft example tried was sharp with a distinct flavour like the end of blackberries. It is a improvement on the otherwise bland Idared.

FUJI from New Zealand is, along with the Braeburn, one of the more interesting apples from the southern hemisphere in early summer. Yellow with binding streaks of red, it is squat, 7 cm (2¾ in) across, with a dimpled top. The yellow flesh is crisp, honeyed and immensely sweet with no acidity, close to tropical fruit.

*GOLDEN DELICIOUS is not an English apple but was developed in West Virginia in 1916 and introduced here in 1926. For many years it has been picked under-ripe and green to imitate the success of Granny Smith, but its true glory only comes out when it has turned yellow. Encouragingly, growers seem to be recognizing this point. BLUSH GOLDEN DELICIOUS is a large fragrant variety of Golden, 7-7.5 cm (2¾-3 in), which arrives in March. Lightly speckled and with a crimson streak, the white flesh is sweet and mild. It is a very temperate and good apple, if a bit sugary and lacking acidity.

EMPIRE, from the USA, is a good example of the American breeders' obsession with looks. About 6.5 cm (2¾ in), it is a soldierly red with clouding in neat stripes, from vermilion to deep pink. Although lovely to look at, the crisp, juicy, white flesh, collapses after the first mouthful. Nevertheless, it has some flavours of lemons and a good first bite.

GRANNY SMITH is named after Annie Smith who was born in Sussex in 1800 and emigrated to Australia when she was 38. When she was in her sixties, she accidentally discovered the world's most famous apple growing from seeds that came from some discarded fruit. First exported to Britain in 1930s, it needs a warmer climate than northern Europe can provide. It has a distinctly green skin, but the flavour is indistinct and acid — it is really just the crunch. An example from South Africa in May was pale green to yellow with a melony smell, short finish and good texture. Another from South Africa a month later was bright yellow, with a saffron hue to the creamy skin, the texture was softish, bursting ripples of mellow caramel flavour, sugars to the fore. By August, all the South African imports were completely yellow. Some brilliant examples in November from **Paille** in France were fully ripened to a deep yellow, with a red sunset flush, about 8 cm (3¼ in), tapering to a small crown, the flesh a cream-hued orange, with a smell of melons, perfect texture and a bready citrus sweetness. Magnificent to look at, this was what it was supposed to be — bravo **Paille**!.

IDARED is sold as a traditional variety, but was bred by Leif Carner in Idaho in 1942. Known for its texture and crispness, it is plump, round and well shaped, coloured with beautifully soft shades of pinks, crimson and yellow. The flesh is white, with a good first bite, but low on juice and with very little actual flavour, only mild distant notes of citrus, although the reputation for texture is well founded.

JONAGOLD was first raised in New York in 1943, a cross between Golden Delicious and Jonathan. Large, 8 cm (3¼ in) across, speckled, turning when ripe to smooth yellow to red on opposite sides. Juicy and sweetish it has a soft texture. JONAGORED is a clone of Jonagold raised in 1980 in Belgium.

*KIDD'S ORANGE RED is a good example of an overlooked British apple. About 6 cm (2½in), it is bright lemon going to deep red, flecked with parchment — sunset colours. There is an orange hue to the flesh, which has a soft bite, but a full wide flavour tinged with flowers, almost spices or vanilla.

LAXTON FORTUNE is available from September. About 6 cm (2½ in) and streaked with red on lime yellow, the sweet white flesh, although a bit soft, has plenty of crunch and is juicy, with a pleasant buttery flavour.

LAXTON'S SUPERB was first bred at Bedford in 1897, a cross between Wyken Pippin and a Cox. First picked late in October, it lasts through to January, although crops tend to be biennial. About 6.5 cm (2¾ in), it is usually speckled green with areas running to polished mahogany red. The greeny cream flesh is soft, very neutral, with muted edges of flavour; the texture is that of cotton wool. Who called this superb?

M. FRIADISE traces its history back to before 1760 as a Dutch variety known as *Knoop* Tubular and resembling a pear in shape and texture, it is scarred from mahogany to lime with clouds of russet. The white flesh is firm-textured, dry, and highly acidic.

PRINSES IRENE is a cross between Jonathan and Cox's Orange Pippin dating back to around 1925. One of the most brilliant-looking apples, streaked from bright yellow to crimson reds, it is a bit dry and soft-textured, but has a swelling sweetness mixed with acidity, almost a citrus intensity.

RED CHIEF, from France, is large, about 8 cm (3¼ in) in diameter with a fat base. Strongly redded, with occasional breaks of yellowish cloud, it has crisp, melon-coloured flesh, and the flavour is clean, juicy and mainstream, which breaks down to a buttery sweetness.

RED DELICIOUS comes from New Zealand, Chile and the USA. The colour ranges from a bright orange hue to the deepest red/purple. The shape is ovoid, with five pinnacles forming a crown around the stalk. An example tasted in May had strong skin and the flesh was mild and inclined to mushiness; one in June had flesh which was disappointingly quick to disintegrate; another in August had white crunchy acid flesh which was pleasantly sour. With a mild to cardboard edge, it had elements of crab apple in the flavour.

REINETTE ONTZ is a mid-season dessert apple, which can also be cooked. Flat and wide, with a Cox-like blush from mahogany to melon, the flesh is white, friable and soft with a light melon taste. The crunch in the skin disappears in the flesh.

ROYAL GALA, from New Zealand, is about 5 cm (2 in) across, with attractive orangey-green skin, speckled with red and lemon and a small crown on the top. With a fresh floral smell and a tart, fruity flavour, it is soft in texture with a Cox-style bite but not the acidity. Handsome examples are available in September from France, about 7 cm (2¾ in) in size and red with yellow to lime flecks round the core, the flesh is lime-white, crisp, sweet, crunchy and juicy with a hint of melons.

SPARTAN was bred in British Columbia, Canada in 1926 and produces a high proportion of class-1 fruit. With smooth dark red/purple skin, it is at its best from September to December, after which it deteriorates. Good examples hint at strawberries and melons, others are vinous.

SPLENDOUR, from New Zealand, are about 7 cm (2¾ in) across, and are lime-yellow to bright red in colour, with a lime hue to the flesh. They have a good bite and sweet honey taste, with no acidity. A bit one-dimensional, but it does have a lovely first bite.

STURMER ORANGE PIPPIN, from New Zealand, is lime yellow to busted orange green-brown in colour, with a pale green hue to the flesh. They are crisp and intensely sour, with Cox tones, and a big distinct flavour.

WASHINGTON RED, from the USA, is a deep red that polishes up into an almost unreal varnish that reflects everything around it, like a soldier's boots. The red skin is streaked with runs of crimson and mauve and is a bit tough; the flesh is lime-hued, crisp and fragrant, with a slight vegetable taste, like sweet cabbages.

**WORCESTER PEARMAIN, often just called a WORCESTER, is one of the great English apples that has survived in the market since 1876. Pistachio-green to deep red and 6-7 cm (2½-2¾ in), it has juicy white to lime-coloured flesh and a soft texture which tends to wooliness, but still with bite. The excellent and distinctive flavour has a beautiful mellow edge.

PEAR

Related to the apple, pears were introduced here by the Gauls. There are more than 3,000 varieties of tree, many of which are extremely long-lived, up to 400 and 500 years old. The wood was an important part of the economy for joiners, wood turners and engravers.

Until the 16th century pears were exclusively a cooking fruit, stewed or baked and sold by street sellers. They were also made into jams and marmalades. Many of the old cooking varieties like *Fertility*, *Bartell*, or *Beurré Hardy* seem to have disappeared completely, although they could still be found in the '50s. Ironically, the quince has survived as the root stock for grafting pear trees. The first eating pears were grown in Italy and France and known as *beurré* for their sweetness, a tag that survives in variety names. Before that — especially in Roman times — they were grown for their medicinal virtues, particularly for stomach ailments.

The original gritty woodiness of the pear has inexorably been bred out in new varieties. *Conference* has become the dominant variety grown in this country to the exclusion of all other kinds. Pears will take on other flavours from things stored nearby and are fragile and easily bruised. **Marks & Spencer** has taken the forward-looking step of creating special polystyrene cases to protect them.

*ABATE FETEL is tall, 6x13 cm (2¼x5¼ in), although developed in France is now available from September from many parts of Europe, and in the early spring from South Africa. Initially rather large and lumpy but now more elegant, it is lemon-yellow to brown with strong freckling; the white flesh has a good crunch and is sweet, clean and juicy — a good all-round pear.

ASIAN PEAR, or *Nashi*, are usually grown in Italy, Chile and New Zealand. The skin is rough and prickly. They are best served chilled, often with cheese. They tend to be innocuous when not fully ripe but the flavour builds up. A pretty example from Italy, with mottled deep yellow skin turning to brown paper, was 7.5x5.5 (3x2¼ in); its white flesh is crisp, juicy, and rich in its sweetness, developing a flavour of honeyed lemons but with a mild aftertaste of something plastic/off.

Another example from New Zealand was large, 8 cm (3¼ in), with a russet skin speckled with white dots; the white flesh had some yellow hues and a taste of ice-cream and crunchy texture — a lovely mellow wet/dryness, but £1.29 each. They are at their best early in spring.

BEURRÉ BOSC from South Africa and Australia, is russet beige with a yellow undercoat, varying widely when ripe from lime-green to leather-brown. With a wide squash-style base, crenellated not perfectly round, it tapers to a volcanic tip from 7 cm (2¾ in) across at the base to 2 cm (¾ in) at the tip. The stalks are usually left on and it has a very small core, only 3 cm (1¼ in) high. The brown-hued flesh is refreshing, citrusy, light and crunchy, with watery features; some refer to it as a pear equivalent of a watermelon.

*COMICE or, more accurately, *Doyenne de Comice*, named after the Comice Horticole at Angers where it was developed in 1849 and introduced here nine years later. 'Incomparable', says **Sainsbury** and the 'finest of all dessert pears' according to **Marks & Spencer**. The European season starts in October, but South Africa supplies in early spring. The best tend to come from Holland where orchards grade and pack better than the English. It has the classic attributes of a pear, a good crunch, not overly woody texture, and a juicy, mild cool flavour. A squat English example, about 7.5 cm (3 in), with rough speckled khaki skin, and translucent white flesh was well-textured and juicy, with sharp notes and good body.

CONCORDE, a cross between a Comice and a Conference, is being tried by selective branches of **Sainsbury** and is getting enthusiastic support in the trade.

CONFERENCE is named after the Pear Conference held in Chiswick in 1885, when it was the only fruit to win a first-class certificate outright. It was developed by Thomas Rivers in 1874, from a cooking pear *Léon Le Clerc de Laval.* It is well known for its long keeping, which leaves it on the market from September through winter. Crab-apple-green, long and spindly with a very thin core and seeds at the bottom. Crunchy and dry, like an apple, they bake well.

FORELLE, from South Africa, is lime in colour with red freckles creating the blush. Elongated, it is about 8x6 cm (3¼x2¼ in). Juicy and in good condition for May, they have a fresh taste of grass and hay; crisp outside and juicy inside, with a swelling of sugars that rinses the mouth. **Tesco** call it a Red. Another example from **Safeway** was pretty, hump-shaped, yellow with orange speckles and blush turning bright fire-engine red in places; woody in texture, is sweet with a sour skin.

PACKHAM or *Packham's Triumph*, originally developed in Australia, is squatter than the Bosc, almost square at 7 cm (2¾ in) across. Some from South Africa were bright lime green speckled with brown/grey pin heads; the mild gentle and sticky flesh had a green/lemon hue with a small core only halfway up the fruit — it is inclined to graininess by the core. Another example, from Italy, was slightly smaller and squat, a dusty pistachio green, lightly marked; the flesh white to melon-coloured and crisp, releasing its juices slowly — a good classic pear taste.

PASSE-CRASSANE, developed in France, is squat and dumpy, speckled russet, the stalks waxed red. It has juicy white flesh, and a good ratio of meaty flesh to rough skin; it had a watery, almost sorbet-like texture, and slightly sour and gritty skin.

**RED ANJOU is firm, mahogany-coloured, with a square configuration. It is a beautiful-looking pear. Examples from the USA still have their short stubby stalks; skin colours shading from a deep cerise to a mottled scarlet in definite streaks. It is sweet and juicy, like distilled sweet wood, superior in all regards.

*RED WILLIAMS, properly *Williams' Bon Chrétien* and originally favoured for canning, is 10x6 cm (4x2½ in), almost rectangular or coffin-shaped, with a beautiful redwood finish and dinky stalk. The creamy white flesh of a French example had soft bites, but perfect pear notes and a bready texture. Another smaller example from Italy was deep yellow/beige, with creamy sweet flesh and a rough skin, giving plenty of high notes.

ROCHA, about 8x6 cm (3¼x2½ in), has the classic look of a small Conference, brown at tip and base and a pronounced pale green speckled brown on the sides. The white flesh of the example from Portugal was crisp and juicy, having refreshing sour edges mixed with sweetness. A new season example in November was slightly smaller and sweet yellow, yet 38p each more than the coveted Comice. It has a granular translucence, with hints of yellow on white flesh, and a soft instant intensity, honeyed and sticky.

QUINCE

This large yellow-marked fruit about the size of an orange, 11x7 cm (4½x2¾ in), has a smooth, lightly furred skin, somewhere between the pear and lemon. It has an intense smell of melons and chocolate and hard white dry granular flesh, with a straw-like texture and a flavour of lemons and almonds. It needs to be baked to bring out its flavour, as in the ruby Spanish **Membrillo** paste, which is more usually sold on the cheese counter.

OTHER FRUIT

This catch-all section rounds up some fairly important fruits which don't happily fall into our other categories.

Grape
Melon
Pomegranate
Rhubarb

GRAPE

Grapes for the table have become the poor relation of those used by the wine trade. For all the hundreds of different varieties, only a handful surface in the supermarkets. The wonderfully named heritage of *Muscat of Alexander, Buckland Sweetwater, Black Hamburgh* and others have been relegated to the province of the gardener. *Thompson* — originally cultivated as the grape for sultanas in California — has been pre-eminent, leading the move to seedless grapes. White grapes with pips are seemingly being phased out as seedless variations arrive from all corners of the world. Prices consolidate around £2 per lb, but can tumble dramatically in gluts to less than half that.

ALPHONSE LAVALLÉE, from South Africa, are handsome round black marbles, about 4x3 cm (1½x¼ in), with a purple hue reflected in the green stalk. Inside there are 3 pips, and the smooth flesh has a well-delineated crunch, although the taste is a shade muted.

BIEN DONNE is fat with thick olive skin, lime flesh and 2 pips. The taste is innocuous, if not dull.

**BLACK MUSCAT is round, about 1 cm (½ in), with a dark blue — almost sloe-black — skin with a smoky blush. The flesh is opaque limy, sweetly Muscat, with three pips. This is a delicate, refined grape with a lovely Muscat flavour — a lady among grapes and expensive at £4.50 per lb.

*DAN BEN HANNAH, from Chile, is tall and

elongated. The smooth skin is black and the juice sweet, with 1 or 2 pips. This is a very good grape, with a lovely sense of balance and contrast of skin, the slightly sweet flesh almost tasting of lychees.

DAUPHINE, from South Africa, is thumb-sized and white to opaque golden, almost translucent. Sweet, with a tough ungiving skin, there are 1 or 2 pips per grape. With a satisfying taste of good wine, this is a good — if not outstanding — grape

FLAME, from the USA, is small at 2 cm (¾ in), rounded, red-brown and slightly sweet with an over-strong skin. The taste is insignificant, but they are fun because they are so small.

NAPOLEON has opal, dark red to black thick skin. The soft, pale flesh, with a single pip, is sweet and lychee-like.

PERLETTE, from Israel, is lime in colour with clouds of white, oval and about 2 cm (¾ in). Crunchy and sweet, it has more fibre and texture than flavour and is good for fruit salads.

RED GLOBE is large, round, plum-coloured and hard, with 2 pips. As they ripen they become translucent crimson, with a sour edge, good juice and texture, and a soft edible skin.

RIBIER, from Chile, is black and clusters tightly. There are 3 pips per fruit. Juicy and sticky, with a crunchy skin, this is a very good everyday grape.

SEEDLESS SUGRAONE, from Mexico, is a translucent lime ovoid, about 2 cm (¾ in) firm and tart, with a strong bite and little taste.

SUPERIOR, from Israel, is oval, about 2 cm (¾ in). Sweet, with a muscat ring, it has a short precise flavour and is better than Perlette.

THOMPSON is now universally grown as if there was no other variety. An example from Australia was a seedless ovoid, pale lime in colour, with tough skin and soft and inclined to pulpiness inside. A batch from Mexico were firm and crunchy, but with not much flavour save a hint of lettuce and a tart finish.

WHITE ITALIA, from Brazil. is large, at around 3 cm (1¼ in), seeded, with a melon-lime skin. They are fat, soft, good, sweet and juicy, with a single pip and muscat-style flavour.

MELON

Of all types of fruits, the different melons have much more variety of colour, size and flavour than you might expect — from the bland to the sublime. The abundance of different varieties reflects the ease with which they can be cross-bred. The Honeydew family alone changes from green to white to orange through the winter.

In southern Spain and Portugal the piles of melons stacked for sale by the roadside suggest the easy abundance growing in the sun. Here — although they have been cultivated since 1570, introduced from Jamaica — they need glass, nurturing and water. Unlike their close relation, the cucumber, these domestic varieties cannot really aspire to the supermarket. Buying melons is about climate: Spain for honeydews; France for the more delicate cantaloupe family. The word cantaloupe is from *Cantalupo* , one of the Pope's country homes near Rome, where they have been extensively cultivated. When a melon is ripe the base will yield readily to pressure and the flesh will smell through the skin.

CANTALOUPE is both a family and its own variety, but the distinguishing marked ribbings have tended to be bred out. Usually round, about 11 cm (4¾ in), and smooth, with shades of lime-green skin and pale marrowy-orange flesh, the circular pod is about 4 cm (1½ in) across. It has softer flesh than the Charentais and is juicy and sweet.

CHARENTAIS are round, about 11 cm (4¾ in) across, with a very pale-green skin streaked with thick white rivulets as if marking where to put the knife. The flesh is markedly orange, with a deep orange rim at the inner skin, and a triangular pod, 4 cm (1½ in) at its widest. Richly honeyed, its ripeness is easily judged by smell. They need to be eaten swiftly as they do not keep well.

GALIA is a modern variety named after the daughter of the Israeli farmer who first developed it in 1976. Squat, like bowling balls, green going to yellow in colour, and streaked with contour-like white craters, they are quite petite by melon standards at 11 cm (4¾ in) across. Greenness of the skin denotes unripeness, yellowness maturity. The flesh is green and the bowl of pips about half the size of the fruit. Creamy and sweet, these melons are plentiful and cheap in late summer.

HONEYDEW encompasses many different varieties of the fruit, notable for their zeppelin shape and size and, for the most part, their disappointingly neutral-tasting flesh; the more so if not perfectly ripe. The percentage of pip hollow in the centre is high. At their peak early in summer, the best come from Spain.

OGEN are grown in Holland — and here — though they are named after the Israeli kibbutz where they were first developed. The English season is late autumn, but they are available from the Mediterranean through most of the summer. The ribbed skin goes an attractive mottled yellow, but the green flesh inside is dominated by the large crater of pips that occupy most of the space. Ripeness is judged by smell and important, because a few days either way and they are wishy and then washy.

PIEL DE SAPO (meaning 'skin of the toad') from Spain are large and oval, about 20 cm (8 in) long. Green in colour, turning yellow with light cratering, which distinguishes it from the honeydew, they have thin skin, white flesh and a large pod about 5 cm (2 in) across and running most of the length of the fruit. They are mild and gentle in flavour with a little tartness.

WATERMELONS are from a different part of the family and have been cultivated in India for millennia. Round, elongated, marrowesque, mottled green or even black, the variety tends to give way to distinct red sorbet-like flesh and myriad pips, varying mostly in the ratio of pips to flesh. There is no sure way to judge the ripeness of a watermelon except by cutting it in half. They are best eaten chilled.

POMEGRANATE

These fruits enliven the autumn with their vivid pips. Along with grapes and figs, they are one of the mythical symbols of prosperity, fertility and wealth. They owe their longevity to being desert foods. The hard crimson shell retains the moisture for long periods. The juice stains badly and was used to colour Persian carpets. The best fruit, from Iran, can measure 10x8 cm (4x3 in), looking like giant apples with deep red skin. Use as garnish or pick over with a pin, discarding the bitter white pith, or make into pomegranate water, as the French do, for grenadine.

RHUBARB

The Victorians popularized rhubarb in fools and crumbles. Previously it had been grown for its medicinal properties across Asia. Most of what we find in the shops is forced over winter, grown in candlelit sheds (mostly in Yorkshire), to preserve the pinkness. Inside the sheds, the rhubarb grows at an extraordinary rate of up to 5 cm (2 in) a day and can be heard eerily popping out of its sheath in the dark. The top of the stem may be yellow rather than green. The outdoor varieties tend to be stronger and need the outer membrane to be skinned off.

Ways with Rhubarb

Its high acidity makes it a candidate for use in more modern dishes in place of lemon — say with salmon — rather than older pudding and wine recipes.

LARDER

The investment in basic larder items, like virgin olive oil wine vinegar, sea salt, premium mustard and fresh root ginger repays itself many times over. The cost is marginal compared to the impact they have. For less than the price of this book you could buy the best brand in each major category and they would last for up to two months, possibly more, even with everyday use. In real terms, compared to the cost of other foods, the larder is the bargain basement. Anyone can afford sherry vinegar and estate-bottled olive oil – even more so if they plan to economize and live for the rest of the month on inexpensive staples like salads, pasta and pulses.

BAKING, BREADS & CEREALS

The influence of the miller has stretched far wider than just bread. The pies, pastries, buns and cakes of the first half of the century point to an alliance with the other great Victorian industrialized food processes in sugar, dairy and fat that stamped itself over the national diet. Breakfast cereals are another offshoot. These powerful monolithic – often government-funded – agencies represent the last great food barons of the Victorian era – sugar dominated by two companies; flour-milling by three; milk until this year a 60-year national monopoly. It is only the power of the supermarkets in the last decade that has begun to threaten the status quo. **Sainsbury** is currently building the largest bakery in Europe, to bypass the culture and, it is hoped, begin a new chapter of baking for the mass market.

FLOUR

From the 1880s onwards, America, Canada and Australia supplied all our flours. These were hard high-protein wheats. The deep rich loamy soil of the Prairies produced high-quality wheats against which the thin overworked top soils of Europe could not compete, except in isolated patches like East Anglia. It was not for 100 years – until Britain joined the EC and work on wheat varieties and the use of nitrates on the soil, and punitive levies on imports – that the pendulum swung back to home production. Today most breads might only contain 10% Canadian wheat, the rest is all home-grown – or at least European. The EC now produces a surplus of wheat.

Half a dozen varieties of wheat are used to make flour, of which two – Mercia and Avalon – are far and away the most common. The seed is registered and approved by the Ministry of Agriculture. More than 60 types were registered in 1986. Standardization, in practice, remains a stern discipline. Of the 32 milling businesses in this country, three supply 80% of the flour for our bread.

The combine-harvester thrashes off the straw and chaff and leaves simply the berry of the wheat. On a traditional STONE-GROUND mill, the berry is squashed and worked out into ever smaller particles. Millers still using stone grinds tend to specialize in more unusual batches of wheat, quite often some of it organic, although the distribution tends to be localized. Good names to look for are **Downfield Windmill** of Ely, **Shipton Mill** of Tetbury (heroically trading on despite a bad fire in May which affected the store but not the mill), **Crowdy Mill** in Totnes, **Letheringsett Watermill** at Holt, **Newnham Mill** of Tenbury Wells, and the **Water Mill at Little Salkeld**, Penrith.

On the ROLLER-GRIND factory system, the teeth actually cut the berries. As the wheat moves through different – ever-decreasing – rollers, different products are extracted: wheatgerm, bran, middlings, semolina, special high-performance flours designed for branded products like cakes, and even pet food.

WHITE FLOUR has always been popularly perceived as the best. The trade in what has been ground out of the wheat has inexorably involved the miller with other large-scale food products, such as sugar, and has been an influence on large areas of the national diet and how – and what – we cook. The innocent tubby little bags of flour on the supermarket shelf seem increasingly like tombstones to different – now mostly dated – eras of cooking.

SELF-RAISING FLOUR is a low-protein,

An independent analysis for this book of six flours bought off the supermarket shelf revealed the following protein contents:

Sainsbury strong white flour 9.4%
Allinson's strong white, soft-grain 10.99%
Somerfield strong white 9.2%
Homepride strong white 10.7%
Sainsbury strong wholemeal 11.9%
Sainsbury strong brown bread flour 12.5%

Neither of the ordinary supermarket white flours were strong enough to bake a loaf and, almost without exception, the branded flours were around the 11% mark. It is probably not too cynical to suggest that a retailer might prefer customers to pay for the added convenience and expense of a ready-baked loaf; or that a miller will make more profit supplying a baker than he will encouraging end-users to bake their own bread. In the case of **Waitrose**, the strong white flour – which one would expect to be the bread flour – only declares a protein level of 10.1% and you would have to go to wholemeal at 12.6% to be confident of a good loaf. *Tesco flours are strong enough to bake bread. The strongest flour is probably **Granary Malted Brown** at 14%, which takes some of its strength from the added malt.

highly refined flour to which a raising agent, usually sodium bicarbonate, and an acid are added (see Raising Agents, page 00). Variations might be still weaker and more refined cake flours, although self-raising is also the flour for soda bread. Self-raising is still said to be the biggest seller, which is perhaps a statistical nicety and paints an unlikely vision of whole tracts of suburbia bent over their ovens baking marble squares, sticky date puddings, gingerbread and peach melba sponges. Can this really still be the case? STRONG FLOUR is, or should be, for bread-making, although most of the examples in the supermarkets would appear at the bottom of a list of good bread flours. Sometimes vitamin

C is added to improve the strength of the protein. If the flour is not strong enough – ie it does not have enough protein – then when the yeast creates carbon dioxide, the protein strands snap and the bread will collapse in the oven. **Waitrose organic plain flour** has a protein level as low as 8%. Bakers would regard 11% protein as low-grade white and expect to bake with a protein level of 12%. Wholemeal flour would be 13.5% in a bakery.

BREAD

Breads provide one of the most convenient forms of eating the complex group of carbohydrates. Although we have the cheapest form of bread in Europe (even cheaper now that bread is one of the loss-leader items in the price war, with a loaf sometimes selling for less than 20p), we eat less than any other European nation. Perhaps there is a connection? The array of supermarket breads is to some extent a deception. For all the Bloomers, Hedgehogs, Parisiennes, Danish and Cobs, the flours conform, the sizes conform strictly to factory batches of 400g or 800 g, and the factory technologies are broadly similar. Variety has been tightly focused so, for the most part, breads are different mainly because of their shape.

Good bread depends on the flour, how it is mixed, and how long the yeast and dough are allowed to mature. As with white flour, the popular perception of quality runs against the known evidence. Most of the flavour of bread is found in the crust and much of if its goodness derives from its hardness. However, soft – even bouncy – and crustless breads have become the norm.

Breads in a supermarket divide into three philosophies. The freshly baked unpacked loaves tend to take their names from their shape. The BLOOMER is baked on the floor of the oven so that it has crusty top and bottom. A SANDWICH LOAF is baked in a tin with a lid on, so it has minimal crust. FRENCH BREAD has suffered badly from this definition – it is merely English bread in a *baguette* shape. However, **Sainsbury's Traditional French** and others are part-baked loaves imported from France, which are more faithful, using French flour which has shorter-keeping qualities. Some traditional loaves will also indicate that the dough has been matured and the flavour will be improved as a result.

The packeted and well marketed breads in the section that includes **Mighty White** or **Weight Watchers** are largely aerated to make them softer. The extra benefit in low calories is more air and less bread. Actual SOFT LOAVES, by contrast, use emulsifiers and fats rather than air to create the softness. BROWN BREAD is no longer a term with much meaning. The trade gives strict definitions for WHITE and WHOLEMEAL BREAD, while brown just inhabits anywhere it chooses in between. Established as far back as 1886, **Hovis** was originally a brown bread flour into which some bran had been put back, but is now a brand name covering any kind of loaf from wheatgerm to granary, country grain to wholemeal.

Speciality breads have become increasingly prominent, although the section is more of a tourist's guide to what bread might have been somewhere once upon a time. Last year's runaway success CIABATTA was originally made with sunflower oil. It was the innovative bakery **La Fornaia** in King's Cross that started to use olive oil to make it seem more authentic. It attracts a premium not just because of its fashionability but because the dough is so sticky it has to be kneaded by hand. It has spawned a generation of sunny

Mediterranean-style breads in which authenticity seems again to be mostly to do with shape. Ciabatta itself is also sold stuffed with olives, sun-dried tomatoes or rosemary. FOCACCIA seems to be the same thing but flatter, while PUGLIESE and the so-called Spanish version GALLEGO are round. There are some very disappointing versions of Italian-style bread around. The variety of other breads is often down to the addition of a few seeds.

There are some glorious exceptions, for example the **Manoucher** breads imported from Canada and **Innes** sour-dough breads. In London, **Sally Clarke's** breads represent the true art of bread-making, which is unfortunately in decline.

RAISING AGENTS

BAKING POWDERS have been used to remove the smells from fridges and even as toothpastes in America – and now relaunched over here – as well as for making cakes rise. Their mix of alkali and acid sets up the reaction which releases carbon gases into the mix through the cooking and makes cakes and pastries rise. The acids were traditionally provided by tartaric acid and cream of tartar, the alkali from bicarbonate of soda. The mixing has always been a professional process to ensure that each tiny particle is properly covered with the other and then left to mature.

YEAST is a microscopic plant that lives on sugar and starchy substances. As it grows, it ferments and gives off carbon dioxide that swells up the dough. FRESH YEAST is hard to find, except from professional bakers, and even the trade has moved towards DRIED YEASTS. The main differences between yeasts are now in the drying. Bakers use COMPRESSED CAKE YEASTS, whereas

yeasts sold in the supermarkets are either pellets, which need mixing with water and sugar, or increasingly EASY-BLEND for 'quicker simpler home-baking', which can be added straight to the flour. Yeast is a main influence in the flavour of bread and all the haste promised on the packet is not likely to encourage well-flavoured bread. By contrast, breads sold on the next aisles have begun to declare the virtue of their matured dough.
*__Allinson's__ dried pellets of yeast produce a more responsive and sensual dough. Packet recipes encourage the speeding up of the process, but the yeast needs time to ferment and allow the flavours to develop – preferably mixed with a small quantity of flour, then left overnight and the rest added the next day.

BREAKFAST CEREALS

The extraordinary rise of the breakfast cereal began with the recycling of what was called the 'miller's offal'. As the miller ground purer and purer for white flour, so he was left with the husks, nibs and rusks and had to find a use for them. The irony of the British and American breakfast is that cereals which now constitute such a part of it are the goodness milled out of the bread which we then go on to eat with butter and jam to make it more palatable. If we baked harder breads out of wholemeal flours there might be no nutritional role for cereals – or, arguably, even butter and jam.

The best thing to be said about the razzmatazz of breakfast cereals with their stupid names, ridiculous offers for ridiculous toys and artificial additions of vitamins and minerals, is that the labelling is impeccably clear. Most of the answers to their precise contents are listed on the sides of the packets. Nutritionally, the most admirable cereals

are *Puffed Wheat, *Weetabix, and
*Shredded Wheat, which provide good
benchmarks against which to assess other
cereals.

Protein content is less of a nutritional issue
than it was, because most of us get enough
from the rest of our diet. Although in an ideal
world there should be more protein than
sugar. The cereals which are the best protein
sources are **Special K** (where it is added), **All
Bran, Puffed Wheat, Bran Buds, Ready
Brek, Weetabix, Swiss Style Muesli** and
Shredded Wheat.

Predictably the sugar levels in cereals span
an enormous range, from 0.5% in **Shredded
Wheat** through to **Sugar Puffs** at a stagger-
ing 56.5%. Salt has crept up as one of the
more controversial issues in cereals.
Manufacturers argue that salt adds a necessary flavour, which given that they are not
working with very much in the first place is
probably true. Their claims serve to underline
the poverty of the nutritional thinking behind
many of the leading brands. One serving of
any of the following would provide an adult's
complete daily requirement of salt: **Rice
Krispies, Special K, Bran Flakes, Kellogg's
Corn Flakes, All Bran, Farmhouse Bran,
Weetos, Crunchy Nut Corn Flakes, Coco
Pops** and **Ricicles**.

The trend continues to be eccentric, with
new launches as varied as the dinosaur mod-
els or free trolls inside. Of this year's releases
from the cereal 'fun factory' **Cheerios** worthily
mix corn, oats, rice and wheats – albeit with
22.9% added sugar. In practice, they are last
year's flavour, **Start**, with added rice.
Squares offer an unlikely promise of packets
filled with hazelnuts and chocolate – at 34.2 %
sugar, not quite as cardinally sucrose as
some. **Tesco** responded by cleverly adding
Apricot Squares, which round off the health

message more successfully than chocolate. On the other hand, **Corn Pops** from **Kellogg's** represent a huge gulf between protein at 5% and sugar at 41%.

MUESLI

This mixture of cereals, fruit and nuts was created by a Swiss, Doctor Bircher-Brenner, and introduced to patients at his clinics in 1897. He wanted a mix that created a strong pattern of B vitamins, a range of A, D, and E vitamins and a blend of cereals that covered the amino acids.

Dr Bircher-Brenner's original muesli recipe was:

1 tbsp rolled oats
3 tbsp water
1 tbsp Nestlé's sweet condensed milk or single cream and honey
juice of half a lemon
1 peach or some strawberries
1 small apple, grated with the skin on
1 tbsp chopped nuts, such as almonds, walnuts, hazelnuts, cashews

Today's all-singing and all-dancing views of Swiss mountain tops or designer polystyrene packets are exuberantly miscalculated. The notion of luxury derives more from the concept of an Alpine health clinic than a top-of-the-line diet.

PORRIDGE

Low in protein and susceptible to individual additions of salt and/or sugar, porridge oats are still rich in important fats that are recognized to be positively healthy – or certainly more healthy than wheat. Oats grow best in cold climates on poor soils, but also at higher temperatures than other grains. Scotland was known as a prime grower, especially East

FOOD *watch*

Muesli Prices

Any supermarket's commitment to the idea of healthy eating as outlined in the Government's *Health of the Nation Report* might be judged by comparing the price of their regular own-label muesli with that of the sugar-infected luxury lines. The regular line should be healthier and cheaper, but in **Tesco** it is 25% more, at **Sainsbury** it is 15p more for 500 g, at **Asda** it is 10p more for 750 g, and at **Waitrose** 62p more. The only supermarket to come out the right side of the equation is **Safeway.** Imported brands seem equally susceptible to coating the health message with sugars and honeys.

The price of branded mueslis varies alarmingly with **Cheshire** consistently the cheapest, **Alpen** on a par with most own-labels and **Billington's** considerably more expensive.

Lothian. The Scottish dependence on oats was akin to the Irish on the potato and was not confined to porridge, as traditional dishes such as herring fried in bacon fat and oatmeal shows. The outer husk is milled off, because it is deemed indigestible.

Oats respond differently in cooking, which renders meaningful comparison of different brands difficult. They are best cooked long and slow, overnight if possible, with regular rhythmic stirring to break down the starch and bring out the flavours. Larger grains take longer cooking. Porridge keeps poorly, losing its taste and taking on flavours from around it, so it is best kept sealed in a dark dry place.

HERBS, SPICES & FLAVOURINGS

The great achievement of the global food market has been to expand our array of flavours and seasonings. These have transformed cooking possibilities and almost rendered redundant old-fashioned staples like pepper. The new spice trade has been like a renaissance, every bit as triumphal in its effect as the ancient routes from Persia to Rome and Venice.

Herbs
Spices
Flavourings

HERBS

Many of the major kitchen herbs originate from the Mediterranean. The exception is basil which is credited to Persia, but that was probably a stopping point on a journey from South-east Asia. It has, however, been so thoroughly adopted by the Italians that it has become a foster-child. Many herbs are grown in hothouses here and in Holland, which has brought fresh herbs back into vogue and added wonderful new dimensions to cooking.

By comparison to good fresh herbs, DRIED HERBS are a waste of time and money, except in long slow winter casseroles where they can revive in sympathy with other flavours. Only bay, oregano and thyme can really be said to dry to advantage. The best mixes of dried herbs are invariably from Provence. Other coastal Mediterranean markets sell comparably excellent reminders of their regions, but these are not commercially developed. The small jars of, say, dried mint show none of the attributes of the fresh except in teas and tisanes. Many dried herbs are also too often disappointingly old and anaemic. At the other extreme, today's new freeze-dried herbs are wet and lifeless.

FOOD *watch*

**Supermarket Fresh
Herb Prices**

Leaf for leaf, the pots of
fresh herbs weigh about
the same as the packets,
but are usually 25p more
expensive. The
advantage is that they
keep, especially chives.
Price differences are
noticeable and subtly
obscured. **Waitrose**
have one price for all
herbs, but different
weights in the packets.
Sainsbury's parsley is
£1.18 for 100 g and 85p
for a pot, while their
coriander is 59p for 15 g,
or nearly four times the
price. By contrast,
Waitrose coriander is
half the price of
Sainsbury. **Tesco** fresh
herbs in the pot have
been 16p cheaper than
Sainsbury.

Daregal package herbs in neat little boxes for the freezer, which can then supposedly be poured straight into dishes. Predictably, the herbs are wet and cold which rules them out of salads – if not cooked dishes. The more delicate herbs, like chives, are disastrous outside of soups and the more robust mixes provide the best alternatives to using dried herbs in casseroles, but lack the same power so are probably best added at the end of cooking to finish a dish prettily.

ANGELICA is the stalks and stems of the upper branches of the large umbelliferous *Angelica archangelica* found in wet banks and ditches across northern Europe. There is a long history of confectionery working with angelica, both in candying and in crystallizing. Like juniper, angelica is one of the main aromatics in some gins. The juice is the prevailing flavour of Benedictine liqueur and the seeds go for vermouth and Chartreuse.

BASIL is a modern love affair. Older books speak disparagingly of a leaf that resembles cloves. Basil has always inspired romantic associations, perhaps because of its brilliant floral, peppery perfume. In Greece it was a symbol of poverty and misfortune, in Italy one of love, and to the Hindus it was sacred. When it first was introduced in France, it was the royal herb and only the monarch could cut it, using gold scissors. Basil is a tropical plant which is native, according to some texts, to Persia and others attribute it to the East Indies. Its first mention here in 1573, by the herbalist Culpepper, was as, 'a soothing leaf to swab into wasp and hornet stings'.

There are different varieties and they perform in markedly different ways. Garden catalogues sell packets of BUSH BASIL, with short spiky leaves which have an intense aniseed edge, quite different from **SWEET BASIL which has a broad deep-green fragile leaf and is the true basil for cooking. There is also DARK OPAL BASIL and LETTUCELEAF BASIL. Commercial growing has introduced different strains, not all of which are successful. Some English pot-grown examples have striped ribs and hints of, 'metal, fresh cut grass, strong texture, not really what we all get excited about'. These are best used with oils in dressings. By September some of these pots can have grown enormous leaves up to 10 cm (4 in) long. There are also good examples flown in from Thailand, which has a profusion of varieties.

To freeze, first wipe in olive oil. A pot on a windowsill will supposedly keep flies away and a tea made from basil leaves is said to be a sedative. Basil needs to be used generously in handfuls, not as a seasoning but as a prime flavour. The pots sold in supermarkets may suggest a dainty good housekeeping, but are a more accurate guide to portion control – use the leaves of the whole plant, and add them towards the end of the cooking – the flavour dies in the heat of the pan. They can be kept in the pot, but will shrivel if the temperature in the kitchen is not right.

BAY is the leaves of the sweet bay tree, *Laurus nobilis*, found across the Mediterranean belt, which will grow to 10 m (30 ft). The younger leaves are more acid, so the mature leaf is prized. Bay has sustained its place in trade because of the hydrocyanic acids, which repelled weevils and other grubs from destroying dried pastas, pulses, rices etc. They are still used in boxes of figs and liquorice. The bitter-sweet flavour seems increasingly old-fashioned and unwieldy, but it is one of the basic herbs in a bouquet garni and in a faggot of herbs, also finding its way insidiously into casseroles, soups, fish, marinades, milk puddings and with rice – but always fished out at the end of the cooking.

Ways With Basil

Pick the smaller leaves, leaving the suckers and the top shoots. Tear them rather than cut to release their oils.

Tomato is its main benefactor, but it is also the crucial influence of pesto pounded with garlic, pine nuts, Parmesan and olive oil.

Ways With Chervil

Like chives, it does not benefit from cooking and is best added at the final moment in deliberate small amounts, as if it was a seasoning. It marries well with eggs in all forms.

CHERVIL has delicate miniature fronds, looking like a lace tablecloth, and swiftly loses its looks as it turns an unappetising yellow. It is one of the four French *fines herbes*, along with chives, parsley and tarragon, and is not out of its class in that company. It originated in the Middle East, but has become naturalized across much of Europe and can still be found in hedgerows here. Very much a favourite in restaurants, where it has displaced parsley as a more feminine and subtle garnish, it has surprising depth of flavour, 'somewhere between a rich fennel and a soft parsley'.

CHIVES, sometimes called CIVET, SWETH or RUSH LEEKS, are the smallest member of the onion and leek family. One of oldest culinary herbs, it was little used as a medicine and always associated with the kitchen. The flowers should be cut in June and July to keep the plant strong and can be used in salads. Use scissors to cut the fragile stems or they mush. Pots raised in Holland sell at 85p against 56p for the herb in the packet, but the pots will keep indefinitely and can be grown usefully on a windowsill. GARLIC CHIVES are a different species, *Allium tuberosum* not *A. schoenoprasum*, with flatter and wider stems than the ordinary chive, and white not violet flowers. Sometimes called CHINESE CHIVES because of their use in Chinese cooking, they are stronger than the European chive and should be used more sparingly. There is some confusion in early summer when Chinese supermarkets sell thick-stemmed but beautifully delicate fronds as long as 45 cm (18 in) to serve as a vegetable, either steamed or stir-fried.

Ways With Chives

Snipped into 1 cm (½ in) strips, they combine well in all salads, go well with butter and have a deep affinity with new potatoes in a salad with a vinaigrette. They do not like the heat and are best used in the final preparation. Chives can substitute for salt in meat dishes and they freeze well.

CORIANDER is the world's most widely used fresh herb, dominating the cooking of the world outside Europe and North America. As recently as the '50s, English text books referred to the 'nasty, disagreeable odour' of the fresh leaf. Writers took gleeful pleasure from pointing out that the name comes from the Greek *koris*, meaning a bug (coriander was supposed to smell like bed bugs). Its main role in this country was as a seed used in gin, in pickling and to disguise less pleasant tastes like senna. The flavour of the fresh leaf is subtly addictive and has an affinity for chilli. In America it is called CILANTRO, from a Mexican and central American plant that is similar but of a different species. Coriander is a herb with bravura and demands to be used with a swagger not a limp, to galvanize parts of cooking too long occupied by parsley.

DILL is commonly called 'false fennel', which is appropriate. The seeds are used in North-African cooking, but in Europe more usually in pickling combinations for gherkins and aromatic vinegars. The fresh fronds are universally stamped with the association of *gravlax*, where the sweet butteriness of the fish and the mustard of the sauce mute the tones of aniseed, but it can also be used sparingly in a salad.

FENNEL is a biennial herb that can grow to more than 2 m (6 ft) in shady corners and is found across the Mediterranean. The leaves are thin green stems that form into feathers. BRONZE FENNEL is more properly thought of as purple. Stumpier in growth and with less delicate fronds, the flavour is less accentuated but in compensation it has the looks of nobility. (See also Vegetables, page 234.)

LEMON GRASS is a grass native to Southeast Asia, *Cymbopogon citratus*, which is grown commercially to extract citronella oil that is used as an insect repellent, for cosmetics and soaps. The young stems (rather than the long brown leaves) are chopped for salads, and the roots crushed to add flavour but taken out before serving.

Ways With Fennel

The flavour is strongly aniseedy and, like rosemary, it is best used to burn up on a barbecue or in the oven to lend its scent to fish or, less often meat.

Ways With Lemon Grass

Lemon grass is widely used in South-east Asian cooking for marinades, curries, soups, stews and seasoning rice. Dried, it needs soaking for a couple of hours before use. Use as a substitute for lemon.

MARJORAM in this country remains largely the province of gardeners, who grow it robustly both in the green form and the variegated golden. There is SWEET MARJORAM, *Origanum majorana*, and the wild *O. vulgare*, more commonly called OREGANO. The sweet combines well with pork, carrots and cucumber, but fresh should be added towards the end of the cooking when its marigold-style flavour is not lost in cooking. The stalks tend to be tenacious and should be discarded. Dried, the flavour intensifies significantly. OREGANO has come to be associated with the cooking of the South-east Mediterranean, for pizzas and tomato sauces, and in Greece with lamb.

MINT grows wild across the world and there are many varieties. The sweet industry favours SPEARMINT, *Mentha spicata*, but more commonly found in gardens and seed catalogues is the round-leafed *M. rotundifolia*. APPLEMINT, *M. suaveolens*, has cream edges to downy green leaves. It attracts flies in the garden and is the least successful of the culinary mints, although it is said to have been the original basis for mint sauce. PEPPERMINT, *M. piperita*, has a purple stem and hue to the leaves, the oil is also used in the confectionery industry. There are other variations, mostly flourishing in different parts of the country, such as the decorative PINEAPPLE MINT or the perfumed EAU-DE-COLOGNE MINT which have commercial applications and flourish better in some areas than others. The best use for the variations is as leaves in a salad.

Ordinary mint is pungent and dominating and needs to be used sparingly or with confidence. The hesitancy of older books seems less valid now with the emergence of more virulent comparable aromatics, like ginger or coriander.

Ways With Mint

Mint is a surprisingly friendly herb, combining well with fish and fruits such as orange as well as more conventional pairings like that with new potatoes.

Fresh Mint Sauce:
Chop 2 parts mint and add to 1 part sugar, blend with 5 parts white wine vinegar and 5 parts water.

PARSLEY is native to the Mediterranean. *Petroselinum crispum* first reached here in the 16th century and was subsequently taken to America. All parsleys are rich in calcium, iron, vitamins A, B1, B2 and C, and deserve to be used more widely in cooking. They are too often miscast as a garnish and have been, rightly, replaced in the French kitchen by the more delicate chervil. The high chlorophyll content sweetens the breath, notably after eating garlic. Heavy parsley eaters are reputed to smell seductively sweet. The densely curled-leaved varieties beloved of garnishes and garden centres – PARAMOUNT IMPERIAL CURLED, which looks like miniature kale, or MOSS CURLED PARSLEY – is an unhappy relative that keeps getting rolled out for the wrong party. Raw, it is bitter and dry and one suspects its reputation is based largely on its bizarre role of livening up food shop window displays, a hangover from its brief moment of post-war fame when it came to be a symbol of a shop for serious cooks. More delicate and interesting is FLAT or ITALIAN PARSLEY, with larger fern-like leaves that have a more definite cutting flavour, edged with aniseed. HAMBURG PARSLEY, *P tuberosum*, looks like Italian but is grown for its flavoured root and recipe history, associated with celery and parsnip. CHINESE PARSLEY is actually coriander (see page 330).

ROCKET, or ARUGULA, is sold as both a salad leaf and as a herb; and, in part, it has the attributes of both. The spindly leaves are peppery and enliven salads with other strong flavours, like that of blue cheese or a very fruity olive oil. It is native to southern Europe, but is easily grown here from seed. It needs to be cut before it flowers, otherwise the leaves become hairy and the flavour almost mustard-strong. (See also Vegetables, page 199).

Ways With Parsley

Parsley is best used as if it were a vegetable, generously filling up casseroles, or where it can star in soups and purées, and salads like *tabbouleh*. The stems are also useful in stocks.

SAGE is a native of the Mediterranean and named after the Latin *salvia*, meaning to be in good health. For many centuries it was grown mainly for its perceived medicinal properties. The purple-leaved varieties are most commonly associated with healing. The leaves are harvested before flowering. Raw, they are delinquently strong, often said to have tones of camphor, but lose their pungency in cooking and have come to be used to underwrite other blander flavours, as in sage and onion stuffing, or to flavour milk dishes. They have other more peripheral uses. Fashionably they are deep-fried as a surprising garnish in restaurant cooking. Sage tea reputedly clears phlegm and was popular before China tea was imported. Chewing the leaves whitens teeth and they can be used as a scent in the bath.

ROSEMARY, *Rosmarinus* or 'the rose of the sea', is native to the Mediterranean and will grow to 1.25 m (4 ft). 'There's rosemary, that's for remembrance,' says Ophelia in *Hamlet*. It was introduced here by the Romans and flourishes well enough in southern Britain, not necessarily by the sea. It likes full sun and well-drained soil. Commercially, rosemary oil is used in eau-de-cologne and toilet waters. In gardening catalogues *Miss Jessup's Upright* is neat and straight; *O'Connell's Blue* needs space and gives spectacular flowers which can be used in salads; there is also a creeping rosemary, *R. prostrata*, which is 'beautiful and functional'. The needle-like leaves are best used to flavour because, unless they are very young and fine and are diced small, they are quite hard to eat.

TARRAGON may have originated in central Asia but was used by the Arabs and the Greeks. Tarragon enjoys a proud place in the French kitchen, being part of the classical repertoire in a *Béarnaise* sauce, in regional

Ways With Rosemary

Traditionally, rosemary goes well with roast lamb, a habit imported from Italy as in their culture with veal, or on the barbecue to flavour fish, but it also goes well with roast beef.

salads and most famously with chicken. In this country, however, it has been largely overlooked except as a flavouring for vinegar. There are two kinds: the paler, inferior RUSSIAN TARRAGON, which can be grown from seed but is coarse and of little merit; and **FRENCH TARRAGON which has to be cultivated by cuttings, but once established will submit to any amount of hacking around. The flavour is subtle, with elements of 'sharp aniseed, greenness and a mild fluorescent anaesthetic'. An aristocrat among herbs, like basil it can transform the mundane.

THYME has a long history: the stalks were used as temple incense; bees are attracted to it and make an ancient dark-brown honey scented with thyme, marjoram and savory, from Mount Heymettus in Greece. It was a symbol of courage, because it is supposedly mildly intoxicating, and was embroidered on the uniforms of crusaders; French republicans used it as a secret symbol of recognition. There are upwards of 50 varieties: common thyme is a small evergreen perennial, growing to 30 cm (1 ft). The leaves are tiny grey green arrows which can either be diligently plucked off individually or, less diligently, the branch pulled through two fingernails.

LEMON THYME has a gold or silver edge, is highly perfumed, prettier and more feminine, and allies well with fish. Dried thyme is one of the most successful preserved herbs.

> **Ways With Thyme**
>
> With parsley and bay, thyme is one of the essentials for a *bouquet garni*, which points to its best use as fundamental to many meat marinades and slow-cooked casseroles, where it can give up its spiced citrus flavours over a long period.

SPICES

**ALLSPICE, which is also called JAMAICAN BLACK PEPPER, is not to be confused with black pepper itself (see page 340). The trees from which the tiny berries come are tall, growing to 9 m (27 ft), and the berries are not so much black as dark brown. They are, 'very hard, with an instant smell of flowers and the obvious affinity – from which they take their name – for cloves, cinnamon and nutmeg'. The berries have to be picked under-ripe or they will turn to a mush. Plantations are known poetically as 'Pimento Walks'. The trees flower white in July and August, the berries picked when they are still greeny-purple and then dried in the sun. There are false and inferior varieties called 'allspice' from Mexico and America, but they lack the powerful and underrated pungency of the original.

ANISEED, or ANISE, *Pimpinella anisum*, is a part of the parsley family. Older books refer to its medicinal virtues as a carminative, and also to disguise the flavour of early drugs. It grows widely across a band running from Malta through Germany to China, which is always said to produce the best. The seed itself is tiny, the size of a pin head, and produces a blueish-tinged oil. Often it is used with other seasonings, especially coriander and fennel, to which it is related and from which anisette is made.

CARAWAY is the deep brown seeds of the *Carum carvi*, which grows wild across Europe but is also cultivated in Germany and Holland and North Africa. The root, like a small parsnip, can also be eaten. The best seeds are said to be Dutch, with a distinctive blue hue to the brown. The oil is extracted and the residue is sold as 'drawn caraway', but this is much darker.

CARDAMOM is the perfumed seed of a reed found originally in Southern Asia, growing as high as 3 m (9 ft). There are a great many varieties of cardamom and they are often mixed together. The three-cornered pods are green unless they have been bleached. They have sustained their reputation as an early therapeutic food and survive pungently in curries and most famously in coffee. Bought in the pod, the sides should be tightly sealed.

CINNAMON is the inside bark of the young shoots of *Cinnamomum zeylanicum*, found especially in Sri Lanka but also on a belt from Borneo to Jamaica. The tree, one of the laurel family, grows to 8 m (25 ft) and will be fertile for as long as 200 years. However, the best is taken from young trees after about four years. There are two harvests, the best of which is in summer. The outer skin is scraped off and the pliant bark left to dry, initially in the shade and then in full sun, when it curls into quills. Sometimes CASSIA bark is passed off as cinnamon, but is coarser, thicker and darker. Good sticks of cinnamon are light yellow, no thicker than cartridge paper and pliant enough to go soft in the mouth. It should be 'sweetly pungent' and 'leave no aftertaste'.

CLOVES are the dried unopened buds of the *Eugenia caryophyllata*, a kind of myrtle, cultivated across tropical latitudes, principally in East Africa. The tree is slender, growing up to 10 m (30 ft) and it flowers in clusters like honeysuckle. The flowers are white, becoming green and then red, at which point they should be hand-picked and dried swiftly in the shade of the tree for a week, or smoked over wood fires. Good cloves should leave an oily film in the hand and will exude a sticky substance if pierced with a nail. A clove where the oil has dried out (or been extracted) will float in water. The best were said to come from Penang and are red in colour.

GINGER is thought originally to have come from China. Its medicinal qualities as a blood-thinning agent that can carry other remedies around the body are enthusiastically supported by herbalists and are a feature in Chinese medicine. Of all the foods listed in this book, ginger seems the most likely success story of the '90s. Just as garlic's reputa-

Gingerbread

A number of towns – Ormskirk, Congleton, Grantham, Grasmere, Wrexham and Whitby – were known for their gingerbread-making. This was a practice found across Europe and it was said you were never really famous until you had had your likeness made in gingerbread. The French *pain d'épice* was marginally different, using rye flour and honey in place of golden syrup.

tion rose on the back of French cooking, so ginger's reputation gets stronger with the assimilation of Asian ideas on cooking.

Ginger is an underground stem out of which stubby hands form, topped with small buds. The roots are in fact cut off before marketing. It flowers, occasionally producing a cluster of yellow and white flowers which are flecked with purple. Botanically, *Zingiber*, with variations found in Japan and Thailand, is closely related to turmeric. It likes hot weather and grows in India, Australia, Jamaica, China and Nigeria. Jamaican ginger coming into Westcoast ports would have been the basis for much early English cooking of gingerbread.

Gingers from different regions are discernibly different. AFRICAN tends to be harsh and camphorous; INDIAN is, 'lemony'; JAMAICAN is, perhaps surprisingly, mild, and was regarded as one of the best; FIJIAN is a, 'melony lemon', COSTA RICAN is, 'deep citrus and tongue-searingly strong'. The best is probably from *HAWAII, first arriving in February, 'Handsome long roots without gnarls, smooth-skinned and almost silvery beige in colour, stalky texture, potent, somewhere between lemon and grapefruit. Very citrus'. Or another sample later in the year, so probably older, 'knobbly, yellowing, rootoid with much stalk, lemon floral smell, not too harsh'.

Supermarket examples tend to be sparse and poor compared to those in grocers, especially Indian and Chinese shops. The price is arbitrary but as the trade deals in lbs, those supermarkets (**Safeway, Somerfield**) that split it up into grams are usually calculating on high mark-ups. Even so, it remains inexpensive for something so potentially influential. It will freeze for up to three months and can be grated still frozen.

Fresh ginger is the first harvest. Ginger for

drying is harvested later when the rhizomes have gained more strength. Drying tends to, 'accentuate the pungency, while reducing the lemon and aromatic tones'. Black or green is the original, white has been bleached. Soft drinks are made with extracts and concentrates of pure ginger. CRYSTALLIZED and STEM GINGER are made from fresh ginger that has been cooked in sweet acid solution several times, topping up with brown sugar: sold in a syrup it is crystallized, or the pieces are taken out and rolled in more sugar to make stem ginger. Stems are obviously more delicate than roots or chips, which tend to be coarser and hotter.

MACE is the outer casing of the nutmeg (see below) and when harvested it is bright red. It is then pressed between blocks of wood and dried in the sun, which turns it a browny-yellow. There are different grades, of which the smaller are said to be the best. The flavour should be of a more delicate form of nutmeg.

MANIQUETTE, or PARADISE SEEDS or PARADISE GRAINS, are tiny brown seeds which are possibly the same as what old books refer to as MELEGUETA or ALLIGATOR PEPPER, originally imported to France from Ethiopia in the '40s as a substitute for ordinary pepper, but later ingratiated itself for its hard mild-scented heat.

NUTMEG is the kernel of the tropical *Myristica fragrans*, which is similar in shape to a pear tree. They will bear about 4.5 kg (10 lb) of fruit after 10 years. The fruit is peach-like and can be eaten. The nutmegs are dried systematically in the sun until the shell can be broken off without breaking the inner kernel. Price is determined by size, the larger being the more expensive.

PEPPER is becoming increasingly defined as an ingredient in its own right, whereas in the Middle Ages the term passed for all manner of spices and was used as a currency, hence the term 'peppercorn rent'. Pepper comes from the vines of the *Piper nigrum*, which thrives in low valleys in hot climates. It is a vine propagated by cuttings and trained either along saplings or stakes to some 3-6 m (9-18 ft) tall. A single fruit will produce 20-50 corns of pepper twice a year, the main crop from January to May and a second smaller crop in September. A good vine can expect to yield upwards of 2.7 kg (6 lb) of pepper in a harvest. The berries are green, turning red when fully – in fact, over- – ripe. Drying in the sun is preferable to kiln-drying. Heat wrinkles and turns the corn black.

Pepper has been accepted in nearly every cooking of the world, and seemingly also into most manufacturing practices. In the '50s it still accounted for half the spice trade to this country. Its pre-eminence is being eroded by other means of preservation, faster transport of foods and the arrival of other, more dynamic, forms of seasoning, notably garlic, chilli and ginger.

The full intensity of flavour comes either from freshly grinding pepper or using good quality berries. Ground pepper stales more quickly than whole peppercorns, so represents a poor buy. STEAK PEPPER is an expensive affectation, as are the packaging promotions for refills. Given the price and how long pepper lasts it is hardly an area that bears economy. The very pretty bottles of differently coloured peppers are mainly designed for recipe dishes, like a colourful mild *steak au poivre* or lending colour to a casserole.

Good BLACK PEPPER should be like 'scented Doc Martins, granulated, hard with elements of cloves'. The mainstay of the trade to London was from Jamaica which has led to some confusion with Jamaican pepper or allspice (see page 335). The south of India also produces excellent black pepper.

**Parameswaran's Finest Wynad Pepper from Kerala, is grown on a 5,000 metres-high plateau and commands a higher price than other peppers. It is, 'perfumed, paler and hotter' because it is left to ripen until fully red and the berries picked by hand each day to ensure the proper ripeness. It is said to improve with age. 'The heat is slow to eke out, quite spiced like cloves mixed with a fire that builds and lasts for a considerable number of minutes'. It is best used to finish dishes rather than in cooking.

WHITE PEPPER is left on the vine until the black pepper turns white inside. The black husk is taken off and this dulls the flavour. 'The heat of good white pepper builds slowly from a scent; the heat comes from the destruction of the cell walls with vicious, tiny crevices of heat filling the mouth and getting sharper and sharper'. The traditional plantations for white pepper are in North-east India, Sarawak and Singapore, which produce a harder pepper, called Muntok, which used to be known as *Coriander white*. White pepper was famously liable to adulteration and is today looking increasingly arcane compared to freshly ground black pepper.

GREEN PEPPERCORNS are completely unripe, but have been preserved in brine and not dried, although increasingly now they are freeze-dried. They are strong in flavour, but the brine diffuses their heat. Good versions, 'smell faintly of herbs, basil even, certainly thyme. The heat is warming, building to a point of fire.'

PINK PEPPERCORNS are not, in fact, a peppercorn at all, but from another tree found in South America. They are a pomegranate pink, 'sweet on the tongue, mild but with a hit at the back of the mouth'. The RED PEPPER is the riper version of the pink, milder and

Ways With Green Peppercorns

They are good for sauces, as in the classic *nouvelle cuisine* dish of steak with cream and green peppercorns, and also in marinades.

subtler than Asian pepper, 'aromatic with lemons'. Good with fish and mousses, they are usually sold in brine or freeze-dried.

BIRD'S PEPPER is a wild pepper, the seeds carried and distributed by birds in the Cameroons. Larger than white, they are beige to cream balls, with a pure floral smell, not biting. 'Hard, nutty, mealy strong, building with dusky sour essences'.

STAR ANISE, *Illicium anisatum*, is a member of the magnolia family, related to – but different from and more bitter than – aniseed, It is native to China, where it is one of the basic five-spices. The star-shaped pods are dried before they are fully ripe. The Japanese variety *I. lanceolatum* is poisonous.

VANILLA is a trailing orchid which attaches itself to any nearby tree and bears greeny yellow flowers followed by slender three-lobed pods up to 25 cm (10 in) long, which curve and become yellow when ripe. The name is from the Spanish *vaina*, meaning a sheath or scabbard. It is only after curing and fermenting that the pods turn black and give off their brilliant clean humid smell. The best comes from Mexico, where vanilla was first used with chocolate, but there are different varieties cultivated further south along the Continent and in Africa across the Tropics. The pods are harvested in November and December, but may not reach the market for four or five months, depending on how they are cured. Vanilla pods must be kept in a sealed bag or container – or in the sugar jar to make vanilla sugar.

FLAVOURINGS

Flavourings are ridiculously cheap, given their long-lasting value. In all these categories extravagance repays itself many times over.

CAPERS

These pungent little objects are the flower buds of the long trailing shrub, *Capparis spinosa*, usually grown along old walls, or even on rubbish heaps, though it is sometimes kept as an ornament in the garden around the Mediterranean rim. It is low and bushy with oval leaves and beautiful flowers, a waterfall of purple stamens against four white or pink petals. The buds have to be picked daily from May as the flower withers quickly in the heat. They are left to dry for 24 hours and then put in good quality vinegar or occasionally (and very good) in salt. Capers used to be graded in seven different sizes: with the smallest, the NONPAREILS, being the most expensive and prized. The acidity comes from the capric acid which is a similar substance, albeit in much smaller quantities, as that which gives goats their distinctive smell.

The best capers were always considered to come from the South of France, though much of what reaches here today seems to come from Morocco, or better, Turkey. The best sell for as much as £9 per lb wholesale. They benefit from decanting if the brine is suspect.

EXTRA FINE CAPERS from Turkey are small, barely 2 mm ($1/12$ in) across, and slate grey in colour, they are crunchy and floral. **Tornatore**, the Ligurian olive-oil-producing estate, also imports very young capers from Morocco and bottles them in wine vinegar: 'Tiny lentil-sized, quite tart from the vinegar. A treat'. **Noel's** are the most widely available brand in supermarkets, bottled in Lancashire, they are conservative, fair-sized, not too tart, restrained, but OK.

Ways With Capers

Capers were imported almost exclusively for sauce to go with mutton or for tartare sauce. The Romans used them for fish sauces. They are also a startling addition in salads and purées.

CHILLI SAUCES

Chilli sauces go under different names as they stretch languorously across the globe from Mexico, through the Caribbean, North Africa and down to South-east Asia. The main difference is whether they are designed for use in the cooking or, as in the Caribbean variations, for the table like ketchups.

The hottest of all are **Koon Yick Wah Kee's Soy Chilli Sauce** from Hong Kong, reinforced with garlic and sugar. Close behind is the enterprisingly **Gramma's** top-of-the-range **Very Hot**, made in Hainault, Essex, rivalled by the West Indian pair of **Encona** and **Grace**, which are both used as table sauces and not as background heat for cooking.

In this company, the fabled Moroccan HARISSA is only tepid, its heat diluted by cumin and equal in strength to **Gramma's Mild**, and the well-known **McIlhenny's Tabasco sauce**, beloved in Bloody Mary's. Slightly stronger for drinks is the West Indian **Pickapeppa Sauce**. The international brand names have opted, predictably, for moderation and safety in the heat stakes but without really compensating in terms of developed flavours.

CHOCOLATE

The word chocolate comes from the Aztec word *chocaltl* and was drunk in Mexico for centuries before the arrival of the Spaniards. Chocolate is made from the roasted seeds of the tree *Theobroma cacao*, contained in gourd-like orange lanterns that hang in clusters off the main trunks of the tree. The kernel is marshmallow-white in its raw state.

Drinking chocolate was first commercially manufactured in this country by **Churchman's**, later taken over by **Fry's**, at Bristol in 1728, but eating chocolate did not appear for another 100 years. It was **Van Houten** in 1828 who discovered that he could press out the fat from the ground nibs and create a butter that would not only give a balanced flavour but also allow the chocolate to be moulded. The first chocolate bars were made here in 1847 by **Fry** and two years later by **Cadbury.** These would have been PLAIN CHOCOLATE. The addition of milk to make MILK CHOCOLATE was not developed until 1876 by a Swiss, **M D Peters**, a well-known brand before 1940.

Chocolate-making is an advanced process, a tribute to Victorian engineering rather than any gastronomic inspiration. The beans are roasted – usually a lighter roast for eating rather than drinking – and shelled. The liquor goes forward while the debris is pressed, then either filtered for the cocoa butter or ground for powder. The liquor and butter are reunited, sugar is added and then the chocolate begins an elongated series of grindings, and conching – where it flows into a warm tank in which a large granite roller moves back and forth, rubbing out any solid particles, sometimes for as long as a week. It is then tempered, flavoured, often with vanilla as the Aztecs did, and moulded. WHITE CHOCOLATE simply omits the cocoa liquor and is cocoa butter, milk and sugar. One reason Swiss chocolate enjoys such a good reputation is that the early plants had access to cheap electricity from the mountain waterfalls which allowed the chocolate to be ground finer and for longer periods.

The romance of chocolate suggests that it is all about the subtleties of different blends of cocoa, whether it be from Venezuela (usually held to be the premier producer), Madagascar or Sri Lanka. To this should be added the grinding, which accounts for the smoothness. The skill of the chocolatier is to blend. 72% cocoa solids is about as high as it goes for something the equivalent of a chocolate version of espresso coffee, so bitter it is almost

FOOD *watch*

Although British chocolate is often snobbishly derided, it has recognized from an early stage the value of blending and not pitching up for a double whammy of cocoa solids. The lack of smoothness from the conching tends to be offset by the combinations and additions of mousses and creams. A **Mars Bar** remains one of the world's greatest reecipes. For plain chocolate the solitary figure of **Bournville** maintains a conservatively sensible level of 34% cocoa solids, adequate enough for general purposes but lacking the intensity that will give the contrast for work using more than one kind of chocolate. In the milk field **Yorkie** is 22% cocoa solids, **Cadbury's Dairy Milk** and **Galaxy 20%.**

almonds, any more points on the scale and it becomes almost tasteless. There is a subtlety here beyond the reach of what is found in the shops. Specialists like *Coco Barry, **Vahlronna** and *DGF will sell variations of climate and intensity that match the recipes – a lower solid percentage for a mousse, higher for the casing. Milk comes in as a welcome diffusion at around 32% solids. To compare the **DGF Le Louis** white couverture (coating chocolate) to **Sainsbury's White Chocolate Drops** is like comparing a Derby runner to an old lag.

As if to retaliate, **Sainsbury** also sells a Belgian version **Deluxe Continental**, at an astonishing 75% cocoa solids, an almost incomprehensible black void of nothing... the culinary equivalent of a black hole – compared to its ordinary at a mere 51%, made in the UK and distinctly less smooth.

Green & Black make a great play of their organic product and pioneered the first laudable Fairtrade Foundation food endorsement for their **Maya Gold** from Belize, which is 70% cocoa solids (as is their mainline bar, but with beans from Togo in West Africa) but tempered wisely with allspice, vanilla and orange. Another Belgian maker, **Martougin** sell a deluxe bar at only 70% cocoa solids, which is still a resounding thwack of chocolate but again underlines the importance of grinding in the sticky smoothness.

Marks & Spencer gets a similar silkiness in its range of **Swiss Chocolate**, less macho in playing the cocoa-solids power game, but compensating with a cohesive approach that underlines the value of the grinding. As impressive is the **French**.

The legendary **Ménier,** which claims gold medals dating back to 1832 – now owned by **Nestlé** and their chocolate made in Switzerland rather than France – balances its cocoa solids at a sensible 52%. It remains an

outstanding benchmark of a finely orches-
trated chocolate, much subtler than some of
the brash new competition. It is as happy as
an eating chocolate as for cooking, where its
long-standing monopoly is only seriously
threatened by the variations of the specialist
professional couvertures.

Bonnat produce a range of chocolate
bars from different regions which reflect the
styles and character of the region – the perfumed tonic of Venezuela, or the mild warm
Sri Lankan. These are more of an educa-
tional course. **Scot's** is actually produced in
West Germany and, despite boasting cocoa
solids at 55% and a sell-by date of 18 months
ahead, was very poor and stale, quite nasty.

Other cooking chocolates in supermarkets,
Tesco, Scotbloc and **Supercook,** are
flavours, not chocolate itself.

HONEY

Bees pre-date man by about 50 million years
and were thought to have come from
Afghanistan. By Egyptian times the cultivation
of honey was advanced, with hives being
moved along the Nile to keep pace with the
seasons and the different flowerings on the
bankside which imbued the flavour of the
honey. Christian countries kept bees through
the dark ages to supply the beeswax for
church candles as well as an original form of
sweetener and, equally important, as a medicine or as a dressing for wounds. The honey,
along with pollen, is the feed for the young
bees. Fields pollinated by bees have been
shown to be more productive – examples on
rape fields have shown a 53% increase in the
yield. Bees will fly within a radius of six miles
and, depending on the habitat, may well stay
with a single type of flower.

Good quality honey is defined by its region
or more specifically by the flowers the bees

are likely to have pollinated. Brand names are something of a generic aberration that has been used to mask the destruction of the environment. CLEAR HONEY has a higher percentage of fructose rather than glucose, which depends on the kind of flora the bees have been pollinating. Dandelion or rape flowers provide most of the pollination for bees in this country and this honey will set more quickly because of the glucose, whereas honey drawn from bees that have pollinated acacia blossoms is nearly all fructose. Essentially there is little difference. Bees that have pollinated rhododendron flowers produce a honey that can cause dizziness and sickness, while those that have pollinated hemp flowers will produce a honey containing cannabis. Scottish HEATHER HONEY was always well regarded but now seems rare. SET or SOLID HONEY can be returned to liquid by standing it in warm water for an hour. Honey is hygroscopic and attracts water so in cooking the amount of liquid used is reduced

Apicoltura from **Devalle Danille** do a range of specialist honeys from different regions – a light granular curd yellow to orange sunflower honey from Aquitaine: lime flower honey from the Auvergne; chestnut leaf honey from the Cevennes, mountain flower honey from the Savoie, and Lavender honey from Provence. In markets in Portugal it is still possible to buy honeys from quite obscure herbs.

ROYAL JELLY, sometimes added back into honey or sold as a supplement, is secreted into queen cells in the hive and its extra nutrients account for the same bees becoming queen rather than worker bees, however there is some doubt as to whether this works in the same way on humans.

The best HONEYCOMBS are VIRGIN COMB, taken from a young hive where the honey flows spontaneously. The bees will not have swarmed. In succeeding years the comb will become brown, or even black.

MUSTARD

There are two principal types of mustard seeds: the WHITE (in fact yellow) *Sinapis alba*, and the more expensive and volatile BLACK, *S. nigra*, in fact brown. The white is said to be inferior, but has properties which bring out the fieriness of the black. This may have had to do with the seeds being much smaller and more difficult to harvest. The blending of mustards has been such a preoccupation that, before the war, whole tracts of Lincolnshire and Yorkshire were given over to black, and acres of Cambridge and Essex for white. Seed and powder are innocuous when dry and only acquire their potency when water is added.

The origins are almost certainly from the Italian *mostarda*, from the Latin *mustum*, unfermented grape juice. The sell-by dates are important on mustard – the later the better. Citric acid or acetic acid dissolved in water cost about 2p against 90p for good wine vinegar, which is why better mustards start their ingredients lists with vinegar, not water.

DIJON MUSTARDS account for half the world production of mustard. Mustard-making was introduced to the area around Dijon by the Romans, and in the 15th century monasteries popularized its use. Most labels suggest Dijon to go with meats, but it is also the classic vinaigrette mustard.

Benedicta à l'Ancienne is made using water and spirit vinegar and has a 'creamier texture, searingly single-minded, very one-dimensional, lacking the subtlety of the Maille as the cheap vinegar betrays it'.

Colman's Dijon is sandy in texture and

Mustard powders are credited to a Mrs Clements of Durham around 1720. She made annual pilgrimages to big cities to take orders for her blends, but these Durham mustards seem to have disappeared. She reputedly discovered that if you let the mustard plant bolt and then sieved it through silk screens the resulting mustard was hotter.

FOOD *watch*

Supermarket Own-brand Dijon Mustards

Tesco is quite a spicy mix, involving turmeric, pimento, pepper, cinnamon and cloves. The impact is 'sweet to begin with a fiery edge... interestingly developed'. **Waitrose, Asda** and **Sainsbury** adopt a disappointing one-dimensional approach with variations, mainly in the level of vinegar, water, mustard seed, spirit vinegar and salt and little to choose between them.

colour, and uses water and spirit vinegar. It is all about the delivery of heat rather than flavour. Hot, it is slow to start but builds into a resounding explosive crescendo.

Maille claims to be the oldest mustard firm in the region, established in 1747. **A l'Ancienne** is their grain version, made with spirit vinegar. It is sharp, with an immediate bite on the tongue, crawling all over the taste buds like jumping beans, different impact from different grains, plenty of vinegar. It is good for saucing: mix with cream and pan juices.

Poupon was established around 1870 and uses white wine vinegar. It is a distinctive saffron yellow and creamy, with shards of heat like a lightning storm striking different parts of the mouth and then cascading down to all parts'.

ENGLISH MUSTARDS are dominated by **Colman**, which may account for the monocultural nature of the definition. The fashionably touristic mixes with whisky or beer have very little history and are mainly affectations, often sometimes quite unpleasantly so.

Colman's Dried Mustard is still sold in the imperial-style tins. Invaluable and without competition for the range of old English recipes, it is all the more adaptable for its purity as a powder.

Ginger Mustard from **Leatham's Larder** is a mild Swedish mix of mustards with a considerable debt to the dill mustard sauce served with *gravlax* (**Leatham's** *gravlax* sauce is one of the best on the market) but in this case invigorated with 17% root ginger for a resounding marriage, 'a creamy warm foil to the pungency and resonating root ginger'.

Gordon's English Vineyard Mustard is, surprisingly, made with malt vinegar. The wine component is considerably smaller. It is a sludgy grainy, very hot to begin with, tones of curry, quite bizarre and out of step with what mustard is supposed to be.

Tesco Tewkesbury is a sludgy gruel reinforced with horseradish and white wine vinegar. Its very wide flavour is a bit imprecise but has more variation than its English. Shakespeare mentions Tewkesbury mustard, so it is certainly traditional.

Sainsbury makes a similar mustard using horseradish that it is very sandy and sludgy, the horseradish very much to the front and only a mild edge of mustard at all.

Cumberland mustard is drenched in honey, but with some fire left in the grains. It is not really a very good idea.

Urchfont was an invention in 1970 by William Tullberg, a sausage taster who got bored and who went on to create **"Wiltshire Tracklements**. His **Original** is all white mustard with chilli and black peppercorns and allspice. His **Spiced Honey** uses black and white, chilli and Mexican honey. His **Strong English** is a more conventional – but still hand-made – mix.

Taylor's Original English claims its recipe dates back to 1830. Made with mustard flour and water, it is conspicuously English: intense, bitter, granular, almost sandy, akin to that Victorian taste of patum peperium... woody, strong and individual.

Taylor's Medieval is made with cider vinegar, mustard flour mixed with honey and turmeric, and olive oil. It has a tight sucking sandy texture, and is sweet with edge of fire, really more honey and turmeric than mustard. Good.

FRENCH MUSTARDS seem to be a breed apart, a brand and colouring without much progeny. The French tradition was to grind the seeds more gently on stone mills, like olives for olive oil. Of all the dark brown mushes, **La Favorite** might claim the parentage and justification for the genre. The wine vinegar is diluted with water and spirit vinegar, but is evident nevertheless, and is reinforced in some instances with herbs like tarragon. It has, 'a sour, damp heat with a sandy texture and an inner sweetness'.

****Beaufor Moutarde en Grains**, from Reims, is a black mustard mixed as a semi-paste. It is like an aristocratic version of Dijon, with a sharp heat and a smooth texture with flecks and very good vinegar. ****Beafour** is the smoother version and is equally good.

***Moutarde Violette** is an unusual and rarely found variation, using the must of grapes which creates a purple paste. It is made in Brive and it is claimed that the recipe has not been changed since 1839. Mildly vinous with a shallow fire at the back, it is unusual but good, although a bit cloying. It needs something moist to go with it. (**Chalice** do an equally interesting mix of **Mustard with Black Olives**, which might, in time, attain the same curiosity value.)

Moutarde de Meaux Pommery has a long romantic history of how it was first served to the King of France in 1632 and then handed secretly to the Pommery family in 1760. Sold in the kind of stone jars beloved of street markets, the contents sealed in with cork and wax, it is, 'granular and sour, familiar from steak-houses, almost a thick sauce in texture, it tastes very old-fashioned and seems to have become more porridgey in the last 20 years'. It needs using swiftly after opening the seal, or its heat disappears.

GERMAN MUSTARDS are diluted versions of Dijon with different seasonings – as are AMERICAN MUSTARDS. **Buckaroo**, a Jalapeño mustard from Texas, is not really a mustard but a Jalapeño pepper mix, using vinegar, water, turmeric, onions and colours. Chilli curry piccalilli might be a better name. Very gloopy.

SALT

Different varieties of salt take their name from the manner in which they are produced. Most comes from underground lakes where the rain water has filtered through the salt strata. ROCK SALT is mined as blocks, mostly in Europe now from the enormous reserves on the Austrian side of the Alps. SEA SALT is either evaporated on natural beds, as at Maldon in Essex, or pumped inshore across shallow reservoirs. The size of the crystals depends on how much the brine is heated. At boiling point the crystals will be pin-head size. Lower heats for evaporation will produce larger crystals. Most English salt is pumped out of underground reservoirs in Cheshire in a process that has hardly changed in 1,000 years. The old Celtic word *wych* or *wich*, meaning a salt spring is still attached to salt towns like Nantwich, Droitwich, Northwich and Middlewich.

Salt is the only pure mineral we eat. Excessive salt intake has become increasingly implicated in raising the blood pressure, which is in itself one of the four major risk factors in heart disease. Much of what we eat insinuates its way into the diet through convenience foods, in breakfast cereals for example, and also in more traditional cured products like bacon or ham. The salt market is also sustained by its wide use in cosmetics, medicine, water softening and road gritting.

The best salts are the FLOWER OF SALT, which is the top crust of sea salt imbued with the flavours of the breeze, and RASSOL, which is rarely seen and is the salt left by the intense cold on the surface of ice fields at the Poles.

*COOKING SALT is the best value salt on the market, differing from TABLE SALT in that it does not have added magnesium carbonate and sodium hexacyanoferrate (II) to

FOOD *watch*

Salt is a example of a market that has expanded to serve its own purposes. Cooking salt is far and away the cheapest and most expedient form of salt to use in the kitchen. The idea of salt cellars on the table is just an echo of a once brilliant marketing scheme. Although most salt grinders claim to have long lives, eventually the machinery softens. Premium salts may seem expensive for the table but, in practice, the investment is long-standing and, compared to other foods, is ridiculously cheap.

SALT SUBSTITUTES

Originally developed for low-salt diets, these have grown substantially on the back of more ordinary health concerns. All use potassium chloride, which is part of the same family as sodium chloride but much more bitter. Ironically, where the Government's *Health of the Nation Report* recommends a reduction in salt intake, it actually suggests an increase in potassium chloride, which is more usually found in fruit and vegetables. Increasingly it is being used to create low-salt convenience products, like baked beans. **Lo Salt** is made by **Klinge** who deal in potassium chloride for the drug industry, where it is used to help kidney patients. The bitterness is offset by 33% sodium chloride, so it is strictly not an alternative but a diluted form. **Ruthmol** is a genuine alternative which adds a minute amount of ammonium chloride to ease the bitterness. Both claim that people can't tell the difference in cooking, even if they can at the table.

help it run smoothly through the cellar. Sometimes the colour errs on the grey side, but in terms of cooking it is as effective as more expensive and better packaged table salts.

Cerebos British Salt is an amalgamation of 64 small salt mines in Cheshire, formed in 1888. The main plant is, in fact, on the site of the old Cerebos packaging station. Chiefly notable for its deep-red packaging and the addition of iodine originally intended to supplement a post-war diet.

La Baleine is from the northern Spanish and western coast of France. The sea water is pumped on to inland reservoirs for evaporation. The grits are tighter and smaller than Maldon. It also contains iodine, which is still currently fashionable in France.

****Maldon Salt** comes from Essex. The Romans established Maldon as a salt town and it remains a family business, following traditional slow evaporation giving crystals that are soft and wide, 'perfectly fragile'. It claims to be purer, less bitter and, therefore, stronger.

****Salines de Guerande** is packed in neat white cloth bags which declare chauvinistically that salt from Guerande is '*autre chose*' (something else). Most usually found here is a small-grained mix with the dried seaweed of the estuary, specifically designed to season fish. 'Intense, characterful, it is almost a self-contained sauce.'

Tidman's was originally developed principally for its supposed health-giving properties. Up to the '20s, salt baths were thought to be effective against rheumatism and other illnesses as various as measles. It was taken under the **Maldon** wing in 1973.

SOY SAUCE & OTHER SOY PRODUCTS

The soya bean is native to China, Java and Japan, where it has been cultivated from the very earliest civilizations. For soy sauce, the cooked soya beans are mixed with roasted wheat flour and salt, and fermented in casks. Two kinds of soy sauce are sold – LIGHT and DARK – though, in some cases, the one seems to be a diluted version of the other, with only the salt levels remaining consistent. The lighter versions are designed for fish and poultry and salads, the darker for more meaty dishes. Many recipes call for both. Good soy is a reasonable substitute for meat stock in cooking. Mainline samples from **Safeway** and **Sainsbury** have the colour reinforced by caramel. There are surprisingly different elements to other brands. **Sharwood's Rich** is 'meaty' but with tones of a flavour-enhancer and their **Light** version comparatively 'fishy'. **Lotus Light** has, 'poignant sour sharp notes' compared to **Amoy Dark**, 'a deep swelling of the sea, like a liquorice oyster'. ****Kikkoman** is, 'a vegetabley treat, like a non-meat Marmite'. Chinese imports also show well. ***Pearl River Bridge Superior** is, 'nutty,

Worcester Sauce

A turn-of-the-century recipe for Worcester sauce called for 2½ gallons of malt vinegar, 3 quarts of soy, 1 quart of lime juice, 1 lb of shallots or onions, ½ lb of garlic, 2½ lb of tamarinds, ½ lb of anchovies (or 2 pickled herrings), 4 oz of red chilli and 4 oz of ground cloves, all boiled for 20 minutes, stirring all the time, then strained and when cold seasoned with lemon essence.

burnt, sharply sweet and sour', while **Fo Shan Superfine* is, 'burnt old vegetables, the smell of the bottom of the junk, very salty, edges of sea breeze with a honey richness at the back of the throat as a second wave'.

Soy sauce was, in fact, a fundamental flavouring ingredient of the first generation of commercial sauces of the last century, from WORCESTER to what was called CAB SHELTER'S SAUCE, although there was an English derivation made with malt syrup, mushroom juice, treacle and salt. Interestingly ****Lea & Perrins Worcestershire Sauce**, which is now such a distinctive product and one of the oldest foods made in this country having started in 1837, does not contain soy but still claims to be a Worcester sauce. This is probably a fair historical perspective on what would have been the most popular of sauces for the Victorians. **Sarson's** also do a **Worcester Sauce** designed for the Far-East with similar ingredients, again ironically without the soy, which is somewhat sweeter and less mellow.

In Chinese and Japanese cultures the soya bean is almost as fundamental a staple as rice or wheat. Products like Tofu, Natto and Miso are made by different applications of the same process as that for making soy sauce. The soy beans are first soaked and then cooked. For TOFU, the mix is then strained and cooled and then mixed with salt. For NATTO, the beans are boiled longer until soft, then pressed into cakes while still hot and wrapped in straw, and then – like cheese – left in a cellar for 24 hours to allow the enzymes in the air and in the straw to work on the flavour. For MISO, the cooked beans are pulped and mixed with salt and boiled rice and put into a vat to ferment for two months. The strained-off liquid from these processes goes to make SOY MILK.

Or more variegated still there is PAR-MAZANO, a dairy-free alternative to Parmesan seasoning, made of soy milk, soy protein, vegetable oil and sea salt which works hard to create a glutamate effect.

SUGAR

Sugar cane is a tropical reed, *Saccharum officinarum*, that will grow to 6 m (20 ft) in a zone 25 degrees either side of the equator. It needs sun and up to 80 inches of rain. The first sugar canes probably came from Polynesia and by 1000BC they were cultivated in India. The Crusaders brought the first recorded samples of sugar back to Britain in 1099. There was sugar at the court of Henry III by 1264, but the first substantial shipment is recorded in 1319. It was Columbus who took the canes back to the Caribbean.

The refining of sugar is credited to the Arabs and reputedly the recipe was bought by a Venetian merchant who started the industry in Sicily in 1503. It was introduced here in 1565, though sugar was punitively taxed and regarded as a luxury until the 18th century. The biggest producers of cane are India, Brazil, China and Cuba, but Europe takes its supplies from Mauritius, Fiji, Australia and the Caribbean.

In 1747, a Prussian chemist, Margraf, discovered that sugar could also be extracted from the white Silesian beetroot, but it was Napoleon who encouraged the widespread planting of beets during the war with England in 1806, when cane sugar could not be got in to France. It was lavish subsidies from the Treasury in the '20s and '30s that established the sugar beet industry here. Europe is the largest producer of sugar beet, but under the Lome Convention it is committed to taking £1.3 million worth of cane production from African, Caribbean and Pacific countries.

Politics and sugar have gone hand in glove for much of sugar's history. It was only in 1993 that the Government lifted the mandate for all soft drinks to contain more than 5% sugar, originally justified to, 'ensure children would gain from energy' but now recognized equally to contribute to tooth decay.

The sweetness of sugars, whether raw or refined, tend to be more or less equal. The difference in taste is said to be down to the size of the crystal: the larger the flake the slower the dissolving. Hence granulated sugars work over a period of time, whereas icing gives an instant perception of sweetness. There are thresholds to tasting sweetness and, say, hot puddings need less sugar than cold and ice-cream mixes need much more. For the most part, **Silver Spoon** will be beet and other labels cane.

GRANULATED SUGAR is ordinary refined crystalline sugar and accounts for 8 out of 10 bags sold. It is the cheapest, but must be used where there is enough time for it to dissolve completely.

CASTER SUGAR consists of crystals which are half the size of granulated and this makes it more versatile for cooking, say in cream mixtures, whisked sponges and meringues, or for sprinkling on fruit or for flavouring with vanilla, cinnamon or rosemary.

ICING SUGAR is best used for quick and easy dissolving, such as cold drinks and uncooked desserts, or to decorate cakes and sweets. It should be sieved first.

CUBE SUGAR was invented and pioneered by Henry Tate around 1890, and it is on this that much of his fortune (including enough to fund the Tate Gallery) was to be based. Designed to go with hot drinks and for ready portion control, they are still useful to grate off the essential oils of the zest of (unwaxed) citrus fruits.

PRESERVING SUGAR is designed to help make jam, jellies, marmalades and chutneys. It consists of large crystals which dissolve slowly, avoiding layers in the jam and also producing less froth in boiling, preventing discoloration.

JAM SUGAR is preserving sugar which has added pectin to support fruits which are naturally low in pectin, like strawberries and cherries, or fruit which in a wet year may be low in pectin or just over-ripe.

REFINED BROWN SUGARS, unlike white sugars where any differences are almost imperceptible, will vary because they are white sugar on to which the molasses are sprayed back.

Billington's deal exclusively in unrefined raw cane sugar from Mauritius, a reviving craft industry over the last 20 years while many Caribbean plantations have been neglected because of tourism. They claim their product is purer. **Golden Granulated** is sold as the all-purpose sugar – free-flowing, grainy and less intense than refined sugars. **Golden Caster** is the cooking sugar for biscuits and baking, and it is claimed to be better than refined sugar in the microwave. Their **Demerara sugar** is for coffee, for toppings and glazes for ham. **Molasses sugar**, the unrefined dark sugar, has a treacly flavour designed for Christmas cakes, puddings, chutneys and savoury sauces. The **Muscovado** is both dark – for fruit cakes and spicier things like gingerbread or barbecue sauces – and light for other baking.

GOLDEN SYRUP was pioneered in 1883 by Abram Lyle as a by product of cane refinery, golden syrup was originally just given to staff. There were golden syrups before this, but Lyle came from Greenock where different forms of treacles and molasses were known, though it may well be that none were as pure

SUGAR ALTERNATIVES

Enormous effort is going into developing alternative sugars. ASPARTAME is the best known, a dipeptide sweetener made up of two building blocks of protein – aspartic acid and phenylalanine – sold out through its trade name **NutraSweet.** It is found in more than 300 products in the UK and 5,000 worldwide – mainly in soft drinks, yoghurts, chewing gum and confectionery, table-top sweeteners, dessert mixes and frozen desserts. It is 200 times sweeter than sucrose and can be used in a limited way in cooking. It does not have the bulk of sugar, but can nevertheless sweeten sauces. Tate & Lyle have developed a new product **Sucralose** from cane sugar in Canada, which is said to be 600 times sweeter than sugar but is still waiting clearance. **Dietade** is a pure form of fructose that claims to be 174% sweeter than sugar.

and that he developed the process that made them palatable raw, not just for use in cooking. The sucrose is broken down (inverted) into glucose and fructose and the flavours come from the 'impurities' and the acid agent or enzyme invertase. It is less sweet than sugar and contains 20% water.

BLACK TREACLE is a blend of molasses and other by-product liquids. The molasses by-product from refined sugar is largely considered too unstable to sell on – different harvests and different crops providing widely different, and often very bitter, results. The result is 65% sugars, 4-9% minerals (and the rest water) and is high in calcium and iron. This was probably one of the earliest replacements for honey in the making of gingerbread, parkin, rich fruit cake and treacle toffee, though the sugar histories do not fully tally with the baking histories.

NUTS & OLIVES

Britain, one suspects, is not one of the first countries in the minds of traders in nuts. Despite our long history of cooking with nuts, much of what is sold here is at best second-grade or, in the case of cashews and almonds, the stale nibs and broken bits at the bottom of the barrel.

Almond
Brazil nut
Cashew nut
Chestnut
Hazelnut
Macadamia nut
Pistachio nut
Walnut
Olives

ALMOND

Native to Africa, the Romans called the almond the 'Greek nut'. It flourishes in countries where the average temperature is about 14°C (58°F). The tree grows to 10 m (30 ft) tall and flowers before it leaves. The fruit is covered with a thick green shell which dries in the autumn and opens to let the almond fall out. They will flower here, but will not fruit, and the blossoms were once prized as wedding bouquets. The first GREEN ALMONDS – sometimes found still with the green shell – begin in May.

There are two kinds, SWEET and BITTER; the difference is indiscernible to the eye, except the kernel of the bitter is thicker. The bitter usually goes for oil, confectionery and cosmetics, and in large quantities can be poisonous. ALMOND MILK and the derivative blancmange figured widely in the public cooking of the Middle Ages. Almond soup was crushed almonds mixed with blanched onions, spices, wine and water. Given the price of sugar and the long distances the almonds came, such dishes must have been precious and revered. Almonds have performed an unusual flip from the end of meals towards the front, graduating out of the Victorian sweet and sugar repertoire, up into garnishing and more inspired combinations with vegetables, eventually into breakfast muesli. Nobody seems to have an explanation as to why they are supposed to go with trout.

Most packet almonds are American. Predictably FLAKED ALMONDS are poorer than whole. **Sainsbury** has sensibly adjusted the idea to selling them either toasted or chopped and are of considerably better quality than other brands.

BRAZIL NUT

The Brazil nut comes from the giant Para chestnut tree, native to the Amazon uplands. The trunk can be as wide as 2 m (6 ft) and the highest branches reaching 50 m (150 ft). The nuts are segments encased in a round thick shell, the *ourico*, up to 15 cm (6 in) across. The rainy seasons of autumn blow them off the top branches and they fall and embed themselves in the soft jungle soil where they are gathered, broken open and washed in the rivers, where the lighter unfertile nuts rise to the surface and float off. Liverpool was the prime port for their importation. They have a higher oil content than walnut, at nearly 60%, but it is a bland and little-used oil. In fresh nuts, the kernel will be white and the taste still sweet.

CASHEW NUT

These great walnut-style trees proliferate in a horseshoe on either side of the Indian Ocean, but were originally found in South America by the Spanish and colonized by the Portuguese who took the word *caju* from the native *acaju*. The nut is encased in a very hard bluish shell, which also contains an oily black liquid that can blister the skin but is neutralized by drying in the heat. The nuts were said to improve the flavour of chocolate. The oil went for a blue marker for linen. Most now come from India in the spring, and some from Brazil's autumn harvest. They are increasingly sold untreated for cooking in stir-fries and curries. When they have been roasted and salted the price leaps into the stratosphere for tiny packets sold in pubs and off-licences, as indeed do the calories. Less than £1 per 100 g is a mean average for the supermarket price. Size is everything – good cashews are big, but many packets are filled with broken pieces off small nuts. The pear-shaped casing that envelopes the nut is the CASHEW APPLE, slightly abrasive but still eaten in Brazil with sugar or in jams and fermented into a sweet wine and a vinegar.

CHESTNUT

The most farinaceous of the nuts and containing the least oil. Ground to a flour, chestnuts were an important staple, especially in Central France around Lyons, in the Alps and the Auvergne. Small quantities of the flour can still be found in specialist shops. The more export-led trade is in the sweeter MAR-RONS, peeled chestnuts cooked in syrup and flavoured with vanilla. Different varieties were recognized until the '50s, the best being the almost round **Marrons de Lyons**. Most chestnuts sold here are now from Spain and Italy. The difficulty of peeling chestnuts has doubtless contributed to their decline in popularity, but it is interesting to see how many tasting notes for other foods refer complimentarily to the tones of chestnut. Vacuum-sealed peeled chestnuts are being imported from France, which is a convenience. **Le Gourmet Français**, in fact a Liverpool firm, sell tins of chestnut purée which is purely chestnuts, water and salt.

The familiar tins of purée with green

Ways With Chestnuts

Chestnuts should be nicked, blanched, kept in hot water and the two skins peeled off, then simmered slowly in good stock.

emblems of **Clement Faugier** is a diluted form mixed with water, but no salt or sugar, at half the price of the newer English competition from ***Bridge House** vacuum-packed **Peeled Chestnuts** which, short of the quality of the stock, are pretty much as good as can be done at home.

HAZELNUT

The fruit of the *Corylus avellana*, a supple hardy bush named after the town in Italy where they were first cultivated, there are about a dozen varieties.

Also known as the KENT COBNUT, this is among the finest nuts found in this country, although only a few hundred acres are now left growing. The Kent Cob was first cultivated by Mrs Lambert of Goudhurst, hence it is sometimes called a LAMBERT. Although it is called a cobnut, it is in fact a FILBERT, *Corylus maxima*. Filberts are longer and the husk completely covers the nut.

The crop is usually harvested in two sessions, at the end of August when the nuts are formed but still green; and then at the end of September when the colour will have turned shades of deep bronze and smoky grey. The best will have a deep red pellicle. In hop-growing districts, they were always harvested very young while still green to stop the migrant hop-pickers taking them. They should be picked on the tree and not taken as windfalls. The outside may even have gone black, but the kernel inside is nevertheless pristine and unaffected. In the 17th century, sailors took them on long voyages as a source of fresh food, while the Victorians savoured them as a delicacy at the end of a meal, with salt. Fresh, they will keep for up to two weeks.

The FILBERT itself was grown in Wiltshire from around 1810, but was an improved ver-

sion imported from the more benign climate
of the Mediterranean.

MACADAMIA NUT

Claimed to be the finest of all cocktail nuts,
which might be a moot point, this nut was discovered in Queensland, but has been cultivated in the past century in Hawaii. It has
been groomed as a gourmet nut, with the
qualities of a milky brazil and a hidden
propensity for a grassy sourness. The packaging in vacuum-sealed bags commendably
keeps them very fresh.

PISTACHIO NUT

Once called the BLADDER NUT or GREEN
ALMOND, this is native to Western Asia, but
particularly favours the high rolling tourist
idylls of the Seychelles and Mauritius. It has
also been notably adopted across the southern Mediterranean rim, from Sicily through
Greece into Turkey and Iran where it has
been a central fixture of the cooking for centuries. The tree is an evergreen, growing to a
height of 10 m (30 ft). The nuts cluster on the
branches and are a beautiful hue of blue, the
more so from southern climates. They are
ripe when the kernels split. Drying destroys
much of their visual beauty, but develops the
flavour. Marseilles was the major trading port
for their entry into Europe and also into
French cooking as a garnish.

WALNUT

The common English walnut, *Juglans regia*,
is native to Iran and the northern mountains
of India. There are many different kinds,
some of which are quite coarse. Walnuts
here at least demand a sense of history. In

Iran, the tree will fruit within eight years, in Spain after 16 years, in England perhaps 24 years – and it may be 60 years old before it reaches its full production. The tree will be 100 years old before the wood is hard enough to be used for engraving. The best nuts are young, when still green, though traditionally many of these went for pickling. The shell should be thin and the skin of young walnuts is quite bitter, but becomes milder as they age. Older walnuts are pressed for their oil which can constitute as much as 50% of their weight. The oil will turn them rancid if they are kept on through the winter. The quality varies substantially from region to region and many will be sulphured to make them last longer.

WALNUT KETCHUP was made with the brine in which young walnuts were kept for pickling, boiled for half an hour with ginger, pepper, cloves and chilli mixed with malt vinegar.

PICKLED WALNUTS are a singularly English product, cured usually with a boiled infusion of malt vinegar, pepper, ginger, mustard, cloves, mace and bruised garlic.

OLIVES

Olives are inedible on the tree and have to be immersed in salt brine with soft water for weeks to render them palatable. Few of the best olives are sold here and even those that carry the right names are often much smaller than in their native countries.

The difference between BLACK and GREEN OLIVES is only that the black are left on the branch longer. Olives deserve to be bought by their name, because anything with just a brand generic term is likely to be low-quality. Usually table olives are distinct from olives grown for oil, except in areas where the agriculture is backward or olives are a marginal crop.

STUFFED OLIVES need to be treated with even greater caution. Stoned green olives tend to be very mushy and lose their texture. Particularly nasty are **Sainsbury's** marinated pipped olives in sunflower oil with garlic. The best green olives in supermarkets are QUEEN OLIVES from Seville, sold as own-label by **Tesco** and up-market **Sainsburys.** ****Tesco Queen Olives** from Spain. ***Taylor & Lake** sell bottles of **Tanche** olives.

The best olives are sold loose. They will have been taken out of the brine – usually just a plain salt solution – and just washed off. The brine for olives in tins and bottles is necessarily very watery, because the olives will absorb liquid and their flavour is diluted.

FRENCH

**COQUILLOS NIÇOISE are the very small, 1 cm (½ in) long, black olives found wild along the coasts of Provence. The colour is purple-black and the skin shines with the ripeness. The season is later and they will be kept in salted brine for six weeks; so later in the year they will have spent much longer in the brine and they will get progressively softer. 'Juicy, clarity, salty'.

**LUCQUE are large ungainly long and thin olives which are emerald green in colour. They are picked early and given a short cure, and are held to be grander than the Picholine.

**PICHOLINE from the Vallée des Baux, are oval, dusky green olives, 3 cm (1¼ in) across, with a good ratio of flesh to pip. They are picked early in September/October and cured only for three weeks. The flavour is sweet and meaty, hammy, bacony.

GREEK

KALAMATA or CALAMATA are usually kept in
brine and red wine vinegar to reinforce the
colour, which can vary from deep beigey-
green to deep black. The flavour is without
subtlety, it is a meat flavoured with salt in various degrees. Check the brine details carefully
– olive oil should be the prime ingredient.

SPANISH

MANZANILLA from Seville, can be excellent,
but absorb the brine and go watery in the bottle if poorly handled. They are also used for
making olive oil.

**QUEEN from Seville, are the largest of the
Spanish table olives. Deep, almost khaki-
green, they can have a 'superb sourness
melting into sweet crunch, large pip, but a
large olive. Excellent'.

AROMATIC OLIVES

Adding aromatics was a way for market-stall
holders to add value to their olives. The traditional Provence seasonings were fennel,
thyme, rosemary, bay and garlic – but these
have now been widened to take in more
southerly influences, like chilli and other peppers. Often the olives will now be imported
from Spain.

The **TAILLADÉE is a good mixing olive
because it is quite sour, picked half ripe when
it is a soft mauve. They are machine-slit,
which allows the marinade to go right through
to the stone. They blend well with the juicier
Spanish Manzanilla. The Ligurian olive oil
estate **Tornatore also exports mixes of the
small Tagiasca olives with different blends of
herbs.

OILS

Culinary oils divide cleanly into two categories: those for cooking and those for
flavouring. The only oils that might be said to
cross this divide are olive and, to a lesser
extent, sesame.

VEGETABLE OILS tend these days to be
made from rape seed, but are largely deliberately denatured to make them as inoffensive
as possible to as many people as possible.

Some SUNFLOWER OILS buck the trend
and retain enough vestiges of character to be
useful in making milder forms of mayonnaise,
but perhaps that is just an illusion fostered by
the sunny label?

GROUNDNUT OIL is peanut oil and is
favoured by the professional kitchen, especially for deep-frying, where it survives longer
at higher temperatures than other oils. For the
same reason it is also the best oil for a wok.
The refining policy for these oils is to make
them taste of as little as possible. The health
arguments are spurious – it would, for the
most part, be easier, cheaper and healthier to
cook without them, using non-stick pans.

NUT OILS far from being outré, were born of
the necessity of making use of good harvests
before the oils turned the kernels rancid.
Taylor & Lake sell an ALMOND OIL, which is
quite rare, and is mainly seen as helpful in
baking. Chemists also sell almond oil under
the **Care** label, which hopefully suggests that
as well as being a good bath oil it can be used
in baking, although the intensity is muted and
the effect diluted. PISTACHIO OIL is a newer
product, which is warmly aromatic for use like
the other nut oils judiciously in salads, though
both command premiums for their rarity.

   PALM OIL and COCONUT OIL share with
COCOA OIL the distinction of having the

Grapeseed oil
Hazelnut oil
Olive oil
Safflower oil
Sesame oil
Walnut oil

Sainsbury's, grapeseed oil from Italian grapes, is 'neutral but drinkable, more pleasant than say sunflower with just an edge of the grapes left'. ***Dufrais** is a lovely deep green oil sold in clear bottles. The taste is of, 'summer, quite buttery and distinct, not oily, but that hint of something vinous...'. It tends to be expensive against supermarket own-labels. **Cuisine Perel** from California illustrates the potential of grapeseed. Sold in designer bottles, one example was delicately flavoured with orange, lemon and coriander, and in another a very pungent chilli.

Safeway's is French and more expensive than other supermarket brands, and 'very creamy, not very subtle, one-dimensional, not very grapey'. **Asda's** is from Italy and 'very thin and poor'. **Tesco's** is also from Italy and 'probably from the same source as **Asda**, same bottle same country, same taste', but cheaper.

highest saturated fat of any vegetable oil, in some cases as much as 90% saturated. Palm oil is mainly used here in margarine but in Africa it is a prime cooking medium, tasting fairly neutral with just an edge of voilets to it, and a reddish colour which is used as a dye.

GRAPESEED OIL

Once used to light street lamps before electricity, this now resurfaces as a cooking and salad oil, possibly somewhat happier in its new more respectable guise. The centre of crushing being Modena in Italy, its composition is similar to olive oil, except the polyunsaturates are considerably higher and the monounsaturates much lower, with only a trace of cholesterol. The label promises that it can be used for everything from shallow-frying to making salad dressings and baking, which makes it an expensive alternative to sunflower or rape oils. It does, however, cook at higher temperatures. It is possibly best seen as an alternative to cheap olive oil with a pleasant distinctive grapey bite which can add interest to salads. It is invariably sold in clear bottles, most of which are tinged lemon, except **Dufrais** which is distinctly green.

HAZELNUT OIL

Why supermarkets package hazelnut oil in clear glass 250 ml bottles is not obvious, but for most kitchens 250 ml will have gone rancid before it is ever used. A small drop is all that is needed to pervade dressings and sauces. It is only stocked by **Waitrose**, **Sainsbury** and ***Asda** is slightly cheaper and the pick of three good examples, 'clean-tasting, slightly toasted'. Mix hazelnut oil with other oils to extend its use and so as not to overpower other flavours.

OLIVE OIL

The olive oil season starts in November and the best oils will be made before mid-December. The first oils will be unfiltered and fruity. Those for export and for longer keeping will be filtered. Most oils mellow and flatten out with age and will be past their best within a year. The olives are either hand-picked or left to fall into nets on the ground.

The traditional stone press crushes these olives along with some leaves (which add colour and bulk). The paste is then laid on circular mats and these are piled one on top of each other around a central axle. The pile is then wheeled into the press and the oil allowed to exude gently under pressure. Finally, oil and water are separated.

More modern machinery has speeded up the process by using centrifugal force to clean, wash, crush and separate the oil from the olive in a continuous process. These machines can produce more oil from premium olives at the height of the year and have been widely adopted in the top Tuscan groves. These first olives have considerably higher percentages of vitamins and antioxidants which are lost as the nights get colder.

VIRGIN OR EXTRA VIRGIN OLIVE OIL is the first pressing, but as with wine the term can cover a multitude of anonymous blends. True quality virgin oils come from single estates where thought and effort has gone into the blend of olive varieties and the timing of the harvest.

FIRST or COLD-PRESSED OLIVE oil is a hangover from washing the paste with hot water to extract more (but diluted) oil. In a few rare instances, like **Affiorato** from Umbria, the olives are left to stand under their own weight before going into the press. This yields a small amount of oil which is scooped off by hand. What is commonly sold labelled

FOOD *watch*

Olive oil suffers from being thought of as an expensive commodity but even single-estate bottles might not, on a portion to portion basis, cost more than 25p a serving, and a good everyday oil would be less than 10p. Compared to wine it is cheap.

as OLIVE OIL, previously often known misleadingly as PURE OLIVE OIL, is made from the paste out of which the virgin oil has been extracted. This is treated chemically to extract more oil and then mixed with an undeclared amount of virgin olive oil.

The northern Mediterranean produces smoother and more elegant oils. Some of the more westerly oils, notably from Portugal, Spain, North Africa and some from Provence, have sharp metallic, petrolly overtones. Greek oils have been largely overlooked, but represent terrific value for the middle of the market. Their reputation for being heavy and greasy stems from the practice of leaving the olives on the trees too long, but the top-quality oils are reshaping this image with fresh, green apple, asparagus-style flavours close to Tuscan and Riviera oils but with softer finishes.

The health-giving reputation of olive oil is centred around the low instance of heart diseases in regions where olive oil is the predominant cooking medium. The level of fat in the oil is high, but three-quarters of it is monounsaturated. There are complementary associations with high levels of vitamin E and antioxidants, and it tends to be used with other positive foods like garlic, pulses and fruit as well as drinks such as red wine.

FRANCE

There are very few single-estate producers in France of any size, possibly because inheritance laws have split up the estates over the years and dictated that villages go over to the co-operative system. The main areas are around the Vallée de Baux, The Bandol, and Nyons, where it is mostly *Tanche* (also an eating olive) that is grown. This has an *appellation contrôlée* although little seems to get over here. Mostly it is single olive production and

Ways With Olive Oil

Most kitchens need two types of olive oil: one for everyday cooking, and one for finishing salads or saucing. It needs to be stored in the dark or the light will turn the oil rancid. In Tuscany, for a light meal a piece of bread would be toasted, rubbed with a clove of garlic, the surface wetted with oil and then seasoned with sea salt.

there is some pressing of Spanish olives. Rarely is there any sign of the pepperiness associated with Tuscan oils.

À l'Olivier is a good commercial blend, typical of the Provence style: catty, buttery, spicy finish, slightly bitter, hints of grass clippings, it is unobtrusive but has character.

Alziari is made by Nicolas Alziari, former friend of Jacques Médicin, the legendary Mayor of Nice, and owner of an olive oil shop in Nice, where the olives and the oil are sold loose. He owns some groves above Nice and presses his own oil. The style is closer to Liguria than Provence: sweet, delicate, some pepperiness... herby, fresh.

Les Alpilles from **Taylor & Lake** is orange-hued like castor oil, and comes in clear bottles. The label recommends it for vinaigrettes, with champagne vinegar. It has an intense more direct impact than Vaucluse (see below)... it is lighter, softly buttered, a scratching of itchiness, perfumed.

Moulin de la Garrigue, from Moulin de Gassac, Verdale, has a petrol smell, is pale lemon, with hints of citrus peel, grapefruit, metallic, closer to Portuguese or Spanish style.

Vaucluse from **Taylor & Lake** comes from the hills above Orange. Sunset yellow in colour, it is like thick grassy meadows, hay and lemons, with a hint of pepperiness, it is quite forceful but lacks the delicacy of Italian oils... quite heavy and unctuous.

Vieux Moulin is made in the southern Rhône on a single estate from a single olive, the Tanche. A popular first stop for initiates, it is characterful and good for cooking with ... sweet, musty in this case from age, earthy, hints of cracked walnuts, green oil, very fruity with little pepper. Other tasting notes included 'Very eggy', 'Not really typical of the Nyons style' and 'High price for the fancy bottle'.

Good all-purpose French olive oils include **Puget** from **Vitrolles**, which – like its plastic bottle – is lemon-yellow in colour and is bright, grassy, one-dimensional but viscous, sweet... with a little pepper and shades of vanilla; and **Plaignol**, in the fancy fluted bottle, which is not quite first division but makes a good mayonnaise.

* GREECE

Much Greek oil is pressed too late. The *Kalamata* olive produces good oil (some are being planted in Tuscany) but only if picked early. The *Koroneiki* olive also produces a good oil, which is notably good value for everyday use and so far unexploited. Many of the best Greek olives go to Italy for processing. Shops also tend to keep them past their sell-by dates. A good Greek oil should taste of torn salad leaves. With the above riders, Greek oils represent excellent value and sensible cut-price alternatives to Italian. **Safeway** first, and then **Sainsbury**, picked up on this, but their prices are still excessive compared to Greek brands in specialist shops.

Chalice is made from Kalamata olives and sold in dainty clear thick-glassed carafes with handles and cork seals (which don't fit very well). Almost emerald-green in colour, it is creamily thick and verdant, with edges of petrol and primroses, silky thick, some pepperiness. An interesting oil, it is about as thick as any I have tasted.

Cypressa is the own-label for the Cyprus-based importer, it is deep yellow to sun-scorched grass, and is buttery with big floral notes, with mild pepperiness on the finish. Creamy. It is very good value for an all-purpose everyday oil – half the price of **Safeway's**.

Iliada is made from Kalamata olives and is deep yellow in colour, luscious, floral, winey,

with hints of vanilla... it is excellent and good value.

Kolymvari from Crete is sold through an Italian wholesalers which is a mark of respect. Floral and buttery, it holds it own well in the Tuscan company as a very good cheap oil. The price of about £3 per litre wholesale suggests some supermarkets are marking up 400%.

Kydonia from the Co-op Kolibari, north-west of Crete, is good value and tastes of fresh clear apples.

*****Mani Organic** from the Mani Peninsula is mill-stone pressed and has, plenty of body and appley fruit, warm earthy, Chardonnay and orange. Sweet, rounded and grass', compare the price, at £9 for 750 ml, to Kolymvari. **Safeway** has been selling **Mani**, the non-organic version.

*****Solon** is widely available in Greece, but to date its sale has been restricted to Greek specialists. Hay-green in colour, it is fruity, luscious, mildly creamy, herbal... with a slight bite... very good for the money. You could not say that top Tuscan was four times better. At £1.89 per 500 ml in specialist shops, it is excellent value.

Sparta comes from three villages south of Sparta. It is suggested for use in *taramasalata,* onion fritters, cheese and eggs with Feta. Linseed, Castrol, texturous, viscous, lime-flecked gold, it is an everyday oil, reminiscent of Portuguese and Spanish oils.

Commercial blends of note include: **Athena** which is, 'sweet and creamy, hint of aniseed' and uses Kalamata olives as in the **Illada**. **Safeway** has pioneered the introduction of mass-market extra-virgin oils in which area the Greeks have been particularly impressive. 'This variation smells of lemons and cut spring mountain flowers, full and viscous, lacking a little of taste compared to the good

Tuscans, but a good all-round oil that responds to lemons.' **Sainsbury** followed up this year impressively with a version that is, 'pure ice-cream... unctuous... lovely'.

ITALY

The Italian supremacy in olive oil is down to the use of three or more blends of olives to create a single oil – either by design or by accident, the groves tend to be mixed. The *Frantoia* is the olive of Tuscany, although the frosts of '85 wiped out many old groves. It is only in the last two years that Tuscan oil has come back on the market. Many more estates are about to come on line, encouraged by the sudden interest. Tuscan oils typically tend to be soloists, best used in salads or on pulses, or just on toasted country bread with garlic and salt. Ligurian oils are more mellow and inclined to be used to create simple sauces for grilled fish or even meat. They are more almondy and closer to the Provence style or vice versa.

Sicily tends to upset the easy rule that the best oils come from the north, where the cooler evenings slow down their growth. The olive there is *Nochelara del Belice*, famously good at the start of the season in December but tending to flatten off through the year. Other isolated examples from different areas suggest there is no monopoly on great olive oil in one region or one style.

*LIGURIAN OILS:

Canto is organic and unfiltered and so is aromatic and expensive. A beautiful pure yellow, it is very pale, delicate lemony... an ultra treatment for a grilled fish.

Carluccio from Villa Nova is sold in small clear wine carafes and is a strong yellow hued with green, sweet and appley... ice-cream soda... brilliant for cooking. Add a little tomato and it creates a velvety sauce. Try it with grilled lobster and lemon.

Prela from Raineri family estate comes in elegant tall slim numbered bottles. The oil is buttery green in the style of old-fashioned Riviera oils and closer to a fine example of Provence than Tuscan, 'warm finish, nutty'. The estate also makes a second oil sold under the family name, **Raineri**, which has little pepper but good body, for half the price. One of the best oils found here while the Tuscans were replanting, it now has some serious competition.

Tornatore is, unusually, unfiltered and comes in imposing large triangular bottles, pale deep lemon in colour it is lightly peppery, sweet... an excellent everyday oil for improving cooking. The same estate also exports superb capers from Morocco and sells the aromatized small Tagiasca olives.

**TUSCAN OILS:

Ardoino, from Vall Aurea, is sold in distinctive gold foil and green bottle. Made from late-harvested (in January) olives, it is light and delicate, with a golden green colour and a smell of peaches and almonds.. use for salad dressings or marinades.

Avignonese, from Montepulciano, comes in elegant slim dark glass designer bottles and is a deep burnt yellow in colour. It is sweet and creamy, with hints of peppers, luscious, mellow.

Badia a Coltibuono is often held up as the benchmark for Tuscan olive oils, but since the frosts of '85 some olives have been bought in. 'Full of style and character, it is herbaceous, bitter evergreen.'

Carluccio from Pistoia, is emerald-green in colour, 'My perfume,' says Carluccio. Delicate... with shades of rocket and mild saffron, the pepperiness building.

Colonna comes from Molise and is said to be one of the most scientific of all the olive farms. The oil is a mix of different olives, predominantly *Coratina*, each grown and picked by hand separately and then blended after crushing. Neat carafe-style bottles with sell-by dates sensibly marked for the end of November. Lemon, hues of grass, it is thick and creamy, with some pepperiness and hints of green leaves and grass. The estate also produces an oil imbued with lemons crushed with the olives in the press which has its enthusiasts. A mass-produced imitation for **Collavita** is destined for the market using essences. **Dell'Ugo** from between Sienna and Florence is unfiltered. Not part of the Laudemio consortium (see opposite), it is similar in construction and uses the same olives. Antony Worrall-Thompson named his Soho restaurant after it. Cloudy green apples, pure olives, vivacious, it responds well to the addition of salt, pepper, chilli or lemon.

Frantoio di Santa Tea from Reggello, Florence, sells two oils – one, **Fruittato-Intenso**, is a marked green, picked early (in November) it is, 'youthful, assertive, crying out for garlic'; while **Dolce Delicato** is picked in December and the oil has become a pale sunset yellow. Cut grass and peppery, it is very typical of Tuscan oil.

Gemma from Arrezo is a good everyday restaurant oil. It is clean, buttery, with a hint of pepper, fruity and full-flavoured.

Monte Vertine from Radda, Chianti is made using the *Correggiolo*, *Maraiolo* and *Leccino* olives. Production is still limited because of the damage from frost in '85, but the groves have been replanted. Stone-milled, it is emerald yellow in colour and comes in fat green wine bottles. 'Thick viscous, peppery, taste of meadows lemons and peppers. Brilliant. Very fruity.'

Ornellia from Marchese Lodovico Antinori who is better known for his wines and who also produces a fine **Laudemio**. The groves are near the sea and, unusually, escaped the '85 frosts. The trees are 80 years old, mostly *Frantoio* and *Leccino*, and the olives are hand-picked before the end of November and traditionally mill-ground. In a tapered and embossed glass bottle, the oil is mown grass yellow-green, pure, clean smell, sweet, nutty, luscious combination, outstanding oil, lightly peppery... with a long, long finish.

˚˚Podere Cogno comes from groves which date back to the Middle Ages. At 500 metres high, the soil is stony. The unfiltered oil comes in clear bottles, syrupy yellow, mild, intense citrus fruits, powerful peppery... not typically Tuscan.

Ravagni from Arrezo is a thick deep emerald-green oil, which is fresh and powerful. Very persuasive.

OTHER REGIONS:

Tenuta di Saragano from Saragano near Perugia in Umbria, comes in numbered and dated bottles and, although Umbrian, uses the same olive varieties as Tuscan, it is 'soft, buttery, delicate pepper, sweet'.

˚˚Ravida from Menfi on the south coast of Sicily is made using three different local olives harvested young, which gives it a warm smooth assertive style, which has been consistent, reputedly, since production began in the 17th century. Herbaceous, with an aroma of tomato skins, the taste of freshly mown meadows, it is expensive but widely regarded in Italy as one of the best non-Tuscan oils.

Other Sicilian oils worth looking out for are the organic **La Biotecha** and **Nochelara**, back to rhubarb, greenest of green; **˚Bottarelli** comes from the west side of Lake Garda and Garda oils have a good reputation but possibly not deserving over Liguria, This is a fine example. Sunset-yellow in colour, it

˚˚**Laudemio** is a form of *appellation contrôlée* self imposed on a group of now more than 50 Tuscan olive producers, led initially by Marchese Frescobaldi and the Antinori family. Half a dozen are imported here – the **Sonnino** estate was the first major olive oil in a supermarket at **Waitrose** last Christmas at a knock-down price of £9.95 against the usual £13.95. In different ratios according to the estate and the year, the olives will be primarily *Frantoio* and the *Maraiolo*, with the fattier *Lecchino* as the make-weight. To carry the Laudemio (meaning 'the tithe given up to the landowner') label the olives must be hand-picked, pressed within 48 hours and submitted to independent analysis before the middle of December. The younger they are the more peppery. **Frescobaldi** is, 'green leaves and green bananas'. 'The **Sonnino** and the **Torre de Caltrona** are not really typically Tuscan. They are great oils but surprisingly different to the others.'

comes in a wine bottle, It is dry, fruity and thick, with a hint of bananas.

*Montiferru comes from a hundred-year-old business in the mountains in the north-west of Sardinia. Orangey-yellow in colour, it is wide, peppery and precise.

Gastrum from Bari, comes in a straw bottle and is pure, very thick, mealy, almost a food, peppery on fish – good second-division oil.

Casa Bini from Reggello comes in an opaque designer bottle and is yellow to burnt umber in colour. 'Tart, short, ice-cream, pepper', it is an unusual and not bad value second-division oil.

Fior d'Olivia, from Bari, has been used in Italian embassies and is pale yellow. It is a smooth, mild minor oil.

Harvey Nichols own-label from Italy, is a deep yellow, sharp, peppery oil, with a short finish.

**Carluccio from Gioia del Colle in Apulia, is sold in a suspiciously fancy ceramic reusable jug and is bright yellow, like all the Carluccio choices, with hints of almonds and chocolate. Thick and bready, it is sweet rising to a serious pepperiness that vanishes swiftly into a creamy sweetness. Revelationary.

Worthwhile brands include La Nonna, a mix of olives from Tuscany which is sweetly buttered and £3.45 per litre wholesale, which puts into perspective the prices of olive oil in supermarkets where tiny phials of less good oils are sold for twice as much. Good examples of widely found commercial brands include Filippo Berio, based in Lucca the centre of oil blending, which consistently heads the tasting tests of mass-market oils, and they have introduced a new 'mild and lighter' olive oil which seems a regressive sop to the culture of other oils. Not to be outdone, Sainsbury introduced a mix of sunflower and olive oil which further complicates the polyunsaturates question. Dante is widely used in

Italy and regarded as a good starting point. **Menucci** is sweet and grassy and well-balanced.

PORTUGAL

The Portuguese tend to leave the olives to ferment and this creates a distinctive, very gutsy muddy petroleum style, which can be off-putting. 'Burnt farmyard' is a common description. As with Portuguese wines, there is a lack of precision.

Gallo from Victor Guedes Abrantes is extra virgin (bought in Portugal as it is not available here as yet). A good example of what Portuguese oils might be: damp yellow grass, mellow nuts, very thick, mild pepperiness, fairly harsh, good body... metallic notes muted here. Compare that to the widely sold **Damatta** from **Envendos**. An olive oil, rather than a virgin, it is metallic, tough with no fruit... very poor.

La Rosa, from the Douro Valley, comes in a clear wine-style bottle. Sunshine yellow in colour, it is cleanly filtered and has a petrolly smell and metallic hints... acid. It bears out the idea that most Portuguese and some Spanish oils have different applications to the Italian and French – they are not really for salads, but should rather be used as a flavouring for thick mealy dishes and for cooking large quantities of onions.

SPAIN

Most Spanish olive oil is from single olive varieties, making them emphatic but simplistic. Some argue that they are underrated. The best tend to nuttiness, lemon hints and freshness. In principle the more northerly estates produce better oils.

****Lerida**, from the Vea family estate in Catalonia, is one of the finest examples of Spanish olive oil made from *Arbequina* olives:

burnt almonds and bitter chocolate, buttery, dark chocolate.

*L'Estornell is single estate from Lerida and made from organic *Arbequina* olives: herbaceous, sweet, hints of chocolate, walnuts and softness. A sample in September was sunset-yellow with some pepper, a very good example of Spanish style.

**Nunez de Prado has been made on the same estate at Baena near Cordoba since 1795. The olives are still stone-milled on the same days as picking to ensure low acidity. Sold unfiltered in distinctive square bottles, this is probably the supreme example of Spanish olive oil. It is unusual for Spain, in that they use a blend of three different olives and only the flesh – not the stone – is milled. About 11 kilos go into each litre, rather the usual five. With hints of passion fruit, lemon rind, hints of petrol, unripe nuts, it is rustic, and intense with a fine peppery finish. A September sample had hints of grapefruit and nuts.

Sabor d'Abana from the Ebro valley, is bright yellow, with primrose edges... OK.

Siurama, from the Agrana Co-op in Catalonia, comes in gold and red label varieties in clear bottles. A clear oil, it is deep yellow tinged with green and gold in parts, With a sweet smell, it is thick, gummy, light but solid, grassy... unusual'. Tomato skins... could be Italian, not typical.

Good brands to look for include Lupa, which is from a single estate in Malaga but is bottled in the UK. The flavour of sweet almond, nuts with passion fruit, is typical of the Spanish style and good value. Safeway own-label has high petroleum notes mingled with sweetness, some fire, good texture, very metallic, meant as a support not as a soloist. Carbonel is well known and considerably more interesting at the start of the year; it is good for cooking and tastes of ripe melons.

SAFFLOWER OIL

Mostly from Holland, this oil is only stocked by **Asda** and **Harrods** – which must be some kind of first – priced on the same level as grapeseed at £1.09 per 500 ml. It is recommended for salads and shallow-frying, and claims to be good for, 'delicately flavoured dishes', but probably is not, and should not be used for deep-frying. It is neutral-scented, seedy and quite creamy.

SESAME OIL

Excessively sold in 250 ml bottles, most of the contents of which will likely oxidize before they are used, a small amount of sesame oil is all that is needed to pervade salads and other dishes. The vogue has been to toast the seeds before pressing as this gives a wonderful aroma and edge but a discernibly different effect of, 'autumn bonfires'. This is a fairly superficial effect that begins to pall in the kitchen. It is usually the product of more than one country, though **Safeway** claim Japan. **Asda** and **Sainsbury** own-labels are markedly superior and evocative, 'beautifully potent roasted smell and pervasive power'. **Waitrose** is milder and subtler. **Tesco** and **Safeway** have been poor, weak and vapid, with a late nagging taste. The best are from Chinese supermarkets, such as **Koon Yick Wah Kee's**, which has a powerfully potent, rich, deep aroma, and a strong nutty element.

WALNUT OIL

The profusion of walnuts in France and Switzerland led to the crushing of the nuts for their oil. Fresh nuts harvested in late September will turn rancid by the end of the year because of the amount of oil they contain. Walnut oil is sold with the health message to the front – flashes denote that it is high in polyunsaturates and low in saturates. However, as such tiny quantities are involved the benefits can only be marginal. In any case, it is best mixed with another oil so its flavour, though less pronounced than hazelnut or sesame, does not go rampant. It should be kept in dark bottles to stop it oxidizing, but unilaterally supermarkets sell it in clear glass. The taste is mild, meek and virtuous, reassuringly homely, with nudges of autumn, a good housekeeperly taste. There is surprisingly little difference between any of the own-brand supermarket oils.

PASTA, RICE ETC

Rice and pata represent the intelligent route to inexpensive eating. Both are cheaper bought in bulk, and rice much cheaper in specialist Chinese, Thai and Indian shops. Nevertheless supermarkets might claim the credit for introducing both to the mainstream UK diet.

Pasta
Rice
Polenta

PASTA

The word pasta is simply the Italian for a 'paste', but that is rather a brutal description for something as old as bread that has evolved into hundreds of different shapes each of which seems to have developed its own school of saucing.

Good pasta must be made with durum wheat, which is high in the gluten that provides the stiffness and elasticity, or semolina which is the same thing but more coarsely ground. Durum's other advantage is that it does not soak in water. The best was always grown in southern Italy around Abruzzi, but now even the Italians import it from America. The hardness of durum wheat needs different milling technology from bread, which is one reason why pasta was not assimilated here earlier. The technology here now is probably as good as that in Italy, which suggests that the more outré and packaged designer pastas imported from Italy are no longer worth the kind of premiums they demand.

The supremacy of dried pasta over fresh is as much about flavour as it is about convenience. Almost uniquely in supermarkets, brand names like **Lilly**, **Sitoni** and **Cypressa** can actually be cheaper than own-labels. The bigger packets are conspicuously cheaper – and spaghetti is the cheapest shape. The

Ways With Pasta

Pasta should be cooked in generous amounts of water to rinse out the starch. There are differences of opinion on when to add oil – if at all. Some say the oil should go in at the beginning to stop the pasta sticking, but if you use enough water this is less of a problem. Others use olive oil after draining to separate the strands before saucing. Pasta should not be over-drained. Allow up to 75 g (2½ oz) per person for a starter, about 100 g (3½ oz) for a main course. Names are used loosely, but within each family there are consistent philosophies of use.

LONG PASTAS: Spaghetti and its variations, and the egg-based flat pasta like lasagne are designed for oil-based and tomato sauces. The thicker the spaghetti the stronger the sauce should be. Egg-based pastas are designed for meat sauces, often made with softer more absorbent flours that can benefit from taking in the sauce.

SHORT PASTAS: the mother of the short family is penne which, in itself, comes in six different variations of thickness but is a robust all-purpose pasta. As the shapes become more pronounced, say for macaroni or farfalle, the tendency is for cream sauces. The coiled fusili or the shell-like conchiglie, need to have thicker and more texturous accompaniments, such as vegetables and nuts.

STUFFED PASTAS: are often best par-boiled before stuffing and need bright fresh sauces so that they do not become bland. Their blandness is meant to take in combinations of seasonings and heavy sauces.

SOUP PASTAS: come in a bewilderingly amusing range of shapes. The smaller ones are for texture, the larger designed to pick up the soup. They should be cooked separately from the stock and added at the last minute so the starch does not cloud the soup. Good stock, fresh vegetables, pasta and Parmesan or Pecorino to grate are the watchwords of great soups.

supermarkets have standardised the price between themselves, leaving whole-food and other shops charging considerable premiums.

Cooking times for dried spaghetti have been slashed from 10-12 down to 5-7 minutes, simply by making the pasta thinner. Most use durum wheat from Italy, though **Tesco's** value range – which almost halves the price of dried pasta – combines durum with plain wheat. QUICK-COOKING PASTA is the same price as a regular, so the saving is not passed on. STONE-GROUND PASTA tends to be 5p more and extra flavours bump up the price – garlic by 10p in **Sainsbury**, spinach by 5p in **Tesco**. ORGANIC PASTA attracts a big premium: **La Biotecha** costs £1.15 for 500g, or almost 75p more. Other good names to look out for are **Ferrare**, from Modena, which is sold in designer plastic bags together with some above average sauces in bottles. **Buitoni** tends to attract a premium.

RICE

There are more than 1,300 varieties of rice and several thousands shades and forms of those according to the climate and soil. No other grain is so widely eaten and rice is still the staple for more than half the world. Rice is a grass, *Oryza sativa*, growing from 25-200 cm (10-80 in) tall, which is similar in shape and colour to oats. It grows in flooded fields and will yield two crops a year. The paddy fields need constant back-breaking weeding. Before harvest the fields are drained to let the sun ripen the heads. The rice is then cut, tied into bundles, sun-dried briefly and then threshed and milled to remove the two outer husks, leaving 60% of pure white husk.

Rice is infinitely flexible and interchangeable in cooking. The general principle is that long- and medium-grain rices are for savoury dishes and short-grain (in the west at least) is reserved for puddings. The Japanese use short-grain rice for *sushi* because of its stickiness and *Paella* contradicts the Western rule by using short-grain. Graders grade by length, although size is no indication of quality. Soaking helps to stop the grains from sticking. AMERICAN LONG-GRAIN RICE is the classic boiled rice and akin to Basmati (see overleaf), although it does lack the aroma. A good general all-purpose rice, it is used in curries and savouries because it separates well and is half the price of Basmati. Cooking time is 12-15 minutes. **Froqual** produce a frozen five-minute rice – although it only takes 10 minutes to cook dried rice – made from American long-grain and acquiring a rather luminescent yellow colour en route, which lingers in the

Ways With Rice
Allow 55 g (2 oz) per person. The usual ratio for cooking is 450 g (1 lb) of rice to 575 ml (1 pt) of water simmered for 10-12 minutes. Take off the heat, pour a fresh kettle of boiling water over it, then drain, add butter and allow to stand, covered with a wet cloth. Another wet cloth underneath the pan helps to stop the rice sticking to the bottom.

Rice Prices

The large 4 kg (9 lb) bag
of American whole-grain
rice represents a
substantial saving, but
supermarkets price
differently with
Sainsbury's being 50p
cheaper than **Tesco** and
Safeway only carrying 2
kg (4½ lb) bags. **Uncle
Ben's** is conspicuously
expensive – the same
money would buy an
own-label Basmati. The 2
kg (4½ lb) bags of
basmati rice represent
savings of almost £1.
With fragrant Thai rice,
Chinese and Thai
supermarkets undercut
supermarkets by a large
measure and buying in
bulk at 4.5 kg (10 lb) can
create savings of more
than £3, even more with
broken grains.

pan/palate. It is remarkably tasteless,
AMERICAN EASY-COOK RICE is American
long-grain parboiled with the husk still on. This
processing makes the grains less brittle and
fewer nutrients are also lost in milling. It is
also supposed to stop the grains sticking and
some brands argue that it cuts the cooking
time, but this is questionable. It does lose
some flavour and pureness of colour. Cooking
time is 10-15 minutes. **Tilda** does a boil-in-
the-bag version which stops the rice sticking
to the pan, but at a considerable premium.

*AMERICAN WHOLE-GRAIN RICE has the
bran layer left intact, leaving much of the fibre
untouched. To compensate, cooking times are
longer – 20-30 minutes. 'More texture,
chewier, nutty flavour.' Soaked overnight,
however, the cooking time shortens. Less processing marginally shortens the shelf-life to
around 12 months. It is best for soups, salads
and vegetarian loaves. Looked down on in
many rice-eating countries where white is
supreme, it is worth rediscovering and not
only for its nutritional virtues. Despite brown
rice's association with the health culture it
remains three times more expensive in wholefood shops than in supermarkets. However,
they seem to grade the price up according to
the increase in nutritional value. Bizarrely, the
boil-in-the-bag brown rice does not seem to
attract the same premium as does easy-cook.

**BASMATI RICE comes from India, mostly
from the area around the Punjab. Basmati,
meaning 'the fragrant one' in Hindi, is also
known as the 'Prince of rice' as it is generally
regarded as the best. It has the longest of rice
grains, thin and opaque at one end.
Traditionally used for curries and most Indian
dishes, it is also right for Middle Eastern cooking. Own-labels are cheaper, but the quality of
*Tilda argues well for a few pennies more.
BROWN RICE has a more intense flavour and

aroma than American, harder to find, as there is no own label, unfortunately. Treat as American whole-grain. The main brands are **Tilda** and **Veetee**, although **Uncle Ben's** does an eccentric can of ready-cooked weighing an unhelpful 277g. Unlike American rice there seems little difference in brown and white Basmati prices. EASY-COOK BROWN RICE is parboiled brown rice, which is very rich in nutrients and has grains which are well separated. Cheaper than whole-grain, it is well worth looking for, although it has slightly less flavour than whole-grain.

*FRAGRANT THAI RICE, sometimes called JASMINE RICE, is cultivated in Thailand. Its aroma is slightly less pronounced than Basmati and it is widely used in South-East Asian and other Oriental cooking. With a slim grain like Basmati, it does tend to stick together more on cooking. Also available from specialist stores are broken grains, which have been damaged during milling; since Fragrant Thai rice is a slightly sticky rice, however, the broken grains make little difference to the final texture. Cooking time is between 8-10 minutes.

JAPANESE RICE is short-grain and glutinous. Due to the roundness of the grain, it becomes sticky on cooking and has a slightly sweet taste. It is traditionally used for *sushi*, mixed with vinegar and sugar then wrapped, usually with raw fish, in *nori* seaweed.

POPPED RICE is a short-grain cooked with sugar and subjected to high pressure. The water inside the grain turns to steam and smashes the outside hull. This is then toasted and the result is **Rice Krispies**.

PUDDING RICE is American and was originally called CAROLINA RICE, although it is often now grown in Italy and in Spain. Pudding rice is a white short-grain rice with very plump grains, intended to produce smooth creamy puddings. It has a similar texture to Arborio but a much blander flavour, and is therefore better for a sweet pudding. Cooking times is 10-15 minutes. It is one of the cheapest rices in supermarkets. There is also FLAKED RICE, in which the white grains are flattened to thin opaque leaves. However, this takes away all the texture of the grains so it is only suitable for creamy puddings. Cooking time is 6-10 minutes. GROUND RICE is for creamy puddings and bakes in place of flour. Cook in milk or water for 6-10 minutes.

RED RICE is a wild rice peculiar to the Camargue. It is a pretty dark garnet in colour and cooks slightly differently from other rices. Add it to boiling water for half an hour, drain and cover for another half an hour. 'Nutty, chewy... very chewy... almost a fragrant wadge.' Use sparingly to add texture and interest.

RISOTTO RICE: the blanket term means Italian fat white grains which can absorb up to five times their weight in liquid, against three times for ordinary white rice. The plump grains stick together and produce a smoother result. The final textures vary according to the rices. Cooking time is 20-30 minutes. An important phase in risotto is to whip in some butter at the end, and be generous. Risotto rice is also useful for rice balls. Prices for risotto rices tend to be higher than those for other rices. **Tesco** does an Italian easy-cook rice parboiled to stop the grains sticking. It still produces a thick risotto, but the texture is not as creamy as a normal risotto. It is best for seafood risottos.

The best rices for risotto are sold under their generic names, but attract premiums of three and four times the own-labels *Arborio* is the most frequently found of the risotto rices. **Carnaroli rice produces a risotto with, 'a slightly nuttier texture'. This is sold exclusively in Italian specialist stores, but is very good quality. A good example is **La Gallinella.** **Vialoni: The plumpest grain of the family, this arguably produces the best and creamiest risotto because of the grain thickness. It is available only from Italian food stores. As with carnaroli, a good name is **La Gallinella**.

WILD RICE is not a rice but an aquatic grass, *Zizania aquatica*, harvested from August to October and mostly imported from Canada. The grains are green and they are cured for 4-14 days to develops the nuttiness. When the grains are brown or black, they are roasted to reduce the moisture, then hulled, cleaned and graded.

There are also mixes, usually with long-grain rice, to get the price down. **Safeway** and **Tesco** do an interesting box of long-grain brown *wehani* (a variety of brown rice, amber in colour, which is grown in eastern America) and black *japonica* (another variety of brown rice, grown in California, which is a very dark brown treacle colour). **Tilda** do a mix of Basmati and wild.

POLENTA

Corn meal was first brought back from America by Columbus and adopted in northern Italy where at times it has been a staple as important as pasta. Variations are endless, although only two kinds are sold: coarse and fine. The end results do not differ enormously, though fine is predictably smoother. Buy maize meal rather than maize flour, which is properly for bread. The consistency of the polenta depends on how much water is added: 1 part water to 2 polenta for stiff (hard work); 1:4 for frying and grilling; 1:6 for creamy; 1:8 for a soft custard. Extend the cooking times as you increase the water. It is cooked when it comes away from the sides of the pan. **Aurora** sells polenta in tubes ready-mixed for frying, baking or microwaving. It tends to come out of the tube as rather wet and pongy, almost scented. It is a bland mix with a strong back-taste of eggs and milkiness. It is pragmatic and easy to use, if lacking in character.

Ways With Wild Rice

Cook it in three times the volume of water (the grains can expand to four times their size). Cooking times vary according to the different dishes: from 45 minutes, until swollen and split showing the white centre, for salads and stews; or longer, 60 minutes, for bakes. To fluff the grains, leave them in the water for a few minutes after cooking. Cooked it will store in the fridge 2 weeks, in the freezer 6 months. It is mostly used in salads, stir-fries or as a side dish.

VINEGARS

Balsamic vinegar
Champagne vinegar
Cider vinegar
Malt vinegar
Raspberry vinegar
Rice vinegar
Sherry vinegar
Wine vinegar

Rather than wine, early civilizations may well have drunk vinegar in diluted form to purify the water – or used it as a dip for bread, as is still the custom in Asia. The Egyptians thought of it as medicine, Moses mentions it and Roman legionnaires certainly drank it. Good vinegars of whatever persuasion will have gone through two fermentations, the first where the alcohol is lost and the second where it acidulates. The character of the original liquid should remain, which is why shortcuts using acetic acid are self-defeating, just acidity for its own sake. Lemon juice is invariably more natural and successful. Vinegar has, however, managed to slip back into fashion and might claim – along with garlic and ginger – to be in the forefront of modern cooking, either souring sauces and gravies, or in its most glorious form as a flavouring like balsamic. Given the quantities used in cooking, it is inexpensive and the investment in good-quality vinegars is worthwhile.

BALSAMIC VINEGAR

Made for about 1,000 years in Modena and Reggio, it is only since the '40s that it has been sold at all. Before that, it was a dowry and a gift for friends and sipped as a liqueur after banquets. Most of what is sold here is a diluted or adulterated form of the original article, which takes decades to mature and might well claim to be the finest – and certainly the most expensive – individual food product in the world. **Fortnum & Mason** sell small phials of genuinely aged balsamic, otherwise we are dealing with scaled-down versions, house claret not Lafite.

The *Trebbiano* grape is harvested at its

peak of sweetness and then dried out in the sun. It is then pressed and the juices simmered into a concentrate over 24 hours. Unlike wine vinegar, which converts alcohol to acid, balsamic converts sugar to acid. The liquid is cooled and put in a barrel in the loft. Some families use a mother, while others discard it in favour of some of the cooked must to start the fermentation. The barrels are chestnut, oak, cherry, mulberry or ash, with holes in the top to allow evaporation and the concentration of flavours. The steamy hot summers and cold winters of the region allow for a cycle of loss and rest. Each year the vinegar is transferred into a smaller cask. There must be at least three transfers to different casks. The saying is that one generation makes vinegar for the next. The flavours are of browned meats, old port, wood, herbs, wild flowers and new hay...

Imitation balsamics are made in Naples and often shipped out in bulk for bottling in other countries. Commercially made balsamics can be good especially in cooking for sauces, soups, stews, salads and marinades. The best are a blend of good-quality wine vinegar, grape must and some balsamic (and sometimes caramel) aged in a balsamic cask. Others are just wine vinegar, caramel, herbs and no balsamic or must at all. The acidity should be 6%.

The artisan-made balsamic vinegars of Modena and Reggio must have been aged 12 years. Each one is judged by a panel of five and the bottling is done by the consortium so it cannot be adulterated. Modena bottles are small globes, Reggio bottles are vase-shaped like small decanters with three quality levels denoted by the colour of the label – gold (the highest), silver and then red. Each year there is a competition for the best balsamic vinegar at Spilamberto on San Giovanni's Day, June 24.

Good-quality balsamic is really a seasoning to be used like salt, sparingly and deliberately. Artisan-made vinegars should not be wasted in cooking, but just used to adorn dishes from pasta to fruits – half a teaspoon will go a long way.

Five Barrels Balsamic Vinegar is bottled in dinky carafes with metal flip-over tops by **Guidetti Fine Foods** and labelled 'extra mature'. It has a fierce nose, giving way to burnt treacle toffee, sweet and caramelized with lovely tartness. It is a good example of above-average commercial balsamic.

Torrione, from the Carndini family, makers of balsamic since 1836; their 'cask 1**' has the sweet taste of red wine, more like a high-quality red wine vinegar tinged with balsamic process. Distinctly different, it is good for salads and dressings, although it is unfaithful to the pure balsamic idea or too young.

*Luigi Ugolotti & Figli from Modena, is sold in **Waitrose** in lovely clouded glass corked bottles. It has a sweet smell of caramel, harsh, but authentic velvet tones, a generous dose of the real thing in there. Its good measure represents good value for the second division. It is easily the pick of the supermarket balsamics.

Fini from Modena, is usually sold boxed in an opaque fluted bottle inside. Aged about five years, it is a good commercial blend.

*Mazzetti from Modena is noticeable by the elegance of the 36 cm (15 in) tall thin dark glass bottle, with a cork stopper. With a deep coffee colour, it is sweet, treacly, crackling... very fine.

Sainsbury Balsamic Vinegar is poor, runny and acid, like balsamic added to tart low-quality caramelized vinegar.

CHAMPAGNE VINEGAR

The sugars and yeasts in champagne create a sediment which forms around the neck when the bottles are stored for the first year. This sediment is taken off by freezing the necks of the champagne bottles, which can then be extracted and the champagne given its formal mushroom-shaped cork. The frozen sediment is what goes for champagne vinegar – one year old in non-vintage and three years old in vintage.

Benedicta's Vinaigre de vin blanc de Champagne is 89p per 250 ml, and is sweet, not bad and cheap. It is a good alternative to their wine vinegar, but not representative.

****Edmond Fallot** is tart, sharp Chardonnay butter, supremely invigorating.

CIDER VINEGAR

The apple juice has yeast added to convert the sugars into alcohol, so cider vinegars tend to be sweeter than wine vinegars and have a lower acidity. Own-labels come in around 65p per 350 ml. **Dufrais** is £1.39 for 500 ml. The best examples come from France.

****Vinaigre des Côteaux Nantais** is outstanding, even the version filled with shallots designed for serving with oysters, Mild and sour, it has the beautiful taste of *cidre bouchée*. Other variations seem to lack the same purpose in life.

MALT VINEGAR

The reverse of the process for wine vinegar is used to make malt vinegar, creating the alcohol in the first place. The grain is steamed with water to create a starch, the barley malt is added to convert the insoluble starch into sugar, then pumped into vats. Yeast is added to convert the sugar into alcohol and fermentation takes 3-4 days. The liquor is then filtered and bottled and the colour added as caramel. Its solitary valid domestic use today is for pickles. The alcohol can be taken off and distilled and is widely used in processing to preserve and retain the colour. **Sarson's** dominate the market, managing to hold a reasonable parity, around 50p per 250 ml, with own-labels.

RASPBERRY VINEGAR

Traditional in the North of England as much as in France, it is made by macerating raspberries in white wine vinegar (though presumably more likely malt vinegar in England), for a month and then filtered. Unfortunately **Benedicta** smells like boiled sweets and is about as acid as a cream cake, and **Martlet** has met with flavours rather than fruit. It also uses cider vinegar as a base and claims to be the 'inspiration behind *nouvelle cuisine*', though it is unlikely the Troisgros brothers used cider vinegar, let alone an English version. A more genuine example is **Taylor & Lake Fresh Raspberry Wine Vinegar** which is unpasteurized and sells at £4.59 per 375 ml – admittedly nearly five times as expensive, but it has a, 'real hit of raspberries backed by a lashing rounded acidity'.

RICE VINEGAR

This is made by adding a starter to *sake* and this is then matured in cedar-wood kegs for 8 months and finally filtered through cotton.
Amoy Red Vinegar is sold as a dipping sauce with ginger for Peking-style food. Brown, diluted malt colour, it is very thin and acid, like an off red wine. Made from rice, E150 and spices, it is not very good.

*Chinkiang Vinegar** is soy-black, with some of the sweetness and caramel of a balsamic. It says 'gold plum' on the label which is appropriate. Good and very interesting, it is made from glutinous rice and is not expensive and no worse than some of the rubbish passed off as balsamic vinegar for a fraction of the price.

Koon Yick Wah Kee's Red Vinegar is flavoured with star anise, just a light boiled sweet sourness, very direct, very refreshing, little complexity just the edges of acidity.

Mitsukan is natural vinegar distilled from wheat, *sake* cake, rice and corn. Pea-yellow in the bottle, it is fragrant with wheaty overtones, gentle, pleasant and sharp but low on acidity.

Yokoi Brown Rice Vinegar claims to be, 'uniquely mellow' but is actually sharply sour, mellow but distinct and powerfully influencing flavours to the east. The acidity corresponds to wine vinegars but the heaviness of the brown rice is evident.

> There is also a CANE VINEGAR **Datu Puti** from the Philippines. It is opaque, the colour of diluted pastis, all acidity and sugar in almost equal parts, sharp, indistinct. Interesting uses to surprise, say with fruit.

☆SHERRY VINEGAR

This is aged in old oak sherry casks. The **Xérès** is revered by French chefs, being mellower, caskier but with the cutting bite of wine vinegar that lends acidity to sauces and dressings, especially those with nut oils.

WINE VINEGAR

Prices for red and white wine vinegars are interchangeable. Red wine vinegars should be aged for at least six months. Own-label wine vinegars undercut brands like **Dufrais** and **Benedicta** by one-third or more. The rage for flavouring cheap white wine vinegars with garlic, herbs or anything else does not bump up the price, nor the quality. Better to do it at home. Check the label to see if it is

> FOOD *watch*
>
> *Sainsbury** own-label sherry vinegar is £1.15 per 350 ml, nearly twice the price of the wine vinegar, but infinitely superior. Likewise **Dufrais** at 95p per 250 ml is a better buy than their white wine vinegar.

flavouring rather than flavoured – either way they tend to be meek.

**Edmond Fallot makes old wine vinegars in the Beaune: red and red with cassis. 'Very good with the taste of the burgundy still prominent', normally good value too at under £3. The quality of this vinegar stems from its origin and method of production, declares the label and so it does. Mellow like good burgundy, the cassis gives a wider accent.

Peloponnese traditionally aged red vinegar is more than 12 months old and sold for £1.29 in larger supermarkets. Vigorous, grape skins and wood in flavour, it is good for marinades, a bit brutal for salads unless the sun was very hot.

*Martin Pouret in Orleans was always known for the quality of its wine vinegars. Pouret also make **La Favorit** mustard (see page 351). Very pale, the vinegar is like thin cheap white wine, but mild and rich-tasting.

Doktorenhof from Germany are wine vinegars made from good German wines, matured in oak or beech and filtered through a second barrel of beech, oak, cherry and mulberry shavings and then matured on for up to a year. The bottles are hand-blown glass and the labels from original oils painted on the estate. The vinegars are intense and sabre sharp, the marketing suggests they might be used as an aperitif, but probably they need a big fat wild duck to go with them. Superb but witheringly sharp. The rosé is from Spatburgunder, there is a very good and faithful ***Reisling and white from the Weisser burgunder. Exclusive to **Harrods**, they are outstanding for dressings and saucing and, despite the designer price, not bad value.

GLOSSARY

ACETIC ACID is the strongest of the kitchen acids, and is now widely used in manufacturing as a preservative. Its most famous applications were as an adulterant to vinegar or as the alternative 'non-brewed condiment' found in fish and chip shops. Unlike malt and wine vinegars, there has been no fermentation. Its addition inhibits bacterial growth in vinegar. It is made from a dry distillation of wood. Naturally occurring, it provides the tang in yoghurts and some cheese.

AGAR, sometimes known as AGAR AGAR or listed as E406, is sold as a vegetarian alternative to gelatine. Found in powder, sheets and shreds it is obtained from boiling different seaweeds and straining off the resultant jelly. It melts at a higher temperature than gelatine – at 90°C (194°F) compared to 27°C (80°F) and sets at about 45°C (112°F) rather than 20°C (68°F). It tends to perform erratically, as does gelatine, and there is a residual aftertaste. Allow 1 teaspoon per litre (1¾ pt) of water. Do not boil too long with an acid food or it will not set. Agar can be used to make fresh papaya and pineapple juice into jellies, however, where gelatine cannot.

ALUMINIUM reacts badly to salt. It is used in some foods as a cheaper alternative to silver – in confectionery especially – and listed as E173. Aluminium saucepans are good conductors of heat, but foil should not be used with salty foods or in a microwave. Links to the wasting Alzheimer's disease have been suggested, but are not proven.

ANATTO is a bright orange/yellow dye that originates from tropical South America but has long been used to colour butter, margarine and cheeses, like Cheshire. It is the red arils around the pod that give the colour and, in South America, the seeds are used as a spice in cooking. Found also in Sri Lanka, it comes from a shrub, *Bixa orellano*, which is an evergreen 2-3 m (6-9 ft) tall but sometimes twice that, and bushy from the top with a single stem. The fruit pods are heart-shaped, about 2.5 cm (1 in) long, red and covered with stiff prickles containing 30-50 seeds embedded in a reddish yellow waxy pulp, which – after the pod is rubbed or brushed off – settle in a tub of water. It contains two colorants: orellin (yellow) and bixin (cinnabar red).

BOTULISM is one of the most lethal forms of food poisoning, usually associated with poorly sterilized food in tins. It survives at a temperature of 120°C (250°F) for up to 10 minutes. Symptoms of dizziness, weakness, breathing difficulty and paralysis come on within 3-36 hours. It is fortunately now rare, most recent case being connected with contaminated hazelnuts in a consignment of yoghurt.

BST, or bovine somnælotropin, is a drug that encourages cows to give more milk. The EC has stopped its use on the grounds that cows are already producing a surplus of milk and there have been welfare concerns about the genetic manipulation of animals. In America the more aptly named BGH (bovine growth hormone) is licensed, which has led to the ban on the import of American animals.

CAFFEINE is found in tea, coffee, chocolate and cola-nut derivatives. It tends to raise the blood pressure and the sense of alertness, hence its reputation for stopping people going to sleep. In large quantities it can cause tremors as well. Coffee beans contain less caffeine than tea, but as more is used the effect is greater. Instant coffee has the same caffeine as fresh, but cocoa powder has considerably less – an almost negligible 0.1%.

CALORIE is the unit of energy needed to heat one gram of pure water by 1˚C. It is so small that it is usually short-handed up to units of 1,000s as kilocalories or Kcal on labels and, in fact, this is what most people mean when they use the word Calorie. A balanced diet for an adult, depending on the level of activity, would vary from 1,500 to 3,000 Kcal a day.

CAMPYLOBACTER is one of the more common forms of food poisoning, leading to vomiting and diarrhoea, usually spread from pets to food.

CHORLEY WOOD PROCESS was developed in the '60s at the laboratories of the Flour-making and Baking Association in Chorley Wood and allows mechanical kneading of softer flours. The level of yeast is doubled, but then fed with ascorbic acid and extra water. The main advantage is the speed of factory production.

CLING FILM will leach its plasticizers into fatty foods over a period of time – as much as 60% in five days on cheese. Microwave brands are excellent for wrapping and cooking fish to retain the natural juices.

COLOURS for food form the E numbers 100-200. *Natural* colours do not necessarily have to be natural to the food they are colouring.

Synthetic dyes, including the azo dyes – notably the yellow TAR-TRAZINE E102, widely used in soft drinks – which are a by-product of petrol refining, have been found to cause allergic reactions, especially in people sensitive to aspirin or suffering from eczema or asthma and hyperactivity in children. Confusingly, the numbers give no indication of progeny, so the equally controversial azo dye BROWN FK used in kippers is listed as 154, while E153 is a carbon-black derived from burnt plant material.

DRIPPING is rendered-down beef fat.

FAIR-TRADE FOUNDATION awards its label to foods avoiding social and environmental damage. The first food product to carry the logo is **Green & Black's Maya Gold** organic chocolate with an agreed price to organic cocoa farmers in southern Belize for three years.

HYDROGENATION was invented in 1911 and allows liquid vegetable fats to be converted into hard fats by exposing them to hydrogen with a nickel catalyst. Widely used in biscuit and margarine manufacture, the process changes unsaturated fats to saturated.

INULIN is the fructose (fruit sugar) naturally present in Jerusalem artichokes and some pulses that is not digested in the stomach and ferments causing wind.

IRRADIATION by gamma rays is widely used to sterilize hospital equipment, but has also been used to preserve and inhibit growth in foods, notably to stop potatoes sprouting in store in Russia and to clean consignments of pepper. Its use is only allowed by licence, but it is only labelled where the ingredient is a component part.

KOSHER indicates food prepared according to Jewish religious rules, ie insisting that meat is killed by bleeding. Pork, game, eels, scaleless fish and shellfish are not allowed. Meat and dairy products must not be eaten at the same meal – which is why the favoured Jewish cooking medium is chicken fat not butter – and cheese must use vegetarian rennet.

LECITHIN, labelled as E322, is found naturally in egg yolks and vegetable – usually soya – oils and is used as an emulsifier and stabilizer. The best example of its natural properties is in making mayonnaise.

LISTERIA was first identified in a laboratory rabbit in 1926. The bacteria are commonly found in the ground, but only cross over into the food chain through poor hygiene. Until 1982 it was believed that the disease spread directly from animals, but an outbreak in Canada showed that it was invariably a food-borne disease. Then 34 pregnant women and seven adults were poisoned by a batch of coleslaw, 16 of whom died. The vegetables came from a field with known listeria associations, had been inadequately washed and had been mixed with a mayonnaise with too little vinegar to kill off the bacteria. Three years later in California, 48 people died in the worst recorded outbreak to date after eating a fresh Mexican cheese. The difficulty with detecting listeria is that symptoms may not appear for 4-6 weeks. The notorious Swiss Vacherin cheese epidemic only came to light four years after the first deaths had occurred. Then seven died in early '87 and the cause was identified as a pasteurised Vacherin Mont d'Or. It was only revealed later that 24 others had died of similar symptoms in the region. In '92, an as yet unattributed epidemic killed 32 people in 46 *départements* in France between April and August, suggesting the agency may have been some widely distributed food product. Foods most likely to be carriers of listeria are soft cheeses (where the bacteria will tend to be in or near the rind), chilled salads and prepared meats. The case against unpasteurized cheese is largely discredited and hard cheese is not a risk. Particularly susceptible are pregnant women, the elderly and those with poor immune systems and low-acidity digestive systems. Microwave cooking poses particular risks if the food is spot-cooked. Research is concentrating on the possible link between listeria and spontaneous miscarriages.

MEAT AND LIVESTOCK COMMISSION is a body funded from a levy on all carcasses killed in the industry. Most of its resources go into meat promotion, but it has developed quality-control schemes for lamb, beef and pork.

MECHANICALLY RECOVERED MEAT, sometimes shortened to MRM, is the gristle, cartilage and fat removed from carcasses by centrifugal force, etc.

MONOSODIUM GLUTAMATE, or MSG or E621, is the salt from glutamic acid, found naturally in foods high in the glutamates like soya, milk, aged hard cheeses and tomatoes. It is used as a flavour-enhancer in the same way as salt. However, excessive dosages – above 0.3% – can lead to adverse reactions (Chinese Restaurant Syndrome).

PDO, or Protection of Geographical Origin, was introduced by the EC in July 1993 for co-operative producers whose craft and product is unique to their area. PDI, or Protection of Geographical Indication, is the slightly lesser recognition for co-operatives that can claim their process is unique, even if the materials are brought in from outside the region.

POLYPHOSPHATES are labelled as 544 and 545 and are used to for their water-retaining properties to bulk up the weight of frozen fish and chicken.

QUINOLINE is a yellow synthetic coal-tar dye, E104, used in smoked haddock and Scotch eggs. Some doctors warn against its use for any-one with a history of asthma or poor reaction to aspirin.

RDA is the Recommended Daily Amount of vitamins and minerals, usu-ally worked out as a percentage of 100 g, or a notional portion size which is more relevant to meat, say, than it is to butter. The calculation is based on raw as opposed to cooked foods, because cooking destroys vitamins.

TRANS-FATTY ACIDS are found naturally in meat and dairy products, but their widest application has been in the fats industry as a result of hydrogenating oils to harden them. They are believed to have worked to increase levels of cholesterol. A 30-year study of 85,000 American nurses by Walter Willet, published in 1993, revealed the link between heart disease and the kind of trans-fatty acids found in margarine. The report suggests that the trans-fats actually increase cholesterol levels. Further studies by Lisa Litin and Frank Sacks at Harvard School of Public Health further argue that the so-called health benefits of not eat-ing butter are almost completely negated by a diet reliant on foods with high trans-fatty acids. They quote as an example someone who might eat a doughnut for breakfast, a small portion of fries at lunch, two tea-spoons of margarine with bread at night and two biscuits. It is widely predicted that margarine manufacturers may reformulate their products as a result. The only non trans-fatty margarines on the market cur-rently are **Granose** and **Whole Earth's Superspread**, both using soya oil, and **Vitaquell** from Germany, which uses palm oil. Going one step further is **Apri-Bake**, only usable in cooking, which is a blend of apri-cots, fructose and lecithin, claiming to be 98% fat-free.

UMAMI is said to be the fifth element of taste, associated with the glu-tamates found in soy, beef stock, tomatoes, mature Parmesan cheese, anchovies and ketchups.

VITAMINS are food constituents essential for complete health. Claims should not be made for foods having any given vitamin unless they contain at least $\frac{1}{16}$ of the RDA (recommended daily allowance) of that vitamin; that the foods are 'an excellent source of' it unless they contain half the RDA; and only if they contain the complete quota of vitamins for a day should any health claims be made.

A is formed in the body from dairy foods, fish, leaf and some root vegetables and pulses. Livers are a good source. Vitamin A deficiency is rare now, except in very poor areas. Pregnant women are usually advised against taking too much vitamin A because large quantities can adversely affect their babies. Children, on the other hand, need slightly more to help the growth of bone and tissue.

B is a complex series of vitamins, found mainly in wholemeal cereals, yeast products and meat. B1, B2, Niacin and B6 are usually easily sourced in a balanced diet. B12 is exclusive to animal products and lack of it leads to anaemia, a problem for vegetarians. Folic acid is important during pregnancy and lactation, and also for the elderly on limited diets, Although widely available, it is harmed in cooking and by nitrates, either used as preservatives in processed foods or even present in the water, and can be at a premium.

C is an important antioxidant and good for all-round health. It is found mostly in fresh foods, fruit, green vegetables, root vegetables and sprouted seeds. The highest concentrations tend to be in citrus fruits, chilli and sweet peppers, blackcurrants, fresh milk (in the darkness of cartons rather than clear bottles). It is destroyed by long cooking and canning. Levels must be sustained when pregnant and during breast feeding. Smokers and older people on restrictive diets should seek to ensure higher levels.

D is the sunshine vitamin, added by law to margarine originally to compensate for the lack of daylight in winter. Deficiency was a major health issue in the North and in Scotland until 1940, when the idea of cod liver oil supplements first gained ground. In children, a lack of vitamin D can cause rickets. Equally, too much can lead to kidney stones. Requirements for pregnant and breast-feeding women increase, which is why doctors usually recommended a diet rich in the oily fish, liver and (pre-salmonella) eggs.

E is the most fashionable of the vitamins, for its protective antioxidants which underpin the enthusiasm for much of the Mediterranean diet. The body tends to store it up, so supplements are rarely used. Ironically, it is found in fats as well as grains, vegetable oils and eggs.

INDEX

INDEX Suppliers & Brands

INDEX PRODUCE

FOOD *watch* FEEDBACK

FOOD *watch* will be updated and published again next year. Obviously every effort has been made by the team working on the book to ensure that all the information it contains is as accurate as possible. We apologize in advance for any inadvertent inaccuracies; some are inevitable and we cannot be held responsible for them… but please let us know if you spot any so we can put them right next time.

Also, If you have comments on foods, would like to endorse or query a rating for a food, notice a significant change in what is happening, can fill in a history with notes from your own experience, or are a food producer and would like to register your product(s) on our data base then I would be very interested to hear from you. Please write to:

Drew Smith
c/o Department LE,
HarperCollins*Publishers*,
77–85 Fulham Palace Road,
Hammersmith,
London W6 8JB